PENGUIN BOOKS

INSIDE THE INNER

D0626517

'With an insight which is quite simply awe-inspiring, it tells us
what it is really like to be poor in this country. I have no
hesitation in declaring that this book will be a classic' – *Time Out*

'A quite uni⬚⬚⬚⬚⬚⬚⬚⬚⬚⬚⬚⬚⬚ sustained and
passionate ca⬚⬚⬚⬚⬚⬚⬚⬚⬚⬚⬚⬚⬚ . . . informed by a
singularity o⬚⬚⬚⬚⬚⬚⬚⬚⬚⬚⬚⬚s own terms is
both definitiv⬚⬚⬚⬚⬚⬚⬚⬚⬚⬚sor to Henry
Mayhew, Ch⬚⬚⬚⬚⬚⬚⬚⬚⬚⬚⬚*y Limits*

'Nobody with⬚⬚⬚⬚⬚⬚⬚⬚⬚⬚⬚ be deeply
disturbed' – S⬚⬚⬚⬚⬚⬚

'He puts hum⬚⬚⬚⬚⬚⬚⬚⬚⬚⬚leprivation. His
book will beco⬚⬚⬚⬚⬚⬚⬚⬚⬚s' – *Marxism
Today*

'A major piece of evidence which demolishes the comforting myth
that modest affluence is universal' – *Sunday Times*

WITHDRAWN

Margaret Danyers College

Catalogue: 04011

4011

uthor:

Paul Harrison was born in Oldham, educated in Manchester, and has master's degrees in languages from Cambridge and political sociology from the London School of Economics. For three years he was on the staff of *New Society*, and his articles have appeared in the *Guardian*, the *Sunday Times*, and the *New Scientist*, among other journals. He is a contributor to *Encyclopaedia Britannica* and writes frequently for a number of United Nations agencies. He has reported on problems of deprivation and conflict from many of Britain's inner cities and depressed regions, as well as on similar problems in developing countries – on which he wrote *Inside the Third World* and *The Third World Tomorrow* (both published by Penguin). He is married with two children. His wife taught in Hackney for ten years.

In 1988 he was awarded a Global 500 Award by the United Nations Environment Programme for his writings on the environment. In 1990, for *Inside the Inner City*, he was made the first fellow of the prestigious Institute of Community Studies, home of the classic East End study, *The Family Life of Old People*. The Institute's founder director, Michael Young, contributes a foreword to this edition.

Michael Young is the founder director of the Institute of Community Studies and co-author of *The Family Life of Old People*, *The Symmetrical Family* and many other books.

Paul Harrison

Inside the Inner City
Life under the cutting edge

PENGUIN BOOKS

PENGUIN BOOKS

Published by the Penguin Group
Penguin Books Ltd, 27 Wrights Lane, London w8 5tz, England
Penguin Books USA Inc., 375 Hudson Street, New York, New York 10014, USA
Penguin Books Australia Ltd, Ringwood, Victoria, Australia
Penguin Books Canada Ltd, 10 Alcorn Avenue, Toronto, Ontario, Canada m4v 3b2
Penguin Books (NZ) Ltd, 182–190 Wairau Road, Auckland 10, New Zealand

Penguin Books Ltd, Registered Offices: Harmondsworth, Middlesex, England

First published in Pelican Books 1983
Revised edition 1985
Reprinted in Penguin Books with new Foreword and corrections 1992
10 9 8 7 6 5 4 3 2 1

Copyright © Paul Harrison, 1983, 1985, 1992
Foreword copyright © Michael Young, 1992
All rights reserved

The moral right of the author of the Foreword has been asserted

Made and printed in Great Britain

Set in Linotron Baskerville by
Rowland Phototypesetting Ltd, Bury St Edmunds, Suffolk

Except in the United States of America, this book is sold subject
to the condition that it shall not, by way of trade or otherwise, be lent,
re-sold, hired out, or otherwise circulated without the
publisher's prior consent in any form of binding or cover other than
than in which it is published and without a similar condition
including this condition being imposed on the subsequent purchaser

'When we have to break into the rent money to pay the milk, that really gets us arguing, and once we start, we're down each other's throats all night. It isn't fair that we have to suffer like this. We don't ask much out of life, just a little money to buy food and decent clothes. But they take every penny you've got, they don't leave you with nothing.'

Bernadette Tsokallis, roofer's wife, on rent and taxation

'They used us here for twenty years. Now they got no use for us. They want us out.'

Young black rioter

'Why have I been left like this? They call it a welfare state. Never! It's not a welfare state no more. You ain't got a chance. What have you got on a Monday morning? You haven't got a tea-bag.'

Sarah Jones, single mother of seven, without electricity for two years

'I'd rather live in the thirties than now. I'd rather be fighting in the war than be like I am now. I wish I was still in school. If I could just stop time, and be sixteen.'

Steve Capes, unemployed lorry-driver and father of three small children

'Oh, it's a free country all right. You're free to starve to death, 'cause there's no sod will help you when you're down.'

Stan Waller, fitter, on strike against redundancy

'I got no plans, I just take it as it comes. What's the worth of thinking ahead? The only time you can think ahead is if you've got money. If you made plans, you'd only be disappointed. They wouldn't work out anyway.'

M.D., petty thief, unemployed

'It's all because I'm a bit small. They always kept me down. I ain't got no push, see, that's why. If I'd been a big bloke, they'd have taken notice. If you're small, they walk all over you.'

Joseph Bowles, night-watchman, in court for rent arrears of £1,110

*For the people
of the inner city
and all those working
to better their lot*

Contents

Contents

Part Two: Private Need and Public Squalor

Part Three: Tensions and Conflicts

Conclusion: Myths, Realities and Possibilities 421

Foreword

This book evokes two contrasting responses. The first is appreciation that it should be written at all. The author is one of the inheritors and transmitters of a great British tradition which stretches from Defoe to Mayhew, from Booth to Rowntree, and now from Orwell to Harrison. All these writers have been both sympathetic chroniclers and withering social critics who dared in their time to set themselves against the conventional opinions of the comfortable classes. The comfortable classes have always kept themselves comfortable in an insidious manner – by denying the extent and gravity of poverty or, if they cannot do that, by blaming those who are poor for getting themselves into such a state.

The denial has been most shameful, and for those who are defending themselves most necessary, in a London which within the space of a few miles exhibits such contrasts between opulence and squalor. The people who are prepared and able to pay thirteen pounds today for a small glass of champagne in the Ritz Bar have to be blind to the condition of other people with the same-sized stomachs who are going hungry in places like Hackney.

The second response is a combination of sadness and indignation. The sadness is that the underside of London could still be so seamy when Harrison first wrote his book – and I have no doubt that conditions are still much the same as in the early 1980s. If there has been any change, I would expect conditions to be worse after local government has taken even more of a hammering, social benefits have been further squeezed and the economy has moved into deeper recession. Only the most blinkered of champagne drinkers could entirely ignore some of the outward manifestations of poverty in the inner city – the garbage piled up against the tower blocks, the graveyards of old cars, the boarded-up shops, the dirt spread all around.

But Harrison takes you behind the flaking façade to the people who are on the other side. He brings them alive – the pretty eighteen-year-old unemployed girl who never dares to walk down the street outside the estate where she lives for fear of being attacked, or to get in the lift in case 'they' jam it between floors – 'Then you've had it.' The homeworker who is cooped up in a cupboard working at her industrial sewing machine for ten or twelve hours every day, not able even to take a lunch break if she is to earn enough to feed her children. The Gujarati man who was granted full resident status in one year but then got caught up in a raid by immigration officials on the Hilton Hotel, where he worked; from then on nothing he said was believed and he was detained pending deportation. The Anglo-Indian teacher with a B.Ed. and a BA from India whose teaching qualifications were not recognized in England, but was then refused a grant to do a diploma course in business administration because he was already a graduate – his qualifications were recognized only when they counted *against* him. The old people whose party was cancelled because the food and drink had been stolen. There are in this book hundreds of other accounts of man's inhumanity to man, and especially to woman, and, amongst them, a particularly welcome (because relatively sympathetic) account of the demanding jobs done by the police.

The local people are victims. They are entangled in a web from which only the lucky or cunning or ruthless or exceptionally diligent can escape. The schools brand too many people as failures. People who have done badly at school cannot get decent jobs and there are hardly any of those anyway in a district without modern industry or commerce. People who cannot get decent jobs cannot get decent housing – their lot is sodden basements, leaking roofs, damp, pharaoh-ant-infested flats. People without decent jobs cannot get decent food. People without decent food or housing are more liable to mental and other illness and this makes it more difficult for them to get jobs. People without cars hardly have any public transport to fall back on, because it has been killed off by the cars of the more fortunate. In Hackney, people who are caught in the web of poverty are not unlike those who are entangled in it in the Third World.

Indeed, one of the features of the book which makes Harrison different from his predecessors is the comparisons he is able to make with the Third World that he has written about so well. Some people in Hackney suffer from worse malnutrition than in some African or Asian countries, and their job prospects are no better. Hackney is dependent on the same labour-intensive manufacturing that is the first to be taken over by developing countries. To survive against this international competition in the same industries, employers have cut real wages down to near Hong Kong levels. Mothers whose children are bent down sticking eyes and tails on to cuddly toys for other children to fondle are like Guatemalan Indians who take their children to labour on the coffee harvest for the benefit of office workers in Paris or Los Angeles.

The indignation is that conditions can be like that, and like that (with their local differences) at the heart of every large city in Britain - yet nothing was done about it, or even proposed. The Conservative Government elected two hundred years after the French Revolution presided over a continuing decline of the inner cities, and contributed handsomely to it, and there was hardly a murmur of protest from the suburbs, let alone the country towns. There has not even been a Bob Geldof for the inner cities. And Labour has not been exactly convincing that public expenditure will be raised enough to make a new start possible in places like this – public expenditure financed by higher income taxes on the people who do not have to live in Hackney. But it would be utterly wrong to give up hope, and while there is a Harrison to stir us, we will not need to.

Inside the Inner City will act as a constant reminder of the need for action to alleviate poverty and social deprivation.

Michael Young, 1991

Preface

This book is in part a sequel to my previous book, *Inside The Third World*. I had no sooner completed this than it became obvious that Britain was, in a sense, underdeveloping, under the devastating impact of monetarism and world recession. Having spent four years looking at acute poverty around the globe, I felt I could hardly ignore it on my own doorstep.

The book that follows has three main aims. The primary purpose is to paint a concrete picture of the everyday realities of life for the disadvantaged in Britain, a worm's-eye view of the welfare state, the mixed economy and representative democracy. The chosen background is the inner city, and the location is not arbitrary, for it it here that the disadvantaged are found in greatest concentration. The second aim, therefore, is to sketch the outlines of the inner-city phenomenon, to try to show the interrelationships of the multiple problems, and to use the inner city as a diagnostic pointer to some of the major problems of British society as a whole. The third aim is to reflect the dark historical moment at which the book was written – to show the human costs of recession and public spending cuts. The historical moment is also germane to the inner-city theme, for it intensified the growth of inequality and the processes of industrial and housing decline that generate disadvantage and create such inner-city areas.

There is no shortage of surveys and academic studies of the fields covered here. This book tries rather to convey the human side of the situation, the private consequences of public policies and institutions. I have chosen to do this within a single community, Hackney, which is in my view the most deprived inner-city area in London and one of the two or three most deprived in Britain. I hope that this will help to show more clearly how the problems interconnect. But the aim is to focus on those phenomena that are of national significance. Hence I do not dwell much on things that are peculiar to Hackney. (This applies particularly to the health service, and to details such as the organization of Greater London Council housing and of the Inner London Education Authority.) The book, too, is about the inner city as a *problem*. Hence it focuses on the problematic and cannot do justice to the detailed local initiatives aimed at improving the local situation.

My subjects do not make up a random or a representative sample of Hackney people. They come overwhelmingly from the groups in greatest need, people whom our system has not served well, since I believe that the pathology of a society can be diagnosed from its victims. In general the approach was to identify the key problems from official surveys, which there was no need to repeat, and then to find case studies of individuals and groups which illustrated the human detail and the concrete mechanics of each problem. Those agencies with wide contacts among the deprived – MPs, councillors, teachers, social workers – provided numerous briefer examples which confirmed the representativeness of the cases chosen. The case-study approach, I believe, is a more powerful instrument for reform than depersonalized statistics or surveys with fixed questions which cannot respond flexibly to the significant peculiarites of each subject.

The portraits in these pages are incomplete: they were taken at a particular moment in time (for most people an unpleasant one), a time in which we all became aware, far more than in the expansive 1950s and 1960s, of the inescapable connection between all our individual destinies and that of Britain, indeed of mankind, as a whole. Our heroes and heroines are caught as if hanging from a cliff face by a slim branch: whether they will fall or clamber back to safety we do not yet know.

I have tried to convey something of their existential plight, wherever possible in their own words, and also to view them against the background of national and international forces that mould their destinies. These are personal odysseys, in frail boats, in which every individual views himself or herself as protagonist. But the reefs and rocks with which they have to contend are founded in the structure of our society, while the storms and tides and currents that buffet them emerge from the interplay – as complex as the climate – of economic and political movements operating on a vast and impersonal scale, certainly outside their control, possibly beyond anyone's.

Altogether I must have interviewed about 500 individuals for anything from five minutes to four hours, and observed many more in social situations. I offered payment in the cases of most acute need, but this was almost always refused. In every case I gave what welfare advice I could. Many people asked to appear under pseudonyms – something I've not encountered much before, but it is an indicator of the extent of anxiety, shame and illegality in the inner city. A number of others who did not request pseudonyms have been given them, either because they were children or to protect them. I have had to do this with the entire 'Davies' family, who appear frequently in these pages, to protect 'Mike Davies'. The story of each individual is told in one place – hence documentary material, especially on housing, jobs, incomes and social security, is found throughout the book as well as in topical chapters. (For the Davies family, see the Index, page 441.)

The research was carried out between May 1981 and July 1982. All statements in the present tense refer to the situation at that time. Social-security rates and many pay rates change around November each year, so I have stated which period the income quoted relates to: 1981 means before 1 November 1981; 1982 means from then until July 1982. Where a date is not given, 1981 is referred to. A guide to some local prices and incomes for 1981 is given on page 436.

Needless to say, I do not agree with all the views put forward by my subjects especially on race and crime, but I record them because, for good or ill, they are of social significance. I have checked what I can of people's stories and am satisfied that all those included correspond to the facts. Statements that cannot be checked are consistent with a wider range of interviews. Some may seem incredible to those unfamiliar with the disadvantaged; to those who live or work among them they will appear routine. For one can say of the inner city, as the choir of angels in Goethe's *Faust* says of heaven, 'The indescribable is enacted here.'

Acknowledgements

This book would not have been possible without the cooperation of many people and institutions. First and foremost, of course, there are all those individuals whose stories figure in the following pages and who, in one sense, wrote this book.

The London Borough of Hackney Council provided first-rate cooperation. I would like to thank in particular John Kotz, leader of the Labour Group at the time the research was done, and chief executive Dennis Woods, whose combined instructions opened many doors; and also research and intelligence officer Robin Morphet, who provided unstinting help with documentation and coordinated the checking of the book. My task was also considerably lightened by official reports from many council departments, economic studies by the Hackney–Islington Partnership, and the crime reports of the *Hackney Gazette*.

I should also like to thank the many officials of Hackney's Housing, Social Services and Technical Services departments who gave me their time, the Staffa Strike Committee, Hackney Trade Union Support Unit, the Springfield Project, the Hackney Cypriot Association, the Hackney Asian Association, Holly Street Tenants' Association, the Edridge Chambers probation officers, Hoxton Hall, Stamford Hill and St Paul's Youth Clubs, Nightingale Lunch Club, Gayhurst Infants School, Clissold Park and Hackney Downs secondary schools, the G district of the Metropolitan Police and Stanley Clinton Davis MP.

Thanks are due to the editor of *New Society* for permission to use a few items first published there. And, finally, thanks go to those who kindly checked through parts of the manuscript and whose comments helped to improve it: Janet Allbeson, John Bligh, John Brittain, Robin Chambers, Trevor Dawling, Ian Haig, Eileen Howes, Commander George Howlett, Graham Hudson, Adrian Lovatt, Alan Macfarlane, David Rangecroft, Mike Seward, Malcolm Rose, Sue Shutter, Jean Wait, Peter Wickenden and Fedelma Winkler. Naturally they bear no responsibility for the accuracy of this book or the opinions expressed in it.

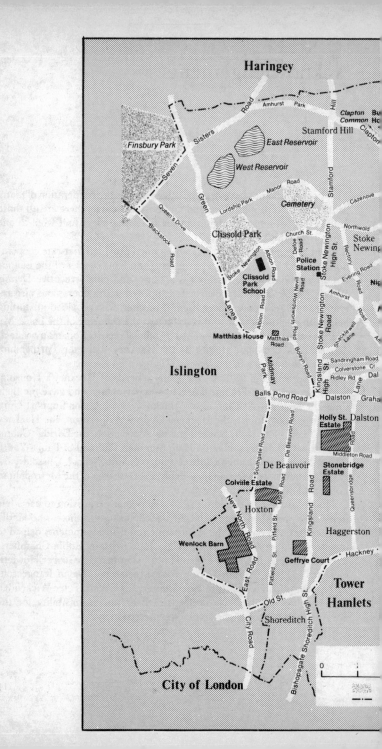

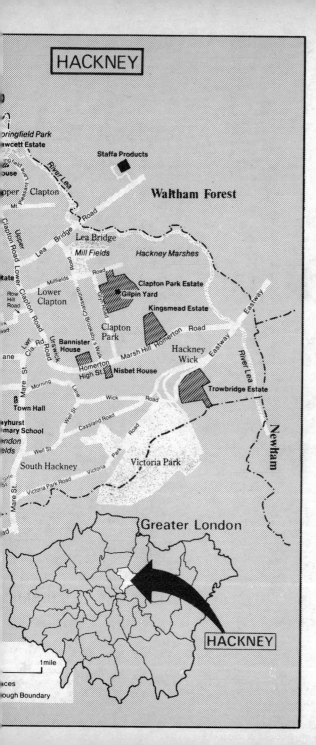

HACKNEY

Springfield Park
Fawcett Estate

Staffa Products

River Lea

Waltham Forest

Upper Clapton

Mt.

Lea Bridge Road

Lea Bridge

Mill Fields

Hackney Marshes

Lower Clapton

Clapton Park Estate

Gilpin Yard

Kingsmead Estate

Clapton Park

Homerton Road

Bannister House

Marsh Hill

Hackney Wick

Eastway

Homerton High St.

Nisbet House

River Lea

Mare St.

Wick Road

Morning Lane

Town Hall

Cassland Road

Road

Trowbridge Estate

Newham

Mayhurst Primary School

Well St.

London Fields

Victoria Park

South Hackney

Victoria Park Road

Mare St.

Greater London

HACKNEY

1 mile

Places

Borough Boundary

Prologue

1 The Inner City:
A Symptom and a Warning

If you stand where the kites fly on the summit of Parliament Hill in Hampstead, on a clear day you will see, about half-way between the spire of St Michael's church in Highgate and the steel-and-glass skyscrapers of the City of London, the six immense tower blocks of Nightingale Estate. They stand, in two ranks of three, almost in the centre of Hackney. It is less than four miles from Hampstead and Highgate in space, but if social distances were measured in miles it would be half-way round the globe. The gulf between the inner city and the desirable neighbourhood is a measure of the wide gap between wealth and poverty in Britain.

The inner city is the social antipodes of middle-class Britain, a universe apart, an alien world devoid of almost every feature of an ideal environment. It is the place where all our social ills come together, the place where all our sins are paid for.

The inner city is now, and is likely to remain, Britain's most dramatic and intractable social problem. For here are concentrated the worst housing, the highest unemployment, the greatest density of poor people, the highest crime rates and, more recently, the most serious threat posed to established law and order since the Second World War. And yet it is not a peculiar, exceptional problem. For all the deprivations found concentrated in the inner city are widespread throughout the country, strongly present in the peripheral northern and Celtic regions, and in scattered pockets almost everywhere. The inner city is therefore a microcosm of deprivation, of economic decline and of social disintegration in Britain today. It is not only a particular sort of place on the map, but a symbol and summation of the dark side of a whole society. I hope, therefore, that this book will be read in the first place as a book about Britain.

I have a personal interest to declare. My home town, Oldham, now rates officially as an inner-city area. If you stood on Oldham Edge and surveyed the horizon, you could count several hundred spinning-mill chimneys: all but a handful of the mills are now closed or converted. All the steep terraces of tiny houses where my school-friends lived have been pulled down and replaced, after a lengthy spell as wasteland, by ugly council estates. The street where I lived my first eight years is now an almost entirely Asian street.

I spent my three apprentice years of journalism in another blighted area, South Wales, and got to know Splott, decaying in the red haze of Cardiff's steelworks, and Butetown, one of Britain's two oldest areas of settled Commonwealth immigration; and the valleys, *urbs in rure*, inner-city areas in the countryside, if you can call countryside mountains of spoil-heaps and Coal Board terraces clinging to steep hillsides, overlooking towns even then, more than a decade ago, crippled by closures of pits and steelworks.

I moved to *New Society* and reported on many other inner-city areas, on race tensions in Brixton, breadline poverty in Gateshead, religious wars in Londonderry, prostitution in Southampton; and from inner-city areas in Southall, Swansea, Leicester, Coventry, Birmingham and Hackney.

For all their manifest differences there was something similar about all these places. There is no clear definition and no definitive listing of inner-city areas, but a useful pointer is the list of author-ities that receive funds under the various urban programmes. They include many inner London boroughs: Brent, Islington, Hackney, Newham and Tower Hamlets in the north and east, Hammersmith and Ealing in the west, Lambeth, Lewisham, Southwark, Green-wich and Wandsworth south of the river. Outside London they were, until 1980 at least, largely concentrated in a few (though heavily populated) areas: Clydeside, Tyneside, south-east Lan-cashire, South and West Yorkshire, the West Midlands, urban South Wales and urban Northern Ireland.

Three closely related factors define most of the problems of these areas. The first is that they are areas of older industry: clothing and textiles, shipbuilding, docking, and, more recently, steel, cars and refining. They are often areas of former prosperity, now upstaged by changes in the pattern of world trade, in technology or in transport. The gradual decline in competitiveness of these industries is paralleled by a gradual shedding of labour and a relative decline in wage rates – and hence rising unemployment and falling incomes among residents. Often firms in these places have been bought up by larger companies or multinationals, or absorbed into vast nationalized monopolies, so that the destinies of local people and communities are increasingly controlled from outside. What determines their prosperity or misery is an impersonal calculus of profit or rationalization pursued regardless of social costs.

Second, these are areas of particularly bad housing, a mixture of old Victorian terraces, often built specifically to house manual workers and now reaching the end of their useful life, and more modern council housing, frequently of the worst possible design; an environment short of parks and access to countryside, full of dereliction and dehumanized concrete, places as if infected by a peculiar physical disease of blight, like a wall patched with mould or a heath scarred by fire.

Third, these are areas with higher-than-average concentrations of manual workers, low-skilled, unskilled, or de-skilled as the industries they worked in have declined; areas of high unemployment and low incomes, where people are effectively stranded by their poverty, unable to travel to work outside the area, unable to afford private housing or to qualify for council housing elsewhere. People, like the places they live in, who were exploited for as long as there was profit in doing so and then abandoned to survive as best they could. The cheap housing in these areas also draws in other disadvantaged groups with low income or little capital: immigrants, single parents, the mentally and physically handicapped. At the same time the gradual decline of the area pushes out those with freedom to move – with savings, skills or educational qualifications.

The concentration of so many disadvantaged people in a single area produces other effects: local government poor in resources and sometimes in the quality of staffing; a poor health service, since doctors cannot find decent accommodation or much in the way of private practice; a low level of educational attainment due primarily to poor home backgrounds and the low average ability in schools; and, finally, high levels of crime, vandalism and family breakdown, and, wherever communities of divergent cultures live together, conflicts based on religion or race.

It is important not to consider the inner cities as unusual or isolated phenomena. The bulk of poverty, of bad housing, of declining industry, is in fact found outside the inner cities. The poor, wherever they live, carry their own inner city round with them, like snails their shells, and every urban area has some district of some size – even if it is only a single housing estate – that shares the interacting problems of concentrated poverty, unemployment, bad housing and crime of the larger inner city areas.

Conversely, a varying, often large proportion of those who live in local authorities commonly termed as 'inner city areas' are not seriously deprived. Every such authority has its more desirable streets and neighbourhoods, and Hackney is no exception. The inner city proper is invariably a more limited zone than the local authority boundary. Its irregular frontiers would in fact coincide with the location of disadvantaged people in sub-standard housing. Thus the inner city is less a precise geographical location than a mode of existence – more diffuse in some places, more concentrated in others – of the poor and disadvantaged. That is what makes it so hard to change, for it is not a surface wound that can be treated locally with a plaster, but the symptom of nationwide processes that create, and segregate, poverty.

The first of these diseases is a chaotic, unplanned process of economic advance, characteristic of British capitalism, that allows companies, private and public, to close down old plants regardless of the consequences for the people and communities that depend on them, in a callous, uncaring way, with little or no thought to prevention or mitigation. Related to this is the persistence of sharp class divisions between manual and non-manual workers, the 'educated' and the 'uneducated', and of long-lasting inequalities in wealth and income, all of these mapped in space in the marked segregation of middle-class and working-class areas. Added to this is the marginalization in British society of other groups – women, immigrants, the handicapped, the mentally ill, the unskilled and the under-educated – who are placed at a disadvantage by law, by social stigma, by discrimination, or by the changing requirements of the labour market.

All these wider structures generate large categories of disadvantaged people, who share a common problem of low income and therefore lowered freedom of choice. They are scattered widely across the country, found in greater numbers in the Celtic and northern regions, and in concentration in the inner city.

The inner city is therefore of far more than local interest. It is the bombardment chamber where the particles generated and accelerated by the cyclotron of a whole society are smashed into each other. It is therefore a very good place to learn about the destructive forces inherent in that society.

The state of the inner city is a warning of what much of Britain's urban future may look like unless there is a radical change in policies.

For the sake of concreteness and coherence, I have chosen a single such area, Hackney, as the source of my examples. But this is not a book about Hackney as such. It is about those parts of Hackney that suffer from the inner-city syndrome, and the examples are intended to reflect the realities and problems of life for the poor within inner-city areas, and in many respects outside them, throughout Britain.

2 The Killing Ground
by the River

There is perhaps only one place within Hackney's boundaries where all its diverse elements can be seen in combination: Ridley Road market. Heading east off Kingsland High Street, it is crowded even in the rain. On Fridays and Saturdays, stalls line the street between the permanent booths, and between the stalls is a crush of people: Asian women with their nylon saris trailing the wet pavement, West Indians pushing double buggies with babies dozing or staring out of plastic greenhouse rain-covers, squeezing past knots of dark-eyed Turkish Cypriot ladies exchanging gossip. A giant Pakistani with a spade beard, skull-cap and flapping *kunta* stands by a blazing pile of boxes and crates. Three teenage black boys nudge each other as they notice two helmeted white police-men peering out between a gap in racks of cheap skirts. Behind, a Bengali staggers down the steps of a clothing factory clutching a huge bale of cut cloth for machining at home. It is a lively place, where people talk freely and you can overhear many a fragmentary tale of drama and woe: 'I've only been in my flat two years and the rent's gone up twelve times.' 'Well, you don't expect him to be a monk, but it's a bit much doing it in front of his daughter.' And a descant is provided by two West Indian ladies, one with a white stick, chanting the praises of the Lord in syncopated rhythm.

Like Hackney as a whole, Ridley Road is a motley collection of human beings gathered together in this particular corner of the world in pursuit of a living of kinds, all of them preoccupied with obtaining a modest and often temporary state, as near approaching happiness as is feasible in Hackney, or perhaps, for most, only with the increasingly difficult business of surviving. Behind those faces lie reaches of space and time, the wheat and rice fields of South Asia, the hills and olive groves of the Mediterranean, the plantations of the Caribbean, the ghettos of Poland,

Russia and Germany, underemployment and poverty in shanty towns and villages; and behind the history of each individual the history of parents and grandparents and ancestors, of Atlantic crossings and slave-masters, of Turks and Greeks, Islam and Christianity and Judaism, wars of imperial conquest, wars of independence, civil wars, pogroms and persecutions, and of oppression in the British Isles, of colonialism in Ireland, of clearances and enclosures in Scotland and England. If you pursued the chain of causes that led these people to be in this place, you would encapsulate much of the history of humanity and of inhumanity. If you investigated the present circumstances of their lives, you would discover much of the reality of deprivation and injustice in Britain today.

Ridley Road has to cater for the tastes and habits of the world. There are stalls, all manned by whites, specializing in tropical fare: red sweet potatoes, log-like yams, green plantains, cocoyams, cassava, okra, papaw, all costing two or three times the price of home-grown staples. And there are gaudy decorations for assorted festivals, incense and Eastern perfumes, curly wigs and tresses for black women, and curious neo-colonial cosmetic preparations with which they can lighten their hue and straighten their hair: Blue Magic Pressing Oil, Dixie Peach Pomade, Leon's Double Strength Hair-Grower and Dr Fred Palmer's Famous Skin Whitener. Ridley Road caters for poverty, too. You can get really cheap meat in the butchers' shops, provided you bear in mind the Arab proverb: 'Buy cheap meat and when it boils you'll smell what you have saved.' When the cheapest decent meat cost £1 or £1·20 a pound, here you could get mutton shoulder for 79p a pound – a joint shaped like a plasterer's float, with very little lean to it. For 50p a pound you could get unidentified and unidentifiable chunks of meat networked with fat and gristle, or the front leg of a cow from the knee down. For 45p a pound you could get pigs' tails floating in buckets of purple brine. For a mere 33p you could get a pound of assorted blackening scraps, not more than one-third lean, the rest fat, gristle, skin and the odd hair. And hanging on display are items you would rarely spot in your Potter's Bar butchers: pigs' trotters, tripe, and even a pair of lungs complete with oesophagus. These types of cut, the majority of them as lacking in nutritional value as in aesthetic appeal, make up at least half the window displays of most Ridley Road butchers. Clothes are cheap here too: 'perfect' tights at 90p for five, children's trousers or sweaters at £1·99 a time, gents' shoes from £8·99 – most things at roughly half the normal high-street price, many of which will, shortly after purchase, illustrate the maxim 'buy cheap and you buy twice'.

Yet there are many people in Hackney for whom even half-price is too much. For them, a few metres from the market, the dingy church hall of St Mark's holds a succession of jumble sales. A jumble sale in a poor district is not like a village bazaar: the queues start forming up an hour early, the doors open like a dam bursting, the customers, mostly women with the odd male pensioner or child, stampede towards trestle tables two feet deep in petticoats, blouses, cardigans. They rummage with desperate determination and an abandon born of need and the devil-may-care attitude of people who have broken with deep-rooted taboos, who do not care or cannot afford to care about wearing other people's cast-offs. The clothes fly, the piles become distorted into tangles and knots. A white woman in her twenties holds a faded denim skirt to her waist to check the length. Two teenage black girls discuss whether to buy a pair of scuffed clogs. At the bric-à-brac counter an air of exploration and discovery prevails, and a man clasping a dusty toaster to himself as if it were a pot of gold examines an old vacuum cleaner dirtier than any floor it could ever be called upon to clean.

Back at Ridley Road, towards the end of the afternoon, the price of fresh fruit and vegetables falls and the traders shout louder and more often, and the bus queues lengthen in St Mark's Rise. A 236 bus for Leytonstone pulls up. Twenty are standing inside and the windows are painted with steam. It pulls away leaving half the queue at the stop. A minute later another 236 comes along empty, and another immediately behind that. The stallholders load up their vans till they can't see out of the windows. By 5 o'clock there is only the big yellow Hackney dustcart growling along while dustmen fling cartons and boxes into its rumbling belly.

Now comes the hour of the scavengers, human beings that poverty has reduced to the level of jackals. A West Indian in a woolly hat rummages through a box of black plantains, picking out those that still have a few streaks of yellow. An old Mediterranean man limps from one pile to another, poking among squashed cucumbers and rotten oranges with his aluminium stick. A man in a corduroy jacket spots a box of cocoyams dumped by a lamp-post. Most are·superficially flecked with mould, nothing serious. He looks around cautiously, then stuffs a few into a green plastic bag. As I pass, he stands up and pretends to be admiring the view. Then he crouches down again, sees that the plastic bag is not big enough, places the bag in the box and walks rapidly away with it, like someone who has just committed a crime.

The Breaker's Yard

Hackney, like most urban settlements of any size, is a patchwork. It exists as a unit only as a local-government entity. It possesses an aorta: the long straight road, once the Romans' route to Cambridge, that begins in the south as Shoreditch High Street and ends in the north at Stamford Hill, changing its name half a dozen times along the way, from Kingsland Road to Kingsland High Street, and from Stoke Newington Road to Stoke Newington High Street. But Hackney is a place curiously without a heart, an uneasy amalgam, still only in its late teens, of three older boroughs – Shoreditch, Hackney and Stoke Newington – themselves formed by the fusion of several parishes.

Hackney is an archipelago of islands, each with its own distinctive geomorphology and ecology. In Shoreditch, atolls of dilapidated small factories, warehouses and offices, cut off by a sea of metropolitan traffic. To the north, Hoxton, a concrete forest of council blocks, still largely inhabited by Cockneys, one of the few places in the borough's boundaries where some networks of community and kinship survive, albeit much weakened and frayed. Further north again, De Beauvoir, whose stately terraces – by far the best built and best laid out in Hackney – increasingly house the upper-middle and professional classes. East of that, Haggerston and Queensbridge wards, more than three-quarters council tenants, and planning-blighted London Fields and Broadway Market, with shops boarded up or burnt out and streets of houses either empty, with doors and windows breeze-blocked up, or housing squats of radicals and feminists: *Why pay rent when they don't give a damn about you?* reads one pointed slogan. East again, Homerton and Lower Clapton, streets of humble Victorian terraces, many of them not much above the level of the Hackney Marshes and the River Lea that bound the borough's eastern limits. The Marshes, Hackney's only area of 'natural' wildlife, are marred by motorbike scramblers, electricity pylons and what little exists of large-scale industry in Hackney – Lesney's Matchbox Toys (closed down in 1982), Metal Box, James Latham Timbers.

Inside the bend of the river, stretching from Stamford Hill down to the flyovers of Eastway, a long succession of council estates, each cursed with its own subtle combination of torments: the rain-penetrated towers of Trowbridge; Kingsmead with its air of a high-security prison; crime-plagued Clapton Park; and a row of grim blocks – like Wren's Park, Wigan House, Lea View and Fawcett. Along the borough's northern edges, bounded by Seven Sisters Road and Amhurst Park, lie the more desirable wards of Hackney, becoming fashionable among radical professionals and long the home of most of Hackney's large Jewish population, including members of the revivalist Hasidic sect whose bearded men wear broad-brimmed black hats, long black coats and hair in ringlets. And in the heart of Hackney lie terraces of the worst Victorian housing, originally dominated by cheap rooming houses, now in the process of changing over to gentrification, housing associations and infill council housing: a chaotic mixture of races and classes where whites, West Indians, Asians, Africans and Cypriots are shuffled like the suits in a pack of cards.

Even a superficial tour would show that most of Hackney is not healthy or prosperous. There are piles of refuse in many streets, and run-down shops with safety grilles left up even when they are open. There is an air about people in the street or in the bus queues: of patience adopted not out of a tranquil mind, but out of necessity, holding in a tense bolus of sufferings. An air, not of open despair, but of lack of hope; not of misery, yet of an absence of joy. An air of aggravation and diffuse anxiety. For the inner city is a sump for the disadvantaged of every kind, a place to which those with the fewest resources sink, and from which those who gain any freedom of choice escape. It is a place of deprivation, of toil and struggle and isolation, a knacker's yard for society's casualties, a breaker's yard where the pressure of need grinds people against each other and wears them down.

You can get a glimpse of the problem from the statistics. Even by Inner London standards, Hackney is an unusually underprivileged place. It has the second highest proportion of overcrowded households in Inner London, the second highest proportion of manual workers (two-thirds), the second highest proportion of households with no car (two-thirds), the second highest male unemployment rate (22 per cent in January 1982), and the second highest proportion of children in care (one child in forty). On all these criteria, Tower Hamlets, usually known as London's East End, pips it to the post. But Hackney leads Tower Hamlets in other indicators: it has the second highest proportion (after Haringey) of people living in households with a New Commonwealth head (27 per cent), the second highest incidence (after Lambeth) of violent street crime. And Hackney leads the field for a string of other factors. It has the highest female unemployment rate in London and the highest proportion of single-parent families (with 15 per cent of children under sixteen). It has by far the highest proportion of dwellings unfit for human habitation – one in five – and by far the lowest educational attainments in London. It has the highest proportion of registered disabled in London. It has the highest level of smoke pollution. And it has the honour of being the only Inner London borough without a tube station. Incomes in Hackney are the lowest in London, and well below the national averages despite much higher than average housing and transport costs. In April 1981, average weekly earnings were £133·50 for men and £94 for women – bottom of the Greater London league in both cases. One in three male manual workers earned less than £100 a week, one in ten earned less than £72·30. These figures are for full-time workers whose earnings were unaffected by absence: average *incomes* in Hackney, dragged down by high levels of part-time or short-time working, by lay-offs and absenteeism, and by unemployment, are far lower. On a composite scale devised by the Department of the Environment in 1983, based on unemployment rates, housing and family conditions, Hackney came top of the deprivation scale in England.

There are, too, subjective measures. In 1978 the National

Housing and Dwelling Survey asked people in inner-city areas what they thought of their neighbourhood. The proportion of respondents in Hackney who were dissatisfied or very dissatisfied with the area was 42 per cent, by far the highest in the country – a full 11 per cent ahead of Tower Hamlets, the nearest London rival, and almost double the highest figure outside London (22 per cent for Manchester).

It is invidious to make comparisons, but I believe that the inner city zone of Hackney is one of two or three contenders for the title of the Most Deprived Place in Britain.

There are many people who live in Hackney who will deny this: middle-class owner-occupiers will tell you aggressively that it is not at all such a bad place to live. And probably it is not, for people with cars, telephones, bank accounts and self-contained dwellings. They do not have to walk along dangerous streets with all the money they possess in their pockets, or queue for hours at bus stops, or search for unvandalized phones when someone falls ill. They do not have to share toilets or baths. They do not have to wrestle shopping and pushchairs up stairs or into lifts that often do not work. They do not have to suffer damp and cold. They do not have to be humiliated in social-security offices or wait months for essential repairs. Above all they are there by choice, not by compulsion. They can leave at any time they want: they do not have the sense of imprisonment, of closed options, that plagues those without the incomes or the saleable skills that would enable them to get out. Whether a place is tolerable to live in, or intolerable, depends on your income; that is as true of Britain as a whole as it is of Hackney. For the poor, the inner city is something akin to the Slough of Despond, a place so terrible that the only recourse seems to turn tail and run. Yet most of them lack the means of escape – the money to buy a house elsewhere, the skills or certificates to get a job elsewhere.

The View from Golf Four

There is no better initiation into the peculiar character of the inner city than a Saturday spent in a police area-car. The police inevitably view a district through jaundiced eyes. For the most part they do not see the ordinary or the agreeable. They are called in when normality breaks down, when peaceful methods of resolving problems have failed. They see the points of conflict and conflagration. Just as the inner city is untypical, and yet symptomatic, of Britain, so these crises are not average for Hackney, but they crystallize the chemicals that are present, in invisible solution, throughout the area. For what sets Hackney apart from Hampstead or Harrogate is not only the appalling state of housing, the low incomes, the insecure employment, the mix of cultures, but also, more than each of these taken singly, the consequences of their coexistence in one place. The result is not an addition of problems but a multiplication. The product is a degree of fragmentation – of communities, families and even individuals – and a level of routine violence against property, against neighbours, relatives, even against the self, that can only be believed if witnessed.

I spent the afternoon and evening of 2 January 1982 in Golf Four, the red-striped white Rover that patrols the Stoke Newington area. The driver is Colin Dryden, a burly, bearded Scot. In the passenger seat is his operator, WPC Karen Connor. Our first call is to a 'disturbance' in a row of new council maisonettes just off Stamford Hill. A Cypriot woman in her late fifties, with an orange flowered dress and a red headscarf pulled down to her eyebrows, welcomes Dryden with tears. Her eighteen-year-old son has assaulted her and punched her in the throat. She complains of difficulty in swallowing and speaking. Her English is poor, but the message comes across: 'He hit me, push me. He very bad boy. I bring him up good, why he like this? All the time he want money, but I get only £22 a week, how can I give him? When he was a baby his father hitting me, now he grow up he hitting me too. Why? Why?' She cries out at the injustices of destiny. Dryden has been called here before; this has been going on since the boy was a juvenile. He tells her simply to lock her door, keep her son out, and phone the police if he comes again. The woman is grateful, as much for the comfort of a visit as for the advice. 'Thank you, thank you. I don't like to waste your time. God bless you. Happy New Year.'

The next call is to a burglary in Mount Pleasant Lane, a row of semi-detached private houses looking out at the back over steep lanes leading down to the River Lea, and at the front across some of

33

the most dismal problem estates in Hackney. The resident had left a back window open and a neighbour had seen two men climb out carrying plastic bags. It is a fact of life in Hackney that any way of entry left open will, with a probability approaching unity, be entered, just as surely as scattered breadcrumbs will be lifted by hungry birds.

Three abortive but typical 'shouts' follow. A female in a fur coat passing a stolen Access card in Mare Street. An attempted mugging in Stamford Hill, where two youths have been chased off by a group of irate Jews (it is rumoured that they are developing a new approach of aggressive group self-defence). In both cases Golf Four is beaten to it by one of the other three area-cars cruising around Hackney. Glue-sniffers, reported to be causing a disturbance at Malvern House on Stamford Hill Estate, have melted away before we arrive. We continue our routine patrol, heading north for Finsbury Park, where crowds of youths hundreds strong are making their way home on foot from a Spurs–Arsenal fixture. Trouble is expected but does not materialize. Along West Bank Karen Connor points out the locations of three murders in the past year, two of them over arguments at a drinking den in a private house.

On to the major red-light district in Hackney, around Queen's Drive. Most inner-city areas have such market-places in human flesh, where the local female poor sell their wares to passers-through with funds to spare. The location of this one is determined by the proximity of an ample supply of the cheaper kind of hotel and of the major trunk route of Seven Sisters Road. Unfortunately, it is also a residential area. As English law hypocritically allows prostitutes to work, but not to make themselves known, all local females risk being propositioned by kerb-crawlers. Tonight five girls are out 'tomming'. When they spot Golf Four they turn on their heels and walk off briskly. Karen Connor stops three for questioning. They deny they were soliciting. Connor asks if they have any contraceptives in their handbags and takes their word when they say no. There is no need to come heavy: a special police 'tom squad' is operating in the area and already driving the trade away, though only to other streets in Hackney.

The radio bleeps again. Down in Shoreditch a gang of forty

white youths are being chased after a mugging. We race down Kingsland High Street, but by the time we get there most of the culprits have been caught and are stamping, like wild horses in a corral, inside a ring of police. Dryden adjusts his speed according to the urgency of the call: slower for a 'disturbance', which could be anything from a neighbours' quarrel to a mass punch-up; faster, with two-tone horn and blue light, for serious violence, robberies or burglaries where there is a chance of catching the offender on the spot.

For the next call he hits 150 kilometres an hour. It is a reported shooting at Portland Avenue, just off Upper Clapton Road, with the wounded victim still on the premises. We are the first to arrive and enter with some caution. The door of the downstairs flat is opened by a lady in her late fifties with straggling red hair and a coat of slightly mangy fox fur. 'I know this woman,' Dryden mutters. 'She's a nutter.' The flat is crammed tight with old furniture, tea-chests, large plastic bags full of possessions and undiscarded rubbish. An alsatian crawls along the passage behind us, dragging its paralysed back legs. In the bedroom a man in a green overcoat is lying on the floor groaning. 'They've shot him in the head,' the woman says. 'They've got illegal weapons upstairs, they've got stolen GPO equipment, for communications.' An examination reveals no trace of a wound. 'It must have been an airgun then, pellets. He fell down the stairs here. I don't know what happened,' the lady rambles. Dryden raises the man's head gently. His eyes open and roll, he extends a hand and says, 'I love you.' 'He's as drunk as a skunk,' says Dryden, then rounds on the woman: 'If you carry on giving us false alarms like this, I'm warning you, I'll take you to court for wasting police time.' We leave her as the ambulance crew arrives. Across the road, Hasidic men in Sabbath outfits, flat mink hats and white stockings, look on. Karen Connor radios back her report: 'Man very drunk. Woman suffering from harmless delusions.' 'That was your typical Stoke Newington nutter – the place is full of them,' Dryden comments as we drive off. Connor recalls the day, a few weeks earlier, when she had to deal with a woman who was found stark naked in the middle of Kingsland High Street eating the flesh of her feet. Hackney has far more than its fair share of mental illness.

We round off the evening with family problems: twice we are called to a low-rise block on Nightingale estate, where a black couple are complaining that the woman's former husband has been besieging them since the day before, kicking their front door, peering from landings into their windows, heaving half-bricks at his ex-wife's new boy-friend and posting ominous notes like the following: 'What I want, I won't give up till I get it, even it cost my life.' What he wants, it transpires, is the child his ex-wife has custody of.

The climax of the evening is a call to all units to proceed to Nisbett House in Homerton, where Golf Three is in trouble and has requested assistance. It is a grim tenement of dark, rectangular, walk-up blocks, five storeys high, arranged around a central courtyard. A black man has barricaded himself in his flat. He is standing at a ground-floor window, clutching a baby. Another child is inside. His common-law wife is out in the courtyard; she is nursing a badly injured arm and has a large purple bruise below her left eye. A white neighbour commiserates: 'Was that the row that was going on earlier?' 'He's been beating me up all day, since this morning.' 'I heard it. You could hear the screams all over the court. I saw at least thirty men walk past, and not one of them lifted a finger to help. I thought it was disgusting.' By late evening an exceptionally public-spirited neighbour finally called the police. Golf Three arrived. The wife wanted to prefer charges. When the officers tried to arrest the man, he lunged at them with a knife. They drew their truncheons and he ran into the kitchen and got a meat cleaver. The police retreated with the wife. The man locked them out, with the children still in the bedroom.

When we arrive, other police officers are talking to him through the window. Two white police minis draw up. Four alsatians leap out and pull their handlers along to the grass outside the window, snarling at the man. Another police van – the Immediate Response Unit, introduced after the 1981 riots – screeches to a halt and ten men jump out with riot shields and crash helmets. Residents hang, silhouetted, out of the upper-floor windows. The man under siege begins to cool down a little in the face of such superior force. He agrees to come out peaceably, under protest: 'There's no right for anyone to break into a man's house and beat his head in.' He is led out, complaining, as a short-sleeved policeman holds him firmly by the arm. 'Get back where you came from,' shouts a middle-aged white man in a bobble hat as the captive is loaded into a dark blue van. The children are carried out and brought to the mother, all three of them crying as they are driven off to the station. Father follows, handcuffed, inside the Black Maria.

So much of the inner city's essence was enacted here: two people, both, as it happened, with no work, imprisoned in squalid architecture, loudly destroying each other and their children. Apathy or passive withdrawal among neighbours. And the grand finale, the police acting as undertakers at the public burial of what, once upon a time, must have been a human relationship.

So it went on, pursuing stolen cars, calming angry disputes between a tenant and his resident landlord, between next-door neighbours and at a noisy reggae party. It has been, according to Colin Dryden, a fairly quiet night, with less in the way of serious crime than average. But it has served well as a guided tour of the inner city's sights, its victims and the victims of its victims. For the saddest aspect of such places is the way they accentuate adversity, setting their inhabitants at each other's throats like rats in an overcrowded cage.

From Country Retreat to Inner City: The Genesis of the Problem

Hackney has not always been such a place. Its first historical associations were, admittedly, resonant of its modern plight. The name was believed by early etymologists to identify the riverside site of a bloody battle. Modern scholars believe it means 'Haca's island', or 'the land in the bend of the river'. In AD 896 invading Vikings sailed up the River Lea, and King Alfred the Great cut a canal that altered the river's course, leaving the Vikings stranded and creating the fertile land that became known as King's Mead. Stoke Newington (meaning 'new town in the wood') rates a mention in the Domesday Book of 1086: 'There is land for two ploughs and a half . . . There are four villanes and thirty-seven cottagers with ten acres.'

Shoreditch, in the south, was first urbanized and early acquired a reputation as a poor, disreputable and dangerous quarter. The name probably means 'sewer's ditch'. The first English stage, known simply as the Theatre, was built here by James Burbage and demolished in 1598 to provide materials for the building of the Globe. That same year a petition of residents complained to the authorities: 'there are divers persons that are owners of small tenements . . . that doe lett the same out by the week . . . unto base people and to lewd persons that do keep evell rule and harbour thiefes, rogues and vagabonds.' The perennial association of bad housing with the bottom layers of an unequal society was already forged. Peter Cunningham's 1850 *Handbook of London* cites a Dryden quote of 1680: 'Courage, I say; as long as the merry pence hold out, you shall none of you die in Shoreditch.' 'To die in Shoreditch', Cunningham explains, 'was not a mere metaphorical term for dying in a sewer.'

In the seventeenth and eighteenth centuries, however, the parish of Hackney proper was an area of country houses, pleasure gardens, farms and watercress beds supplying the City of London with dairy produce and vegetables. Samuel Pepys records a trip to Hackney on a warm and pleasant day in June 1664: 'There light and played at shuffle board, eat cream and good cherries, and so with good refreshment home.' Daniel Defoe moved in in 1708, and wrote *Robinson Crusoe* in a residence off Stoke Newington Church Street. A travel writer of the eighteenth century commended the place: 'Anciently celebrated for the numerous seats of the nobility and gentry, it so greatly abounds with merchants and persons of distinction that it excels all other villages in the kingdom, and possibly on earth, in the richness and opulence of its inhabitants.' Highwaymen were attracted by the traffic of fine coaches; on Stamford Hill, where his less gentlemanly successors roam the streets today, Dick Turpin is said to have held up many a carriage, escaping to the White House, an inn on Hackney Marshes.

Shoreditch crept northwards and filled up in the first half of the nineteenth century, taking in elements of the City of London's proletariat, driven out by demolitions and developments, and many of the labourers working on London's docks. Its population expanded from 34,766 in 1801 to a peak of 129,364 in 1861, crushed into an area of just over 250 hectares or one square mile – it is still crowded today with a quarter of that number. To the north, the parish of Hackney had grown from a mere 12,730 in 1801 to 53,589 in mid-century. But the growth of the railways provided the stimulus to its fastest period of expansion. In 1850 the North London line linked Bow with Islington via Hackney. The year 1865 saw the opening of a branch line from Dalston junction to the City, and seven years later the Great Eastern Railway ran from Shoreditch through Hackney to Enfield, with a branch to Walthamstow via Hackney Downs and Clapton. Thus, between 1861 and 1891, Hackney added no less than 122,000 people to its population, finally reaching a peak of 222,533 in 1911.

But Hackney's hour had come and gone within a couple of decades: the railway lines built in the 1870s made it easier for those with a little extra cash to live out in the greener suburbs beyond Hackney. Had Hackney boasted an ample supply of decent housing, it might yet have remained a decent place to live; but it quickly acquired far more than its fair share of bad housing. The Lords of the Manor, the Tyssen-Amhurst family, sold the land to developers in smallish parcels, on building leases. The developers – larger builders or small-time speculators – would in turn spread the capital risk by subdividing the work between half a dozen or more smaller firms, building only three or four houses each. The developers and builders were out for a quick return, and the more corners they cut, the bigger their profit. Much of the land had been used as clay-pits to make bricks for the City. Other parts were marshy or had a high water-table. But Victorian builders, far from building more securely to compensate, often knocked together dwellings as shaky as their subsoil.

This was the decisive moment that determined Hackney's destiny, creating the legacy of bad housing that, by its low rents, in its turn attracted the disadvantaged. This was the key to the mystery of how a desirable suburb becomes a social dumping ground. An anonymous journalist styling himself *Flaneur* (Stroller), whose talents were far above his humble column in the *Hackney and Kingsland Gazette*, took a perceptive look at some of the houses being built in 1875, at the height of the development boom. Some houses were built on clay-pits infilled with public refuse. Even where the sites were solid, builders would dig out the sand

and gravel to a depth of two or three metres and sell it, replacing it with soft parish ashes and road-sweepings and sometimes worse. On one site our observer noticed bones being tipped: a human skull, which the workmen hastily covered up, indicated that these were remains removed from condemned churchyards in the City. In some cases rotting vegetables were dumped, and sewer gas was always escaping from under the floorboards, where colonies of rats held 'perpetual grand carnival'. 'On this soft and yielding bottom, dozen of houses were erected, and the processes of putting in the footings might be compared to that of a hen scratching a slight hollow of nest in the road to lay her eggs in.'

The superstructures were hardly better than the foundations. Old rotten timbers and green, sappy ones were used for joists and rafters. Often they were far too thin for the loads they had to bear. Floor joists, instead of being set into the brick walls, were propped up on loose piles of half-bricks. As for the walls: 'The bricks are of the most inferior quality and, save only those which constitute the front or exposed parts, are utterly bad and worthless. The interior walls are mostly of the bricks of old houses bought at sales in the city.' Thus, Stroller concluded, all the houses in each terrace had 'a mutual dependence on one another – together they stand and together they'll fall'. All these malpractices were going on 'within sight of the parochial rulers, some of whom had a direct or indirect interest'. Hackney today is still paying the cost of that speculation and that public laxity.

The new Hackney began as a middle- to lower-middle-class suburb, but the poor quality of the construction soon led to social decline – a process that greatly intrigued Charles Booth. In his mammoth survey of London, Booth wrote in 1900, 'The first tenants of a newly built street are usually of a fairly good kind. They quit when the freshness of the house wears off.' A 'lower stamp' of tenant follows: 'By this time the houses are much out of order. Money must be spent. This is the crucial moment.' If the money is spent, a decent, stable sort of tenant emerges. 'But if the houses have been badly built, no patching avails, and, a worse class of tenant succeeding, the street, and it may be the whole neighbourhood, falls irretrievably.' Some of the larger houses intended for families with servants had to be let by the room almost as soon as they were built. Many terraced houses were built right from the start with multi-occupation in mind.

It is remarkable how many of Charles Booth's comments are still applicable to modern Hackney, underlining the long-term nature of the fate of stigmatized localities. 'Hackney is becoming poorer,' he wrote. 'The larger houses are turned into factories. The better-to-do residents are leaving or have left . . . Their places are taken . . . by a lower or middle grade. Each class as it moves away is replaced by one slightly poorer and lower.' In the south of Shoreditch, housing was already giving way to warehouses and factories, and the houses that remained were mostly sublet and grossly overcrowded. Hoxton was worse then than it is now, but in degree rather than in kind: 'Wall off Hoxton, it is said, and nine-tenths of the criminal population of London would be walled off . . . About a quarter of them are chronically out of work.' Booth also noticed 'bands of boys, named after this or that street, making themselves the terror of the neighbourhood'.

Outside Shoreditch, the worst poverty, marked in black and blue on Booth's hand-coloured street maps, was concentrated in Homerton and Hackney Wick, where the low lie of the ground, not much higher than the rain-swelled level of the Lea, made housing particularly unattractive: 'It would seem as though the rejected from the centre have been flung completely over the heads of the rest of the population to alight where no man had yet settled, occupying undesirable ill-built houses on the marshy land that is drained or flooded by the River Lea.' Hackney Wick, commented Booth, 'consists largely of failures who have drifted there from other districts. Dirty, shiftless, helpless and undisciplined, but not criminal, they lack the sturdiness of offenders and are rather to be described as crushed and downtrodden . . . We are told that those who can and do improve, leave.'

Stoke Newington was spared the fate of the inner city for much longer. In 1871 it was still a suburban retreat for gentlefolk with only 9,841 residents. By 1901 it had 51,247, and has remained at that level ever since. On Booth's maps Stoke Newington's streets are coloured mainly in red, for well-to-do, while along Upper Clapton Road and around a few of the parks there are even some streaks of yellow, signifying the wealthy.

Hackney's predicament has been shaped as much by the character of its local economy as by the state of its housing. Since the latter half of the nineteenth century the mainstays have been clothing, and to a lesser extent shoemaking and furniture. All three were notorious for 'sweating' their workers – that is, squeezing out a prodigious amount of labour for a minimal reward. As the largest settlement of poor people in the country, the East End had been the heart of the second-hand clothing trade since the sixteenth century. It became a natural site for clothing manufacture when the invention of the sewing machine in 1846, and the growth of fashion houses and chain stores, made possible the ready-to-wear revolution. But the factory system never really caught on in the rag trade. The essential equipment, the sewing-machine, was cheap, compact, and could be accommodated, with some discomfort, in homes and tiny workshops. And the fashion business demanded an infinite and rapidly changing variety of styles and sizes, requiring a flexible and seasonal supply. Mass production was impossible. Large-scale factories employing a stable workforce were – and still are – at a positive disadvantage. The seasonal ebb and flow of orders led to a seasonal pattern of employment, with extra workers being taken on in spring and autumn and laid off again in summer and winter.

The nature of the local labour force lent itself readily to exploitation. First there were the wives of builders, labourers, dockers, porters – men in irregular, low-paid jobs for whom the wife's earnings were indispensable for survival. The sewing-machine allowed many of them to combine earning with their duties as mothers and housewives – albeit often at the cost of their own wellbeing and that of their children. The second source of labour was immigrants: the Jews, especially after the pogroms of 1881–6 in Russia and Poland; then, from the 1950s on, West Indians, Asians and Cypriots. Immigrant and female workers are harder to organize into unions than indigenous males and will generally accept lower wages: immigrants because they are often used to lower living standards or very long hours of work, women because their wages are seen as a supplement to those of the male breadwinner. The rag trade was based – and still is – on the exploitation of female and immigrant labour.

The small scale of operations did, however, allow many locals to make good – to work hard, save hard and invest in a little business. Those who took their chances were the immigrants with a tradition of independent farming or commerce: the Jews, the Asians and the Cypriots. Those groups long accustomed to labouring for others – the English working class, the Irish and the West Indians – were much less successful in breaking through to entrepreneurship.

By 1900 then, the lines of Hackney's fate were already drawn. Bad housing meant low rents and low house prices, attracting people on low incomes – less skilled workers and immigrants. The local population in turn helped to determine the kind of employment that would predominate. Thus a vicious circle was outlined in which Hackney is still trapped: sweating industries pay low wages, and that, in its turn, ensures that the housing stock will deteriorate further because funds are not available to pay for the scale of repairs needed.

Eighty-odd years of the twentieth century, two world wars, massive efforts in public housing, a decade and a half of government programmes to help the inner cities – all these have made essentially no difference to Hackney's plight. Indeed it has worsened. The total population of the present borough peaked in 1901 at 389,000. It declined slowly to 363,000 in 1931, but over the following two decades it lost 100,000 people. After a plateau in the fifties the decline continued and accelerated: 14 per cent down in the sixties, 19 per cent in the seventies. The 1981 population of 180,000 was less than half the 1901 level. The social sifting that Booth had noted carried on. The building of Greater London Council housing in Outer London and Essex, and the growth of the new towns, gave many people a chance to move. Those who moved were mainly the most mobile: people with skills or school qualifications to offer employers, or with enough cash to buy houses elsewhere, the able-bodied in the twenty-five to forty-five age-group. They left behind many of the old, the unskilled, the handicapped.

Newcomers were moving in, too: as always, the lower-paid, the disadvantaged in various ways, and immigrants. Small businesses continued to arise out of their savings and ambitions – and to go under, too – but no sizeable new industries moved in. The

Victorian housing stock continued to decay. Many slums were cleared by blitz or bulldozers, but the public housing that replaced them was in some respects worse. Local government was poor in resources, with a narrow and declining base on which to levy rates. Officers were reluctant to serve in Hackney and quick to move on to greener pastures. Educational results were spectacularly poor, perpetuating the shortage of qualified labour. Redevelopment, emigration and immigration progressively ate away at the community, the extended family and even the nuclear family. Socialization and social control of the young began to fail. Crime and vandalism blossomed. Good neighbourliness gave way to apathy or open conflict.

Similar tales could be told of most inner cities in Britain. The precise reasons for housing and industrial decay varied, but the results were depressingly familiar. They became not only places of concentrated deprivation, but places of violence, in a Hobbesian condition of 'war of everyone against everyone . . . continual fear and danger . . . and the life of man, solitary, poor, nasty, brutish, and short'.

Part One

Economics and Incomes

> When will you pay me,
> Say the bells of Old Bailey.
> When I grow rich,
> Say the bells of Shoreditch.
>
> *Nursery rhyme*

The Inner City in the World Economy

The inner city, like the depressed regions, is the inevitable result of the unplanned, destructive way in which the British economy adjusts to changes in the global economy. The most radical change in the international division of labour over the past decade and a half has been the entry of developing countries on to the manufacturing stage hitherto hogged by the developed countries. It began with goods such as clothing and footwear; they require a lot of labour to produce, and labour is much cheaper in the Third World. But the process has continued, extending to the production of more complex consumer durables and processed materials, from assembled electrical products and cars to textiles, ships and steel. The newly industrializing countries like Hong Kong, Singapore, Taiwan, Mexico, Brazil and Argentina are emerging as competitors over a wide range of traditional British industries.

The more progressive and adaptable developed countries, such as Japan, West Germany and the United States, have shifted their economies into the kinds of activities in which the Third World cannot yet compete – those that require a high level of capital investment and a highly skilled, well-educated workforce: the production of capital goods, communications equipment and computers, and the more sophisticated consumer products. Britain, too, is making the shift, but not as smoothly, swiftly or completely. She thus finds herself caught in the middle and squeezed at both ends, undercut by cheaper Third World wages in labour-intensive industries, outmanoeuvred by higher levels of investment and applied technology in her developed-country competitors. The blame for our lag is widely spread: among financiers who prefer oil, property or foreign countries for investment, managers who do not modernize fast enough, workers who resist improvements in productivity, educationists who cling tenaciously to academic ideals, politicians who have been unable or unwilling to involve government in the forward planning of the economy.

At the end of the seventies, deep world recession arrived on the scene to complicate matters. To some observers it is merely the second hiccup in post-war expansion produced by a wave of oil-price rises. To others it is a far more sinister affair, a repeat of the Great Depression, the downturn of the fourth Kondratiev wave of long-term expansion and contraction since the first beginnings of capitalism (named after the Soviet economist who postulated such waves back in 1919). But this recession was more complicated. Inflation, the symptom of the intensified scramble of competing social groups for more pie and of the unwillingness of governments to control the share-out, had come to stay. The conventional ways of combating recession by increasing government borrowing and spending seemed only to stoke inflation. Keynes fell out of fashion, Friedman came in. And so recession was deepened by deflation, high interest rates, public-spending cuts. Conservatives in Britain and America hoped to compensate by cutting taxes, but growing budget deficits forced Thatcher and Reagan to renege on their promises, except for the rich. The overall result was a steep decrease in world and British demand, and a further increase in the severity of competition.

Some British companies adjusted successfully to the new cut-throat environment, though their 'success' has meant shedding labour and shutting down uneconomic factories. Others adjusted negatively, without investing, simply by pushing workers harder and paying them less in real terms. Others still, in the hardest-pressed industries, simply closed down and recovered what cash they could from the sale of their premises and equipment. Organized labour, especially the manual working class, was hammered in the process. In the expansive fifties and sixties union strength had grown considerably, and unions were able to increase real wages and reduce the share of profits. One of the attractions for Conservatives of monetarist deflation was that it reversed these trends; deep recession clobbered the unions and cut real wages.

All of these processes had a particularly destructive impact on the depressed regions and the inner cities. For these were often the sites of prosperity in earlier phases of industrialization, and have more than their share of industries now being upstaged by the Third World. They have many antiquated, badly sited premises that are incapable of adaptation to new modes of production and new channels of transport. To these problems the inner city adds others: clogged roads, high crime rates, a less disciplined work-force, and frequently, especially in London, high rates and rents to boot. As the new competitive climate made more industries and premises uneconomic, a new generation of depressed areas and inner cities began to develop.

But the process of adjustment is not only a problem for communities; it is above all a problem for people. It is not only machinery and factories that become outmoded, it is also trades and skills. With the new microchip technologies, economic adjustment is progressively destroying manual and low-grade clerical jobs and marginalizing increasing numbers of workers, not only the unskilled, but also the de-skilled who cannot find local openings for their skills, and those with skills that are no longer highly prized, such as tailoring. It has not been common British practice to care overmuch about those people whom economic change has left standing – to guarantee them retraining, further education or new jobs. In recession, far from expanding to meet the greater need, our education and retraining systems contracted. A sub-proletariat has been produced and is growing in numbers: under-educated, unskilled or de-skilled, unemployed and increasingly unemployable, and dangerously concentrated in poor regions and inner cities.

The economy of Hackney was shaky enough before recession and monetarism began to bite. Factors that had worked in its favour in the past – the proximity of London's docks and railheads – ceased to be advantages as roads and container ports came to handle most freight. And the ever-increasing flow of commuter cars and heavy lorries made access from Hackney factories to motorway networks more and more difficult. Many firms simply closed. Others were drawn out, along with their skilled workers, by the new-town movement and government programmes to relocate industry and offices outside London. Capital and training grants – unavailable in London – attracted other firms to development regions. Redevelopment demolished not only slum housing, but many of the small workplaces as well, and no provision was made in new public building for the businesses thus thrown on to the street.

Virtually no new industries or large-scale enterprises moved in to take the place of those that had closed or left. Potential newcomers were deterred by poor access, lack of suitable premises, above all by the local shortage of skilled manual and educated non-manual labour and, more recently, the high rents and rates. The industries that remained were precisely those most threatened by changes in world trading patterns: Hackney had the misfortune to specialize in those labour-intensive manufactures that are the first to be taken over by developing countries.

And so the 1970s saw a rapid decline in Hackney's manufacturing sector, paralleling a national decline that dragged Britain's manufacturing output in 1982 to 12 per cent below the level for 1975. The number of manufacturing jobs in Hackney dropped precipitously from 45,500 in 1973 to only 27,400 in 1981 – a fall of no less than 40 per cent. Non-manufacturing jobs fell much more slowly, at only 5 per cent over this period, but there were heavy losses in those non-manufacturing sectors that provided work for the two-thirds of Hackney's population who were manual workers – in transport, public utilities, shops, printing and, hardest hit of all, construction. By contrast there was little change in the numbers of professional and scientific jobs, while the number of jobs in public administration rose steeply to 1977 and fell by only 10 per cent in the four years after that.

There was thus a growing mismatch between the kinds of jobs available in Hackney and the kinds of people resident in Hackney who were seeking work. Hackney had to rely on commuters from other boroughs for the more qualified workers it needed. Four out of five professionals, managers and employers who work in Hackney live outside the borough, along with two out of three junior non-manual workers and 55 per cent of foremen, skilled manual workers and self-employed. Thus most of those who earn the highest incomes from Hackney's economy spend those incomes, and pay their rates, outside Hackney, after the fashion of imperial rulers expatriating tribute from the colonies, with a depressing, deflationary effect on local shops and services.

At the same time, the manual workers who make up two-thirds of the local population find fewer and fewer jobs locally, and are increasingly unable to travel elsewhere to work, or even to look for work: two-thirds of Hackney households have no car, and public transport is increasingly expensive and unreliable, largely because of commuter traffic. Hackney's manual workers find themselves marooned on dry land, forced into unemployment, or into low-grade, low-paid service jobs.

As the home of dying industries and increasingly marginalized workers, Hackney's modest former prosperity entered a tail-spin in recession. The unemployment rate rose much faster than national or local trends (see page 114). As the demand for local labour dropped, local incomes fell in parallel, relatively and sometimes absolutely. In 1976 average gross weekly earnings for Hackney men were 4 per cent above the average for Britain – five years later, they had fallen to 5 per cent below the national average, despite much higher rents, rates and transport costs in London. In April 1981 the Hackney male average was £133·50 – £7 a week below the national average, and no less than £30·30 below the Greater London figure. Hackney's working women earned £13·40 a week less than the London average.

As a result the overall incidence of absolute poverty reached serious proportions. There were the growing numbers of unemployed – one in four males by the end of 1982 – who were living on or below the official poverty line. And there was increasing deprivation among the working poor. In 1981, no less than 35 per cent of Hackney's adult male manual workers earned less than £100 a week, equivalent to the supplementary-benefit poverty line for a married man with two children paying £5 per week in fares (see page 436). Indeed, one in ten earned less than £72. One in every three working women earned less than £75.

Thus the declining demand for the inner city's 'exports' is reinforced by weak demand – held down by poverty – for its locally consumed products and services. The inner-city economy, like that of the peripheral regions, is to some extent in permanent recession. In times of severe national recession, the economic crisis of the inner city and its residents reaches the proportions of catastrophe.

51

3   From Rags to Tatters:
The Agony of an Industry

Is there any difference between killing a man with a knife and killing him by misrule?

Mencius (tr. D. C. Lau)

The rag trade permeates the fabric of Hackney. Firms sprout up and wither like fungi on a fallen branch, working out of tiny premises, often not designed for industrial use, identifiable, if at all, only by little hand-painted signboards with slots where vacancies, if any, can be advertised. Take a short stretch of just five houses in Frederick Terrace, Kingsland Road: they were built as elegant town houses, three storeys and a loft, but today the roof slates are crumbling, window panes are broken and the end property is propped up to prevent it collapsing. Name-plates cluster thickly around the doors and over the ground-floor windows: KSN Fashions, Dresses, Suits and Slacks; C & S Fashions; Cash and Carry Dresses and Separates; J & D Footwear; Taylor Clarke auto repairs; Nichan Dresses; Evren Fashions; Steam Electrical Services Ltd; Falkson's Mantles Ltd; Lucky Thirteen Ltd; M.B. Signs Ltd; Etchport Skirts and Slacks; J. Y Fashions; Vallance Cutting; Hora – Cutting To The Trade. Fifteen firms in five houses: about one floor, two or three rooms, per firm on average.

In the early 1980s it became increasingly difficult to distinguish moribund industries from healthy ones. Some, however, were clearly more moribund than others, and the clothing industry – provider of one job in eight in Hackney, and one in three manufacturing jobs – was obviously closer to a terminal phase than most. In 1970 Britain – once the world's biggest exporter – still enjoyed a rough trade balance in clothing. By 1978 she had a deficit of £251 million, and imports were taking more than a quarter of the home market in clothing and footwear, double the proportion of ten years earlier. The threat came primarily from developing countries, especially Hong Kong, but also from low-wage developed countries such as Italy and Ireland.

The formal sector of the rag trade – the larger-scale operations, paying tax and national-insurance contributions and PAYE – was hard hit by competition from three sides: on one side, high-technology industry in Germany and the USA; on another, low-wage employers in the Third World; and at their backs, the informal British sector, increasingly using Third World methods. For some, the crunch came suddenly: one company employing ninety-three people had relied for years on the orders of a single large client. One day the client walked in and informed the manufacturer that henceforth he would be placing his orders in Paraguay.

For others, like Emmen Garments,* the agony is prolonged. Emmen's speciality is tailored outerwear. It is a fastidious business. In the cutting room, thousands of paper patterns hang from pegs like a collage frieze. The owner, Michael N.,* cuts them all himself, and it is no mean task; his current order for 750 garments takes up a single-spaced foolscap page of twenty-seven different sizes, each one with a different combination of waist, chest, height, arm and leg measurements. For every size a set of dozens of patterns must be cut, anything from the waistband to the lining of the breast pocket. Everything has to be done in small batches – in some of the sizes only ten garments are required. The most needed of one size is seventy.

The cutters work on two long, broad tables, outlining the patterns with chalk on a plateau of layers of cloth as deep as the required number of that size. The marked-up cloth, looking like a complex engineering drawing, is sliced through with band-saws and circular saws leaving only thin slivers of waste. In the machining, pressing and tailoring departments Hoffman presses wheeze vapours on one side, sewing machines whine on the other, while tailors work by hand with needle and thread on mahogany tables in the centre. The windows are opened to let out the muggy heat, and sheets of curtain are pinned up to keep out the sunlight. The

* All names in this section have been changed.

machinists work briskly, their pace dictated on the one hand by the supply of cut components in the wooden boxes by their stools, on the other by the demands of the trouser manager and the jacket manager, who call out for certain items when the tailors are running short. On the day of my visit, there is a 'rush' on to get a delivery to a major client by 2 p.m. the next day.

Before 1979, Emmen was a success story and a model employer by Hackney standards. The firm was almost completely unionized, wage rates were competitive, nationally agreed rises were paid on the dot, without query or quibble. But by the end of that year the chill winds of monetarism were beginning to blow and demand was falling fast. At the same time, overheads were rising faster than ever before: rates and rent doubled in two years, the price of electricity and petrol soared. 'I'm one of the few top-quality manufacturers left,' Michael N. remarks. 'But these days the world won't beat a path to your door just because you're better than anyone else. Whatever you've done in the past counts for nothing – you can't save up goodwill in a competitive tender. People are looking at price, price, price, all the time. I've had to reduce my prices lower than 1978 to compete, but firms up in Leeds can still do it cheaper – they can pay people less up there and push them harder. They can charge £6 or £7 less per article. On a contract for 5,000 garments that makes a difference of £30,000 plus. Nobody can afford to ignore that.'

Without adequate funds to invest in new cutting and basting technology, N. was forced to hunt for savings. He gave up the largest of the three spaces he rented and moved his jacket department in with the trousers, slashing his rate, rent and fuel bills. He saved a driver's salary by drafting his son to do the delivering. And he was forced to hold his wage costs down. In March 1980, Emmen's workers received a union-agreed rise, the second instalment of a settlement that had been agreed in October 1979. That brought basic wages for most of them up to between £65 and £100 per week, which was not bad at the time. In October 1980 the National Union of Tailors and Garment Workers negotiated a national rise of 17 per cent. Not many employers paid more than half that. Emmen could afford no rise at all. A year later the union rise was 7½ per cent. Emmen, after months of pressure from the workers, finally gave a rise of 5½ per cent in December 1981. Over a period when national statistics assured us that average wages were keeping up with inflation. Emmen's workers had missed out on 19 per cent of the union rise over two years, and their real wages fell by around 20 per cent. Michael N. would have liked to pay more. 'But what can I do? I'm caught between the devil and the deep blue sea. If I pay them more, my prices would have to be higher and I couldn't get the orders. If I don't pay them more, half of them will leave – they're only staying on in the hope of getting redundancy money anyway. I can't work out a way to cope, I can't see that there's an answer.'

The real incomes of most employees fell by even more than their gross pay indicated, for deductions for tax and national insurance increased; and, towards Christmas 1979, the lay-offs began: half a dozen workers were laid off for six weeks. Lay-off pay worked out at about half of normal wages. The following Christmas, all but a handful of workers were laid off, this time for fourteen weeks – the maximum permitted before workers can claim redundancy money. Again at Christmas 1981, seven people were laid off for nine weeks. Why did Emmen's workers accept such a deep cut in their real incomes? Certainly they did not do so willingly. 'They raised the matter of pay almost every day for a year,' shop steward, West Indian-born Jim J. told me. 'They kept asking, what use is the union? This is a union shop, the union should make him pay. I told them, you are the union, the union can only be effective if you are forceful. But when it came to talk of striking, they didn't want to.'

The sad fact was that the poorer they became, the weaker they became industrially. Debts were mounting, savings dwindling, the margin over mere survival shrinking. The more they needed a pay rise, the less they could afford to take industrial action: deep recession emasculated the unions far more effectively than any anti-union legislation. The same context prevented many of Emmen's employees from seeking better-paid work elsewhere. Openings were fewer than ever, and many could not afford to lose pay for time taken off for interviews.

Talking to individual workers at Emmen provides some idea of the human costs of industrial decline and recession. Jim J. himself takes home only £58 a week out of a basic wage of £73 (1981), less than his twenty-year-old daughter, a Post Office wages clerk, and can only survive because his mortgage is paid off and his three children work. Others get by because their wives or husbands work, because they live with parents or have savings. Others do not get by at all. Georgos G., a Greek Cypriot Hoffman presser, takes home £59 out of a basic £74. His rent and rates after rebate come to £21 a week, heating, by paraffin, costs £6 to £7 a week. Surplus over housing and fuel costs: £22 a week plus £10·50 child benefit, £32·50, to cover all other needs of a non-working wife and two children at school: £1·16 per person per day, enough for a large loaf and twelve ounces (340 grams) of cheese. Elizabeth C., a youthful forty-three-year-old machinist from Mauritius, takes home only £48 a week (£64 gross), and out of that spends no less than £9 a week in fares from Ilford. For the previous three months the remaining £39 a week had been the sole income for herself and her husband. He normally works evenings as a minicab driver – the couple hardly see each other – but three months before he collided with a car coming the wrong way down a one-way street. He said the car was a write-off, the insurance company did not agree: 'And all this time he is without car and without money: because he is self-employed, he can't get unemployment benefit.' She would like to look for a better-paid job: 'But I can't take time off to look. I can't afford to lose money – we have mortgage to pay, electric to pay.'

Most of the staff at Emmen are no strangers to redundancy, and have lived through many of the company deaths and departures that have decimated Hackney's clothing industry. James N., a melancholic measure cutter of sixty, takes home £51 out of a gross of £72: 'It's a dying trade, well it's dead really. I worked for thirty-six years at Hector Powe's. When they moved out of Hackney to Dagenham, I moved with them. I was down there seven years, then they said "you're redundant", and that was it. Then I was eighteen months at another firm before they went broke. Then I came here. I can't wait till I retire, that's what I'm looking forward to.' Machinist Cath M., a spinster in her forties, worked at Simpson's, one of the biggest clothing factories in Hackney, for twenty-five years. It closed in 1972, leaving only its elegant art deco building, now a banqueting hall, to grace Stoke Newington Road. 'All I got out of them was a watch,' she laments. She worked for Moss Bros for three years, then they, too, closed their Hackney factory. She came to Emmen in 1975. 'I take home £50 a week. If you gave your wife that for housekeeping, she'd laugh at you. The rates on our house are £600 a year. I live with my parents – if I lived on my own, I'd have to sell the place.'

Perhaps the saddest victim of the slump is tailor Andreas T., a fifty-six-year-old Greek Cypriot with a mop of curly greying hair and a friendly, rounded face. His job is basting collars and lapels by hand – sewing them together with loose stitches to hold them in place for machining. He suffers from muscular dystrophy, a wasting of the muscles that has weakened his legs.

'My hands are all right. Once I get there to my table, I can do as much work as anybody,' he says proudly. 'But my legs, they are like jelly, I can't walk up steps, I have to use my hands going up and going down I go on my seat. It's very hard for me to look for another job. There has to be a lift, there has to be a place to park my car: not many clothing factories have those.' Andreas lives in a three-bedroomed post-war semi in West Finchley, with roses in the front garden. But the house stands out on the street. There is a distinct line between the brilliant white pebbledash walls of next door, and Andreas's, now a dirty grey, and the gloss paint on the window frames has flaked down to the bare wood. The house was bought in 1970. In those more prosperous days Andreas was on good wages and his wife had no trouble finding machining work to do at home. But as the clothing trade contracted, the family had to pull in their belts as their real earnings began to slow, halt, and, since early 1980, decline steeply. Holidays in Majorca gave way to holidays in Blackpool and, five years ago, to no holidays at all.

Andreas has been laid off at Christmas time every year for three years, for six weeks in 1979, three months in 1980, and nine weeks in 1981. The first two occasions he did not claim supplementary benefit, though he would have been entitled to around £15 a week extra on top of his lay-off pay. 'To tell you the truth, I feel ashamed to go there [to the social-security office]. Each time I thought it would go on only for a few weeks and it would pass and everything would be all right. But this time I had to claim social security. All these years we been in England, we saved, not much, but something. Over the last three years we had to spend it, all of it, and we had to cash two life-insurance policies. Now we got nothing. All my bills are behind: I still owe £100 off my last gas bill and the new one will come soon. I had nearly paid off the mortgage – I had to see the building society and stretch it out for some more years. I can't paint my house, I haven't painted it for seven years. Two years ago I asked a painter how much it would cost, he said £300. This year I'm afraid to ask anybody, believe me. We make do now with old clothes, we don't eat meat. This year we planted a few vegetables in the garden. I feel very depressed when I'm laid off. With my legs, I can't go out for a walk, I have to stay home, just watching television, I stay in bed more just to pass the time. Before this I'd never been idle in my life, not even for one hour.'

When I interviewed Andreas (1982) he was taking home £71 a week out of a basic £87. With child benefit for his nine-year-old daughter, his net income was £76·25 a week. Mortgage, rates and fuel took more than half of that. But his heaviest costs are for running his car, without which he cannot get to work. Repayments amount to £17 a week. Petrol costs £10 a week, insurance and road tax £6·50. He gets a mobility allowance of £16·50, which is supposed to provide for the special transport needs of the disabled worker, but in fact covers less than half the actual cost. Surplus for all other needs of three people: £22, or just £1·05 per person per day, enough for a packet of cigarettes. His two older sons work, but the £7 a week each they contribute barely covers their food. Asking for that modest sum goes against the grain for a Greek: 'I don't like it. They will need it to save, to buy a flat when they want to get married.'

Andreas's situation could only get worse. In 1983 he would have to either renew his car or face mounting repair bills, and he can afford neither. With no car, he could not get to work. He would be £10 or £13 a week better off on the dole, given his high transport and housing costs. 'But I don't want to give my work up. I don't want to be a parasite. If I can't work, I'm going to be so depressed I would die.' For a disabled man, work is an indispensable ingredient of dignity: take that away, and all that is left is helpless dependence. Andreas T. spends a lot of time thinking about the injustices of life. Although he is still in work, recession has sloped the ground beneath his feet, so he is sliding inexorably down the scale of his own social values: enforced idleness, increasing debt, inability to keep up appearances, compulsion to claim benefit which he regards as humiliating charity. Andreas is precisely the kind of sensitive soul that recession could destroy. Worries gnaw at him: 'I have bad stomach, and whenever I am upset, my legs leave me. When I was laid off in 1981, I was parking my car and my foot slipped on to the accelerator. I hit two other cars and lose my no claims bonus. My doctor say all this worry makes my illness worse.'

Perhaps the deepest hurt lies buried in his heart, with his furthest memories of Cyprus. His father owned a small farm with sheep and goats and orange and lemon trees, in the village of Yialousa near Famagusta. Andreas worked on it for ten years, between leaving school aged twelve and coming to Britain in 1948. 'The Turks used to help out on our farm with fruit picking. When I was a boy I would take a glass and fill it up with water for Turk, and take the same glass and fill it again for Greek: that is how friendly they were. What happened later was all politics, my friend. Politics is a very bad thing.' The two Cypriot communities lived intermingled under Ottoman rule. From 1878 the British ruled by dividing, using Greek administrators to break Turkish power, then Turkish special police to combat Greek terrorists fighting for union with Greece. After independence Greece and Turkey, seeking military advantage in the Mediterranean, set extremists on each side in Cyprus at each other's throats, and alienated the two communities further. In 1974 the Greek nationalist coup on the island was followed by the Turkish invasion and occupation of the north of the island, where Andreas's farm lay. That year the farm was taken over and Andreas's mother, eighty-six and already ill, was evicted. She died after only one night in Britain. 'This land, it was in my family for generations. Now Turks live in my parents' house, they use our farm. When my boys finished school here, I was planning to go back to live in Cyprus. I would have been there five years ago. But I can't even go to see it now.'

A Family Affair

The informal sector of Hackney's rag trade has on the whole weathered the storm in better shape than the formal, all-in-one factories like Emmen. Where the formal enterprises are complex animals, that die when dismembered, the informal ones resemble single-celled colonial animals like sponges, which quickly reform into their old structure if disturbed. That structure is pyramidal in shape. At the pinnacle are a few large wholesalers or retail chains that buy direct. These place orders with 'manufacturers' – a misleading name, since most of them do little more than cut the patterns and buy the cloth, putting out the actual work of making the garment to contractors. The contractors cut the cloth. Some of the machining is done on the premises, by indoor workers, some by outworkers and homeworkers, who form the base of the pyramid. No one employs a large staff, no one carries a massive burden of ongoing overheads, no one faces a huge bill for redundancy payments if they close. The structure is flexible, well built to withstand economic gales: while many of its component firms may go to the wall, others pop out of the woodwork and take their place and the structure itself survives. In a climate of intensified competition, the informal sector is much better placed to lower prices. The going rates for most types of clothing made in Hackney came down steeply from 1979 to 1981 and 1982. The prices paid to manufacturers for lower-quality work halved in many cases: from £4 to £2 for a fashion dress, from £1·50 to £0·75 for a fully lined skirt. The drop for quality work was less, but still significant: from £13 to £10 for a two-piece suit, for example. These cuts of 25 per cent to 50 per cent were passed on, as we shall see, to workers' wages, leading to cuts in living standards or increases in hours of work.

The informal sector, too, is freer to exploit the booming black economy. The National Union of Tailors and Garment Workers reports that practices like the use of 'lump labour' (legally self-employed) inside factories are spreading: this helps the worker to evade tax, and enables the employer to avoid national-insurance contributions and all liabilities such as sick pay, holiday pay, lay-off pay or redundancy money. A similar practice is the growth of 'off-the-book' payments, cash in hand, for overtime and wage rises. As these are not taxed, they make small pay rises worth more to the worker. Many factories use illegal immigrant labour, though less so than in the late seventies when many Cypriot refugees, unable to return home and not yet allowed to settle in Britain, were technically illegals. In 1976 Yasher Ishmailoglu, of the Hackney Cypriot Association, visited more than a hundred small clothing factories in North London and found that a high proportion of the indoor workforce were illegal immigrants, whom employers were able to push hard and pay badly.

More than half of Hackney's clothing firms employ fewer than ten people. Many of them rely on family labour, like Pluto Fashions.* There is no name on the plywood street door, between two shops in Stoke Newington. You enter along a passage of ancient lino, up resounding bare wooden stairs. Only on the first floor is the name scrawled, in felt-tip pen, on the wall, with an arrow pointing upwards. The stairs end at a hardboard door. Behind it lies the 'factory', a single large room about 5 metres by 8 metres, crammed with skirts on racks and hanging from the ceiling, light-blue, dark-blue, dark-brown skirts, plaid and pleated skirts. Electric wires spiral along strings to machines around the walls, which are patched with damp and peeling paper. On untidy shelves are dozens of coffee and jam jars containing assorted buttons, and hundreds of bobbins of coloured threads stacked high in triangular wooden frames.

The owner is a resourceful thirty-year-old Cypriot, Mullah Ahmet, with close-cropped hair and bandit moustache. The five other employees are his wife and her in-laws. Mullah is alternately and simultaneously entrepreneur, manager, salesman, accountant, delivery-man and, when the occasion demands, also presser, machinist, cutter and overlocker. His brother-in-law Zuhti Abdullah, aged nineteen, is the main cutter. Mother-in-law Kamar is sewing buttons on the skirts and arranging them on the racks. Her daughter Ayse, a plump twenty-two-year-old, and Mullah's wife Fatima, work at the window at overlocking machines (overlocking means sewing along a cut edge so it doesn't fray). In a corner,

* The names in this section are pseudonyms.

cousin Saban Ali is pressing skirts with an ancient hand iron attached to a compressed air cylinder, emitting sporadic bursts of steam.

It is a damp day towards the tail end of winter, and the view from the window is of blackened Victorian façades opposite. On the wall behind the cutting table, two large tourist posters of Cyprus are like windows on another world, views of classical ruins on ochre hills: *Cyprus, where Spring is eternal, Cyprus, island of Venus*. The island itself is unattainable, a sunlit memory in gloomy exile. Zuhti pines for it: 'Our life in Cyprus was better than here. Here it is like you are free, but you are in a gaol. We just work, go home, sleep, come to work again. We can never go back to our home because the Greeks have it. We just have to think of this as our home now.' The Abdullah family came from a village near Episkopi on the south coast. Turks in the Greek zone, they lost their home and homeland in the same 1974 upheaval that cost Andreas T., a Greek from the Turkish zone, his dream of growing old in the land of his forefathers. They spent six months under canvas in a refugee camp, followed by two weeks in a dormitory in Turkey. Then they were resettled in the Turkish zone of Cyprus. But they were far from home and economic prospects were poor. In 1975 they decided to come to London. Father got a job as a security man in the civil service, mother became a home machinist, the children, after a couple of years in school, got jobs in the clothing trade. Mullah Ahmet came over in 1976 on a holiday, met and married Fatima, and stayed on. After four years as a Hoffman presser, he started his own business in 1981 with £3,000 in savings.

Pluto Fashions, like most small firms, does not sell direct to department stores. Mullah deals through middlemen: he makes up to orders, mainly from two Jewish-owned wholesalers who, in turn, sell to two major chain stores. The wholesalers supply him with ready-cut patterns and uncut cloth. Zuhti cuts the cloth and linings, the women do the overlocking, then Mullah packages up the pieces in bundles, wrapped in paper and string, piles them on the back seat of his ten-year-old red Morris Marina, rusting around unrepaired dents, and delivers them to his five homeworkers. They are paid by piece-rate, 35p a skirt. On average, they machine about 200 skirts a week each and earn £70, but for that they may be working up to sixty hours, and out of it they have to pay their own taxes (or, more likely, not pay them) and the cost of electricity and upkeep of their sewing-machines. Mullah collects the batch of completed skirts at the same time as he delivers the cloth for the next batch. Back at the factory, the family team put in the buttons, finish the hems, cut off the loose threads and press the skirts. Once a fortnight Mullah delivers the finished garments to the wholesaler. He has to pay a stiff penalty if they are late.

The flow of work is uneven. At flood, when deadlines are close, the normal family workday of nine and a half hours is extended to twelve or even fourteen. At ebb, when orders dry up, there is nothing to do but sit around. At any one time, Mullah has anything from a couple of weeks' to a couple of months' work in hand. In November 1981 he ran out of orders completely and had to chase around a dozen wholesalers touting for business. And it is a buyers' market. The price for the high quality of skirt Mullah makes has dropped from £1·40 in 1979 to £1 in 1982. Mullah was reticent about the details of his finances, but provided enough information for a rough estimate. He turns out around 1,000 skirts a week. The homeworkers are paid £350, his wife's four in-laws about £370 including tax. Add £26 for rent, £7 for rates, £50 for electricity and £25 for running the car. Total expenditure per week: £828. Income per week: £1,000. Profit: £172 per week, before tax, and that has to cover the full-time labour of Mullah and his wife and the cost of maintenance and new machinery. The flexibility comes from the family: none of their wages are fixed. When times are good, they may be paid more. When they are bad, they are paid less. They get the same pay whether their hours are short or long. 'Whatever he can afford to give me, I don't mind,' says Ayse philosophically. 'I know he pays us as much as he can afford. We are all the same family.'

One Big Blackmail: The Homeworkers

Scattered throughout Hackney's terraces and council estates is a hidden, silent and largely female army whose presence is detectable only by the growling of industrial sewing-machines and the daily toing and froing of small vans delivering and collecting bundles and sacks of varying sizes.

The homeworkers have three main functions. One is to provide cheap labour, working at piece-work rates so that any loss in productivity is a loss to them rather than their employers, paying their own overheads of electricity, purchase and maintenance of machinery, and receiving no social overheads such as national insurance, sick pay, holiday pay, industrial-injury benefits, compensation for negligence, or redundancy money. Second, they provide a flexible pool of labour which can be used when there is a rush on and discarded when times are lean – essential ballast in a seasonally rising and falling trade like fashion, just as casual cane-cutters are to the sugar-cane harvest in Third World countries. Third, they are scattered and unorganized: for the most part they never meet each other or the indoor workforce of their employers and thus cannot combine to force rates up. They can be used as a perennial counterweight against attempts to organize and unionize clothing factories. They are, in short, the ideal labour force of primordial, free-market capitalism, of the kind favoured by the Tory government of the time, whose wages rise and fall in line with demand for their product, regardless of their own social or even survival needs.

The homeworkers themselves, of course, also derive benefits. Homework, when properly paid, suits many women: women who wish to stay at home with small children, women who dislike the discipline and timekeeping of factory work and wish to work at their own pace, Muslim women observing semi-purdah. It provides extra money to supplement the wages of low-paid husbands or the niggardly rates of supplementary benefit, pin money for clothes or family treats, tax- and national-insurance-free money to cock a snook at the increasingly devastating ravages of the Exchequer.

Finding homeworkers who would talk was the hardest task in the researching of this book. They are a secretive and retiring species, for they are usually flouting a number of laws: doing industrial work at home without planning permission, evading tax, some of them claiming as well as working, some of them illegal immigrants. For obvious reasons, I have given them all pseudonyms.

Mary is a forty-five-year-old English woman with five children, living in a council block in Hackney Wick. Her eldest girl is married and her eldest boy 'a guest of Her Majesty' (in gaol). The eighteen-year-old girl has gone to live with her boss, and the seventeen-year-old boy recently left home because he wouldn't lift a finger to help out. Mary's common-law husband is a Hungarian refugee and a skilled sample-cutter – he cuts the cloth for the crucial sample submitted to secure an order. In 1979 he was taking home £120 a week, but in 1980 he was laid off, at £54 a week, for so long that he had to look for other work. All he could find was a job taking home £76 a week. Thus his money wages fell by 37 per cent.

Mary herself, after a spell homeworking while her children were young, worked in factories until 1979. 'But they all went bust, one after another. The only factory job I could find recently was for £50 a week. All I brought home out of that was £39. You couldn't live on that. So I've had to do homework for the last three years. I can't declare my money. If they taxed me and stamped me on it, there'd be nothing left. I've got no alternative. I did go to evening school in 1980 to do a secretarial course, but I was so tired from work in the day that I couldn't concentrate. I couldn't keep it up, and my spelling wasn't good, not having had such a marvellous education. I've been machining since I was fifteen, and with thirty years' experience I'm really fast now. I can do buttons, buttonholes, felling [stitching seams] and overlocking. I should be at a time, at my age, where I can take it easy.

'But I'm having to work twice as hard to earn the money. The governors used to go on their knees to get you to take work if they had a rush to meet a delivery date. But they're not begging no more. It's take it or leave it. If you argue about the price they say we can always find others to do it. It's like one big blackmail. Three years ago we used to get 35p to 40p for a blouse, but now [1982] you only get 15p to 20p. For a skirt you'd get 15p to 16p, now you only get 10p or 11p [this is for overlocking only – the 35p a skirt mentioned earlier is for flat machining]. And now they want you to do overlocking and flat machining as well, to save them having to pay two people. I had to have my machine converted to do both – that cost me £125.

'I used to get my work done in five hours, now I work ten or twelve hours a day – all day really, from 9 in the morning to 10 at night. I have to work that long to average £70 a week, allowing for the weeks I don't get any work. I don't take a lunch break, I just eat a sandwich at the machine. I stop at 6 to make the dinner and start again at 7. The kids say, mum, I don't know why you sit there all those hours. I tell them, I don't do it for love, I've got to feed and clothe us. I won't work Sundays though. I have to think about the noise. The neighbours are quite tolerant, they say, well, as long as it keeps you out of the social-security office. They always say they feel so sorry for me, but I can't stand that. It's bad enough that I've got to do it, without them poking their noses in feeling sorry for me. They don't understand what it's like. I'm cooped up in a cupboard all day – I keep my machine in the storage cupboard, it's about three feet square with no windows. I get pains in my shoulders where the tension builds up. I've got one lot of skirts to do now, I've got to do sixteen in an hour to earn £1·75 an hour, that means I can't give myself more than four minutes for each one. I can't let up for half a second between each skirt. I can't afford the time to make a cup of tea. With that much pressure, at the end of the day you're at screaming pitch. If I wasn't on tranquillizers, I couldn't cope. I'm not good company, I lose my temper easily. Where I might have been able to tolerate my kids' adolescence, with this I haven't been able to, I haven't been able to help them – I need someone to help me at the end of the day.

'I never dreamed the time would come when I'd be scrounging for work. I buy the *Hackney Gazette* on the dot every Friday morning and look at the ads. There's no regular work any more. I don't know who I'll be working for from one week to the next. You work for one firm for a couple of weeks, then they won't have any more for you. Homeworkers are the last ones to get work, we only get the overload that the factory can't handle. In May and June, when the weather's good, there's plenty of work in blouses, but winter's a bad time. Sometimes I don't even get paid, that's happened to me a few times recently, and there's nothing you can do about it. You haven't got a ticket to produce. They just pretend you never did it. They know you're working without cards or tax, so you can't go to the police. All you can do is go round to their place and have a fight and a scream about it, but that doesn't get you anywhere. People say, if homeworkers refused to do the work, the governors would have to pay more. But we're not in a position to bargain. There's always someone they can find to do it, there are so many illegal immigrants. If they're only paying 50p a hour, that's wealth compared to what they're used to.

'All the old family firms have gone bust. Today they're all Greeks and Turks and Asians. I don't know how they survive – it's dog eat dog. Some of them watch where the others deliver their orders to, then they go in and talk to the owner and offer to do the same work for less. Another thing they do is go bankrupt and open up again straight away under a different name. The firm where my husband worked went bankrupt, but they didn't even close the doors, they just went on working, with the same workers. They changed their name three different times.'

Repeated liquidation becomes a novel way of cutting costs by writing off losses – often at the homeworkers' expense. 'Joyce', from Haggerston, echoes Mary's complaints: 'When I started homeworking three years ago, you'd get 60p or 70p for flat machining a fully lined skirt. I used to be able to make £150 a week working eight or nine hours a day; mind you, that was six days a week and the machine more or less ruled my life. Now they only pay 35p or 40p a skirt, if you can get it. Some of the cutting and overlocking is so bad now that it's much harder to machine it properly. And they're very unreliable. Sometimes they say they'll come and they don't. If they come, you just take the work and hope they'll pay you for it. I've been cheated of my wages four times now – three times the firms went bankrupt, and one just refused to pay. The last time it happened I thought, "that's enough" and I stopped doing homework. I'm looking for a shop job now.'

There are many other types of homework in Hackney: making handbags, stringing buttons on cards, wrapping greetings cards, filling Christmas crackers, assembling plugs and ballpens, sticking insoles in shoes, threading necklaces. Rates of pay vary enormously according to the type of work and the speed of the worker, but it is rare to find any that better the average female hourly earnings in the clothing trade in 1981, £1·75 an hour, itself the lowest for any branch of industry. And many work out worse than the Wages Council minimum for the clothing trade of £1·42 per hour (in

1982). Among the rates quoted to me (1982): sewing lampshades at £5·76 for 288, taking four hours: 2p per shade; 50 seconds for each one; £1·44 an hour. Gluing the silk into jewellery boxes for £3·60 a gross, taking eight hours: 3 minutes 20 seconds for each one, 45p per hour. Assembling bracelet-type watchstraps at 25p per strap, taking 20–30 minutes each, 50p–75p per hour (the rate was cut in 1981 from 30p per strap, which had been paid since 1974). Given these rates of pay, sometimes the whole family, kids and all, are dragooned in, in the same way that Guatemalan Indians take their children to coffee harvest to increase their piece-rate earnings: one mother had her three daughters and son helping to stick eyes and tails on cuddly toys.

Some women pass rapidly through a succession of different trades, in a vain attempt to find one that is tolerable or durable. 'Michelle', who lives in Clapton with her market-trader husband, preferred to do homework because she wanted to be at home when her six-year-old daughter came home from school, or was off sick. In 1979 she was making earrings: 'You had to stick pearls on to the base with glue. They paid £1·50 for a thousand, and it used to take me about six hours [20 seconds per earring, 25p per hour]. The glue used to get all over my hands, and you had to lay them out on trays and wait for them to dry. It was hard to get it dead right. If you didn't put enough glue on, the pearls wouldn't stick, and if you put too much on, it went all over the side. And you had to pick them up yourself and take them back, and it was miles away. With the fares, I was losing out all the time. I stuck it for five months. They didn't pay me for one lot, they said there was too much glue showing round the edge of the earring, but they still took them off me. So I said you can stick it, I'm not doing it no more.

'After that [1980] I was stripping rubber rings out of their mouldings. I've no idea what the rings were for. They paid £2 a thousand and it took six hours [33p an hour], but they used to pick them up and deliver them. The only thing was, you'd have all this rubber piling up in your house. The best job I had was addressing envelopes [1981]. Me and my cousin did it together, they paid £10 per 1,000 and we could do it in about three hours, writing them by hand [£1·66 per hour each]. You had to pick them up and deliver them to Liverpool Street. But that firm moved out of London. The last thing I did [1982] was screwing nuts on to brass taps. They paid £1·20 for 1,000 and it took me about four hours [8 taps for 1p, 14 seconds per tap, 30p per hour]. My hands used to get all black and sore and cut. And you had to collect the work and take it back. I used my daughter's pushchair, but the stuff was really heavy and it buggered my pushchair up. I've not been able to find any homework since I gave that up. I keep ringing up about adverts in the paper, but the jobs are always gone; they just say, yeah we'll put you on the list, then you never hear from them again.'

Homework requires dexterity, speed, application. It involves bodily pains, mental and family strains, untidiness about the house. I have seen it in Hong Kong too: a mother on a train through the New Territories, with a bag of bits on her knees, assembling five components to make light switches, fingers trembling; an old woman squatting in a courtyard on Cheang Chau island, putting the wheels on toy jeeps. The parallel is no superficial resemblance. It is precisely the same phenomenon, at precisely the same level of low-technology, labour-intensive economic development. Hackney and places like it are competing directly with the Third World.

The developing countries, with their low wage rates and low or non-existent social overheads, have the competitive edge in labour-intensive industries. The only rational way for Britain's enterprises in these fields to compete is to convert to other products, to head up market towards high quality and high fashion, and to invest in more productive machinery. But instead of shifting their terrain, many manufacturers are competing with the Third World on the Third World's own ground, by reducing real wages to not much better than Hong Kong levels. The workers, in their turn, have adjusted by working harder and longer hours, by moonlighting, by cutting their living standards, and often by passing outside the law into the black economy, evading tax, or claiming social security and working at the same time.

It is precisely the weakness of labour organization, undermined by recession and by the use of female and immigrant labour that is harder to unionize, that determines this path. The clothing trade in Hackney is not more than 10 per cent unionized. Wage bargaining is a jungle of privately struck bargains between owners and individual workers. The class conflict between management and labour, so evident in larger concerns, is here muted and confused. The immediate employers of labour – the contractors – may be as much exploited by those above them in the pyramid, as exploiting those below, for the biggest mark-ups occur at the wholesaler and retailer level. As with Third World cash-crop growers, the primary producer gets only a small percentage of the final selling price, as little as 10 per cent or less.

If the unions were stronger in this sector, and if wage rates were higher, employers would be under greater pressure to invest in new machinery or to move into more profitable lines. The assault on union power, the constant call from Conservative Party ministers for stagnant or falling real wages, would lead to Britain becoming an economy specializing in labour-intensive manufactures.

This is creeping underdevelopment, in which parts of the country regress towards an economy of coolie labour, the creation of a Third World country in our midst, in the inner cities and the peripheral regions. Like most developing countries, Britain is becoming a dual economy, with a backward sector of low-paid, labour-intensive industry and a vast reserve army of unemployed, and a more modern, well-paid, capital- and knowledge-intensive sector. That division reflects and deepens social and geographical inequalities, between inner city and suburbs or new town, between the north and the south, between Celtic fringe and Anglo-Norman heartland, between manual and non-manual workers, between Labour areas and Conservative areas. That dualism is likely to be as unhealthy in its consequences as it is in the Third World.

4 Modernization by Destruction: The Death of a Factory

If one's aim is wealth one cannot be benevolent.
If one's aim is benevolence one cannot be wealthy.
Mencius (tr. D. C. Lau)

Just across the marshes of the Lea Valley from Hackney lies Lea Bridge Industrial Estate. It is one of those bleak and utilitarian places where town planners have hived off the noisy, smelly business of manufacturing. An intriguing variety of industry exists here: heavy machinery, drums, wood veneers, button and buckle manufacturing, colour printing, paint making, banana storage. Although it is nearly a kilometre outside the borders of Hackney borough, many Hackney people work here. Or rather, used to.

For by 1981 the place, like so much of British manufacturing industry, was coming to resemble the aftermath of a neutron-bomb strike, with the people gone but the buildings still left standing. As all over Hackney, factories that once produced shoes, steel sheets, cords and cables bore 'To let' or 'For sale' signs, while one structural engineering firm, still pegging on, advertised 'Industrial Units for Letting, Shortly Available'. Machinery gathered dust and rusted, roofs leaked, paint flaked. Idle plant here, idle workers signing on the dole there.

At the back of the estate, at the end of a dead-end road, stands the factory of Staffa Products Ltd. The visitor who approached the place in October 1981 found the orange-painted gates closed. Outside, pickets with arm bands, blowing their hands in the blustery wind and driving rain. Inside, a makeshift hut has been erected, a flapping tarpaulin slung over walls of tea chests. Behind it, a scene of haunting symbolism: strikers breaking up packing cases with a sledgehammer to feed a fire held in by four massive metal plates, consuming the future to warm the present.

You identify yourself, the gates open, your exact time of entry is logged and you have entered occupied territory. There is a constant bustle of comings and goings: sympathizers from political groups, Right To Work campaigners, trade unionists from other workplaces. Bundles of cyclostyled leaflets, collection sheets for contributions, badges, posters, stickers, move in and out. On the blackboard, notices of important meetings ahead and the exhortation: 'To the temporary management: we will win this struggle. Staffa stays.'

Almost everywhere else in Britain, workers had simply lain down as the juggernaut of recession and mass redundancies rolled over them. At Staffa they stood up and held the pass, like the 300 Spartans blocking the Persians at Thermopylae, in a battle that encapsulated both the long-term problems of British industry and its fortunes in recession. The issue was stark. The management had announced that they would phase out the Lea Bridge site starting in 1982, with the loss of around 350 jobs, and transfer production to a new and more efficient plant at Plymouth where they would need only 300 employees. It was a rerun of so many previous closures in and around Hackney: owners shut down old factories, throwing many of their employees on to the dole, and opened up, slimmed down, on a new 'greenfields' site far away from the jungle of the metropolis. The planned Staffa closure was part of the ongoing process, accelerated by recession, by which inner cities decline – but all the more worrying because this was not, like clothing, and shoes, a long moribund industry. It was an advanced engineering company, with a skilled workforce, and a good deal of the latest high-technology machinery. It showed how fast recession and rapid economic adjustment were working to spread the inner-city phenomenon to areas that had hitherto been spared that fate.

Staffa Products started life half a century earlier under the family firm of Chamberlains. Good labour relations and the ploughing back of profits into new investment built the company up into a product leader. Its hydraulic motors, used in forklifts, cranes, oil rigs, anchors and fishing tackle, had a world-wide reputation for high quality. By 1975 Staffa accounted for no less than 9 per cent of the total world production of hydraulic motors.

In January 1979 the holding company, Chamberlain Group Ltd, was taken over by the US distributors of Staffa motors, Brown & Sharpe. The new owners reassured employees that their interests, job security, conditions of employment and pension rights would not be affected by the takeover.

By the late seventies, the company – which so far had managed to make up for sluggish growth in the UK economy by selling harder abroad – was facing much stiffer competition: the number of companies and countries producing hydraulic motors had increased, while at the same time demand was growing more slowly than before. Staffa's managers faced the problems that confronted the whole of British industry: high interest rates and export prices artificially inflated by an overvalued pound sterling (high mainly because of North Sea oil). Between 1976 and 1981 the price of Staffa's motors rose by 55 per cent and Kyaba, the most dangerous Japanese competitor, was selling similar motors in the USA at prices 30 to 50 per cent lower than Staffa. One US fisherman, confronted with the choice between a Staffa B200 motor at $3,375 and a Kyaba MR190 at $2,300, told a salesman: 'I like Staffa quality, but I don't like it to the extent of $1,000.'

Staffa's managers were forced to seek ways of keeping prices down by controlling costs. This meant, above all, improving productivity, not just by increasing output per worker, but also by rationalizing machinery, work flows, transport. But between those goals and their achievement lay the deteriorating state of labour relations.

Officers and Men

Those relations had always contained the potential for conflict: there were the traditional caste divisions of British industry, the traditional polarity of management and labour, the traditional distrust and day-to-day hassles. Staffa after the takeover was no better and no worse than the general run of the mill in Britain.

I had an introduction into the state of industrial relations from Dave Rankin, a forty-five-year-old maintenance builder with straight blonde hair and in a scruffy donkey jacket, who showed me round the occupied site, past rusting racks of components, baths of

73

caustic soda, lathes, grinders, drills, with filings and corkscrews of shaven metal underneath, hot-oil baths, testing rigs, and stacks of the Staffa motors themselves, neat and self-contained, like over-sized children's tops.

We leave the cavernous, smelly, greasy and usually noisy works for the offices, in a white-painted block just inside the gates. They are by no means luxurious, but the contrast with the works is stark: carpeted entrance hall, indoor plants, trophies of staff v. worker football matches. On the top floor is the higher managers' dining-room. 'I bet half the workers don't even know there is one,' Rankin comments. 'I only know because I done work in there. It's got nice tables and chairs, waitress service. They got their own cook. They can get nice food, like pineapples and that.' He sounds like a boy with no pocket money staring in a sweetshop window. Downstairs to the staff dining-room, painted in orange, with white mouldings and yellow striped curtains. Next door is the workers' canteen, white painted, with no curtains, and spartan tables. Until recently, there was not even a door to communicate with the adjoining staff canteen: the rules of the British caste system frown on commensality between labourers and scribes, two classes, indeed two separate cultures, with precious little contact or mutual regard.

Rankin's attitudes to management seep out: 'If they're feeling cold up there in their offices, they'll get heaters straight off, but when there's a hole in the factory roof, it's "We'll get that done when we get it done". There's a lot of people here producing nothing, supervisors and super-supervisors. They don't know nothing about my trades, brickwork or painting. They just think you stick a coat of paint on and that's it. They don't understand you have to strip, prime and undercoat first. But you got to do what they tell you, even if you know it's wrong. They think they know everything and look on you as if you know nothing, but if you think of something good they'll claim it as their brain-child. It's like when I was in the army, I'd never rely on an officer to get me out of trouble. I'd rely on the sergeant, 'cause he knows the ins and outs. It's the officers that get you blown up.'

A much more detailed view of shop-floor relations before the occupation comes from the shop stewards' daybook, kept in a drawer of the stewards' office in a tiny cell on the edge of the valve-and-piston shop. It is magenta-covered, lined foolscap. The writing is in a variety of hands from block letters to illegible scrawls. The bottom edge of the pages is black with thumbing and reeks of oil and metal. The book is used to transmit messages between the stewards on the day shift and those on nights: the two groups never meet on normal days because there are gaps between the end of one shift and the beginning of the next. Several entries show the typical problems of a multi-ethnic workforce assembled from the far ends of former empire. One undated summer's night in 1980, probably during the Muslim fast of Ramadan, steward Ron writes to his day colleagues: 'Good morning bros. We have had a small problem here tonight re a moslem religious time, which means they must fast all day and only eat after sunset, by which time they are starved. A. [a manager] found them stopped work and sitting down to eat approx 9 p.m. Can they have a different meal break? There is quite a large number of them and they were quite upset by it all.' The next evening it is agreed that the men can eat at their machines.

The bulk of the daybook is the record of the routine conflicts between workers and managers engendered, with tragic inevitability, by the structure of British industry. In companies where workers have no share in control or in profit, the interests of workers and managers are, of necessity, directly opposed. The contradictions arise out of the rules of the game as surely as they do for two opposing teams of footballers. Managers seek to maximize their power over workers, workers to minimize it. Managers seek to maximize the workers' output and to minimize their earnings – workers seek to minimize their effort and maximize their earnings.

Labour discipline is a continual source of problems: no one submits willingly to externally imposed orders that bring no personal gain.

May 1980 (unsigned): 'Re recent warnings on nights. It seems to me A. [a manager] has told his foremen to have a go. I think it is worth fighting one or two discipline cases just to hold them off. Disturbed by the number of people who don't want union representation – especially Asians.'

September 1980 (Ron writes): 'A funny sort of thing came up tonight. A. said "We caught Gordon asleep in no. 2 toilets. Would you like to come over and be witness?" I replied, "Are you asking me to climb on a seat and look over the partition because I will not do that. And how do you know he is asleep or it is Gordon in toilet? Did you look over?" He replied, "No." Gordon naturally takes a dim view of managers acting like peeping Toms. I said maybe the police would think this an odd thing to do. A. now claims he said, "I believe", not, "We caught.""

Much day-to-day conflict is over pay: workers on lower grades feeling they are doing the work of higher grades, and asking to be upgraded; arguments over the standard times allowed for different operations, used to calculate bonus earnings; short payment; and, on one occasion, a complete absence of wages for the night shift, who duly walked out at 10.30 p.m. Plus, of course, the game of bluff and counterbluff, threat and counter-threat, of the annual wage round, the *danse macabre* of a society that still has not learned how to distribute its rewards with equity and without destructive conflict.

The Battle over Productivity

The main conflict which contributed to the management's decision to move to Plymouth was over productivity. It is a battle that goes on inside most factories daily, even hourly: arguments over new machinery, over target times for operations, over cover for absent colleagues, over the pace of conveyor belts, over minutes or even seconds lost in tea breaks, lunch breaks, clocking in and out, even excreting.

At Staffa the major issue related to flexibility: workers' readiness to cover for machines other than their own, or to operate two or more machines simultaneously. There was ample scope for multi-machine manning. For example, although one of the valve-grinding machines allows a basic cycle time of between 1 minute 39 seconds and 5 minutes 2 seconds for each valve to be ground, for anything between three-quarters and nine-tenths of that time the machine is grinding away on its own and the operator is twiddling his thumbs. In theory he could use that idle time to work a second or a third machine, if they were laid out so he had only a few paces to travel between each one, and a flowing sequence of operations was designed. It would, of course, mean a greater mental and physical strain on the worker.

A wage incentive scheme, agreed with the unions in April 1979, provided for multi-machine manning where the worker agreed and was suitably compensated. But multi-machine manning never got off the ground. Even modest attempts at increasing flexibility were resisted with increasing force as the recession deepened: it was the workers' way of protecting jobs.

In August 1980 the management tried to get the day-shift fitters, who assemble the finished motors, to work on the rigs used for testing the motors, a job they were not normally called on to do. Pete pointed out the implications in the daybook: 'Recruitment of replacement labour has stopped. Flexibility means loss of jobs. Please do what you can to stop it.' Shop stewards did their best. A note at the end of August: 'They threatened the assembly workers with short time if they refused to work the rigs. The assembly fitters on days voted six to none with two abstentions in favour of short time rather than run the rigs.' Management withdrew the threat of short time and replaced it with a more severe threat of four redundancies. The day-shift fitters reluctantly voted to accept some degree of greater flexibility, but still stuck out against running the test rigs. They were, Pete wrote 'extremely annoyed at the attitude of some night shift members who operated the test rigs and fucked us up'.

Shortly thereafter, under the threat of widespread redundancies, the shop stewards' committee for the whole factory reluctantly agreed to accept controlled flexibility rather than strike. The agreement gave management discretion to move workers around within their 'normal' work areas. They could also move them to 'other work areas' provided they consulted shop stewards and showed that there was a shortage of work in the normal area. But disputes began again almost immediately about the interpretation of the agreement. Shop stewards sought to limit it as narrowly as possible. Ron took the hardest line, interpreting 'normal area' as a single machine. At the other extreme, one of the managers defined it as an entire shop and all the machines in it. As the talk of re-dundancies grew, shop stewards became more and more inflexible on a whole range of issues. In October 1980, when the storeman was on holiday, manual workers refused to go into the stores to show the foreman where tools were. About this time management began calling men in for more overtime. Shop stewards quickly realized that this would make it possible to shed labour, and tried to organize resistance.

27 October 1980: 'A number of machines were called in for overtime this weekend. I can't make out why the men agree, with the threat of redundancies it doesn't make sense.' Gordon, on nights, replies, 'Men on 19/case line were asked to work Friday nights. Men refused this overtime.' Mick, next morning, congratulates: 'Re overtime: well done!' A few days later, unsigned, after No. 3 shop did some overtime: 'We on nights are pissed off with the attitude of No. 3 shop and something should be done to stop this disease.' Pete, on days, replies, 'There is no ban on overtime. However, we agreed to explain to the membership the problem, that is that they would work themselves out of a job.'

The behaviour of Staffa's workers over this period may seem negative, and even suicidal: all these petty obstructions, in the midst of deep recession. Here they were wrestling with British managers while the Japanese were battering the doors down. But resistance to technological progress and to more flexible working procedures are the inevitable result of the British approach to economic change. In a socialist economy, change can be planned so that full employment is maintained. In a country of paternalistic capitalism, like Japan, the worker is guaranteed lifelong employment with his company and knows that if his present activities are no longer needed, another position will be found for him. In Britain there is no effective planning and private and public companies still have the unchallenged right to throw unwanted workers on the scrap-heap, where they are left largely to their own devices to find work, or not to find it. The taxpayer picks up the bill for their subsistence, and the social costs frequently exceed the private benefits of redundancies to the companies. In a society where redundant workers are abandoned, workers will inevitably do whatever is in their power to maintain the number of workplaces in their factory by resisting increases in productivity.

The shop stewards had agreed to the principle of flexibility in the hope of avoiding redundancies. They had resisted the practice of it in the same hope. But in November 1980 the management announced that there would be forty redundancies. Among them were about half the shop stewards' committee. Even so, the workforce swallowed the redundancies without a strike, in the further hope that they would result in a more secure future for those who remained. That hope, too, was to prove misguided.

How Do You Drop a Bombshell without Doing Any Damage?

Top Staffa managers had already begun to consider more drastic solutions to the combined challenges of recession, heightened competition and the growing resistance of their own workforce. The old Lea Valley site was becoming a major handicap to increasing production and efficiency. 'It was a jumble of buildings,' general manager Ted Nailon explains. 'It was never planned, it just grew like Topsy. We had twenty fork-lift trucks working permanently just carrying components between areas.' The buildings were in poor physical state. Renovation would be costly and would disrupt production. Access was poor, down narrow side-streets filled with parked private cars, and the closest major road, Lea Bridge Road, the main route in from Essex, was one of the most notoriously congested in London. It was the familiar story of antiquated premises and poor accessibility that had driven so many firms out of Hackney.

A move came to seem essential. Foreign sites were considered – in Singapore and Eire in particular. But the site that eventually seemed most attractive was at Plymouth. Brown & Sharpe already owned a substantial machine-tool factory there, plus a large adjoining plot of vacant land. Wages in the area would be lower and, as it was a development area, substantial grants would be available for capital investment and the training of new workers. On 10 October 1980 top managers received a report entitled starkly: *A Programme for the Relocation of Staffa Works*. It concluded breezily: 'A fresh start on a new location with new people would allow optimum manning arrangements and minimum labour costs.'

Consultations with the Department of Industry followed. Statutory grants of up to £4 million for investment would be available. Desperate to avoid losing Staffa to Eire, officials took the unusual step of offering 100 per cent training grants. A detailed company report at the end of March 1981 made out an irresistible economic case for moving to Plymouth. With a new factory, purpose-designed for a smooth flow of production, only 300 employees would be needed – 90 fewer than in London. Wage rates would be 10 to 20 per cent lower. These savings would add more than £1 million a year to company profits. The cost of the move to the company, given a government grant of £4 million, would be £5 million, providing a handsome rate of return on the investment of 20 per cent. Without the government grant, it would be only 11 per cent. The role of the Department of Industry seems a dubious one: here they were, negotiating in secret, several months before the affected workers knew, to pay out £4 million of taxpayers' money to destroy more than 350 jobs in one place and create 300 in another. The catch, of course, was Brown & Sharpe's option to move Staffa out of the UK entirely.

Thus a depressed region would be helped, but only at the cost of inflicting deeper damage on an inner-city area. A multinational company was able to play off one needy community against another, one country in recession against another.

Having taken the decision in principle about the beginning of April, Staffa's managers still had to await formal planning permission from Plymouth, expected early in June. But their major problem was how to break the news to their London workers without causing massive disruption to their operations. The build-up in Plymouth would take two years, and in the meantime production had to continue at the Lea Bridge site or Staffa would lose its market presence and give ground to its competitors, hovering like kestrels for any sight of an opportunity to swoop on their customers. Managing this delicate transfer presented problems beyond the ordinary capacities of most managers.

So, in April 1981, Staffa hired a management consultancy firm, Hay Communications Ltd. Hay's eventual reports were discovered by the occupying workers in a manager's office. They provide a unique insight into the thinking of a not untypical British management. They contain nothing illegal, yet they outline a strategy of concealment and countermeasures worthy of a Machiavelli or a Churchill, with the workforce cast in the role of the enemy to be outmanoeuvred. Phase One of the report, submitted on 24 April, outlined the main tasks. The decision to move was to be announced early in June, immediately after planning permission came through, seven months before the first redundancies and four months before the company was legally obliged to tell the workforce. In preparation there was a long list of precautions to be taken to forestall any possible resistance by the workers. Strikes, go-slows and even a factory occupation were considered, and brainstorming sessions held to plan responses. All rumours and inquiries were to be stalled until the day of the announcement. Sensitive documents were to be moved – technical drawings and customer and supplier records that might be useful to competitors, personnel records that might stir up trouble among the workers. A stockpile of motors was to be produced, over and above normal requirements, and moved off site before the day of the announcement. There would be a study of alternative sources of production in the event of a strike, and of an alternative timetable for speeding up the move to Plymouth if there was serious disruption to production in London. Phase Two of the report, dated 22 May, consisted of a thorough and brilliant timetable for D-Day. In the morning, managers from outside the charmed circle of those who were in the know were to be briefed on the reasons for the move and trained to deal with workers' questions. This session would also help them to get over their own emotional reactions to the news. Indeed, it would be essential to monitor and intervene with 'disaffected' managers and supervisors who might exert a strong negative influence on the workforce during the transition. At 1.30 p.m. trade-union reps would be informed: managers were urged to be calm and patient, helpful, courteous and concerned. If the unions threatened a strike, managers should point out that this would not help, and that the unions' proper role would be to drive the best redundancy deal for their members 'at a realistic cost'. Then, at 2 p.m. the workforce would be told, not in a mass assembly where ugly scenes might result, but in small groups, by their section managers. The report even included verbatim texts of a letter to employees, notices, model questions and answers for media interviews. There was a press release for Plymouth, leading, in true public-relations style, with the positive, 'Upwards of 300 new jobs will become available in the Plymouth area.' For London, not surprisingly, there would be no press release. The strategy would be to respond to press inquiries. Only the two top managers, who had received training in handling press, television and radio interviews, were to speak to the media. They were urged to be 'helpful in manner but not in fact', to beware of reporters who assume false identities, or who use pregnant pauses to try to get managers to carry on talking and perhaps reveal unfavourable information.

Everything was ready. The managers knew. The Department of Trade and Industry knew. Hay Communications knew. The only group still in the dark were the workers whose lives, families and aspirations would be most disrupted. For our advanced democracy does not grant workers any right to information about current company profits, prospects or plans, even if their whole destinies lie in the balance.

Scenes from Occupied Territory

June the 5th – as it happens, the eve of the anniversary of the original D-Day – arrived and its programme was enacted almost exactly as planned and rehearsed. The Association of Scientific, Technical, and Managerial Staffs (ASTMS), representing staff, began negotiating for an improved redundancy deal, and were eventually offered more than double the legal minimum of one week's pay for each year of service with the company. The manual workers, belonging to the Amalgamated Union of Engineering Workers (AUEW), refused even to talk about redundancies and took a series of actions: overtime bans, one-day stoppages, blacking of goods destined for Plymouth. But management would not budge an inch on the decision to move.

Finally, on Tuesday, 29 September 1981, AUEW shop stewards called a meeting in the workers' canteen to vote on whether they should start negotiating for redundancy, or take other action. The vote, by a five-to-one majority, was to occupy the factory. Work stopped immediately. Staff and managers were allowed to stay till the Thursday, so pay cheques could be processed. Staff were told not to report for work until further notice. Afraid that they would be dismissed and rehired again on short-term contracts, ASTMS members decided to join the occupation. The following day, ASTMS headquarters declared their dispute official and started paying strike pay of £25 a week, provided the strikers moved outside the gates so as to remain on the right side of the law. The AUEW was not to follow suit until later, leaving the occupying workers without strike pay for several weeks.

The AUEW shop stewards had their own equivalent of the Hay report. They had been planning for an occupation for all of three months. Occupying offered distinct advantages. Hydraulic motors worth some £2 million would be immobilized. The organizers would be indoors, in the warm, with a pay phone to arrange support. There would be none of the hassle with police and blacklegs involved in picketing. Provided no damage was done, and no disturbances caused, they could only be evicted by court order. And so a code of conduct was drawn up: no alcohol to be drunk, no damage, regular cleaning and maintenance – and a copy sent to local police. Committees were set up to organize finance, food, rotas, entertainment, delegations and security. Speakers went out to trade-union branches and workplaces all over the country with sheafs of collection sheets.

I visited the factory in the second week of occupation. The tables had been moved from the manual workers' canteen and the floor covered entirely with mattresses and blankets for the night rota. The staff canteen was now being, as it were, ritually contaminated by the untouchable caste of workers with the hand. A group of West Indians played cards, marking up their scores with matchsticks. Three young, turbaned Sikhs sat on a table, backs against the wall. The food committee had laid on cheap refreshments: tea 3p, cheese sandwiches 10p. The entertainments committee filled a window-ledge with highbrow reading material, from Sherlock Holmes and E. M. Forster to the war memoirs of Lloyd George.

Morale was high and rhetoric expansive, yet there was a realism and a fatalism about. A group of men at the gates, sheltering from the autumn wind, aired their feelings.

(*A man in his fifties, with a lumpy nose and red hair*) 'Sometimes I see a pot of gold at the end of the rainbow, sometimes I'm not so sure. The thing is, we've got nothing to lose. There are no other jobs about. There was only one job this week in the *Hackney Gazette* and the *Walthamstow Guardian* – one job, and there are two hundred of us on the shop-floor here.'

(*A tall light-skinned West Indian*) 'You should see the wages on offer down at the Jobcentre – £70 to £100.'

(*Red-haired man*) 'The thing is, I'm a skilled engineer. I've been doing it for thirty-four years. Why should I go now? If I wanted to change to being a road-sweeper, I'd have done it years ago.'

(*Tall West Indian*) 'We won't even be given that privilege, because there are no road-sweeping jobs around.'

(*Red-haired man*) 'They want me to sell my job for three thousand quid, well balls.'

(*Tall West Indian*) 'It wouldn't be so bad if you found another job.'

(*Red-haired man*) 'If there was work about, what we're doing now wouldn't be taking place. Everywhere is closing down round here. I reckon Thatcher will go the way of Sadat [assassinated earlier that week]. We're worse off now than in the thirties.'

(*Tall West Indian*) 'But the degree of poverty is higher psychologically. If you have a kiddie, now they want Space Invaders. You never had that before, our expectations are greater.'

(*A Young Socialist, visitor in orange bomber jacket*) 'How long are people gonna take it? Trade unions have got the muscle to get her out, why don't they use it?'

(*Tall West Indian*) 'We got used to good times. We got flabby. You don't change *that* quickly.'

(*Red-haired man, carried away*) 'What right has she [Thatcher] got to make my life unhappy because she refuses to make a U-bend? What is inflation anyway? It's only money. Why shouldn't we borrow the money now, and when we're back on our feet, we pay it back? Why should people be governed by the mind of one person? You're put on this earth, but surely it's not just to be kicked in the bollocks?'

Outside the gate the ASTMS pickets, sheltering in a zinc

workman's hut, are also talking. A little man, muffled in a sheep-skin coat, expatiates:

'It really is very difficult when the government goes and gives people grants to do this type of thing. The chances of us keeping the work here is very much diminished. We don't seem to have any rights. I wonder what's happening to this country, I think they're going to rename it Chicago. We got Japs in, Germans in, Yanks in, Arabs in. The people here are not militants, but they're so bitter with the treatment. I've never seen anything like it and I spent six years in the army.'

There is humour – the humour never gives out, not even in de-feat. It is the last refuge of working-class defence. At the same time, there is a grim determination, verging on desperation and tinged with bitterness. Their predicament seems to have opened a deep vein of reflection. Stan Waller, a gaunt fellow in a brown parka, a machine-tool fitter at Staffa for five and a half years, was under-standably bitter. His marriage had just broken up, he was living with his ten-year-old son in a small room in a hostel, and without strike pay could not pay the rent: 'What about us in our forties, we got twenty years of working life ahead, how long will we be in the wilderness of the dole? This government wants a working class that's starving, so they can say: here's two per cent, take it or leave it. Oh it's a free country all right. You're free to starve to death 'cause there's no sod'll help you when you're down. But when a person has got to the bottom of the barrel, that person will fight as they never fought before.'

Dave Rankin echoed his feelings with an apocalyptic remark: 'We might not win this fight, but if we go down, we'll take them with us.'

Roger Owen, a fitter with a wiry, lined face, joined in. 'The people here used to work hard, they would never let a shitty motor go through. I used to file a bore down to make sure the motor wouldn't come back for repairs. That's something they'll never have again, the will to work. My attitude now is, fuck it, why should I bother, they don't give a monkey's bollocks about us. People think us shop stewards are all Commies. I'm not even a leftie. If there's a choice between the union and my family, it's no contest, it's my family all the way. When I talked to Leyton County

High School about our occupation, one boy said, "What right have you got to tell the management what to do?" I thought and then I said: "If you're a working man, you're there for your family, to defend them, and that's what right you got."'

'I Never Seen Trouble Like This in My Life'

Gaurishanker Maru has a shock of black hair, a trim moustache and a long black overcoat, and looks at least a decade younger than his thirty-nine years. Although his English is shaky, he was throwing himself into the struggle with gusto, offering to drive speakers to the Midlands in his ageing Ford Capri.

Under his youthful exterior he carries the history of another segment of empire: he is a descendant of the Indian navvies, junior clerks, artisans and traders that the British imported into East Africa to help them rule the natives. When Kenya gained her independence in 1963, there was widespread resentment among Africans about the Asian predominance in commerce. There were no mass expulsions as in Uganda, but in 1967 Asians who had not opted for Kenyan citizenship were allowed to work only on a temporary basis. The result was a flood of migrants to Britain, among them G. K. Maru.

Maru's father, a labourer in Nairobi, died when he was twenty. Maru never went to school and never learned English. He spoke in Swahili to the bosses of the big garage where he worked as a mechanic.

He arrived at Heathrow without any contacts in the country, illiterate and speaking hardly a word of English. Hence he had no other method of looking for work than to wander the streets calling in at any establishment that looked promising. It was not a productive method, and he spent eight years on the dole. In 1974 he married a distant cousin whose family had settled in Ashton-under-Lyne. They had a baby and got a Hackney council flat. In 1976 he heard of a job going in an Ashton mill and moved up there on the strength of it. It was a disaster: all the family got bronchitis, Maru's aggravated by dust in the air at the spinning-mill. His wife spent six months in hospital while pregnant with their second child, and almost lost it. Maru had an accident at the mill and had to give up his job. As soon as his wife came out of hospital, they called an end to the Ashton episode and returned to Hackney. After another two years of unemployment, Maru found his present job, as a fitter assembler, by pure chance: he was repairing the car of a friend who worked at Staffa and heard there was a vacancy.

It was the beginning of a brief episode of relative prosperity. He bought the Ford Capri for £450 and restored it himself, had a phone installed, began to dress reasonably. By 1981 however, rent and electricity rises had begun to erode the Marus' living standards. 'This winter electric coming kill me,' he complained. 'Electric meter chop my neck. My kids got bronchitis so paraffin heater worse for me. Before we got meter, we got bills more than £300, nearest £400 one time. Every week now I pay here, pay here, pay here, nothing left. Milkman take it, electric take it, petrol take it. Nearly road tax go seventy quid, insurance go £180, but without car you never coming job in the bus: fares go kill you. Before this trouble, I'm very good life here at this company. I'm very happy. I like this company. I settle down all right. I'm good fitter for this company, I'm old man here. Pieces of motor all coming to me, I build. I know these motors like a carpenter. I look after this company like my own. If I see tap on, I turn off. If I see heater on, I turn off. I get cuts on my fingers for this company. I get bad chest from oil bath for this company.

'But now this company go finish here. They give me bad heart. At night I never sleep, I think, what I go eat with my family? My wife say, I never seen trouble like this in my life. My wife very nice, look after me, look after babies. This is worst time now coming for me. I got no money, no any money coming from anywhere. I lose my life, believe me. Yesterday my small baby call in the night – this cold weather catch your baby. If you come my house, you see, very old house, very damp house. What you do? If I put money all day electric meter, no money for food. I no go to social security, I no speak proper good, I no read forms, no write. I hope only, this company no go finish here. I pray for God this company no go finish here. Usually I never go to temple, but I pray God, I say him, if company stay here, I will come in your temple and put in your temple something.'

The Retreat

Meanwhile the machinery of the law was already in motion against the occupying workers. On 6 October the company had been granted an injunction requiring the strikers to vacate the factory within fourteen days. The staff, on ASTMS instructions, ceased to occupy and began to picket outside the gates. The manual workers remained inside the enemy citadel, expecting it to be stormed at any time. A further hearing was scheduled in the High Court for 16 October.

Four days before that, a shop stewards' meeting was held to hear advice from Paul Mennell, a union convenor at Metal Box. Mennell, black hair swept back from a high forehead, was the deputy convenor at Crosfield Electronics in north London, which was occupied in 1975 to forestall redundancies. They start by discussing the forthcoming court case.

(*Geoff*) 'We know we ain't got a leg to stand on. We'll lose the case even if we have a lawyer, and then they'd ask us for costs, which we can't afford.'

(*Mennell*) 'I'm worried about your attitude to the legal system. The law in this country is still the law of lords and peasants, it ain't changed. Your only chance of winning is to delay legal proceedings.'

(*Chris*) 'They've already got a writ to come in here, why haven't they done it? They don't want to stiffen feeling. They want to wait till we're weaker. The main problem is to keep up our morale and fighting spirit.'

(*Dave*) 'We talked about the law last week, and all that legal wrangling had a demoralizing effect. That's what worried them most.'

(*Bearded visitor*) 'Well, the law is designed to screw you, it's in the nature of the law to triumph.'

(*Dave*) 'Once we're slung out of here, the danger is that people will trickle back to work.'

(*Roger*) 'If they can get eighty per cent of us back to work, they'd say fuck the others. They might not even want all of us back. This has put us in the management's sights.'

(*Alan*) 'Our people are getting demoralized that the EC [the executive committee of the AUEW] hasn't given backing yet. They can see the ASTMS people outside the gate getting paid their £25 a week. They're sitting pretty. Our people are losing confidence in the leadership. There's guys wandering about out there who haven't a clue what's happening, because we're not telling them.'

(*Bearded visitor*) 'It's got to be explained to them that they're not personally under threat, that they don't risk losing their cars and their houses. They need to know they're not going to gaol. Otherwise they are just standing as individuals before the law.'

Mennell launches into a lengthy description, with photos, of how the Crosfield occupation was organized. 'Another thing you should do is keep out political factions. If you get them in they'll destroy you. They think you're the leading torch to start things off, they think the fucking revolution is gonna start here. Some of these types would see it all fucked up in the hope that at the end of it all they'd manage to get a few extra party members. You got to remember, the average person has a fear of Moscovites and Commies. Your line has got to be: you got the right to work.'

(*Roger*) 'At the end of it we'll have another battle on our hands. The management will be trying to pick us stewards off.'

(*Mennell*) 'When it's all over you'll win something, you'll definitely win something, even if it's only memories.'

(*Alan*) 'I don't care if I walk out of this company with nothing, because at least I'll know that I've cost those bastards money. You reach a point where you've got to say: enough's enough.'

The hearing four days later went in the management's favour. At around 5.30 a.m. on the morning of Saturday, 17 October, with only eight workers on duty at the factory, about three hundred police arrived at the gates. There was no resistance, and no arrests were made. The managers drove in in a convoy. A fleet of lorries followed, loaded up the £2 million of finished motors, and drove out.

The occupation was over. The long picket began. Every day, round the clock, ten or twenty people were on duty. Every Monday a hundred or more turned up for a mass picket. Shop stewards continued the essential work of spreading the dispute: Staffa motors were blacked by dockers and miners. Hackney North MP, Ernie Roberts, tried to get the government grant withdrawn. The Greater London Council made noises that it would consider a loan or grant to enable Staffa to stay in London. But the management would not budge one millimetre. The decision to move was irrevocable and, just as the engineering workers had refused to talk redundancy, managers would not talk of staying at Lea Bridge. The strike, indeed, and the disruptions that preceded it, had forced managers to speed up preparations for the move to Plymouth.

The Staffa workers held out for nearly ten weeks. On Wednesday, 2 December, they assembled for a mass meeting at the Labour club in Grange Park Road, Leyton. They voted against continuing the strike. The majority was six to one. They had surrendered, having won virtually nothing except a marginal improvement in the redundancy offer, and memories.

Why did they lose? Certainly, the leadership was inexperienced. Perhaps the mass of workers was not kept fully in the picture, perhaps some timely legal help might have given them a week or two more inside the factory. But their main enemy was the historical moment. The climate was quite different from the winters of discontent of the seventies. A new ice age had moved in. Trade-union picketing rights had been reduced, supplementary-benefit support to strikers cut back. Trade unions were being routed right across the country: union membership falling, real wage cuts being accepted, massive lay-offs and redundancies being pushed through with only sporadic resistance. Managements were taking the opportunity of union weakness to rationalize, increase flexibility and raise productivity. Though many workers were being hammered as never before in their lifetimes, days lost through strikes plummeted, nationally, from more than 29 million in 1979 to one-seventh of that level in 1981.

What hit Staffa's workers hardest were the simple economics of striking during an inflation-ridden recession. The regulations were tough enough: no social-security benefit for strikers, and an assumed £12 in strike pay automatically deducted (whether or not it was being paid) from their families' entitlement. Even after the AUEW began paying £12 a week, a family man with two children and a wife at home would get only £33·40 a week, plus rent or mortgage interest and rates. G. K. Maru, who could just about keep his head above water on his take-home pay of £100 a week, took a drop of £45 a week for ten weeks. Dave Rankin, single, had to get by on £12 a week when his rent alone was £18. Many did not even get the meagre social-security benefits they were entitled to. Some social-security offices took the initial line that the men were unemployed, and required them to sign on at the unemployment-benefit offices first. There they were informed that they couldn't sign on as they were on strike. And there were the usual delays in the processing of claims and the arrival of giro cheques. Towards the end, most of the workers had accumulated debts of £400 to £500, virtually everyone was in massive rent or mortgage arrears, some had been threatened with eviction, had had electricity cut off or suffered the repossession of hire-purchase goods. Christmas and the cold of winter lay ahead. Wives were turning on the pressure to return. Many workers, too, no longer had any desire to go on fighting for the right to work for a company that had treated them as it did.

It was an industrial tragedy that illustrated graphically the British style of economic adjustment, which allows companies, whose centres of control often lie far away, in another region, in another country even, the unquestioned right to destroy old factories, marginalize and de-skill their workers, destabilize their families, devastate their communites. No democratic account-ability limits this power: no requirement to consult the workers, to consider their alternative plans, to consult the local authority or the central government. Only owners and shareholders are con-sidered, only private profit is accounted, not the massive bill in social costs picked up by the taxpayer and above all by the victims. It was a tragedy that was being enacted all over Britain, with public enterprises like British Steel and British Leyland, behaving increasingly like private-sector companies, contributing more than their share.

The strike cost Staffa more than £1 million in lost production. The workers lost up to £1,500 each in lost wages. Thanks to the engines they had wisely stockpiled, Staffa kept up their market presence, and they accelerated the move to Plymouth. The bulk of the managerial staff planned to transfer to Plymouth. Though they were all offered jobs there, only a handful of the workers agreed to go: one condition was the acceptance of Plymouth's lower wage rates. Many were long settled locally, or did not want to interrupt their children's secondary education. The first workers were made redundant in June 1982, the last left in December of that year. Nearly all of them were destined for the dole, for Staffa took with it almost a third of the engineering jobs in Leyton.

5 Death by a Thousand Cuts: Working in the Public Sector

When I labour, they take away my reward. When I increase my efforts, who will give me anything?

Ancient Mesopotamian proverb

In an area with a moribund private sector of antiquated industries and factories, and low and insecure pay, the public sector acquires a special importance, both as a provider of services to a place that desperately needs them and as one of the few sources of employment that offers reasonable pay, conditions and security. Hackney Council itself provided nearly 5,000 full-time and 1,000 part-time jobs in 1982, and was by far the largest employer within its own boundaries. But the attractiveness of those jobs began to pale when the Thatcher government came in, committed to cut taxes and public spending and to reduce the size of the public sector in comparison to the private. It failed in all three aims: the rising toll of unemployment raised public spending higher than ever; taxes and national-insurance contributions had to be raised to pay for it; and private-sector workers on the whole suffered worse, in terms of job losses and real wage cuts, than their better-organized public-sector colleagues. Nevertheless, the Tories still inflicted grievous damage on public services and employment.

The largest single council department providing manual jobs in Hackney is the building division of the Department of Technical and Contract Services, which employed around 1,100 workers in 1979. The Tories seemed to regard virtually all types of council activity as 'wasteful', but special venom was reserved for the direct-labour organizations (DLOs) which many Labour councils used to do most of their building work. DLOs were set up partly to ensure reliable, accountable construction work, partly to provide decent employment for construction workers otherwise cursed by the insecurity of casual, seasonal work and lump labour. But Conservatives saw the DLOs as the embodiment of creeping municipal socialism or nationalization from below. Some well-publicized instances of excessive costs made them a symbol of council wastefulness.

The Local Government and Land Act, passed in 1980, aimed to convert DLOs into privatistic enterprises, or to drive them out of existence altogether: the Act compelled councils' building divisions to compete for all works over £10,000, and to make a 5 per cent profit, or face closure. This was at a time when many private firms were taking on jobs at a loss just to keep going, and when massive cuts in housing expenditure – the heaviest hit of any sector – greatly reduced the demand for construction work, public or private. Manual jobs in the building division were cut by 27 per cent between 1979 and 1982 – a loss of more than 300 jobs, including the only redundancies that Hackney made during this period.

The requirement to make a profit inevitably intensified the conflict between management and labour, as managers' jobs came to depend on squeezing a maximum of value out of their workers. In a country as class-ridden as Britain, public ownership *per se*, without changes in the distribution of power between management and workers, does very little to mitigate class conflict. Managers retain almost all the powers, perks and pay differentials of their private-sector counterparts. There is the same deep divide between manual and non-manual workers – and curiously it is often at its most intense between the manual workers and the lower-level officials and supervisors, for that is the interface at which conflict most commonly arises.

Listening to Hackney's manual workers talk about their masters, you would think they worked not for a public service run by a socialist council, but for the most grasping of capitalists.

(*Derek Hill, convenor of the building workers*) 'If the bonus surveyors [responsible for calculating bonus payments] get a reputation for keeping the rates down, they get promoted.'

(*Terry Basra, deputy convenor*) 'Some clerks can't tolerate the idea that a manual worker might be earning more than them. They're

94

often caught cutting the bonus target times. If one of them shows he's a dirty no-good snake and knows how to stitch blokes up he's promoted to being a contracts surveyor.'

(*Derek Hill*) 'But they're not animals when they start out: it's people above them putting pressure on them.'

Or listen to some of the workers themselves:

(*A*) 'They're one hundred per cent against you. They've got to stop you making some of your money to justify their existence. They don't give a monkey's about you.'

(*B*) 'The governor sits himself in front of his window so he can see people go in and out. If you're ten minutes late, he says to the foreman: how much money will you stop that guy?'

(*C*) 'On Monday it was pouring with rain and freezing and two guys were sheltering in a little hallway. Then one of them said, come on, let's have a cup of tea. Then the governor happened to drive past and saw they weren't on the job. He stopped them four hours' pay. He stopped me three hours once for nipping to the shop to get some fags. He speaks to you like a lump of shit, swearing at you. But when he wants to push off, he says, "I'm just going to the other office." You can't win with these people, they've always got the upper hand.'

Working the System: The Carpenter's Tale

At 7.30 a.m. on a dark October morning, Hackney's streets are already busy, with workers in battered second-hand cars, in bus queues and on bikes, heading home from the night shift or off to the morning shift. The rain is sheeting down. By 8 a.m., the windows of the site office at Gilpin Yard are running with steam. Carpenters, brickies, plasterers, tilers, roofers and their mates tramp in and out in their council-issue donkey jackets, muttering about the weather, the shortage of drivers or the attractiveness or otherwise of the job tickets that foreman George Tinguey hands out: all these are factors that will affect their earnings that day.

Gilpin Yard, in the middle of the massive Clapton Park estate, is one of the many specialized depots of Hackney Council's building division. It handles maintenance of council properties for about a quarter of the borough, excluding plumbing, heating and electrical work, which is done by separate depots.

All the toings and froings, all the arguments that take place here between managers and men, are coloured by the payments system, which is typical of the sort of donkey-and-carrot pay arrangements that manual workers have to contend with, but which few non-manual workers suffer. The building workers get a low basic wage of £83 to £95 a week (1981), depending on skill and craft. This is made into a living wage by guaranteed overtime averaging £16 a week, but above all by bonus payments ranging from nil to £60 a week. Like most similar systems, the bonus scheme is complicated. It works roughly as follows: for every detailed type of job, a target time is fixed by time-and-motion study. It is more or less the length of time that a rather slow worker would take to do a job of average difficulty. For every hour the worker takes less than that target, he earns a bonus of 88p to £1: for every hour he takes more, he may lose a similar amount off his bonus payments. 'Waiting time', when the worker cannot get on with the job because he is waiting for supplies, is paid at that man's average bonus. But 'Wet time', when rain prevents outdoor work, is paid at the basic rate, and so is sick pay. The bonus makes all the difference between a mere existence on the brink of survival and a life bearing some resemblance to the social expectations of the time.

Brian Duggan, a thirty-one-year old carpenter, is an expert at working the bonus system to good advantage. He reports for work that day in a blue parka and a smart trade-marked sweater. His job is to repair a front door and lock at 91 Redwald Road: the door has been split from a failed attempt to break in, and partly burned in an arson attack by a neighbourly teenager: typical Hackney repairs. Everything Duggan does is designed to speed up the flow of his work so as to maximize bonus. Instead of waiting for the yard driver to deliver, he loads up his own blue 1970 estate with the materials he will need: door, two lengths of beading, two glazing panels, a huge tub of putty and a lock. He made sure he would get access by visiting the house the evening before. A neighbour brings the key, drags a whining pointer into the kitchen and bolts him in, while Duggan unloads his big magenta trunk full of tools and tunes his portable, for company, to Capital Radio. He works in a sweater, despite a chill breeze, and works briskly, virtually without pause.

He unscrews the old door from its hinges and hammers off the weather-board, cursing as it splits: it will take time to get another – time lost off his bonus. Luckily the house has a phone so he rings the yard to order another. Next he saws off the horns of the new door, sizes it up in the frame, and clamps it into his portable workbench, planing the sides down till they fit. 'It's not a bad measuring job,' he comments. 'If they don't fit you've got a lot more work planing or building them up, and the foremen don't like you to write that down on your time-sheet: it shows they haven't measured it up properly.' He pencils in the shape of the hinges, chips out a space for them and screws them on. Now he bores three holes with a gimlet where the lock is to go, chisels out the hole and inserts the lock. It doesn't fit: he's been given the wrong type. Again he curses, but luck is on his side: the storeman has just arrived with the new weather-board, so Duggan orders the right type of lock. The cold is blowing through the lobby, numbing my hands so that I can hardly write, but Duggan ploughs on, hardly seeming to notice it, screwing the door hinges into the frame. The storekeeper arrives with the correct lock. Duggan slots it in. Then he fits the glass panels into the door, grabs a fistful of putty from the tub and pushes it on, rapidly, feeding it from the palm of his hand to his thumb which marks it like the crinkled edge of a pastry pie. He squeezes the glass against it and slices off the surplus putty. Finally he bores and chisels a hole for a second lock, which the tenant wants fitted for security. Three hours from the start, the job, which carries a six-hour target, is virtually complete: Duggan has earned an extra £3 for his pains. The council has saved about the same amount: for that saving is the real reason for the scheme.

But the work is the least of his headaches. A lot of the time he is working, he is thinking of how he can manipulate the bonus system so as to get paid the bonus he has effectively earned and get a living wage, in view of his experience of the managers' propensity for reducing bonus earnings.

'The bonus target times are fine,' Duggan explains. 'The trouble comes with getting to the job, getting in, getting the materials you need. All that time you can't be earning bonus. We're only allowed eight minutes travel time for each job – anything extra is added on to your time for the job, so you lose bonus. So you have to work faster to cover for travel time. That's why I use my car, though I'm not supposed to. Blokes who use the bus can take an hour or more to get to a job. You've got to have all your wits about you to earn bonus. One flooring job I had, all the joists were rotten, and there was cementing and bricking to be done. I insisted on getting the bonus surveyor down from the town hall. I said either we come to an arrangement or I go no further. He said all right I'll pay you your average bonus on this one. Sometimes a man might be given a right stinker of a job, that he might even make a bonus loss on. With jobs like that it has been known that people just happened to lose the job ticket and didn't do the work.

'I work a personal limit to my bonus of forty hours a week – that means doing every job in half the target time. I never book for less than half the target time, because the management will say, "How come this cunt can do it so fast? The others must be doing fuck all." It makes the target times look too long. Then next thing they'd have a work-study man watching how you do it.'

Every Thursday evening Duggan spends an hour and a half of his own time carefully constructing his time-sheet with a novelist's skill: 'The problem is that governors don't like you to write down the time you spend waiting for materials, because that shows them up, it shows up their inefficiency. They don't like you to claim for pre-inspection – measuring up and that, which we often do to make sure it's right – because that is their job. So you're forced to falsify your time-sheets – you've got to make up for all that time they've made you lose. You've got to tell a few white lies just to keep clear – make the job sound a little bit harder than it really was. You've got to give them a whole life story to make any money out of it. And you've got to have a good memory. You get the bonus payment three weeks after the week you earned it. If I ain't happy I get in touch with the guy who works out my bonus. At one period I kept getting my pay-sheet with less than I expected on it. I phoned him up every time, and I got them back with £17 extra. He doesn't make mistakes any more: he must be going through them properly. If you're all right on paper work and got a little bit of brains, you do all right. You got to be a bit of an accountant. But there are some guys that can't write too well or don't put down what they're entitled to put down.'

Duggan's cunning plus his fast work pace earn him a gross of £160 a week, of which he takes home £120. He is far worse off than a year earlier – his wife gave up her job to have a baby, and he lost around £20 a week when overtime was cut back in April 1981. But he finds he can survive on his money, as his mortgage repayments, on a semi in Barnet, are only £20 a week allowing for his tax rebate.

Risking Your Neck: The Roofing Gang

Workers who do not tinker with their time-sheets, who do not protest enough when managers and bonus surveyors whittle down their earnings, do not manage so well. Graham Chandler, roofer, and his mate Andrew Tsokallis, belong to the latter category. In hard times they have to risk their health, and in their particular trade their lives, to try to beat the bonus system and make up for stagnant real wages.

Chandler is twenty-nine, and wears a parka with a belt and a pouch for nails. He looks as if he shaves about once a week. Tsokallis, twenty-five, born in Hackney of Greek parents, wears a council donkey jacket and a pair of trainers with the sole beginning to part company with the uppers. His long black hair protrudes from under a red ski hat.

'28 Median Road: Investigate/remedy suspected rain entry, roof' reads the job ticket. The house is part of a Victorian terrace: the ground floor is a spartan doctor's surgery, the upper floors council flats. The roof slopes away at a forty-five-degree angle. At the back is an iron platform that shakes when you walk on it, overlooking tangled, weed-ridden gardens, one piled high with hundreds of old television tubes, the next with an alsatian barking up at the roofers. At the front, nothing but a plastic gutter stands between the roofers and a sheer drop to the pavement 12 metres below. The roof itself is in typical Hackney condition: slates crumbling at the edges, flaking around the nails, slipping in parts and giving rise to leaks.

Graham tells me this is a 'nice and easy' job from a safety angle, though it turns out to be a bad one for bonus. He unpacks his tools

– a spike hammer, with one end elongated and sharp; a lath axe, for chopping through wooden battens; a slate clipper; and a slate ripper, like a scimitar with a hooked end, which is inserted under the slate to cut the nail through. The duck-run is in place from the previous day: a steel ladder with rubber-covered stays to support it, wheels to roll it up the roof and a large bend at the top to fit over the ridge. The men are working on an area of broken slates on the open, street side. Graham moves with the caution of long experience: he climbs down the duck-run backwards. Andrew follows, walking upright, facing forwards down the duck-run and carrying, cradled in both arms, a stack of ten or so heavy slates. He slopes his feet backwards on the rungs, but the slightest forward moment could tip him over the edge. There is a certain bravado about his movements: he shows no sign of nerves. Graham now edges across the bare roof, grabs the parapet between this roof and the next and monkeys up it on all fours, fingertips deftly grasping the edges. Lying on one side and holding on with one hand (roofers are only supposed to work with one hand) he slips his ripper under a slate, then pulls and shoves vigorously until the slate comes out. The battens are exposed. He feels them: they are rotten. He curses gently and looks away in disgust: new battens are needed, and he has none with him. It means a trip back to the yard. It's always like that: unforeseen problems and lack of supplies to deal with them slow the roofers up and cut into their bonus, even though they're working flat out all the time.

He drives back in his twelve-year-old Triumph 1500 and talks on the way. If this job was easy, I ask him, then what were the hard ones like? He pointed to the wide, steep-tiled roof of the five-storey block we were just passing: 'That sort there. The duck-run would only reach half-way. And there's nothing to grab hold of if you slip. We had one like that last week – I fell and had to hang on to the TV aerial. Then we had a chimney job, the stack was seven feet high and the pot was four foot on top of that. We had to put a new cowl on and there was no way up. I had to squat down, put Andrew on my shoulders, and straighten up slowly. Then he had to grab hold of the edge of the stack and haul himself up.'

Accidents in their trade are commonplace, and the need to boost bonus earnings often tempts roofers to cut corners and take risks.

Some work without duck-runs on small jobs, to save the time it takes to get one up a steep ladder to the roof and over the ridge. One roofer at the yard showed me the blue mountaineering rope he often used to lash himself to chimney pots. His mate was off sick. Theoretically he should sit around at the yard doing odd jobs on basic pay. But he couldn't afford to lose his bonus and was working without a mate.

And the routine risks are high. Slate roofs are always slippery with slate dust, which pours out when old slates are removed. In the rain, the surface becomes treacherous. Roofers are not supposed to work in the rain: they can book 'wet time' but they get no bonus on it. And they are unofficially discouraged from claiming overtime on days when they have had more than four hours of wet time. So they work in the rain. Snow and ice are even more dangerous. Cold air, too, that numbs the hands so they cannot grasp firmly. 'The council give us gloves,' Andrew explains, 'but we don't wear them. You can't get a grip on anything, and if you slip, you can't grab nothing tight.'

The job is riddled with hazards, like an assault course designed by a sadist. Slate edges are razor sharp and it is easy to drop one or more when you are humping them up a tall ladder at a ninety-degree angle, holding on with only one hand. Graham and Andrew's hands are grey with dust and scarred with blue cuts and wedges where slate splinters have pierced the skin: like so many manual workers, they carry the marks of their toil, like horses with sores where the halter rubs them. They can't afford to take time off when sick, as sick pay is only the basic rate. In 1980 Graham's previous mate fell right through a roof on a conversion job that had been left with no support for the joists: 'Everything fell in on him, slates, timbers, bricks, the lot. I was in hysterics with laughter, but it wasn't because there was anything funny, it was out of fear. All his back was done in. You know how much time he had off sick? Two days. I cut the top off my finger with a slate the other week. I had to have an anti-tetanus injection in my leg, I could hardly walk for four days. But I couldn't afford to go off sick. Andrew had to do all the work for me. If I have two weeks off sick, I have to borrow £50 off my mother to survive.' Graham picks up the battens he needs from the yard and drives back.

Andrew has removed all the slates from the area with the rotten battens. Standing right at the bottom of the duck-run, only a metre from the drop, Graham saws through a batten with a short, rectangular saw. His body shakes as the grain resists and then gives, suddenly, to the blade. With one knee resting on the rotten battens, he stuffs a new length of batten under the concrete fillet, along the side of the roof, takes a nail out of his leather pouch and nails it down with his hammer. To remove the next piece of rotten batten he has to smash about a metre's length of the fillet. A few chunks of concrete slide down and over the edge. He shouts a warning: 'Below!' He pulls out the larger pieces of concrete with both hands, without holding on to the duck-run. Andrew takes them and rests them precariously on one rung. The next batten is a really tough one: Graham has to apply his full weight, with one foot on the duck-run and the other pressed against the side of the parapet. Then he chops off the remaining fragments of wood with the lath axe, spitting and turning his face away as slate dust and sawdust fly up into his eyes. Andrew passes him a new slate. It doesn't fit the hole, and the slate clippers have been left on the other side of the roof. Once again Graham lets go of the ladder altogether, holds the slate under one arm and with the pointed end of his spike hammer chips bits off along one edge, his body juddering with each blow and splinters leaping into his face. Then he fits it and nails it down. That done, he leans right over, reaches down with his hammer and gingerly retrieves a sizeable piece of slate that has slid down to within 15 centimetres of the brink.

Roofers have to think continually, without letting up for one second, of other people's safety as well as their own. Both depend on the most delicate balance of body and work-load, and on an unceasing vigilance that has to become instinctive to be tolerated. Roofing is one of the riskiest jobs, but pay is not commensurate. Graham, in fact, earns much less than carpenter Brian Duggan: about £136 gross, take-home pay £95 to £100. His bonus earnings vary between £10 and £20 per week. Unlike Duggan, he is no expert on the bonus system: he is not acquainted with the target times, never works out what his bonus should be so as to check his pay-slip, and never complains to the bonus surveyors. He compares his earnings enviously with the £60 or so bonus that roofers on conversion work earn, because they can work without interruption on large areas with all supplies to hand – and they have scaffolding up to protect them.

'I can only just manage on what I get,' says Graham. 'Every week I usually borrow £5, I'm down £280 at the moment. My wife is one of those women that can't wait for anything. She's just had double glazing put in, which we can't afford. She's had to start up as a part-time dental nurse, working evenings, so we don't get much of a social life. I have to leave home at 6.45 in the morning, before she's up, to avoid the traffic jams on Lea Bridge Road. As soon as I get in in the evening, about 6.15, she goes out. I cook the kids' teas, put them to bed and get her tea ready. Then we have an hour or an hour and a half together, then that's it till the next day.'

The High Life

'As for Andrew,' says Graham, 'I just don't know how he survives. What he takes home is less than what I give my wife for housekeeping.' Andrew Tsokallis goes home from a day on the roof-tops to a flat 100 ft up, on the eleventh floor of Seaton Point, on Nightingale Estate, where he lives with his wife, Bernadette, and their two small children, George, nine months, and Peter, just a year older. Bernadette is a pretty twenty-two-year-old of Irish extraction, with a Greek silver ornament holding back her brown hair. She is jumpy, nervous, from the strain of holding herself together under heavy pressure.

Three documents define the narrow boundaries of their existence. The first is Andrew's pay-slip. For the week ending 29 November 1981, his gross pay was £107·08, made up of £83 basic pay, plus overtime, bonus and bus fares between jobs. That sounds reasonable, until you look at the deductions, for tax, national insurance and graduated pension, which siphon off £22·29. His net pay is £77·79. Already we have encountered the first root of the family's poverty: the staggering level of deductions. Add on £9·50 in child benefit to get the total family income: £87·29 a week. Now look at the second document, the rent book. The rent is £19·28, rates are £12·64, and there is a £7 a week charge all the year round for background heating. Knock off a rent rebate of £9·46. Net cost of the flat: £29·46. Thatcher's heavy hand is visible here too: council rents were pushed up mercilessly, and local rates had to soar to make up for cuts in total government grants. The third piece of paper is the electricity bill, for cooker, light and bedroom heating: £119 for the previous year's winter quarter, or £9·15 a week. In winter, housing and fuel costs consume 44 per cent of the family's income. Because his pre-tax income is not too low on paper, Andrew is way outside qualifying for Family Income Supplement and hence does not get the other benefits available to FIS claimants: free milk for babies (worth £3 a week), free school meals when they are older, and so on.

The lounge is tastefully furnished: smoked-glass wall units, steel-and-glass table and coffee table, velvet three-piece suite, colour television. But all of it was bought with £700 collected from guests at their wedding, a traditional Greek wedding, three years earlier. But for that, they'd be sitting on wooden boxes. The flat itself is tiny and cramped and the babies have to be watched constantly. Pharaoh ants and cockroaches get in through the hot-air ducts. 'One night we found George's cot full of cockroaches,' Andrew remembers, 'and they were all over the beds and cupboards. Bernadette was crying. We couldn't sleep here, we had to go to my mum's place.' Small flies cluster round the rubbish chutes on each floor, and smoke seeps out from them when children set fire to the piles of rubbish far below. The Tsokallises moved in two years earlier when Peter was on his way.

'I didn't want to move in,' Bernadette explains, 'but they said we had only one choice, and we had nowhere else to go. I don't like heights, I feel closed in, I get very depressed. I hate this area. I know everywhere is rough these days, but Hackney is *really* rough. I hate the thought of my kids having to go to school here. I got attacked in the lift once. This coloured bloke stopped it on the ninth floor. I said it's going up, but he came in, then he put his hand across the door to stop me getting out. He said "What's your name?" I tried to get to the buttons but he pushed me back across the lift. I said listen, I'm married, my husband is waiting downstairs, he'll be up looking for me in a minute. Then he left me alone. I have a terrible fear of getting stuck in the lift. If our lift [serving odd floors] is broken, we have to use the other [serving even floors] and walk down from the twelfth floor. Andrew carries the kids and I carry the double buggy. You shouldn't have to do that sort of thing just to get in at your own front door. My gran who's seventy-seven, she came one day when both the lifts were broke, she had to walk up twenty-six flights of stairs. There's glue-sniffers using the top of the staircases, and there's people who dirty in the lifts, they go to the toilet in there. One time it was all over the walls, and you have to take your kids in there. And there's the music upstairs. You'd think it was in your own flat . They have parties right through till the next morning, and that wakes the babies up.'

The couple have had their name down on the transfer list ever since they moved in. They have repeatedly asked for a transfer, on medical grounds, because of Bernadette's nerves, and on economic grounds, because they cannot afford the rent, but the GLC housing office has informed them that their application for transfer 'does not possess a high priority'. Another obstacle to transfer is the fact that they owe £200 in rent arrears. They have always paid the sum written on the rent book, and Andrew has always declared his wage rises as soon as they came through. The problem arose because a wage rise due from October 1979 was not paid until March 1980, with a lump sum for back pay: over that period Andrew was drawing a rent rebate higher than he was in theory entitled to. By the time the mistake was discovered, they had already spent the back pay. The GLC took Andrew to court for the arrears. 'I took a bottle of 200 cockroaches along, to show the conditions, but the judge just didn't want to know. He just said, well I think you do owe the money, you'd better pay off £1·50 a week. I told him we couldn't afford it, but he said we'd have to.'

The couple have just £48·68 a week left after housing and winter fuel. The court order takes £1·50 of that. Other major items are: rent of a colour television, £2·70; disposable nappies for two babies, £5; milk, £7; cigarettes, £3. Thus only £29·48 a week is left to cover all other needs: food, clothing, entertainment, domestic goods, durable goods, books and newspapers, alcohol, travel. In practice read only: food and domestic goods. Everything else is cut. Bernadette explained how they make out: 'I have to spend £5 a week on disposable nappies, because I've never been able to put by the £24 I'd need to buy two dozen towelling nappies. I used to be a heavy smoker – twenty a day – but I have to make that last two days now. I know I should give them up, but I can't do without them, I'd go berserk. I have tried, but I got more depressed, and I had more fights with Andrew. I've got so many worries on my mind the fags calm me down.

'For food, I'll go and buy us a pound of chops, or ten beefburgers for £1, that does us a couple of days. We can't eat corned beef or ham any more. I can't buy biscuits or cakes – I had to buy two cream cakes today because George grabbed the packet off the shelf when I wasn't looking and chewed at it. I only buy tea, never coffee. I used to make trifles, but I can't now. The kids don't even get custard. I just buy meat, carrots, peas, eggs, margarine and bread. Nothing for sandwiches. Andrew goes out in the morning without breakfast, and he can't afford no dinner at work. Sometimes he complains that his belly hurts him, he's that hungry. I just had tea and toast for breakfast this morning, and it'll be tea and toast tonight.

'I cry sometimes that I can't afford clothes for the kids. Everything they've got is what's been given them, or second-hand. Andrew's got trousers with the zip bust and he can't afford to have a new zip put in. These boots I've got on were given me, this skirt was given me, this T-shirt was given me. None of my clothes are new.

'We've never been out since we got married. We're just stuck in here every night watching telly. When you first get married, you don't think about things like that. The only place we ever go is to my parents, but usually they come here 'cause we can't afford the fares. My mum brings me butter and sugar every week. My dad helps us out sometimes. He does crazy paving and pebble-dash walls. He advertises in the papers. He goes far away sometimes. He's loaded half the time. Andrew would love to do something like that, but at the beginning, when you're building it up, it's hard and you don't make much money. So he can't do it, because we couldn't pay the rent.'

'I'm skint the same day I get paid,' Andrew complains. 'I have to smoke Graham's fags, I can't afford to buy any. I walk to work every morning. It takes me about half an hour. My brother gave me his old car, and my brother-in-law lent me the insurance, but I can't afford petrol to run it. I've only had it three weeks and I've had my radio cassette nicked out of it and the headlights smashed. That's what it's like on this estate.'

'We used to pay our rent fortnightly,' Bernadette says. 'The week we paid it we'd get low shopping. Then the following week we'd put money away for our bills and get extra shopping, with a few luxuries. But as we are now, if we paid two weeks' rent at a time that would only leave me with £12. We're just starting to get into arrears now, on top of that money we owe from two years ago. We're up to £76 in arrears now.'

The constant strain of paying the rent, of being unable to escape from the tower because of low income, is driving Bernadette to the edge of breakdown and telling on their marriage. They have seriously discussed divorce three times, and money is always the cause of their disputes.

'When Andrew's wage packet is low, that's when we start fighting. He cleared £91 a few weeks ago, and we were so delighted. But recently it's been £75, £73. One week he took home £61. But I can't stop my shopping. I've still got the rent to pay. When it's low we pick on each other. I start saying: how am I going to manage on this? When we have to break into the rent money to pay the milk, that really gets us arguing, and once we start, we're down each other's throats all night.'

'Christmas is coming now. It isn't fair that we have to suffer like this. And now they're putting everything up again [the day before my visit, it was announced that council rents would go up by £2·50 the following April, and national-insurance contributions by £1·50 a week. That would more than cancel out Andrew's anticipated wage rise]. They know we can't afford it, so why do they keep on doing it? We don't ask much out of life, just a little money to buy food and decent clothes. But they take every penny you've got, they don't leave you with nothing.

Bernadette had it right. For their poverty – by no means extreme by Hackney standards – sprang primarily, not from inflation in the cost of food, clothing or manufactures, not from excessive wage demands by greedy workers, but directly from government actions.

6 The Idle Poor: Unemployment and Inequality

'To obtain employment, be willing even to wash dogs' feet.'
Bengali proverb

It should be clear by now that it is misleading to assume a stark contrast between on the one hand those fortunate enough to be employed and on the other the unhappy legions of the unemployed, condemned to perpetual futility. In the inner city, and in recession, those in manual employment are not too fortunate either: they find themselves with low and declining real wages, unpleasant work conditions and growing work-load, reduced security and weakened trade-union protection. And the growing reserve army of the unemployed is the principal threat through which this position is maintained: the destinies of the employed and the unemployed are inseparable.

Indeed they are usually linked in the same individuals. For most people in the inner city and the depressed regions neither employment nor unemployment is a stable condition. There is a constant movement on and off the register of unemployed. Recession does not bring unemployment out of the blue as something unfamiliar and new: rather, it increases the frequency and the duration of the periods of unemployment. Most people you meet in Hackney have been on the dole a number of times. For casual labourers in construction and homeworkers, recurrent unemployment is a permanent fact of life. Workers in the rag trade and other small businesses are subject to the seasonal flux of orders and the endless birth and death of companies. Workers with poor health, handicaps or mental illness, women workers with small children and unreliable child care, are forever losing jobs through absenteeism, low productivity or indiscipline, and finding new ones. In the inner city, unemployment is, more than anything, an intensification of tribulations that are commonplace: powerlessness, low status, low and fluctuating incomes are the lot of the unskilled, the uncertificated, the unorganized, in work or out of it.

Rites of Passage

The rigid division between manual and non-manual workers is maintained out of work as well as in work: even in unemployment, scribes are not expected to rub shoulders with labourers. The clerical, professional and executive unemployed in Hackney sign on at the smart Jobcentre in Mare Street, with wall-to-wall carpeting, recessed lights and a bright shopfront in a busy shopping thoroughfare.

Those who labour with their hands must sign on at the unemployment-benefit office in Spurstowe Terrace, an altogether bleaker place. From Hackney, you approach it under a black Victorian railway bridge that shelters a sheet-metal workshop, a small dye-and-chemical factory and a garage that smells of vulcanized rubber. Past a building site whose hoardings have been decorated with Young Socialist posters – *Three Million Reasons to Smash the Tories*; *Ascot, the Idle Rich, Hackney, the Idle Poor*. Through cast-iron gates and a picket of activists peddling the leaflets and newspapers of half a dozen left-wing sects attempting, with precious little success, to mobilize this vast army of unemployed. Down a long, concrete alley-way with high brick walls and a herbaceous border of refuse, like the entrance to an abandoned army camp. There is an air of decay about the place. The notice *Unemployment – Signing On and Pay* is painted over 'Kerby and Jimbo was here', while the blue gloss door is scarred with dozens of carved initials, some framed in decorative boxes.

Inside, a vast semicylindrical hangar, like a Nissen hut, with a vaulted roof in off-white. Fluorescent lights hang on long chains. The floor is utility-grade blue lino, scuffed to patches of black by the shuffling forward in queues of innumerable pairs of shoes each week. The array of signs confronting the newcomer is as confusing as an Indian railway booking office: 'Paypoint 1, 2, 3; P_24, P_25, P_26 Sign On, Pass to Paypoint; Enquiries Box Z and W_3; Tuesday Late Signers.' Another notice warns: 'You will experience considerable delays if you do not report at the time allocated. In your own interest please sign on in time.' Whatever you do you are unlikely to escape delays, for the queues are long. There is a constant movement in and out of people of varying degrees of presentability from barely passable to almost indecent. There is an atmosphere of the days of rationing, of spartan utilitarianism, above all of bureaucratic impersonality. The individual is merely one of a very large set of numbers. People are here because the government does not give a damn about them, and the way they are treated underlines that indifference. The sheer press of queuers prevents any exchange of pleasantries with staff. There is no time for anything but the basic act of signing on as to one's readiness to work, an act which most participants know is a futile, almost farcical gesture. Move forward and sign on, move forward and sign on, like dies being stamped in a production line. It is a caricature of the industrial capitalism of which it demonstrates the failure.

After signing on, the person who has not yet lost all hope passes out through the iron gates again and round the corner to the employment exchange, in the other half of the same building. Here the atmosphere is quite different. There are no queues. A self-service system operates: you circulate around the easels where jobs are displayed on typed postcards, your eyes flitting from opportunity to opportunity as a butterfly flits on a buddleia. Select the card of your choice, take it to one of the counter staff, and they will ring up the employer to fix an appointment. Notices express friendly optimism rather than hectoring insistence on regulations: 'We have new vacancies daily. If you do not see the job you want, come in again tomorrow.'

But it is all show: the buddleia blooms are plastic. The optimism is delusory. In view of the bleak realities, it comes across like a bad joke, like taking the mickey. At first sight you might think there was no slump: there are plenty of job cards here, every board is full. The first problem is that most of the vacancies advertised here have already been filled, for in recessions this deep they are snapped up like midges by martins. Nevertheless, there will be a few still going. But you have to read the cards with the eyes of a typical Hackney job-seeker, underskilled, undereducated, and requiring, for a breadwinner with two children, an absolute minimum gross wage of £90 to £100 a week for the merest subsistence. Remember, too, that in April 1981 when these vacancies were advertised, average national weekly earnings for a full-time male manual worker over twenty-one amounted to £121·90, and to £163·10 for non-manual.

Virtually every job card demands experience or skills that most, especially the young, do not possess. A would-be belt sander for Tottenham, who can earn £100 a week, must have at least three years of belt sanding behind him. Here is an offer of £150 a week as a carpenter, but he must have full experience and a full chest of all his own tools. An Islington firm of solicitors seeks an audio typist 'with experience in conveyancing and litigation'. With so many applicants on offer, employers can afford to insist on the most exacting requirements. Other vacancies require exotic skills, niches in the habitat of the economy of such specialization that, unless you are pre-adapted, like an insect with special probes to reach inaccessible nectars, you cannot hope to fill: roving intruder alarm engineers (£80 per week); statistical typists (£90); silver-lacquer sprayers (£80); meat inspectors (scale rates); rising damp/dry-rot operatives (£100); mughlai chefs (£110 plus a share of the tips). All demand experience – even the most humbly paid like special machinists (£65 per week), shoe machinists (£60 per week), overlockers (£65) or wages clerks (£75).

Those few jobs that offer training, or that do not insist on skills or experience, pay a pauper's wage or involve other drawbacks: chamberstaff, live in, Paddington area, £30 a week all found; hall porter EC4, £58 per week; cellar assistant and driver, £60 a week; trainee window cleaner, £45–£85 a week, must read and write well. At the bottom of the ladder, for young people *in extremis*, are the government-funded Youth Opportunities jobs paying £23·50 a week, with a high probability that you will find yourself unemployed again within three to twelve months, and many of them being used blatantly by employers to get free labour.

If you had very good educational qualifications, or skills and experience in those trades that were still flourishing, you stood a reasonable chance of finding a job before too long. If you had none of these, you were unlikely to be offered the chance of acquiring them, and were caught in a vicious circle.

Taking from Those Who Have Not

The combined impact of recession and accelerated adjustment cut swathes through Hackney's industry. The roll call of closures for the twelve months from June 1979 reads like a remembrance book for Hackney's traditional trades. In women's and girls' tailored outerwear: A. Sable Ltd (with the loss of twenty-nine jobs); Elgee Coats (eighty-seven); Natall (thirty-six); Mono (155); Noral Fashions (thirty-one); Kleanthous (five). In men's and boys' tailored outerwear: P. M. Wilko (eighty-seven jobs lost); Raminax (sixty-seven); H. Green (fourteen). In footwear: Quality Shoes (four operations, with a total loss of 375 jobs). In furniture: Barrett & Bolton (thirty-five jobs); M. Woolf (sixty-six); M. Levin (eighty-eight); A. M. Rosenberg (thirty-four jobs). In stationery: T. Keeley and Whitehead Letterfiles (eighteen and thirty-five jobs lost respectively). Plus Huxtable surgical instruments (fifteen jobs), Dovene Jewellery (twenty-eight), Autocovers Plastic (ten), Odeon Cinema (thirteen), Bonsoir Pyjamas (eighty-five) and the move of Glaxo Operations (pharmaceuticals) to Greenford, with the loss of forty-six jobs to Hackney. Over the same period, many other firms made extensive redundancies: companies in printing, shipping, records and tapes, catering, printing, tea trading, light engineering and, of course, the clothing trade. The biggest redundancies were at Hackney's biggest private firms: Metal Box cut 111 of its 379 jobs in December 1980. Lesney's, makers of Matchbox toys, cut their 2,000-strong workforce by half in January 1980. In 1981 they began to rehire again, but in 1982, burdened with debts, they closed down with the loss of 1,400 jobs.

The impact of redundancy was grossly unequal. A few strong unions in well-established firms avoided compulsory redundancies and struck hard bargains for voluntary ones. The workers at the British Oxygen Co. depot on Eastway successfully fought the threatened closure of the local acetylene plant and won an agreement that there would be no compulsory redundancies. But the inducements offered for volunteers were irresistible. Payments ranged up to £30,000, raising the rewards for egotism to the point where class solidarity was cast to the winds. Shop steward Mick Boulter explains: 'We told them: if that job had been sold before, you wouldn't have a job now. But there was no way we could force them to stay: we couldn't hold a gun at their heads. Most of them had already lined up other jobs to go to.' The net result of such voluntary deals was profoundly regressive. The job-sellers made a handsome profit, sometimes greater than a lifetime's savings. The cost was borne, in a reduction of the openings available, by the unemployed.

Most redundant workers got no more than the statutory minimum, a week's pay for a year's service, and as long service is not too common in most Hackney jobs, that did not amount to much: perhaps enough to buy a colour television or pay a winter electricity bill. Many in Hackney didn't get a farthing. Some small factories shut up overnight and their owners disappeared. Others went bankrupt or into liquidation, so employees could only recover a small percentage of their dues. Many workers were sacked without ceremony, notice or redundancy pay, and in the case of immigrants or others unaware of their rights, employers often got away with it. I was told of cases where employers deliberately harassed workers into resigning, or provoked quarrels that would provide an excuse for dismissal, to avoid having to pay out redundancy money.

Unemployment became a vast engine for increasing the existing inequalities in British society – a welfare state in reverse gear. There was no question of equality of sacrifice in the fight against inflation. The belts of those who were thinnest had to be tightened hardest. The most disadvantaged areas and the most disadvantaged people were hit most brutally. The Hackney figures tell a sad tale, paralleling national developments. Unemployment hit manual workers harder than non-manual: between 1979 and 1980 14 per cent of jobs in the 'operative' category disappeared, but less than half of 1 per cent of office jobs. It hit women harder than men: between 1979 and 1981, female unemployment rose at twice the rate of male. Black unemployment rose twice as fast as white. Recession hit the young harder than the old, the unskilled harder than the skilled, the disabled harder than the fit.

Equally germane to our tale, unemployment hit disadvantaged areas harder than the advantaged, the already lagging Celtic and northern peripheries and the inner cities suffering by far the highest absolute rates, with the Midlands, hitherto unaccustomed to the problem, also severely hit. The reason for the heavier impact was the underlying weakness of local economies, overdependent on industries and plants that were most vulnerable to intensified competition, and the vulnerability of local workforces, overweighted with those groups being marginalized by economic change.

Until the mid-seventies, Hackney's male unemployment rate was roughly on a par with the national average: in October 1973 it was a mere 2·4 per cent, rising to 5·4 per cent in October 1975 after the first oil crisis. From 1976, as monetarist policies began to bite, Hackney's unemployment rates gradually pulled ahead. By 1977 it was 7·8 per cent, 25 per cent above the national level. In October 1980 it was 10·7 per cent, now 44 per cent higher than the national average. A year later it was up to 17·1 per cent (50 per cent above the average). Hackney also lagged further and further behind her region: in October 1971 the unemployment rate had been only 14 per cent higher than the Greater London average: ten years later it was 60 per cent higher. And the true unemployment figures were even higher than these official figures. The census, in April 1981, showed that 18·3 per cent of economically active males were out of work, at a time when the official figure was 13·8 per cent. Thus, almost one unemployed person in four did not bother to register. On this basis, the real male unemployment figure for February 1983 was a staggering 26·5 per cent. The registered rate was higher than that for any of the depressed regions including Northern Ireland, right up front with such devastated one-industry towns as Corby, Ebbw Vale and Irvine.

Falling to Earth

In hard times, disablement is much more likely to become a socially crippling handicap than in normal times. In April 1981, registered unemployment among the disabled in Hackney was no less than 38 per cent, more than two and half times the average rate. In among those statistics the fortunes of Iain Johnstone were quantified. He does not look disabled: a well-built thirty-year-old from Glasgow, with a shock of black hair, a bandit moustache and tattoos on his thick forearms: cross, heart, bluebird, thistle, the words Iain and Mother, and his army number. Having left school at sixteen without a single qualification to his name, he joined up and spent three years in the army, including a spell in Northern Ireland that left him with a slightly gammy leg and a three-inch scar under his left shoulder. He was an artillery man: 'We were on the ranges practically every day practising, with the guns going off in our ears. They supplied little rubber earplugs, but they were always getting lost.' After leaving the army, Johnstone worked as a casual labourer, then as a barman. His last job was as foreman in a small factory: 'I was only taking home £60 a week, but whenever the manager decided he felt like a holiday, he'd hand me the keys and put me in charge. The last time he was away the owners came round, complaining about everything, so I said, here's your keys, to hell with it, and I walked out. That was in April 1980.'

It was not an ideal time to throw in a job. In a slump, sensible workers eat humble pie or, as another of my informants put it: 'When they tell you to jump, you jump.' But within a week Johnstone had lined up a promising interview for a warehouse job at Metal Box. The personnel manager was already explaining the details of the duties and Johnstone was sure he'd got the job, when the phone rang. 'It was the doctor to say I'd failed my medical. I couldn't believe it. I went to see the doctor. He said, "I'm sorry, you're deaf." I laughed in his face. Then he showed me the audiogram: I couldn't hear the higher notes. I went to a consultant at St Leonard's and he confirmed it. He told me I had to find a job where there was no noise or I might lose my hearing completely. Well, where can you find that?'

Johnstone attributes his deafness to his three years with the artillery. He didn't apply for, and in any case wouldn't have been given, industrial-injury benefit or disablement benefit for his deafness. This is payable only to people who have worked for twenty years or more in specific, very noisy jobs which could be shown to have caused the deafness. Firing heavy guns is not one of them. Johnstone registered as disabled on 21 January 1981 in the hope that this would help him get a job. Employers of more than nineteen workers are legally obliged to employ a minimum of 3 per cent of disabled in their workforce, but this law has never been backed up with prosecution of offenders. The green card of the

registered disabled, designed to improve the lot of the handicapped, became a massive handicap in itself during the recession,
when there were plenty of able-bodied workers around to
choose from.

'When you show employers the card, they look at you as if you've
just landed from Mars. They say, "I'm sorry, we can't take you on,
we've already filled our quota of disabled." And there's not a thing
you can do about it. You can't go inside and check who's disabled
and who isn't.' Johnstone landed one job in the interim, as stores
manager in a cash-and-carry. But much of the work was in the cold
room, and the noise of the coolers was giving him headaches. He
had to give the job up after six weeks. Now he has a buzzing in his
ears twenty-four hours a day. He has been tempted to give up his
green card and to conceal his disablement, but he is afraid that
might disqualify him from compensation were he to lose his
hearing completely on a job. In fact, he would be most unlikely to
qualify for compensation anyway in view of his history of deafness.

He'd been out of work for fifteen months when I met him. 'It's
made me very quick-tempered. I lose my temper just like that [he
snaps his fingers]. I get bored very easily, I prefer to be on the go all
the time. If I got a job I'd want to do it every hour of the day if I
could, to stop me being bored. Just loafing about gets right up my
nose. You can't even watch TV in the day, there's nothing on for the
unemployed. As time goes on, I've got very pessimistic about
getting another job. You reach the point where you get to the
door of the interview and you say to yourself, what a waste of
bloody time. The Jobcentre is useless: you spend quite a lot of time
looking till you find a job you really like, you think great, then you
get the girl to phone up. But it's always gone. It's really heart-
breaking. You pick out any card you like in there, and I'll
guarantee you won't get that job because it will be gone.'

Johnstone lives in Hackney with his sister and her family. He
gives her £10 a week, leaving only £9·20 for himself (less than the
part-time earnings of many schoolchildren I met). That means no
new clothes, no entertainment. But the state itself provides the
most distressing experiences of unemployment. 'When you're
signing on, if you're time is 11 and you get there dead on, you'll
never be out before noon or even a quarter to 1. I can't see the point

to it. When you get to the window you hand over your card and they give you a slip of paper and you sign it. No one reads it. I don't even know what it says. But the worst thing is social security. You sit there for three hours waiting, and when you get to see them they talk to you as if they're not interested in anything you've got to say, as if they don't want to be doing the job. You can make an appointment by phone, but you just try getting through to them. I spent £1·50 once in a call box. The switchboard lady kept saying, "Sorry to keep you waiting", and when I finally got through it took just four seconds.

'My giro is due on Thursdays, but sometimes it doesn't come till Saturday, then you're right up the creek. I went up there one day, waited my three hours, and saw this geezer. He said if it's not come tomorrow come back and I'll give you a form. I said why wait till tomorrow and make me queue three hours again, give me the form now. He said that's not our procedure. When I complained, he went and checked it with the supervisor. I asked him to let me see the supervisor. He said, "I'm sorry he's busy." I said, "How can he be, you've just left him." He said, "He's got someone else with him now." I said, "OK I'll wait till he's free." He said, "He'll be busy all afternoon." It's always like that. Their attitude is, here comes another scrounger, another lazy so-and-so on the dole. They give you the impression the money's coming out of their own pockets. You get some clown talking to you as if you're a big lump of whatsit. Things are bad enough when you're getting fed up with not having a job, without them treating you like that. You really feel like bashing somebody.'

A Season in Hell

'Enjoy being unemployed' proclaims the leaflet of the Dalston Youth Project, offering training in leisure skills. In theory that is not half as silly as it sounds. Employment, for most of Hackney's workers, is drudgery, routine, exploitation, subjection to arbitrary authority, and for many add noise, danger, chemicals, unsocial hours, all this sandwiched between two harrowing odysseys on public transport. Unemployment could be a liberation from all this, a chance for people to cultivate new interests, to join in community action and politics, to improve their home or their neighbourhood, to be with their children, to relate to their spouse in a more liberated way.

In reality it rarely delivers. For in our social context it raises a series of practical and personal problems. Income is usually reduced and with it the ability to satisfy social expectations. The state's handling of the unemployed entails a series of frustrations and humiliations which we shall explore in Chapter 8. Unemployment offends the puritan ethos that socially useful work is essential to spiritual wellbeing, and disturbs or reverses deeply established sexual roles. Men in particular are wide open to, and more sensitive to, taunts from wives and children, having lost their status in the family as well as in society. The unemployed person falls victim to boredom: most manual working-class modes of passing time involve the spending of money, and the money is not there to spend.

I know the subjective feelings well, for in 1972 I was foolish enough to give up one job before securing another and spent three months on the dole. For the first weeks a feeling of freedom prevails. After a month, doubts begin to crystallize. The postman's round is awaited with mingled hope and fear. You become superstitious and for the first time begin to read the horoscope columns, placing the most optimistic interpretations on the vaguest of ambiguous hints. You start to believe in omens and placatory rituals: if you can get down the street without treading on a crack in the pavement, a job offer will arrive the next day. The mind invents elaborate fantasies: 'Here I am walking along not knowing that on my doormat lies a letter.' You chide yourself for being silly, then imagine that, as a reward for your pragmatism, the letter will be there after all. Hope bursts forth against every attempt to stifle it.

At first you confront your friends, still wage slaves, with bold complacency. As time creeps on you grow shamefaced, you cross the street to avoid harmless questions that now seem intrusive. You become envious: the successes of others cut you to the quick. You become touchy: an ordinary remark becomes an attack on your dignity which, having so little of it, you must leap to defend. Your performance at interviews declines: you begin to smell of failure. You feel the need to explain and justify your joblessness, you overstate your qualities, you are more easily provoked into emotional self-defence by probing or critical questions. You begin to imagine that there are conspiracies afoot, that someone has fingered you, that damaging files exist against you. Now despair begins to undermine every attempt at hope.

Beyond three months I did not go: from then on the unemployed person, especially male, sinks into demoralization, lethargy and deadness, punctuated by spells of anger and violence out of all proportion to the provocation, magnified by sensitivity and repressed aggression. It is an accentuated form of that feeling that characterizes so much of life in the lower reaches: the feeling that there is virtually nothing legal that you can do that will alter your circumstances.

The impact of lowered status and income is harsh whether you live in Hackney or Harrogate. But the inner city adds its special refinements to torture: the peculiar immobility imposed by the cost and inefficiency of public transport; the unusual unpleasantness of the environment for those forced to hang around in it; the lack of amenities; the tempting subculture of crime.

No single story can sum up the experience of unemployment. Each person responds differently and adapts differently to the problems of lost income, of gained time, of altered roles. The worst affected are those cursed with the puritan work ethos, a concern with status, a traditional view of the place of the bread-winner.

People like Lawrence Robbins, B.Ed. (Mysore), B.A. (Kathmandu). He is a dapper forty-five-year-old Anglo-Indian with a clipped black moustache and black hair Brylcreemed neatly back. His grandfather, a British foreman on India's vast railway system, married an Indian. His father was in the British Army. Robbins worked his way through university, supporting himself with full-time jobs as railway booking clerk, ticket examiner and sales clerk. In 1969 he began teaching at a private boarding-school near Bombay. He married another Ango-Indian teacher, Nancy, and they had two sons.

The Robbinses came over to Hackney in 1976. Robbins told me why: 'I was afraid there wouldn't be much future for my boys in India. There is a lot of discrimination against Anglo-Indians. Ever since the British left, they have been telling us we must stop wearing ties and change to dhotis and saris. My brother was already in England. He said, come over here, there will be a great future here for your sons. But I must say he gave a very wrong impression.' The Robbinses left India because they were not accepted as Indian by the Indians. Having come to England, they soon discovered they would not be accepted by the English as English: belonging by descent to both nations, they were accepted by neither. In Britain they found themselves the victims of a bewildering range of discriminations. Their Indian teaching qualifications and experience were not recognized here (though they would have been in the early seventies), and they were forced to go for more humble occupations. Nancy got a job as a machinist, Lawrence became a clerical officer at Pentonville prison. He left when he learned of the civil-service ruling which barred anyone over twenty-eight from sitting exams for promotion to the executive grade – discrimination by age. In July 1977 Robbins got a clerical job in the Post Office. The following year his wife visited her sister in Llanelli, fell in love with the place and persuaded Lawrence they should move. They left for Wales in November 1978.

It was the start of a journey through the lower depths. Robbins had been told by a supervisor that he would have no trouble getting a Post Office job in Llanelli. Once there, he found that preference was given to Welsh-speakers (discrimination by language). Moreover, the unemployment situation in Llanelli at the time was worse than in Hackney. There were no clerical jobs to be had. Lawrence Robbins had to descend another rung of the social ladder and began applying for manual jobs: barman, baker's assistant, bricklayer. In March 1979 he found a job as a labourer in a paint factory. 'I felt absolutely humiliated,' Robbins told me in his slightly Victorian English. 'I had to mix with ruffians. The language, even among the ladies, was appalling. Although I didn't show I was different, I could never engage in obscene talk. And the toilet, oh, it was unspeakable, the floor was slippery with spittle, there was grease over everything.

'But all the time I was asking around for office jobs. We used to shop at a big supermarket, so I went to the manager and asked if he had any jobs. Finally he offered me a job as assistant chief cashier. It was a good job. Within three weeks my chief cashier went on holiday and I was in charge of the safe keys and had to hand the money to Securicor. If I had taken out £10 a day, nobody would have noticed, but my conscience stopped me. But after five months the manager called me to his office. He said, "Report for work at the warehouse." I said, "What for?" He said, "Don't question me. If you don't like it there's the door." At the warehouse the man said put on this overall, push this trolley. Then my friends saw me, they said what are you doing here? They began to make me feel bad. So I went back to the manager and remonstrated. I asked: "Why do you do this to me?" He was absolutely dictatorial. He said, "All right, leave that job, go to the car park and collect the trolleys there." My wife came shopping and saw me there, she said "What is the matter?" I just cried, I could not help myself. She said, "No Lawrence, I wouldn't like to see you in this position. If you'd started here, that would be different." I was being squeezed, humiliated. I had to resign. That was in February 1980. I found out later that the manager had been planning to make me redundant, but the chief cashier had pleaded for them to keep me on, to give me an alternative job. Now if this had been explained to me at the time, I would have been immensely grateful.

'I was unemployed until September 1980. Then I did a government training course in secretarial work. It seemed incongruous: I was the only man among twenty young girls. When that finished in March 1981, I asked if I could go on another course, but they said you can't do another for three years. Then I actually secured an offer of a place at a college to do a diploma course in business administration. But the education office wouldn't give me a grant because they said I was a graduate. Then I said to them, well, do you recognize my Indian degrees if I want to get a teaching job with you? They said no. I said if you don't recognize them, then how can you refuse me a grant because I'm a graduate? But they still wouldn't give me the grant.

'So all of 1981 passed without a job. I felt absolutely terrible. I went after many jobs. I asked to deliver leaflets. I went after a secretary's job at a builders' merchant's, but they never expected to see a man. The advert says man or woman, but when they see you they tell you they would prefer a woman [discrimination by sex]. Some employers said I was overqualified. When I asked for a milkman's job the manager was suspicious. He thought I would be looking to move on quickly to a better job. I was even so desperate I offered to make a contract with him to say I wouldn't leave the job. If I told you some of the things I tried to get money, you would be surprised. I tried selling chips from a van; I put in eight hours a night from 5 p.m. to 1 a.m., and I took home only £5 or £6 a night. I planned to go round knocking on people's doors and say, I've got a car, I'll do your shopping for you. I used to ask people if they would like me to write a poem about them, for their wedding or anniversary, for just £1, but I got no response, although I used to do this in India and it was extremely popular.'

Robbins was plunged into a trauma in which his established status in the eyes of the family and his in-laws was transformed. From being the chief bread-winner and the brains of the clan, he became the humble factotum and the butt of oblique remarks that stung to the core.

'For the first year, until February 1981, I was entitled to unemployment benefit of £25, but then my entitlement ran out and I had to apply for supplementary benefit. We were allowed only £65 in all. Now my wife was again working as a clothing machinist, she was taking home £50 to £60 a week. If she brought home £60 one week, I would only get £5 from social security. So my wife took over the purse-strings. She gave the boys their pocket money. They would say, "Mum, I need a pair of trainers." She would say, within hearing distance of me, "No, we are beggars, we can't be choosers." Or if they were hungry she would say, "Oh, dear, the fridge is bare." That would prick me. I would be inflamed and would confront her and say, "It is no fault of mine that I am unemployed. I have made great efforts during which I have met with many rough characters." It hurt our relationship, we were arguing more. Always money was the central thing. If I got a giro for only £3 or £5, she would complain. But I told her: "The reason I'm not getting anything is because you are earning. If you stayed at home, I would get the full £65 and I would be the head of the family." Some people at her work said to her, "Why are you working? You would get the same money if you don't work." She was driven so much by this that she resigned. But a month later she got a tax rebate, and we got no supplementary benefit for a while, and she felt so cheated that she went back to her job again.

'All this made me feel very dejected, and to justify my existence I had to take over the household chores. Among my relatives I used to be looked up to as the clerk of the family. But now I was asking them, even though they were less qualified than I, about cleaning jobs at the places where they worked, and they were keeping me hanging about for news. Gradually over the months they only came to me because they knew I could chauffeur them around. From being a clerk I became a man Friday, drop me here, drop me there, and at the end of the day they would say, "Here keep this", and give me £1. This hurt me very much.

'Even my sons said they would rather I didn't visit their school, because my shoes were worn out. It came to a point when I said, "I've had enough. Without a job I'm no man at all. I'm going back to India." Nancy said, "Lawrence, I won't stop you, but I won't go back to that shit (that was the word she used) with all the flies and the mosquitoes. You can ask the boys individually if they want to go with you, but I'm not coming." So it came to the choice of going back alone and breaking up the marriage and the family. I said, well I won't do it. I'd rather be a nobody, a nonentity, unemployed all my life.'

But he persisted doggedly in his efforts to find a job. He decided he would have to look further afield, in other towns. He came up to London for interviews, paying his own fares and expenses. The venture succeeded: after about a dozen interviews he got a job as secretary to a training project run by the Hackney Asian Association.

'Then I learned that you could get up to £2,000 if you moved to a job in another town. I inquired about this, but it had to be a job that nobody in that other town is suited for. That was the catch you see. How could I prove that? It is impossible. So I failed to get that money. My family will stay in Llanelli. They are safer there, and my boys love the cycling, the fishing. I go down once a fortnight. It costs £17 each time, and I must take some goodies with me, presents, Indian vegetables you can't get in Wales. I take home £375 a month, and I give my wife everything that is left over after my rent and food. It has really done the trick, it has worked magnificently. My wife is happy, our relationship has improved tremendously, the boys have more respect for me.

'But still I am not over the moon about it. This job is only temporary. If I were given the chance tomorrow, I'd go back to India. My boys were brilliant in school in India, they used to get merit cards all the time, they would have gone to college. But here they only went downhill. My eldest son is eighteen. He left school at sixteen. All he has done since then is a three-month engineering course and six weeks labouring building Llanelli town hall. Since then he has been at home, sleeping late, listening to music. He is not too depressed. He is a bit lazy – that is a bone of contention between us. I say he is not trying hard enough. I came here to better my children's future, but their future has been blighted: as well they have acquired disrespect and a sense of the obscene, all things which are taboo in India. I have never ceased regretting that I came here. But my wife, like any other woman, is taken up with the material things of this world, a well-carpeted floor, fridge, television. She will never go back.'

7   Youth on the Dole

I wish I were not of this race, that I had died before, or had not yet been born. This is the race of iron.

Hesiod, Works and Days *(tr. D. Wender)*

The injustices of time and history are superadded to those of our social structure and its expression in space. Those who grew up in decades of expansion could nurture youthful hopes, with a fair chance of success in achieving ambitions, in enjoying the pleasures that the media and advertising led them to believe were necessary to happiness.

But the young people of the early 1980s blossomed in a withering climate, of contraction, of rumours of war, of the closing up of opportunities of every kind, the blockage of personal advancement, the denial of the means to satisfy socially generated needs. Yet those needs, for the youth of today, are geared higher than ever before and cost more than ever before to satisfy. Never has the gap between youthful desires and reality been wider.

Unemployment hit the young harder than any other age group. The practice of last in, first out victimized them. Firms choosing whom to make redundant picked on those with shortest service that would qualify for least redundancy pay, and in choosing whom to take on, preferred the ready-trained rather than those they would have to train themselves. The young, too, tend to change jobs much more frequently than the old, as they get to know what kinds of work they like, or rather, don't like. But if you leave one job in a deep recession, you are less likely to find another.

The census gives the best idea of the level of unemployment among different age groups. In April 1981, when the average rate for Hackney males was 18·3 per cent, it was 29·2 per cent for sixteen-to-nineteen-year-olds, the highest rate in Greater London, and 22 per cent for twenty-to-twenty-four-year-olds. For each successive five-year age group the unemployment rate was lower, averaging only 14 per cent for the over-fifties. Among females, the overall rates were lower but the effect of youth even more disproportionate: 24 per cent of sixteen-to-nineteen-year-olds were out of work, almost exactly double the female average.

The pattern seemed purpose-designed for maximum social damage: to alienate a large minority of teenagers and create an embittered generation which would probably never recover lost ground; to hurt those in their early twenties just forming their families; but to give favoured treatment to older workers, whose families have grown up, who have acquired most of the possessions they need, and whose spouses are more likely to be working.

The outlook for Hackney's young people grew steadily more gloomy as the years of the Thatcher administration progressed. By December of each year the bulk of June's school-leavers have normally been placed and the competition for jobs has fallen. In December 1979, Hackney's three careers offices had three unemployed youths on their books for each vacancy. That was bad enough, but twelve months later, there were thirty-two young people chasing every job. By December 1981, each job-seeker had an average of no less than 138 rivals for each vacancy.

Divisional careers officer Daphne Stewart noted the steady darkening of the outlook. Employers were upping their requirements, demanding better exam results, showing much greater reluctance to take on the types that Hackney supplies in generous measure: misfits, school drop-outs, educational failures, kids who've been in trouble with the law. Youth Opportunities placements were increasingly short-term, without prospects. 'And the youngsters themselves have changed so much,' says Stewart. 'We used to get stubbornness, people insisting that they must be a motor mechanic or an astronaut. Now they come in and say, "I'm ready to take anything." They are so despondent, they look like death warmed up, so sad and upset. Many of them can't afford the fares or decent clothes for interviews.'

A Chapter of Failures

In a well-worn, echoing church hall in Homerton, on a Thursday morning in June, four unemployed lads are playing two-a-side football, using battered radiator covers for goals. An unemployed girl is playing solitaire in a corner, while two schoolboys – one truanting, the other suspended from school – are playing pool. St Paul's Youth Club lets in the type of youngster that other clubs throw out. It began opening its doors in the daytime in May 1981, in response to rapidly mounting unemployment among its members.

When the football is over, Tony Risveglia comes over. He has acquired the look of a loser: overweight, hair uncombed, two days' growth of beard, and somewhat shabbily dressed in grubby sneakers and jeans (both are his only pairs) and crumpled sweatshirt. He is eighteen and has been out of work for three months, but the experience is not new – this is his fourth spell on the dole since he left school in July 1979. Tony is the son of a Sicilian couple who came over from the village of Santa Margherita near Palermo, fifteen years ago, little knowing that they were leaving one under-developed area for a place that was fast becoming one. Father is a civil-service messenger, mother has just lost her job as a factory machinist. One of their three daughters is unemployed. The other two work as secretaries – the family couldn't survive without their wages. They live on Kingsmead estate.

Tony told me the sad story of his career in life so far. 'I used to be brainy. I used to enjoy school. But I slacked off in the fourth and fifth year. I really fucked it all up for myself. I took three CSEs [Certificates of Secondary Education] but I failed them all. If I could have any job I wanted, I would like to be a sports reporter. Or an actor – I'm good at that. But I've never really enjoyed myself at any of the jobs I've had. My first job was as a porter, but I left after two months to stay with relatives in Rome. I did a bit of casual labouring over there, but I couldn't make out, so I came back. I spent three months on the dole, then I got a job as an office boy in the City. The wages were poxy. I was taking home £32 a week and had to spend £6 of that in fares. I told them I couldn't manage on it and asked for a raise, but they wouldn't give me one, so I left. I had to do without unemployment benefit for six weeks, because I'd left on my own accord. After a couple of months I got a job at a petrol station. I was getting £72 a week for six nights, 11 p.m. to 8 a.m., but I was lucky if I took home £30 or £40. They kept docking me money, £20 or £25 a time, because every time they checked the pumps, they said the till was short. I said the machines must be faulty, but they said they were working all right. They gave me the sack after three months. I was supposed to put the cash tin down a chute every night, but one night I forgot. There was £150 in it, and it got nicked. They docked the £150 off my wages. They really rooked me. And I had to do without unemployment benefit for another six weeks, because they said it was my own fault I'd lost the job.

'I was out of work for another three months, then I got a job in a clothing factory, cutting loose threads off dresses for £47 a week. I used to get up at 6 to get to Dalston at eight because the buses from Hackney Wick are terrible. The boss there was always threatening me. If I dropped a dress off the coat-hanger, he'd say "Do that again and I'll punch you on the nose." I said, "Come and try it." I wanted to flatten him but I daren't. I got the sack from there because I took one afternoon off. It was the smell of the steam presses and irons, it was making me feel sick. But in the evening I had a football match. I had to go – I couldn't let my mates down or I'd have been chucked off the team, that would have been it. But I sprained my ankle in the game. Next day the boss saw me hobbling in, so he asked me what was wrong and I told him the truth. He said, "How come you're not well enough to work but you're well enough to play football?" So he sacked me. I had to go another six weeks without money. And I've just heard that they're going to do me for social-security fraud, over that petrol-station job. I signed on social security as soon as I left it, but it was one week in hand – they held over a week's wages from the beginning, to be paid at the end, and I'd claimed social security for that first week. I never got paid that first week's wages anyway – it was part of the money they docked me for the cash box that got nicked. I paid back the supplementary-benefit money last September, but I chucked the receipt away, and now they're saying I didn't pay it.'

Tony was getting £41·30 a fortnight (1981), on a Friday. When it arrived, he was usually in debt to the tune of £10 or so to his mother and £4 or £5 to one or both of his sisters. By the time he's paid his debts plus the £20 he gives his mother for his keep, there's only a few days' cigarette money left and he has to start borrowing again. He possesses a meagre wardrobe: two pairs of trousers and one pair of ragged jeans fit only for wearing around the house; one pair each of shoes and sneakers; and a fair supply of T-shirts and pullovers, all of them gifts. His one luxury is smoking, thirty a day, which consumes almost his entire surplus: 'The longest I've been without is three hours. I do it out of boredom, to have something in my hands. The days are really boring, really bleak. I knock around with my mates who are unemployed. When you're out of work, you can't mix with boys earning £70 a week, you can't keep up with them. We don't do nothing, we just go to each other's houses and have a game of dominoes. In the nights you can't even afford to go out, you can't go down the pub, you can't take a girl to a disco or cinema, you just have to make do with standing around on the balconies with your mates.

'It really annoys me when people say I'm not looking for work. I've looked day and night. In the first few weeks after I lose a job, I try really hard. But after a few weeks you give up. It's not worth it, getting no, no all the time. Now when I wake up in the morning, I don't feel like going looking any more, deep down I know I won't find anything. It has come into my mind to do crime, but I know it's wrong and I couldn't do it. The only crime I do is burgling my mum's purse. I can't see any future. It's not going to get any better.' He says all this without bitterness, rather with resignation.

Tony is a typical unqualified graduate of Hackney's education system. As experience ages him, he is willing to swallow increasing doses of authority and humiliation, but he still has his limits. Employers will suffer such quiet rebels in times of labour shortage, but in a slump they opt for the reliable, the obedient, the certificated. People like Tony are dispensable and quickly dispensed with, condemned to a youth far out of line with the expectations of the times, a prolonged adolescence of inability to pull girls, to buy clothes or outside entertainment, a prolonged infancy of dependence on the charity of relatives.

The unemployed girls I met seemed, for the most part, less deeply demoralized than the boys: as they are usually expected to shoulder a share of the housework, they have more to occupy their time than boys; their expectations of life are less heavily geared to career and earning power; and the option is open to them to resolve the problem of inability to afford a night out by going out with boys who are in work. Even for them, unemployment remains a distasteful, distressing experience. Caroline Weymouth, a pretty eighteen-year-old, was still in her dressing-gown at 3 in the afternoon when I called at her parents' home on Nightingale estate.

'I always wanted to be a ground stewardess. Two years before I left school I wrote to all the airlines and they told me to start off in a travel agent's. But the careers teacher told me I hadn't done well enough at school and the only job I could do was shop work. I got a job at British Home Stores, but I chucked it in. Some of the customers who came in treated you like muck. That's why a lot of the girls don't like serving and you see them standing around talking. I am looking now for another job, but I can't afford to go for interviews. One interview in Great Portland Street [in the West End] cost me £3 to get there and back. Well I only get £15 a week and I give my mum £10, so what does that leave me with? I can't afford to go to more than one interview a fortnight. The employers have got the pick of the bunch now. They want O-levels and CSE even to work in a sweet-shop. They expect you to talk proper and nice, but I can't talk posh, I can't put on a voice.

'It costs so much now for a night out that I can't afford to go unless the man pays. But I don't like that, I'd rather pay myself so they can't make out I owe them anything. It never costs less than £10 for a night out. Even if you just go to a pub for one drink it costs £7 in cab fares and £2 for a pint of lager and a vodka-and-coke. Then if we want a meal on top, that's at least £5 just for a kebab and rice, or if you want steak it can come to £20. I have to travel by cabs in the evening. I wouldn't ever walk down Downs Park Road [which flanks Nightingale estate] on my own. A girl friend of mine, she walked me home from bingo, and on her way back she got mugged. They smashed all her leg up, she was off work for five weeks. If we wear jewellery, we have to tuck it in out of sight, or they'll rip it off your neck. I just can't come home unless someone walks me right to the door. I've come back at 2 in the morning and had to walk through forty coloured boys downstairs in the entrance hall. They have these big cassettes, they make so much noise you wouldn't even hear a person screaming. And if you get in the lift, they can jam it between floors. Then you've had it.'

Unemployment and the high cost of an increasingly commercialized leisure combine to cheat Caroline Weymouth of her carefree years. Much of the risk of crime she fears arises, as we shall see in Chapter 17, from the clash of these same two factors.

Beat the Clock

Black youths, especially boys, face the roughest job outlook of all. A continuing, concealed discrimination compounds the effects of a low average level of educational attainment, and there is, too, a greater sensitivity to some of the routine humiliations of employment which, when overlaid with a racial dimension, take on more offensive weight. And unemployed black youths live more of their lives on the street, where questioning and confrontation with the police are a perennial hazard.

I met Michael, a black seventeen-year-old, at the Stamford Hill Project, a youth club that works out of a large Victorian mansion in the heart of Hackney's Jewish settlement. It began to open its doors in the daytime in 1980. Inside, the balls on the pool table click all day long and a video game plays a concerto of bass bleeps. The game, ironically, is called *Breakout*, the object, to smash down a prison wall brick by brick. The young black unemployed who pass their time here are past masters at it, though they have had less luck, in real life, in breaking through the brick wall that seven years of monetarism have built around them. Michael wears a Wrangler sweat-shirt (brand marks are mandatory), blue track-suit pants and a flat cap over his open, ingenuous face. He talks, like so many black youths of West Indian descent, in an uneasy mingling of Cockney and island dialect, shifting from one to the other as if unsure where he belongs. He left school in June 1980 with five low-grade CSE results; followed it by six months on the dole, then a twelve-week Youth Opportunities course in electrical work. The pay of £23·50 a week plus £2·50 towards fares shrank to virtually nothing after he'd paid out £10 a week for food and transport to work and £10 to his mother. After that, the dole again, but as he gets £19·20 (1981) a week and has no work expenses to pay, he is considerably better off than when he was on the training course.

'But money is giving me a hard time. My parents help me out, but I feel bad about it. My mum was a nurse, but she's not working now. My dad's a carpenter, but he's been complaining he can't even afford a new pair of boots. He keeps pestering me to find a job. I say find a job where? I wrote to every electrical firm in the yellow pages, they say they're not recruiting, try again next year. The careers office is always offering me rubbish jobs, the Jobcentre sends a hundred people before you so you got no chance. But I still go to interviews just for something to do. Now I hardly got no money for to take me anywhere. I come here and play a game of pool and thing, I walk around the streets, I go home and play music, I get fed up. Sometimes I go to shop to see my friend, just to kill the time. I got no clothes. The fashion now is thiefing and dressing nice, but I don't bother about them thing, them cause me too much trouble. It's just a rat race you can never win. However fine you dress, one day you will meet a man with all gold round his neck. All of them black girl want money, money make friends like that. You got no money, they don't want to know you. Crime? Me think of that whole time, rob bank and thing, but I no got courage to go and do it. If I see a woman walking up the road, I always think of taking her handbag, but then I think, it might be my mother, and I don't do it.'

Time weighs heavily on the shoulders of those without work. It loses all positive potential, it is no longer time in which to earn money, to spend, still less time to realize ambitions, to work towards goals. Time is a wasteland to be got through and got over. A day becomes a yawning chasm between two spells of sleep. Time, effectively murdered by work, resurrects when work is lost. Either you kill time, or time kills you. Michael's friend Jah, a single dreadlock dangling elegantly from under a peaked cap 30 centimetres high, put it another way: 'When you got a job, you're doing something. When you got no job, you just grow dead nearly. You got to do something to make yourself feel alive.' Jah, now eighteen, has not worked for a year and a half since he gave up a job as a carpet cutter.

'Time has no relevance for these boys,' says Stamford Hill project leader Irwin Horsford. 'There is no difference for them between midnight and midday. They just wake up and exist and sleep. They have no purpose and no aim.' The diurnal rhythm shifts forward, out of joint with light and dark. You get up close to lunchtime, go to bed in the early hours of the morning. The capacity for timekeeping decays. Appointments are not kept, and when by a miracle a job does come along, it is often lost because the organism cannot readjust to early rising and clockwork regularity. Thus the unemployed become unemployable.

Trampling on the Seed-bed

Press concern and political initiatives have concentrated on alleviating unemployment among the under-twenties. But the problem of unemployment among twenty-to-twenty-five-year-olds is in many respects more serious. Among manual workers, this is the crucial time of family formation, of heavy expenditure on home-making or house purchase, and, most important, of the rearing of vulnerable and impressionable children whose physical and mental development can be retarded by poor nutrition, whose moral and emotional development can be blighted by conflicts in the home or by family breakdown.

Yet there is no social group that has been worse affected by crisis than families with young children. High mortgage rates, high council rents, the removal of tax allowances for children, the ending of social-security payments to renew clothing, all these factors increased the expenses and reduced the income of young families.

Steve Capes, a slim, angular twenty-three-year-old, belonged to the labour élite of skilled workers, earning hard, spending hard, owning his own home, building up savings. But within the space of a year he and his wife Irene saw their life with their three small children Lee (aged four), Mandy (three) and Steve (eight weeks) reduced to wreckage. Capes started work while still at school, at the tender age of thirteen, putting in an illegal thirty-two-hour week in a belt factory, where he got a job when he left school: 'I used to fiddle the governor wicked, I'd buy my own materials and go in after hours for another two or three hours, and I could make 2,500 belts extra a week: stitch them one night, buckle them the next, pack them another. Sometimes I'd make only a few pence on each belt, but it came to a nice amount.'

He was always working, evenings, weekends, three nights a week in a pub, Saturdays and Sundays with his father's small building firm, then a Sunday stall in Brick Lane market. At nineteen he started building on his own account, but couldn't make a living. He went on the dole and at the same time took driving lessons to get a heavy-goods-vehicle licence. He soon got a job with a big haulage firm, working long hours, taking home £180 a week, sometimes as much as £275. They bought a house in Northampton. 'This time a year ago I had a stake, a nice mortgage, all the clothes we needed, a nice car – I had a Triumph Stag, the insurance on it was £360 a year. I was going to sell it and get a Jensen, I've always wanted a Jensen, but there's no chance now, I couldn't even afford to buy a bike.'

In November 1980 things started to turn sour. Overtime was cut at Steve's firm, then a three-day week came in. His earnings dropped to £140 a week, then to £54. Then in March 1981 the firm laid off 120 of its 800 staff: 'They didn't do it right. Instead of saying, right, this guy's only got two more years before retiring, so he can go, they picked on all those who'd been there less than two years, so they wouldn't have to pay redundancy money. A lot of them had kids and mortgages. We talked about striking, but if we'd done that they would have just sacked us, and those who were staying wouldn't stick up for us because their jobs were all right.'

They couldn't keep up the mortgage repayments, sold their house with a profit of only a few hundred, and moved back to Hackney where, after a few months in a reception centre for the homeless, they were offered a three-bedroomed flat in Bannister House, Homerton. 'I didn't apply for supplementary benefit – I couldn't face all the questions – and I was sure another job would turn up from day to day. We had savings, £845, so we lived off them. I did go along to the social-security office once, but the queue was so long I thought, 'Sod this.' My wife even pawned her wedding ring for £10. We didn't want to put it in for too much in case we couldn't get it back out again.

'Last Monday we were down to our last 11p, so I had to go and sign on. Our life's been ruined. We used to have a bath every day, but we can hardly have one a week now. We used to go out to the zoo or the seaside, now we walk over to Hackney Marshes and catch frogs in the old filter-beds. I used to think nothing of blueing £25 on a meal out with a bottle of wine, now I couldn't even afford to go to the fish-and-chip shop. My life is like this now: I get up, go to the Jobcentre, go round a few firms asking, come home, watch telly, feel sleepy 'cause I'm bored stiff, fall asleep. That's my life. I got my name on five agencies for casual driving, but I've only had one day's work in two weeks. There's no building work going, and the employers are really taking advantage. A year ago they were paying £15 or £20 a day, now they're offering £8 or £9 and some of them are using school-leavers for £4 a day. A lot of my friends have been forced to claim social security and do casual work without declaring it – they've got hire-purchase payments to keep up and the sosh won't pay them. They say Thatcher's made villains of them. I hate Thatcher. I'm not a violent person, but if I saw her I'd whack her. I can't even watch if she comes on television. The kids just know her as "the old cow". My personal opinion is, they should close the country down and everyone march to Downing Street. But no one will stick together. It's all individuals. I don't think the country will ever get back on its feet. We've had it. If I had the chance to emigrate, I'd be gone tomorrow. I'd rather live in the thirties than now, I'd rather be fighting in the Second World War than now. I wish I was still in school. If I could just stop time and be sixteen.'

It was sad to hear such a resourceful young man lapsing into escapism. Redundancy had hit him like shell-shock: a sudden explosion entirely beyond his power to control or mitigate, revealing in him an impotence he had never suspected. The unrelievedly harsh world of slump produced an almost infantile regression, a desire to be back in the womb. A black boy of eighteen, unemployed since he left school, expressed the same feeling: 'My life was easy when I was small and I didn't have to worry.'

8　The Modern Poor Law: Social Security

Outside the law stands a doorkeeper. A countryman comes to the
doorkeeper and asks to be allowed access to the law. But the doorkeeper
says that at present he cannot allow him to enter.

Franz Kafka, Vor dem Gesetz

One of the factors that most sharpens the edge of unemployment is
enforced dependence on supplementary benefit which, far from
guaranteeing a tolerable existence to those whom recession and
misrule have deprived of work, casts them in the medieval role of
beggar. The Department of Health and Social Security, catering
also for single mothers, the disabled and ill, and pensioners, is a key
institution in the inner city, and determines the incomes of between
two-fifths and a half of its residents.

The largest of three DHSS offices serving Hackney is in Sylvester Road, down a narrow turning off Mare Street, past an empty
warehouse and a burned-out factory. The DHSS occupies a
modern block opposite Second Hand City, a junk store that
proclaims ominously 'Flats and Houses Cleared', and next to a
dismal row of blackened Victorian tenements. Supplementary
benefits is on the first floor, in an echoing hall floored with marbled
tiles, with fluorescent lighting and heating on full on a warm
summer's day. Along with the unemployment-benefit office and
the council's housing-advice centre, this is one of the hidden and
depressing shop-fronts of the welfare state. Common to them all –
as to the bus-stops, the hospitals and the doctor's waiting-rooms –
is the queue, long suffering, joking to pass the time away, occasionally breaking out into loud, embittered complaint.

The service is not designed for the comfort of customers; indeed
it seems expressly planned for their discomfort and discomfiture,
as if in punishment for the sin of being needy. To the left wait the

lucky few who have been able to get through by phone to make an appointment. The rest wait on the right. The very joinery of the place expresses the social interactions that take place here. There are three rows of benches in red Formica, with grey steel frames. They are bolted rigid to the floor. This is not so much to frustrate thieves, but to prevent clients picking them up and hurling them bodily at the officers. Opposite the benches is a row of four booths faced in thick, unbreakable Perspex, pierced with circles of little holes for speaking. The officials sit safely behind these screens, their voices muffled and distant. The clients who have reached their turn sit in front, on a cushionless stool (also bolted to the ground). It is like a high-security-prison visit, with just as little dignity and just as little privacy. The most intimate personal questions, the most insulting allegations, are put and answered in the full gaze and hearing of upwards of a couple of dozen spectators.

The clients can expect to wait anything from two hours to four hours, but little thought is given to their bodily needs during that time. The toilet, downstairs, is often locked. The numerous notices on the walls are peremptory, lacking in compassion: *You are Requested Not to Smoke*; *Please Do Not Consume Food or Drink or Leave Litter on the Premises*; *Children Should Not be Left Unattended at Any Time, Not Even During Your Interview*. Manacles are not provided. When I arrive, about thirty people are waiting with varying degrees of patience. A lady fans herself with a magazine, while the man next to her checks his betting slip against the racing results in the *Daily Star*. A plump woman in black trousers sends her friend out to buy canned drinks from Mare Street. A man behind me complains: 'You'd think there'd be a coffee machine in here.' 'Oh no,' says his mate, 'that'd be too luxurious, wouldn't it.'

To while the time away, the office does, however, provide clients with an entertaining bill of street theatre and real-life drama. Queuers exchange tales of woe. A burly man in a check shirt complains he's just been made redundant: 'My rent is £39·40 a week and I've got two young kids. But they say they can't do nothing till my papers come through and I'm already two weeks in arrears.' A young black with a short beard trips in and laughs to see a friend: 'You need money too? I can't get money out of them. I need a bus fare to Shoreditch. How far is it walking?' He takes a look at the queue and decides to walk. The music-hall up front provides a succession of acts. An old lady in a butterfly-blue cardigan has misplaced her pension book: 'I won't do it again. I've had my lesson. I'm awfully sorry being such a nuisance to you.' She smiles as she leaves: humility such as hers elicits considerate treatment.

But all this is merely warming up, for more thrilling fare is presented at least once in every client's wait. Many people arrive at these offices without a penny to their name, because of lost, stolen or delayed giro cheques or benefit books. They sit there for hours, fighting down their children, wondering where the next meal will come from. When they finally reach the front of the queue, their patience is exhausted, their blood sugar low. Then, all too often, they meet with bland excuses, fob-offs, interrogations and insinuations. Abusive and often violent outbursts are commonplace. People try to smash the Perspex screens and assault the staff. In September 1981 one man, whose giro was two days late and who hadn't eaten in that time, pulled a replica Magnum gun when he was refused an emergency payment.

At 12.30 p.m. on the day of my visit, with three of the four booths closed down for lunch, the plump lady who had sent out for the drink reached the front of the queue. The officer is a pretty girl of about twenty in a smart purple dress, with a golden locket round her neck. What she says is inaudible, drowned out by the juggernauts grinding along nearby Graham Road, but the plump lady's reactions give an idea of the full proceedings. After a short exchange of questions and answers the plump lady explodes in loud abuse. 'You're fucking starting me off, ain't you? You are. My money was due on Tuesday [two days before]. Well you'd better check. No I ain't got no money. Blooming cheek.'

The officer exits and is away for a full ten minutes. Another client paces up and down impatiently. A baby babbles and clambers on the bench. The officer returns with a supervisor, a young, mustachioed man in blue shirt-sleeves who does not sit but stands, leaning over intimidatingly. The client cannot believe what he tells her.

'Fucking ten quid for a week? What am I supposed to do with

that? Fucking cheek. My book says £24 a week. Why did they cut my money then? Could you live on £10 for a week? I bet you fucking couldn't. And make sure you send the next lot on the right day. And when they send my hospital fares they don't send the proper money, they send £1 less, and they say they've included for a cup of tea on the way, the fucking liars. It's been over a year now so you should fucking know. Jesus. My son? He's eight years old. I thought you knew all about my kids. So when will you send it out then? Make sure it reaches my place by Saturday. What am I supposed to do if it doesn't, come up here again on Monday? I'll tell you something. This'll be the last time I have to come here because my husband's coming home next week, thank God.' She is overcome with emotion, with offended pride, and finally decides on a gesture of futile, self-destructive rebellion. 'I'll tell you what you can do with your fucking £10. You can stick it up your fucking arse!'

She strides out shaking her straight, greasy hair. It is always like that. Submission or rebellion is the choice: there is no question of dealing as equals. The girl officer screws the woman's form into a ball and throws it on her desk in disgust.

The lady's performance sparks off a lively debate.

'Civility doesn't cost anything,' says one lady in her late fifties, referring, of course, to the claimant.

'Yes,' says a well-spoken Indian. 'But she's only getting £10 a week for herself and the child. I only get £21 a week, but I got £100 a month mortgage, my rates are £350, how can I manage? It's better in other countries. The government should change its policies.'

'Ten pounds is nothing these days,' says the old lady. 'It's gone just like that, and that's without the bills and everything. There was another lady like that in here on Monday. But then you don't know what's behind it. You see, people don't come here unless they have to. The system's wrong, it's all wrong. It's not fair, it's not fair the way they do it. But some of these people, even when there was work to be had, they didn't want it. I'd love a little job. There's nothing worse than being lonely. I've got a family, but they've got their own lives to get on with. You can't beat working to keep yourself busy.' She grows apocalyptic. 'I can't see it ever picking up again, not in our lifetimes.'

Pinching Pennies

Welfare benefits are typical of the 'rights' that the citizen enjoys in Britain. They are not guaranteed rights: there is no one taking care to ensure that everyone automatically gets what they are entitled to. There are no loudspeaker vans touring the streets broadcasting their existence, no itinerant social-security officers knocking on doors to check that no one is forgotten. The benefits exist, but people are left to their own devices to find out about them and to apply for them. Many stumble on them by chance. Many pass them by unknowing.

There is a scatter of leaflets at various points in Hackney, like clues to a treasure trove: a few slots, frequently empty, at post offices, a sampling at Citizens' Advice Bureaux, and a very comprehensive and complete array at Hackney Council's housing-advice centre. But at the DHSS offices themselves, the place where they are most needed, there are none on display.

Finding a leaflet is only the beginning of your problems. The fullest guide, *Which Benefit?*, promises a bonanza of sixty ways to get cash help. But the average poor person in Hackney would have considerable difficulty in following its complexities, its cross-references to an infinity of other leaflets, and the daunting pilgrimage round countless agencies which a claimant might have to undertake: no less than twenty-eight agencies are listed.

Not surprisingly, there are many poor people in Hackney who do not get the benefits for which they qualify. Frequently – especially with immigrants whose English is poor – this is out of ignorance. Giash Uddin is a diminutive, softly spoken young man who came over from Sylhet, a poverty-stricken region of arid mountains and swampy lowlands in north-east Bangladesh, in 1968. He lives with his wife and three small children in a single tiny room measuring 3 metres by 2·75 metres. All five of them sleep in one double bed, and there is so little room to move in the rest of the room that the eight-month-old baby burned its hand on the paraffin heater. Uddin had been working on a press at a small pleating firm, earning an average of £60 a week. By luck, he happened to live opposite the office of the Hackney Asian Association, whose secretary, Raman Bannerjee, advised him that he would probably be entitled to about £10 a week in Family Income Supplement, and helped him to fill in the forms. By the time his processed application came back, he had been made redundant and therefore no longer qualified.

In other cases, like that of Andreas T. (whom we already met in Chapter 3) the reason for not claiming is pride. Others, like Steve Capes (Chapter 7) simply cannot face the hassles of claiming. At the time of writing, no survey had been done on the extent of non-take-up in Hackney, but it would probably not differ markedly from, and if anything might exceed, the figures provided by other surveys between 1977 and 1979. These suggested that no less than half of those eligible for Family Income Supplement and free milk were not claiming them, along with two out of five people entitled to one-parent benefit, worth £3 a week in 1981, and a quarter of those entitled to supplementary benefit. This latter figure became more significant as the real value of unemployment benefit, which it supplements, dropped further and further behind it, and as the numbers who had been out of work for a year or more, who no longer qualify for unemployment benefit, mounted.

Supplementary benefit is central to maintaining the incomes of the claiming poor. The only fair and humane way to administer it would be for DHSS officers to make a thorough check, with each applicant, of the full list of benefits they may qualify for. But that does not happen. It is left to the claimant to ask. What they don't know about, they usually don't get. Roy Eames, Hackney Council's welfare-rights officer, once witnessed a raw DHSS trainee naïvely telling an applicant everything they might qualify for: 'The supervisor tapped the trainee on the shoulder and said, "That's not our business. You should only answer questions that are put to you. We don't want any more on our work-load."'

Even the person who, by a miracle, gathers in their full entitlement would not be well off. Supplementary benefit covered rent and rates. After deducting a typical electricity bill of £9 a week, from the basic-scale rates, a single pensioner in 1981 would be left with £18 a week to live on; a couple with two children under eleven would have only £10·05 per person per week, a single parent with two children under eleven only £8·96 per person, or a mere £1·28 each per day, to cover all other needs, including clothing for pre-school children. It would be instructive to see how Mrs Thatcher would make out on this. For those unfortunate enough to be fitting out a home on social security, the DHSS generously provided cash to buy a table, one bed and one chair per person, and a cooker (all second-hand), curtains and lino. They would not pay for a fridge (owned by 95 per cent of households in 1981, and helping to save money on food) or for television (owned by 97 per cent of households, and indispensable, in the inner city, for the safe amusement of children). Nor would they pay for items that have become part of minimal social expectations, such as carpets, washing-machines, holidays or entertainment.

Adding Insult to Injury

The basic aim of our modern poor law is to allow a bare survival, but also to ensure that claims are genuine. Its operation is such as to involve not only deprivation, but the systematic humiliation of clients. First, by denying them a basic rate which would enable them to buy for themselves the larger essential items for the house, it casts them in the role of supplicants and beggars. Second, because the state is grudging with its gifts, and because social-security offices are grossly overworked, there is a tendency, again systematic, to reduce all claims to a minimum, to deny them or to beat them down as if haggling over prices with a shifty bazaar merchant. The claimant's credentials, willingness to work, sexual arrangements and honesty are subjected to scrutiny in a way that most claimants I met found deeply offensive and provocative. The stories they tell are so common, so concrete and so consistent that one has to conclude that the abuses they reflect are widespread.

Jean Clements has eleven years' experience of the system. She has the quiet, melancholic manner of a person for whom life has few pleasures. The grey car jacket and flat-heeled shoes she wears are her only ones, and her crumpled pink skirt is one of two in her meagre wardrobe. At eighteen she married a twenty-year-old labourer who was forever in and out of work, and had two girls and a boy, all now in their teens. After six years of terrible rows, flaring up whenever there was no money for the rent or for the baby's milk, she got divorced. She's now thirty-five, and lives with her three children in a flat on the gaunt Bannister House estate. All the rooms give off a long, draughty corridor, so the place costs a lot to heat. She has a low opinion of social-security officials.

'Most of them are just pigs. They don't care about you. They seem to think it's your fault you're poor. They think you're piling it on to get more money out of them. They just like being awkward. I lost my purse once, about eight years ago, with my week's money in it, and I went to the office. The man told me I should be more careful. He said he couldn't give me cash, but he'd give me a food voucher for Sainsbury's. I said, "The nearest one is at Stamford Hill, that's miles away. How am I going to get there with a baby, a boy in a pushchair and an eight-year-old? How can I cope with them and all the shopping on the bus?" But he wouldn't give me any cash, he said, "You'll just have to scrimp for this week." I said, "I scrimp every week." It makes you feel so degraded.

'Last year I got an electric bill for £132. I went to the social-security office and told them there was no way I could pay it. They sent a visiting officer round, but he said they couldn't help. He said, "You should save for your bills." I said, "You must be joking." He said, "Well, you're not a very good manager, are you?" I said, "On the money we get, how can you be?" After three weeks they agreed that they could stop me money weekly towards the bill. Why couldn't they have done that from the start? They took so long, we got disconnected and we were five weeks without electricity.

'Just now I've been asking them for money for lino, but they won't give me any. My lino is eight years old. It's worn through in about six places [there are jagged holes about one metre square] and there's none at all in the bathroom, just the wooden planks. The visitor came and measured up the holes and said he could give me £2·75 to buy little offcuts of lino to put into each hole. He said I could cover them up with a mat. I didn't appeal. I've never appealed, because I know people that have done: you just get shown up and made to feel stupid.

'When they used to give money for clothes, one visitor came and told me I couldn't have a grant. As he was leaving, he said, "Don't you want to know why?" I said no. He said, "Well I'll tell you anyway. It's because your kids are too well looked after. If they'd been in rags, they'd have stood a better chance." Now I get clothing vouchers off ILEA [the Inner London Education Authority] every two years, but you can only spend them in one or two shops, and their prices are dear. I paid £16·75 for a blazer for Gary [thirteen] but you can get one for £8 or £9 down Petticoat Lane. I never buy any clothes for myself. Tights are the only new thing I ever get.'

Life is pared to its essentials. The children are allowed to go to a community disco (entry 30p) every couple of months, but never at weekends, because that is when the week's money runs out. While I was there the three children were sitting in the kitchen, watching a fuzzy grey picture on a small second-hand black-and-white television. There have been no holidays since the time, seven years back, when the council social-services department paid their fares to go and stay with a friend in Derby.

The System Begins to Collapse

The activities of the Thatcher government, compounding the effect of world recession, greatly increased the work-load of social-security offices, not only by the massive leap in the numbers of the unemployed, but also by the frequent rises in rents and rates, which local councils were compelled to levy, and which altered claimants' entitlements. Yet at the very same time, the Department of Health and Social Security was expected to contribute its share towards the pruning of 'waste'. In April 1979, there were 98,369 DHSS employees dealing with social-security claims. Three years later, with an extra 1·5 million unemployed to deal with, staff numbers had fallen to 95,543. The result was not, as ministers might boast, a great increase in productivity or efficiency, but a massive increase in unnecessary hardship among claimants.

There was a slowdown, particularly pronounced in areas of high unemployment, in the rate at which staff could deal with individual changes and demands. Social workers in Hackney, approaching the DHSS on behalf of clients, spoke of 'administrative lunacy' and of 'drastically deteriorated efficiency'. Callers were having to hang on the phone for anything from twenty to forty-five minutes before being put through. People in desperate need were having to wait for several months for home visits to assess special needs and single payments. Giros were arriving unsealed through the post, more prone to loss or theft. Claimants reporting losses often found themselves being treated as the prime suspect, and having to wait up to two months for refunds. More common than losses were delays, due to staff shortages again, but also to temperamental computers, deteriorating postal services, or industrial action. Giros were arriving two or three days late. New books of milk tokens or child-benefit books sometimes took months to arrive. For people already on the breadline, such delays could often mean going into debt for rent and fuel bills, and facing eviction or cut-off.

As the system became more centralized and computerized, it became at the same time more vulnerable to industrial action. In July 1981, as part of a campaign of selective strikes to secure a higher pay award, civil-service unions halted the printing of unemployment-benefit giro cheques. Civil servants in some offices refused to write cheques out by hand. Hackney was one of the unfortunate areas where the supply of printed giros ran out earliest. Claimants began to miss their cheques around Thursday and Friday, 9 and 10 July – the days, incidentally, of the worst street rioting in Hackney. The needy turned to the social-security office for help, but social-security workers blacked the handling of emergency claims arising from their colleagues' action. Indeed, to avoid the possibility (indeed the probability) of violence, the offices closed their doors to *all* claimants from Monday, 13 July. Some were canny enough to know that social-services offices had emergency moneys they could pay to families with children: but the social workers' union, the National and Local Government Officers' Association, also backed the civil-service strikers and closed the four area offices.

The destitute found themselves with nowhere to turn, and ugly scenes were beginning to develop. At the Sylvester Road DHSS office a group of irate women tried to force their way in at the staff entrance and threatened to smash windows when they found it locked. There was talk of organizing groups to go shoplifting. I spoke to many of those affected as they milled about in anxious confusion. On Wednesday I met John, a curly red-haired Irishman in his late twenties, whose fortnightly giro cheque for £44·10 was due on the Monday. He normally ran out of cash a few days before the next giro was due. On Monday he'd borrowed £10 from a neighbour. 'I've not got a penny, and I've a wife and two kids at home.' John was a painter by trade but had been unable to find work for the past six months: 'When I came over from Eire two years ago, everything was grand, you could walk into four or five jobs and get £20 a day easily. Now there's no work around, and they're offering you £12 a day take it or leave it, but I'd need at least £20 to make me turn out on a cold morning.'

The following day I met Richard Bryant, a tall, gaunt sixty-three-year-old with sallow skin and brown instead of white around his pupils. He is the sort of ageing 'social inadequate' that Hackney abounds in. He'd eaten his last meal on the Monday, three days before. On the Tuesday he'd had just enough money left to buy a cup of tea and a slice of bread and butter. He'd spent the week walking from one DHSS office to another, each one passing the buck for his survival. He had no idea how he would pay the rent for his lodging, due that day, and planned to spend the night on the streets. He had been off work sick the previous week. He worked as a kitchen porter in the canteen of a big bank office, taking home £46 a week from a basic of £62. An incident at work had precipitated an attack of bronchitis: 'This Chinese bloke, the other kitchen porter, was shouting at me for standing there doing nothing. Him and the other porter were telling me I was too old. They said, "Can't you read yet [Bryant is illiterate]. You're mental, you should get out and give someone else the chance." So I came short of breath. You see, my own family turned me out when I was twenty-one because I couldn't read or write, they didn't want nothing to do with me. I did get married, on the nineteenth of March 1944, but it only lasted for a day. I had an accident and an old war wound opened up in my stomach. She didn't want to know, and walked out on me. I never seen her since.'

Many of those who arrived at the offices had nothing to do with the dispute over unemployment cheques. There were women who had lost their child-benefit books, redundant workers who had just spent the last of their capital, pensioners who had been unable to cash their pensions at the post office because it had run out of cash, tenants of private landlords threatened with eviction. It was a frightening portrait gallery of social need and neglect in the collapsing welfare state.

There is no doubt that if the situation had continued for more than a week, all semblance of law and order would have broken down in Hackney and hunger riots would have compounded the anti-police riots. It was the nearest Hackney came to the mobilization of the unemployed in mass action that many considered justified by the government's brutality. Significantly, it took no less than total destitution and the threat of imminent starvation to get the masses on to the street in any numbers. As soon as that threat was removed, they withdrew into their more customary passivity. For the immediate crisis did not last long. By the Thursday afternoon Hackney Council leader John Kotz and South Hackney MP Ron Brown had secured the agreement of the DHSS and the unions to allow Hackney Council to make emergency payments. Payments began at 3 p.m. For the rest of the day a shifting queue of two or three hundred shuffled forward to collect their cash. The long trail of waiting poor, down the town-hall steps and right across the tree-lined square in front, was a sorry symbol of dependence and vulnerability in contemporary Britain. The hand-outs were a pittance – £20 for a single householder, £33 for a married couple, nothing for children. It was enough to buy food, no more, and it continued for three weeks before the civil servants' industrial action was ended by government concessions. Life for claimants then returned to 'normal', that is, a state of permanently revolving debt, not infrequently aggravated by unpredictable delays, intolerable waits and arbitrary decisions.

On the Inevitability of Scrounging

Hackney has always had more than its share of those determined to defraud the social-security system. Neither the level of benefits, nor the level of local wages, have ever been high enough in relation to social needs to remove that temptation. Casual work of the kind that is so common in Hackney provides the ideal cover. Low-paid, insecure work and social-security fraud fuel each other and feed off each other.

But deep recession and monetarism greatly increased the

temptation. The British social-security system, never generous, became Scrooge-like, and acted as an incentive and a provocation to abuse. There was the widening gap between the basic rates of benefit and basic needs, especially for clothing and fuel – and the even broader chasm between the rates and the level of social expectations generated by the media. There was the often arbitrary denial of entitlement: if the system did not play fair with its dependants, it could hardly expect them to play fair in return. And there was the suspicion and scepticism about claims: if people were treated as potential scroungers even when they were honest, then they might as well be scroungers for real.

The worsening state of the labour market also stimulated social-security fraud. Real wages had declined in some cases below subsistence level. Rates of pay for casual labouring and homework fell to such a low level that they almost assumed that the worker would also claim social security. As the formal economy slumped, the black economy expanded to fill some of the slack.

None of this is to excuse scrounging. Although it does not have the same direct destructive impact as conventional crime, it does help to make the social-security system more unpleasant for the majority who do not scrounge. Just as high crime levels lead to heavier policing of the whole community, so high fraud levels lead to tighter checks and investigations of all social-security claims. It is impossible to assess the true scale of abuse. Small-scale abuse – doing the odd casual job or low-paid part-time work – is probably fairly common and fairly harmless. More serious fraud is constantly being reported in the columns of the *Hackney Gazette*, taking virtually every form that human ingenuity is capable of devising: claiming and working; cohabiting and claiming separately; claiming under two separate names; altering giro cheques to higher amounts; fraudulently claiming that books or giros have been stolen and cashing them oneself; or selling a benefit book at a discount and then claiming it was lost.

I did not directly ask any of my interviewees if they were cheating on social security, but three of them openly volunteered the facts and hence must appear under pseudonyms. 'Barbara' is a bright-faced twenty-five-year-old unmarried mother, one of those women, so numerous in Hackney, who uses all her wits to survive and give her children some kind of life. She left school at sixteen, and worked both as a lampshade machinist and as an office girl. She had her first child, John, when she was eighteen. Two years later her second, Joyce, was born. She got a council flat and faced the problem of furnishing it. 'The social security gave me three cups and saucers, three plates, cutlery for three, three chairs and a table, two beds and a cot, and £35 for curtains. But the place was half empty. So I went to work for three months, using false names. A friend looked after the kids. I worked from 5 till 7, mornings, cleaning, then from 8.30 till 5 p.m. in a shoe factory, then 6.30 till 9 cleaning again. It nearly killed me, but I managed to save up enough to buy a three-piece suite, television, pots and pans, extra crockery, a clock, things like that that you can't do without, but they won't give you a penny towards.

'Even with more furniture, the flat was still terrible: there was damp in every room. There were seventeen repairs I just couldn't get them to do. There were robberies day and night – I had seven break-ins in two years. I moved out at one stage and squatted in another flat. Then I said if they didn't move me, I wouldn't pay the rent. They said if I didn't pay, they'd kick me out. I didn't pay. So they kicked me out. I spent six months homeless, in a bed-and-breakfast place, then they offered me this place [on a run-down pre-war estate].

'I still find I can't get by on my money. I get £35.90 a week, plus my rent. My money was running out by Thursday. I was borrowing £10 every week. So now I do a bit of baby-minding in the mornings. I get £10 a week. That carries me through over the weekend.'

But life is still hard. 'I was one of eleven children, but my mother managed better than I can do now with my two.' She buys her own clothes second-hand at a charity shop – £2 for a coat, 60p for a pair of trousers. 'It does bother me, but it's a case of having to.' The children go through clothes and shoes at breakneck speed. 'They've just been away on an ILEA holiday. John busted his shoes. Joyce went through a pair of plimsolls and a pair of shoes. She's been going to school for days in a pair of flip-flop sandals, but she can't keep them on her feet. I went to see the education welfare officer. She managed to get £10 off a charity, but that will only buy a jacket for John, and I can't buy for one without buying for the other. I only found out that ILEA give clothing grants a couple of months ago, when my sister got one. Nobody tells you what you're entitled to.'

Meals are transport-café fare: egg and chips twice a week, macaroni cheese, sausage stew, toad-in-the-hole, cheap beefburgers, occasionally a hand of pork. But she does make sure the kids get fruit every day. She has only a single two-bar electric fire for the whole house. When the living-room is warmed in the evening, she puts it in turn into the two bedrooms to take the chill off the air. Throughout the day, and in the night, even in winter, she has no heat. Her only luxury, though an expensive one, is smoking, twenty a day, but like so many of the women I met, she found it an essential aid against stress and all her attempts to give up had failed.

She too has had her share of difficulties with the Department of Health and Social Security: 'I lost my family allowance book last year. I had to wait ten months before I got another. All they sent me was this [she showed me a brown card with the message, *The receipt of your recent communication is acknowledged. It is receiving attention*]. Then some of the slips turned up, signed. I had to see the fraud officer. He said: "How are you going to feel if your kids have to go into care?" – he said it with my son sitting there next to me. I grabbed him by the tie and pulled him down to the desk, I said to him: "I'm a human being not an effing dog." He said, "I'll have you in court for this." But he didn't. They're all like that. One day they asked me who I had sex with, and when, and where. I said are you sure you wouldn't like to know what position we do it in? Another time my giro was late, the officer said, "If you want money why don't you go and ask your babies' fathers?" He said fathers, so everyone there could hear my babies had different fathers. Some of the officers are really young, just out of school, and there they are telling you how to run your life.'

A Tour of the Black Economy

The most thorough scrounger I met was 'Terry', who lives with her three daughters in a flat on an unpopular estate in Dalston. Stray dogs, weeds breaking through paving stones, and flats boarded up with corrugated tin to keep out squatters give it a wartime austerity look, adorned with the graffiti of a multiracial society: 'Ku Klux Klan Rockers', 'Up the riots'.

Terry is a plump twenty-eight-year-old in a pink keep-fit suit, living with her three daughters through the aftermath of ten years of marriage to a Turkish Cypriot. 'My parents came to live in Stoke Newington eleven years ago. I met my husband the first night I went out: what a way to go. It was love at first sight and all that stuff, the real thing. He was a compulsive gambler, always in the cafés around Newington Green: that's where all the action is. I was with him two months, then I left him because I couldn't take the gambling. He agreed to stop it, he really tried, and I went back to him. He was working as a TV engineer, and while he wasn't gambling, he saved and built up the business. Then he went into buying and selling stuff to cafés. He had a really big business, hundreds of customers.

'We moved to this estate five years ago. It's a dump: the fire engines and the police are always round, nearly every night. We had pram sheds but you could never use them, there were always fires in them. People were using mine as a dump for nicked stuff – I found a telephone answering machine in there once. The worst problem when we first moved in was the break-ins. The front doors are a piece of cake, all you need is a plastic card to open the lock. We were broken into six times in three years. The first time we lost £700 – he'd just been collecting from his shops. That was taken from a handbag in the bedroom we were sleeping in. Then we lost a stereo worth £300. Twice we disturbed them, my ten-year-old found them. Ever since then the girls have been really nervous in the night. They leave their door open so I can hear them if they call me.'

Meanwhile her marriage was deteriorating. 'When my husband's business got big, he started gambling again. Usually it would be when he was under a lot of strain, like sometimes his customers owed him £2,000 and he had to take them to court. When he wasn't gambling, he'd give me money, lots, £70, £80, £90 a week. But when he was gambling, if I wanted £1 or £2 I'd have to fight him for it. Those weeks I just didn't feed him or myself, just the kids. He was out most evenings. I couldn't stand for that. I got a lot of beatings, too, but I'm no angel, I probably provoked them. It must have been hard for him, he was always torn between his parents and us, they never accepted me or the kids.'

She threw him out in July 1981, and started claiming social security for herself and the three girls. She managed until January 1982. 'But all of a sudden the children needed a lot of clothes. One of them lost a shoe in the market and I couldn't find it, so that was a new pair that was needed. I went to the social security to ask for clothes, but they wouldn't give me a thing. [She would have been entitled to cash for the lost shoes.] When they refused that, I sat down and cried. I don't want second-hand clothes for my kids: they've never done anything wrong that I should have to put second-hand clothes on them.'

Her needs and her income simply didn't match up. Her total income was £75·83 a week (1982). Of this £28·88 went on rent and rates, £14·50 on gas and electricity (including £1·50 a week repayment of arrears), leaving only £32·45 – a mere £8·11 per person, £1·16 a day – for all other needs. 'There's one hundred per cent no way I could ever manage on social security without a little side job,' she comments.

So early in 1982 Terry entered the world of the black economy, a world of low pay rates and unsocial hours, of cash in hand and no written contracts where the individual worker is alone, without protection of laws or social insurance: 'I've always got to do casual jobs, with no [national insurance] cards. If I did a regular job with cards, I'd get caught. I started doing demonstrations for a pottery firm – you know, in people's houses. You'd get nine or ten women together and show them the stuff and they'd place orders. You had to use your own car and your own petrol. You didn't get any wage, just commission, twelve per cent, on what you sold. If you damaged any of the pots, they took it out of your commission. You'd take half an hour to drive there, an hour to unpack it all and set it up, an hour to demonstrate it and take your orders, an hour to pack it up again, and half an hour to drive home. The most I ever got in commission was £19, that was at Christmas time when people were buying presents. Usually I'd only get £5 or £6 for four hours' work, not counting what I spent on petrol. I didn't stick it for long – it was costing me money sometimes.

'Then I got a job as a barmaid. I was working from half 7 till midnight or later. I got £6 a night. But I wasn't seeing the kids. The governor kept taking liberties asking me to stay till 1 or 2 in the morning clearing up. Then I'd have to get up the next day and get the kids off to school. My eldest girl suffered a lot, she's a bit puritanical, she didn't like the idea of me working in a pub where other men were coming in. Every night she'd cry and ask me not to go. And you get your name blackened if you work in a pub, even if you don't do anything.

'While I was still working there I started doing homework. I met a lot of Turkish people through being a barmaid. Some of them owned factories, and gave me some work. I hired an overlocking machine – I paid £69 deposit and the rent is £5 a week. It's very noisy, so I can't have it in the bedrooms next to the other flats. I have to have it in the small bedroom which is right at the end of the block, so the little one has to sleep in with me. I got more homework through adverts. I just do overlocking. Normally I get 8p a skirt. I can manage 230 in a day if I work from 10 till 7, but normally I'd only work from 10 till 4 because of the kids, so I make about £12. I got an ulcer with doing that and the pub job at the same time. It was getting me down, I was getting irritable with the kids. So I stopped the pub work. But now I can't get any homework. It's all dried up. Yesterday I phoned six or seven adverts. I was at the box by 11, but they'd all gone.

'We're getting low now. We've got food for today, but there's none for tomorrow. Last week we ran out of money for the electric meter. We had to hunt round the house for pennies to make up 50p. I make sure the kids eat all right, they get fish fingers and beefburgers, and if we're lucky once a week we'll have mincemeat. I just have one meal a day, sometimes I don't eat at all, sometimes I have soup or boil up potatoes and put cheese with them. I've had to get the little one out of nappies – I couldn't afford them any more. For my ulcer, the doctor told me to eat boiled fish, eat this, eat that, but I couldn't afford it. When he said are you still on this diet, I had to say yes, I'm not going to sit there and tell someone I can't afford it.

'We're going steadily downhill. This week I started thinking of things I could sell to get a bit of money together. I don't like working and claiming. I'm not greedy: if I could get just two days' homework a week that would be enough. I don't want to get rich, just to feed my kids. I feel bad about it, I don't like doing it. If I could get a full-time job that would pay me enough to come off social security, I'd give my book up straight away. If my husband came back, I'd probably go back with him and take the consequences, just to stop having to do this.'

Social Security and Crime

In theory, social security, by providing an essential minimum for someone to survive on, is designed to prevent crime. But the advanced state of decay reached by the system in the early 1980s made it yet another cause of crime. The gap between a Poor Law subsistence and a socially acceptable minimum is keenly felt among claimants. Some gnash their teeth and bear it. Some bridge it by fraud. Others, by crime.

Others, again, are driven to crime by the sheer necessity of survival. For it is not only during civil-service strikes that people are left without money. In our admirable welfare state there are an increasing number of people who are totally destitute, literally without a penny to their name, many of them for days, some of them for weeks on end. The regular exhaustion of funds, two or three days before the next payment is due, is routine for many claimants. Delays and losses of giros add to their number. And there is the outright denial of unemployment benefit for six weeks to those who leave a job 'voluntarily' because they can't stomach it any more, or those who are considered by DHSS review staff not to be seeking work with sufficient diligence. In 1980 another group of potentially destitute were created: people who left school after Easter could not draw benefits until September (unless they were living away from their parents). Then there are those who are considered to be cohabiting. Cohabitation is assumed to involve financial support though frequently, especially among young black people, it is an informal arrangement with no specific expectations about maintenance.

Tony is an articulate twenty-five-year-old living with Julia (see next chapter). He left school at fifteen with a few low-grade CSEs.

He trained as a motor mechanic for three years, but developed dermatitis and was told to keep away from oil. He was an apprentice carpenter for two years but didn't like it. Then he started work at Ford's in Dagenham: 'I stuck it for three years. I was doing assembly work on shifts. You had to be there on time if you had a cushy job. If you arrived two minutes late, you'd be loaned out to another section. So I'd have to leave home two hours before clocking-in time, to be sure of getting there on time. I stuck it for three years, then I couldn't cope any more, eating my dinner at 3 in the morning one week and 4 in the afternoon the next. The Friday night shift was hectic. I'd get home and have to do the shopping right away, so I'd have to sleep on Saturday evening and most of Sunday.'

He left in January 1980 with a good reference and high hopes of getting another job. In the event he was out of work for more than a year. After twelve months his automatic entitlement to unemployment benefit ran out. 'That was when the social security started messing me about. If you are living together with a girl and you are both working, everything is OK. But when one of you loses your job, that's when they give you a lot of hassle. I was living at this place with three other people. One of them used to be my girlfriend but we broke up and we had separate rooms. The social security wrote to me and said I wasn't entitled to any money because the girl was working, so she should support me. I wrote saying we had separated. They sent a visitor round, he looked in the kitchen and saw our plates in the same place – everyone in the flat used the same kitchen – and he decided we were still living together. Then I wrote again, asking why she should support me if we had nothing to do with each other. They said they might send another visitor, but I'd waited for weeks and weeks for the first one, so I wrote them a reply with just one word, "Bollocks", signed, "Tony". I spent five weeks without any money at all. I borrowed £5 off friends every now and then, but I reached a point where I couldn't borrow any more. Then I had two choices: either go and find work or go and steal something. I thought seriously about stealing, but I thought, I'll just try one more time to hustle myself a job, so I just went walking and went into this builder's yard and got a job as a painter. I was working on one contract for six months, but then the contract ran out and they didn't have enough work to keep us on. I tried for a few jobs since, but most of them want more than one trade, like I rang up for a painting job and they asked what else I could do. I moved out of that girl's house to save the hassle, so now I'm getting social security. But I still think about nicking, I think, if I had some money, I could buy this or that, but where you going to nick from? And there's the chance of getting caught. Is it worth it? You always come back to the same thought: is it worth it?'

A System without Checks and Balances

Perhaps the most telling indicator that something is seriously wrong with the social-security and supplementary-benefits system is the difference that is made when a poor person secures the help of an articulate person, usually middle class by occupation and education, who knows the rules and regulations. Paddy Digney, the coordinator of the Family Centre, an advice agency in Rectory Road, often helps people with social-security problems: 'The people on the counters are often immature and inexperienced, and they're so arrogant, even over the smallest and pettiest of claims. But they pay a lot more attention when people have advocates who sound as if they know what they're talking about.' One of her clients had a part-time job helping in a play group during school term, but when she claimed supplementary benefit for the holiday weeks, for which she was not paid, she was refused. Her husband was admitted into Bart's Hospital: the fares for herself and her children amounted to £8 per week. That claim, too, was turned down. When her husband came out, he had to go on a special diet, but his claim for the £1·20 a week diet allowance also got the thumbs down. Yet in each of these instances the claim was conceded when Paddy Digney pressed it.

Other social workers and welfare-rights advisers of all kinds have similar tales to relate. Social-security cases provide the largest single category (along with housing) of surgery cases for Hackney Central MP Stanley Clinton Davis. His interventions here have a high success rate, which is, paradoxically, a bad sign. It means that a large number of the original decisions were mistaken.

Many reasons contribute to the incidence of error and insensitivity: the mounting burden of overwork; the low pay and status, youth and inexperience, and rapid turnover of clerical and counter staff; the sheer pressure of demand from clients, exceeding the supply of resources; the level of personal abuse which staff themselves are the target of; the lack of managerial concern about the quality of the service; and informal staff methods for reducing the work-load – at the expense of the client. But there is a deeper and more fundamental reason. Every agency has an inbuilt tendency to generate error and injustice. Those that function best have, by the same token, some inbuilt mechanism to detect and correct error. For most public services that mechanism is simply the vigilance of the consumer. Where the public are aware of their rights and aware of the ways to assert them, maladministration will be more easily detected and officials will take more care to avoid it. When the clients are inarticulate and ill-informed, as a large proportion are in poor areas, bureaucrats rule OK, and the laborious indirect mechanisms of representative democracy can do very little to control them. In all this, as we shall see, the social-security system exemplifies the behaviour of so many agencies, from health and housing to the police and the law, that dominate the lives of the disadvantaged.

9   Into the Whirlwind:
Financial Crisis

The mouse that has but one hole is soon caught.
Arab proverb

Families in poverty live perpetually on a pinnacle between financial precipices, performing the most delicate of balancing acts. Timing is crucial. The days between each giro, each child benefit, each pay-day, each day when larger payments fall due, are carefully counted. Borrowing becomes an essential element of budgeting. The poor are forever negotiating bridging loans, to be paid back when the next lump of cash comes in, to be borrowed again the same time next week, next month or next quarter. The loans come from family or friends, or, informally, from those agencies to whom debts are due: robbing the milkman to pay back mother, skipping the rent to pay the electricity, delaying the hire-purchase instalment to pay the gas bill.

Of course, an outsider might moralize, all this borrowing should not really be necessary. If the head of the household planned ahead, he, or more usually she, could lay aside the anticipated moneys for the appointed time and even, if they were prudent, draw interest in the meantime. But on the breadline this is possible only for people of iron will-power and forbearance. If there is £5 or £50 in a jam-jar on the mantelpiece, or in the Post Office, it is sure to be taken, for a necessity or for a luxury. Borrowing becomes unavoidable, because saving is impossible.

Yet borrowing is a very dangerous business, especially if incomes fluctuate from week to week, as many low incomes do. There is always the risk that you may be unable to pay back what you owe. In a life of constant self-denial there is always the temptation to exceed the limits of your purse, to buy an extra packet of cigarettes to calm nerves rubbed raw by multiple stresses, to buy an extra pint to drown a sorrow or a humiliation, to buy a cake or a toy for kids who never get any treats. Then there are sudden, uncontrollable expenses, the cost of dental treatment, the need to pay for a school trip or the clothes required for it, and uncontrollable income losses due to sickness or bonus or overtime changes. There is, too, the fact that the poor generally pay more for the same goods or services: they lack the surplus to buy or store in bulk, they lack the capital to spend in order to save higher running costs, they lack cars to enable them to shop around and freezers to store their bargains.

With prevailing levels of rents and fuel prices, debts pile up suddenly and unexpectedly, like tropical storm-clouds, quickly reaching unmanageable proportions. If you have to pay just two weeks' milk money, you can't pay the rent for the week. If you owe one week's rent, you are up to your neck; if you owe two weeks, it is already above your head. Then you face paying three weeks at once, which often exceeds the week's total income. So you let the debt ride. Demoralization sets in, perhaps a certain abandon. One month later or three months later, it happens again. All this time the centre of balance is gradually shifting away from the pinnacle and the subject is leaning over further and further. Then suddenly the balancing act comes to an abrupt end and the acrobat plunges into the abyss. Social catastrophes of this kind, where quantitative change becomes qualitative, are part of the dramatic fare of the inner city. The most disruptive of financial crises, fuel disconnection and eviction, jeopardize the most fundamental human needs for warmth and shelter. In recession they became commonplace.

Kept in the Dark

In the era of expensive energy, a new concept emerged: fuel poverty. It hit unevenly and arbitrarily, picking out especially those with poorly insulated, draughty homes, and those using electricity as their fuel for cooking and space heating. There are plenty of both types in Hackney, where 32 per cent relied on electricity as their main source of heat in 1978, compared with only 12 per cent in England and Wales as a whole.

The better-off could adapt to higher energy prices by paying for double glazing or cavity-wall insulation and shifting from electricity to gas. The poor could afford none of these measures, while council tenants, even if they could afford them, were not free to take them but had to wait for action from the council, which could not. There was, however, one form of adjustment the poor of Hackney often made: they shifted to paraffin heaters, often second-hand. What they saved on fuel, they paid in damage to their health, through massive condensation – 5 litres of water for 5 litres of paraffin – literally streaming down their walls; through the risk of burns and chest complaints; and through the risk of fire.

Other and often bizarre stratagems are used to save on electricity. Rudolf Carrington, a Guyanese who came to Britain in 1966, takes home £86 a week as a maintenance engineer. But he can no longer afford to run the immersion heater: instead his family boil up pans of hot water on the gas stove and have stand-up baths. The Calane family, whom we shall meet in Chapter 19, run one bath, which costs 50p in the meter, then get in one after the other, using the same water: father first, wife and baby next, ten-year-old boy last.

Many families which get into insoluble difficulty with quarterly bills have slot meters installed: they cost more per quarter and are vulnerable to theft, but at least a meter allows customers to regulate their fuel consumption according to their income. This often means that they go without electricity for a day or two each week, like the Cooper family. Maureen Cooper is the eldest daughter of Doris Davies, whose family we will meet repeatedly in the following pages.* She has the Davieses' unmistakeable turned-up nose and her mother's toughness, unflappable in spite of the frequent crises that punctuate life for the poor. When I interviewed her in 1981, she was earning £35 a week as a school cleaner (with a 6.30 a.m. start) and her husband, a foreman packer, was bringing home £67 to £74 a week, depending on overtime, out of which he gave her £55 to £60. (He was made redundant a year later.) The Coopers were, by the standards of most families I met, relatively comfortable. Her husband Frank's 'pocket money' of £12 to £14 is,

* See page 441. These are not their real names.

for her purposes, inaccessible, but with child benefit for her two children she disposes of around £100 a week. Rent, rates and hot water charge come to £24·54 a week – the rise over the previous year exactly swallowed up the couple's pay rises. For electricity she reckons around £9 a week in summer and double that in winter – fuel poverty is a seasonal matter, the British equivalent of the lean months before the harvest for subsistence peasants. Food, milk and school dinner money cost her £35 a week. The surplus, for clothes, modest entertainments (the odd drink or a day out with a relative), household goods and so on, is £20 in winter, £30 in summer. It is almost exactly enough to manage on, without any luxuries. Maureen has never had a holiday in ten years of marriage, nor before that either, and until recently bought most of her clothes from door-to-door salesmen, common in east London, and often hawking stolen goods. But electricity is her biggest headache. 'I was on the quarterly bill, buying stamps towards it. You go along each week, and you feel good inside because you've bought £5-worth of stamps. But meanwhile you're using up £10 or £15 worth of electricity, and then the bill comes along and you've got £100 extra to fork out. Before Christmas [1980] I was £300 in arrears. I nearly got cut off – the men actually came to the door to do it. Luckily I made an agreement with the LEB [London Electricity Board] the day before to pay off £10 a week. Since then I've had to ask them to cut that to £5 a week.

'After that scare, I got a meter put in. I put £4 or £5 a day in there on winter weekends. I don't feed the meter, I wait till it goes out, that way I know exactly how much I'm using. Once the kids are in bed we turn the fire off and sit with blankets round us. I don't heat the bedrooms at night, I can't afford to, not even in winter. Many a time I've had to send round my mum's for a tin of soup or I knock at Ellie's for half a bar of Oxos, because I've put the dinner money in the meter. [Doris Davies is a perennial source of revolving loans for all her children.] We're usually without electricity every Wednesday, that's when the money runs out, because I get paid Thursdays. If I don't have more than 50p left, I use it to cook the dinner. Then we go without electric for an hour or two, sometimes all evening. Sometimes I'll read a book by torchlight, sometimes we go to bed early.'

Economizing on heating has another drawback, beyond discomfort: damp. Water streams down the Coopers' bedroom windows in winter and has to be soaked up by towels left on the floor. Maureen has complained to the council about the damp. Like many of the poor families I met, she likes to believe that the damp is structural, rising, or penetrating, and therefore the council's responsibility to remedy. Complainants are invariably told – and it is usually the case – that it is condensation, due to their living habits. Another breed of middle-class moralizer preaches at them: they should keep the place heated throughout the day and night, they should leave windows open for ventilation. In cold weather, the poor can afford to do neither. The damp and condensation they suffer is structural, in a social sense: it is the inevitable result of placing poor families in poorly insulated homes with high energy prices.

Maureen suffers a self-imposed, weekly electricity cut. But many families are without heat and light for months on end. There are no separate Hackney figures for electricity cut-offs, but London-wide statistics showed an alarming leap as raised prices and stagnant incomes collided head on during recession. Disconnections rose from 11,016 in 1978 to 16,463 in 1979 and a staggering 37,648 in 1980. That was the crunch year, when London Electricity started to get tough with debtors: shock treatment that brought the number of cut-offs down to the still high level of 19,775 in 1981. Social workers noticed the problem in the number of families coming for help with fuel debts: one in ten of all new cases asking for help at the Shoreditch office in 1981 – and the sums involved were massive. 'A couple of years back', says intake team leader Peter Cole, 'there would have been ructions if a debt was over £60. Nowadays we sneer at a bill of £100. They're coming in at £500 to £1,000 a time.' Social services could offer modest cash help, though only to families with children, and negotiate with the LEB to stave off disconnection. But an increasing number could not be helped at all, especially if the debt was more than £400. One woman with a child of five was cut off when she could not pay a bill of £1,000 for a single quarter – for the previous three years all her bills had been estimates. In an area like Hackney, meter thefts are common, and the householder is responsible for making good the losses. One single mother was cut off for a debt of £382, owed because her meter had been robbed twice.

London Electricity's code of practice recommends that old people and families with small children should not be cut off in the 'closed season', the cold months between October and March. But there is nothing to stop them being cut off in the open season and remaining cut off indefinitely thereafter. Julia, a nineteen-year-old black single mother with a two-year-old daughter, Chantelle, had been without electricity for seventeen months when I visited her. When you call at her council flat, you have to flap the letterbox: the doorbell does not ring. Her troubles started soon after she moved in to her two-bedroomed flat on De Beauvoir estate. The flats have an expensive-to-run underfloor heating system, and Julia was given no instructions on how to operate it. Her first bill, for an incomplete quarter to December 1979, was £100. She couldn't pay it. That was followed up, in April 1980, by a devastating bill for £275 – over £21 a week, more than three-quarters of her weekly social-security income after the rent had been paid. Hackney social services were prepared to pay out £75 to bring the debt down to the level of £300, below which the electricity board would accept direct payment of arrears from the Department of Health and Social Security. The problem was that the electricity board were insisting on a payment of £15 a week to cover the past debt and the expected future use. Julia's weekly social-security money by now (1981) was £35·85 plus rent and rates – and this included an extra allowance for the expensive heating system. She wouldn't agree to that level of deduction. There was stalemate, and she remained without heat or light (though the LEB would have lost nothing – and could have recouped some of their losses – by installing a slot meter). Over the summer of 1980 she stayed in the flat using a paraffin heater occasionally and lighting by candles. The hardest thing to bear was the absence of television. She and Chantelle would go out in the evenings to visit friends and come home at bedtime. But in the winter it was too cold in the flat and she went to stay with friends, sleeping in their children's bedroom.

Her boyfriend at the time was Tony, whom we met in the last chapter. His unemployment is holding him back from the idea of marriage: 'If I get married, it would be my responsibility as a man to provide. I couldn't say, well today I got no money. Like we are now, at times I can help out, sometimes she can help me out. And say things don't work out, and she thinks someone else can take care of her and the kid better, then there would be no ties to split up.' Even so, they were, for the moment, a couple, and this was their stake in society: they had no light, no heat. Neither had a job. The flat was bare and echoing. In the lounge, only a carpet, a battered sideboard belonging to Tony, and an old television set that can't be used. To sit on, nothing but a bedspread laid out in one corner. In the kitchen, a gas cooker – an extravagance, bought on hire purchase repaid at £1·88 a week – and a fridge belonging to Tony, but unusable. A bed in one bedroom, a cot in the other.

But the saddest deprivation was for the child. She faced the danger of burns from candles and paraffin heater. She has not a single toy, and no playmates – Julia cannot get her a place in a nursery and won't let her play out because of traffic through the estate. Chantelle was improvising her own amusements, playing with her mother's yellow comb and mirror, stomping round the room in Tony's shoes, babbling to herself while the couple sat and talked in the falling dusk, camped out like war survivors. I asked them how they viewed the future. 'There's nothing you can do,' Tony replied. 'You can raise your voice, but who is listening?'

The Punitive Ritual

The middle-class moralizer is often correct: financial crisis is often due to unwise budgeting, to wasteful, irrational spending, to choosing the wrong priorities. But it is easy to moralize on an ample income. It is no accident that the poor spend more than they can afford on smoking, drinking, gambling: all three are modes either of coping with stress or of attempting to escape it. And when the choice is between clothing your child and paying the rent or the electricity bill, who can say which is the right priority? Only the poor are forced to make such choices.

Just as frequently, financial collapse is due to excessive demands being made on incomes that are unnecessarily low, either because of an unjust distribution of income and taxation, or because due benefits are not being received. It is often the result of sudden, unexpected calls: by 1981 the electricity bill for a single winter was sufficient to ruin a family.

The poor are essentially abandoned in the welfare state: no one reaches out actively to ensure that their benefits are maximized, or their expenditure minimized, by helping them to switch to more efficient forms of energy and insulation. Official agencies first become involved at the point of crisis, when things have already gone too far for simple measures. At best they can mitigate the crisis, though that often means mortgaging the future, paying off arrears at £1·50 a week or more out of incomes that, even without deductions, are inadequate to cover basic needs. At worst the victim of financial crisis is subjected to treatment that reeks strongly of punishment, or of teaching them a lesson, of bringing home to them the consequences of their folly. The unwelcome visit of bailiffs, to repossess or to evict, the arrival of LEB men to cut off the electricity: these are the means of retribution for failure to make out on incomes that make success impossible.

As the combined outcome of stagnant or falling wages and steeply rising rents, rent arrears owed to Hackney council climbed from £825,000 in 1978–9 to £1·37 million in 1980–81 – an average of almost £50 for every property. By one of those strange paradoxes that abound in Britain, the local authorities who evict families with children for non-payment of rent are generally also responsible for rehousing them as homeless families. After having been evicted, the family spends an indeterminate period in a hostel or hotel, at great expense to the council, and is eventually given a single offer of another council dwelling which in the old days used to be of the worst, but nowadays involves pot luck, and can sometimes be better than the previous tenancy. The whole process achieves nothing, saves not a penny of public money, indeed wastes it, and has no other purpose or meaning than to serve as a punitive ritual.

If a badly designed heating system was Julia's downfall, recession and public spending cuts were the root of Sonia Lewis's problems. She is a big twenty-five-year-old who came over from Jamaica when she was seventeen. She brought with her her first child, Nadine, now eight: 'Then I got mixed up with a man and have Emily [aged five] and now I'm expecting this one [pointing to her stomach]. This last one was a problem thing, you know, you get involved and things just happen.'

I met Sonia at the Finsbury Hotel, in Queen's Drive, one of the bed-and-breakfast places that Hackney Council uses to accommodate its homeless families. She had been working as a school canteen assistant and was training to be an assistant cook. Her take-home pay was low, £43 a week in 1979. Family Income Supplement, maintenance from Emily's father and child benefit brought the total up to £66 a week, and she was getting rent and rate rebates. But Emily was constantly ill, and Sonia had to keep taking days off work to look after her. Education cutbacks meant a reduction in auxiliary staff, and she was made redundant early in 1980. Her income immediately dropped by £20 a week. Sonia could not budget on the reduced income and drew heavily on the rent money to pay for food, clothing and electricity bills. Her landlords, the Greater London Council, spotted her problem and referred her to Hackney social services in March 1981, but because of staff shortages her case was not taken on. Now threatened with eviction, but quite unable to pay the arrears of more than £800, she approached the Department of Health and Social Security and asked them to pay her rent direct to the GLC – so she would not be tempted to draw on it for other needs – along with £1 a week towards the arrears. Had this been done from an early stage, the problem would never have reached insoluble proportions. But now it was too late: it would have taken sixteen years to pay off her arrears, and the GLC would not agree to the arrangement. 'They said they would evict me. I went to court for the case, but when I got there the case was already gone. Then they sent me a letter telling me to take my things out. I packed them all in black plastic bags and left them with my neighbour, and I left all my furniture in the flat: they said they would put it into storage and charge me. I just packed a suitcase with a few things.'

She moved out on 2 June. Hackney Council agreed to rehouse her temporarily but the offer came with a nasty sting in its tail. The letter – typical of the official communications people showed me – put the position in bureaucratese that did not make the slightest concession to the reader's educational level.

Housing Emergency Section,
302 Mare St, London E8.

Dear Sir/Madam,

In accordance with section eight of the Housing (Homeless Persons) Act 1977, I am required to inform you that your application for rehousing as a homeless person has been considered. It has been decided that you are homeless and in a priority need group, but that you became homeless intentionally. This has been decided as you recently left your home because of wilful and persistent refusal to pay rent, and it is understood that the arrears at the time of your eviction totalled £803·88 plus £87 costs [for the court case].

I am required to inform you that, when a person is judged as becoming intentionally homeless there is no legal obligation on the local authority to rehouse the family but only to provide temporary accommodation for a limited period to enable the family to solve its own housing problem.

Your booking will terminate at twelve noon on the 4th of August. However, should you be able to clear the debt owed on your former tenancy, this you should do. In this event it is suggested that you approach the housing authority and ask to be reinstated. If your request is granted you are earnestly advised to maintain your tenancy by paying your rent regularly each week to avoid similar difficulties recurring in the future.

Yours faithfully,

A. J. P., Homeless Persons Officer, for Director of Housing.

Bureaucrats have a predilection for a polysyllabic, Latinate style, which is guaranteed, if not designed, to confuse working-class clients. Translated into Anglo-Saxon, the letter meant that, come August the 4th, Sonia and her children would be thrown on to the street. She did understand enough to reapproach the GLC: 'They told me they want at least £400 or £500 in arrears. They asked if I could sell something, but the only valuable thing I got is a cooker and a fridge, and I am still paying them off. If I sell everything I have, I would just get £40 or £50 and it wouldn't be worth it.'

Enclosed with the letter, clipped with a 'with compliments' slip, was a list of places she could try to find other accommodation: far from helping, it simply underlined the hopelessness of her situation. The first sheet of the list included night shelters, Salvation Army hostels, Rowton houses and DHSS reception centres, all catering for down-and-outs and drunks. A second sheet listed private accommodation agencies: 'I phoned a few of them. They say, no chance of getting a place with two children. To get a furnished place with more than one bedroom would cost £60 or £70 a week and they want a month's rent in advance.' The third sheet detailed bed-and-breakfast accommodation in Hackney, costing from £25 per person per week. But Sonia was already in a B & B hotel and did not consider a cheap hotel a proper home for her children.

For the time allowed her, she found herself in a curious, quiet pause between nightmares. Her room was cold and cavernous, a single bed for her in one corner, bunk beds for the girls in another, a television in between. As we talked, Emily and Nadine watched the children's programme *Blue Peter*, danced a jig to the music, and played a game with little pieces of torn paper. Emily, paternally deprived, came over to me, rested her head on my arm, and sucked her thumb. 'The children don't mind it here,' said Sonia. 'They think it's a holiday. But I am scared, because they told me, if I can't find a place for us, they might take those two into care. But they ain't gonna get them. They can send the police, they ain't gonna get them, unless they knock me out first. I know they give them food, but that's not enough, is it? It would damage the kids, don't they think about that?'

Sonia was kept in suspense for three months. August the 4th came and went, and she was not turned out on the street. Her booking was extended on a day-to-day basis. Her case was considered by a committee of directors and chairpersons for social services and housing. Her ordeal of anxiety ended on 3 September 1981, when she was told she would be rehoused by Hackney Council in order to give her 'one further opportunity to conduct your tenancy in a proper manner'. By December, and by now the mother of three, she was still awaiting an offer.

Part Two

Private Need
and Public Squalor

Thus the public ruin invades the house of each
citizen, and the courtyard doors no longer have the
strength to keep it away, but it leaps over the lofty
wall. And though a man runs in and tries to hide in
chamber or closet, it ferrets him out.

> *Solon, c. 600 BC, on the evils of bad government*
> *(tr. R. Lattimore)*

The Inverse-Care Law

Where domestic poverty is more concentrated, the need for public spending is greater than normal. The poor are less able to finance their own full needs, in housing, health, education, transport or leisure, and less able to supplement public provision where it is inadequate. The potential demands on public services are greater in a deprived area. Because Hackney and places like it gather in the social and physical casualties of British society, there are higher proportions of people in need of support: single parents, the mentally and physically ill and handicapped, old people isolated because their children have left home. But a higher level of public spending can also help to tackle the central weaknesses of the inner city. It can – if properly directed – provide direct and indirect employment to help stimulate the local economy. It can improve the bad state of housing, which, because it is cheap, is the principal magnet attracting the disadvantaged. It can enable education to compensate for poor home backgrounds and to raise the general level of skills and qualifications available locally.

These benefits apply only to the extent that public spending in a poor area is financed from outside, by central-government grants or transfers from wealthier areas. To the extent that finance has to be raised locally, it can become a drain on already tight family budgets and further weaken the local private-sector economy. Yet, despite the greater need for public services, poor areas usually suffer from a lower level of public provision, in quantity, in quality, or often both. Welsh physician Tudor Hart has expressed this succinctly for the health sphere: 'The availability of good medical care tends to vary inversely with the need of the population served.' This inverse-care law has a much wider field of action and is valid for almost all forms of public service. Concentrations of poor people tend to be found together with poor public services.

Private squalor and public squalor go hand in hand, accentuating each other.

There are a number of reasons for this. Voluntary work, and community action, which in middle-class areas supplement (and complement) the public services in funds and in manpower, are usually much weaker in working-class areas, because these are lacking in surplus finance, organizational know-how, and often physical and nervous energy. Private contributions to schools and hospitals are scarcer. Community involvement, although more needed, is harder to get off the ground and keep going. Community care of children, the old, the mentally and physically ill and handicapped – so much cheaper and more humane than institutional care – is made more difficult by the lack of foster-parents and of community solidarity.

The neediest areas also have difficulty in attracting and keeping a good quality of staffing – with the exception of the unusually dedicated. The lack of decent private housing and 'good' schools, and the higher crime levels and general unattractiveness of the environment, tend to deter professionals and higher bureaucrats from living in deprived areas, so that the majority of those who do work there commute in from more desirable neighbourhoods. But the intractability of local problems in the inner city, and the often disagreeable clientele, discourage many from travelling in. In education the staffing problem is compounded by the low average intake of ability of pupils and poor home backgrounds, which affect school ethos and academic results.

A more general factor is the political weakness of the poor. There is a lower level of public vigilance, owing to widespread ignorance about rights and means of asserting them. Local representatives on council and other governing bodies are likely to be less well educated and less able to scrutinize or criticize the activities of bureaucrats and professionals. Laxity, offhand service, and bad management can thrive more easily and grave errors, sometimes on a large scale, are more easily perpetrated and perpetuated.

The British system of parliamentary representation by single-member constituencies has restricted awareness of the depth of problems in poor areas, so that the flow of national resources to local government and industry has never been adequate to compensate for the obstacles.

Finally there is the relatively low rate base of poor areas. Until 1974, when there was little central government compensation for this, this meant they could not afford a decent standard of local services. From 1974, government grants did compensate, but the legacy of the past meant that poorer districts were starting from a lower base.

Hackney was very seriously affected by all these problems until quite recently. In 1979 the council, to combat the staffing problem, introduced the 'Hackney factor' – paying its non-manual staff £300–£500 over the going rate. The recent gentrification of some of the better parts of Hackney may have helped staffing, and certainly raised the educational level of councillors dramatically, from a majority of manual workers in the sixties to a majority of graduates in 1982, but at the price of working-class districts being represented by middle-class councillors. Hackney's rate base per capita is above the national average, but well below the London average, and insufficient to compensate for higher costs in London.

Cut and Come Again

Deep recession tends to increase the shortage of resources in poor areas by reducing government funds. The process is self-fuelling. The more unemployment grows, the lower is the government's income from tax and national insurance and the higher its enforced spending on social security. Keynesian policies of borrowing to get out of recession worked for minor business cycles, but their ability to cope with a major international slump has yet to be proven. Only carefully coordinated action by all major western economies could work, yet recession has made governments more and more introspectively concerned with maintaining their national self-interest. In the absence of an international assault on deficiency of demand in the world economy, there is a limit to what individual governments can do, and western governments of all political colours have found themselves cutting back public spending on goods, services and investment, thereby intensifying the world recession.

Thus the periodic economic crises of capitalism spill over into the social and political spheres: the retreat of the welfare state is an inevitable consequence of economic collapse. However, the spread of monetarist doctrines led to public spending cuts being pursued with greater vigour than the slump's effect on government revenue called for – to the point where they became an additional factor unnecessarily intensifying the recession. The Labour government of 1975–9 adopted monetarist policies reluctantly after a heavy run on the pound forced them to seek loans from the International Monetary Fund. The IMF, as usual, insisted on deflation of domestic demand and on public-spending cuts.

The Tory government of 1979 inherited a healthy balance of payments and a handsome flow of revenues from North Sea oil. Nevertheless, it too espoused monetarism and with an almost religious fervour. Public-spending cuts, it believed, would automatically help to bring down the rate of inflation, and they were also seen as worthwhile in themselves as a means of rolling back the frontiers of the public sector and enlarging the sphere of action for the pursuit of private profit.

Labour and Conservative cut back where it was politically easiest to cut. Central-government spending actually rose in real terms between 1975/6 and 1981/2 – and faster under the Tories than under Labour – largely because of the huge growth in payments to the unemployed. But local-government expenditure was savagely cut, by one-fifth in real terms, over the same period. Current expenditure declined by only 3 per cent. The brunt of the attack fell on capital expenditure, which dropped by 60 per cent during this period. Capital investment in housing was cut back by two-thirds.

The Tory approach to local-government finance, however, was much more draconian and much less concerned with the impact on poorer areas. The years from 1979 saw an unprecedented degree of central-government interference in local government – and an overall shift away from democracy towards centralized state regulation, the opposite of the Tories' professed ideals. The prime motive was an obsessive concern with monetary targets and the desire to make local government play its part in achieving them. There was also a feeling that rates – especially commercial and industrial rates – had risen too high and should be reined in. Local authorities were required to cut the volume of their spending in 1981/2 to 5·6 per cent less than the 1978/9 level, and by another 4 per cent the following year. Councils that did not comply were punished with financial penalties. At the same time the government's overall contribution to local government spending, the rate-support grant, was progressively cut, from 60 per cent in 1980/81 to 56 per cent in 1982/3.

From 1981/2 a new system of calculating the government's grant was introduced that had a profound effect on the inner cities. Until 1974 grant had been primarily related to population, so that, as people moved out to the suburbs and beyond, the cities' grant declined at the same time as their social problems increased. To correct this, in 1974 a new system was brought in which related the grant to indicators of social need, and increased the cities' share of resources. Once the IMF freeze of 1976–8 was over, this enabled city authorities like Hackney to increase their spending rapidly. The block-grant system introduced by the minister, Michael Heseltine, aimed to reverse the flow of funds, turning it away from largely Labour city authorities and back to the largely Tory shires: the cities suffered twice over, getting a smaller share of a shrinking cake. Basically, the block grant meant that, instead of accepting councils' own estimates of their need to spend, Whitehall calculated how much it thought each authority should be spending, on the basis of social need and the average national cost of providing services to each type of client. Another innovation was the introduction of penalties for 'overspending'. If councils spent above their assessed level, the government contribution to the excess would gradually tail off. Indeed some authorities with a very high rateable value, including the Inner London Education Authority and the Greater London Council, risked seeing their government grant shrink to nil if their spending exceeded a certain level.

The methods and indicators used to calculate how much each authority should be spending were so complex as to be virtually incomprehensible to anyone but statistically gifted accountants, and inaccessible to public debate. But many of the assessments were biased against the cities. The outcome was that the most-needy city areas were categorized, generally, as 'overspenders', although the poor state of services suggested that, if anything, they were underspending.

Hackney, like many other inner-city areas, was very severely affected by the combination of overall cuts plus regressive redistribution. Over the financial years 1981/2 and 1982/3, Hackney's grants from central government were £27 million down, in real terms, compared with their grant in 1979/80 – a loss of £418 for every household in the borough, or £4 a week. The borough itself made some cuts, though not deep ones, in its own services. Staff numbers fell by 8 per cent from 1979/80 to 1981/2 – characteristically, losses of manual jobs were twice as heavy as non-manual. The council operated a policy of no redundancies, so the staff savings came from leaving many vacancies unfilled, with chaotic effects on services: streets in some areas were not swept, toilets and baths were often closed outside working hours, pot-holes in the roads deepened. We shall see the disastrous effects that this has had on the two largest departments, housing and social services, in subsequent chapters.

Inner London boroughs are only partly masters of their own financial destinies: three providers of common services, the Metropolitan Police, the Greater London Council and the Inner London Education Authority, have the right to precept (levy) funds from the boroughs for their own purposes, which the boroughs must then charge to the rates. The GLC and the ILEA suffered very heavily from government penalties: ILEA lost the entirety of its grant of £125 million in 1981/2 and again the following year, but it refused to cut standards of education and had to raise its precept dramatically. The GLC's grant fell from 27 per cent of its budget in 1981/2 to nil in 1983/4, and its precept, too, went up.*

* In 1984 the Thatcher government passed controversial legislation to abolish the elected GLC and the other metropolitan authorities within whose boundaries the worst of Britain's inner cities lay – and to replace them with bodies appointed by lower-level local authorities. It also gave itself legal powers to prevent high-spending authorities from raising their rates to compensate for reductions in central government grants. This would force them to make deep cuts in already inadequate services and would result in large numbers of redundancies. Hackney Council, along with a number of other Labour councils, threatened to adopt a policy of no cuts, no redundancies, no rent or rate rises – which would quickly make the local authority bankrupt. The impact of the legislation, and the outcome of the political struggle, were still uncertain at the end of 1984.

It was a political battle between a Tory central government and Labour councils which refused to collaborate in dismantling their services and making their workers redundant. The overall outcome was paradoxical for both parties. On the one hand, rates, instead of falling as the Conservatives intended, registered record rises in many inner-city areas. On the other hand, Labour councils, committed to expanding local employment and assisting the poorest, found themselves (though many would not admit it) dealing local businesses and family budgets heavy blows. The rate bills of shops, offices and factories in Hackney almost trebled in the three years from 1978/9 on, raising costs, reducing profits, helping to drive many firms out of business or out of Hackney, and cutting local employment opportunities further. The average domestic rate bill grew even faster, from a mere £2·23 a week in 1978/9 to £7·71 in 1981/2 – a rise of 244 per cent. Non-take-up of supplementary benefits and rate rebates meant that many, especially low-paid workers, bore the full weight of the increase. In 1981/2 only 13 per cent of Hackney ratepayers were receiving rate rebates.

The lesson was clear: whether they cut services, or maintained them, there was no way local councils could protect the interests of their residents against a central government determined to undermine them. To the extent that local services were maintained, it was at the expense of the private welfare of poorer families – a transfer of personal income from essential private goods to essential public goods. Educational standards in inner London, for example, were kept up only by reducing the amount of cash local families had to spend on other things. The cost of keeping the schools going was often sending the children out without breakfast.

But most services were not maintained at their previous standard. Thus ratepayers paid out more than ever before – and received less in return. An increasing share of the cost of catering for need fell on the shoulders of the needy themselves – central government's contribution to Hackney Council spending fell from 57 per cent in 1977/8 to 36 per cent in 1982/3.

The second slump increased the need for public services by raising the pressures of poverty, pushing people towards family breakdown, homelessness, and physical and mental ill-health. Yet at the same time support services were reduced. The inverse-care law was seen to operate in time as well as in space: *when* the need was greatest, the service was poorest. Indeed, most of the government's actions served not to alleviate, but to intensify, the impact of the slump on the poor. Low demand and high unemployment had slowed, halted and in many cases reversed the growth in real incomes. The Thatcher government reduced disposable incomes even further by unprecedented rises in the incidence of direct and indirect taxation and national-insurance contributions on the poor – this from a government elected on a promise to cut taxation. And while private-sector essentials such as food, clothing and manufactures registered only modest price increases, there were steep rises in the prices of public goods and services. Compounding the rate rises were a series of government-ordered rent rises aimed at reducing the subsidy from the rates to council tenants. The average Hackney council rent almost doubled, from £5·68 in 1978/9 to £10·51 in 1981/2. Energy prices also rose fast, partly because of arbitrary government requirements for profits from nationalized industry. A typical weekly heating and hot-water charge for a Hackney council flat rose from £3·51 in 1978/9 to £9·09 in 1981/2, and the tenant would have had in addition to pay perhaps £2·12 a week, rising to £5·50 a week, for other energy.

Thus an average Hackney council tenant, who paid out only £13·54 a week for rent, rates and energy in 1978/9, was paying no less than £32·81 a week just three years later. The rise of £19·27 swallowed up many people's take-home-pay increases, and at 142 per cent over the three years was almost treble the rise of 50 per cent in the Retail Price Index (thereby demonstrating the RPI's insensitivity to the impact of inflation on different social groups). The conclusion is inescapable: the Thatcher government, which sacrificed the jobs and hopes of millions of people in the battle against inflation, was itself the major source of inflation for the lower-paid and council tenants.

The slump tended to increase inequalities, between those in work and those out of work, between earnings from industries, services and skills that were still in demand and those that were not. Instead of trying to alleviate those inequalities, the Tory government deliberately intensified them. The shift in government subsidy from the cities to the shires was only one element in this change. In addition, housing subsidies for council tenants were cut. In 1979 the average government subsidy for each council tenant had been £445. Five years later it had dwindled to nothing. But home owners – better off, on average, than council tenants – continued to enjoy subsidies worth an average of £170 a year in tax relief, ranging up to as much as £2,300 a year for top rate taxpayers with mortgages of £30,000 or more. Taxes on the rich were reduced, and those on the poor were greatly increased. A married couple with two children earning three-quarters of the national average income saw their taxes increase by 17 per cent from 1978/9 to 1982/3, while a similar family earning five times the national average enjoyed a cut of 6½ per cent. From 1979 to 1984, cuts in the real value of social security payments amounted to £6.5 billion, a loss of about £600 for each recipient – yet over this same period higher rate taxpayers received tax concessions worth £12.9 billion. Taken together these trends amounted to a very significant shift in the distribution of income, from the poor to the rich – a shift which occurred with surprisingly little publicity, public discussion or protest. Had the opposite shift occurred, how many outraged articles would we have read about the threat to freedom and to the incentive to work and save!

Thus poor families, like poor districts, received a double blow: stagnant or falling real incomes, plus a smaller share of the national cake. Absolute poverty and relative poverty, private squalor and public squalor, advanced simultaneously.

10   I'll Blow Your House Down

It is easier to build two chimneys than to maintain one.

English proverb

British cities are segregated by class just as surely as British factories, though more discreetly. There is some mixing in the middling areas. But those areas that have the best-built housing and the most attractive environment and amenities are over-whelmingly middle-class, while those with bad housing and poor amenities are overwhelmingly manual working-class. No laws of apartheid are needed to enforce this separation: it occurs as naturally as oil divides itself from water, by the play of unequal incomes and savings in the housing market.

The mechanism is simple. It is the state of the housing stock and the desirability of the neighbourhood that determines the level of rents and house prices, and these, in turn, determine the type of resident. Bad housing is cheap to buy or rent, and attracts the low-paid, the unemployed, immigrants, single parents, and the mentally and physically disabled. A concentration of bad housing in one area produces a concentration of disadvantaged people in that area. This fact by itself helps to make the place even more un-attractive to those with any choice, by generating high crime levels and lowering the academic and behavioural standards of local schools. Local residents with savings or incomes high enough to buy or rent in a better area, skills to find jobs in a better area, or the luck or manipulative ability to get themselves offered a council house in a better area, move out. What is left behind is a virtual social ghetto, where the problems generated by our social system are found in supersaturated solution.

Whereas the state of the local economy is decisive in the depressed regions, the state of housing is perhaps the single most important factor in creating the inner-city phenomenon. For it is low rents rather than the existence of low-paid jobs that induce the poor to come here and to stay here. Work is less intimately tied to the locality: many people travel outside the immediate area to work, just as, conversely, many of those who work in an inner-city area, especially those in the better-paid jobs, commute in from more desirable residential areas. The housing indeed may influence the local economy, for the presence of a pool of low-skilled, less-educated workers with low housing costs permits local enterprises to pay lower wages, and allows industries that would otherwise have been killed off earlier by competition from the Third World to survive longer than they would elsewhere.

But the state of housing is also the dominant feature in the landscape of daily lives. Home is where people spend half their waking hours – more than that if they are housewives or unemployed – and the quality of the home has a heavy impact on the quality of existence. The last two decades have seen some dramatic changes in Hackney's housing scene. In 1961, Hackney was predominantly an area of cheap, privately rented accommodation: 58 per cent of households lived in this type of dwelling, while 30 per cent were council tenants and a mere 12 per cent owner-occupiers. Twenty years on, after the massive rise in mortgage rates between 1978 and 1980, parts of Hackney had become targets for rapid gentrification. Teachers, lecturers, social and community workers, no longer able to afford houses in more fashionable Islington, began to move in, but not enough to alter more than marginally the basic social make-up: in 1981 owner-occupiers still accounted for only 16 per cent of households in Hackney, against a national average of 55 per cent. The major change was that the relative importance of council and private tenants had reversed under the impact of slum clearance and redevelopment, and restrictive Rent Acts that made many landlords prefer sale to continued renting. By 1981, private renting had dropped by more than half, to 26 per cent of households (still twice the national average), while the proportion of council tenants had almost doubled, to 57 per cent (the national figure was only 32 per cent).

This massive shift from private to public renting led to some improvements, most notably a halving of overcrowding and of the proportions lacking or sharing bath or toilet. But it did little to alter the social make-up of the borough, for the expanding council sector merely rehoused the poor from private rented accommodation. Indeed, as mobility from council housing is much more limited, this may have locked in the disadvantaged and drawn more permanent walls around the social ghetto.

And Hackney's housing remained, by national standards, appalling. In 1979–80 one in five dwellings in Hackney was unfit for human habitation – by far the highest of any London borough and more than twice the London average. Another 22 per cent of dwellings were in substantial disrepair. In material terms that means sodden basements, leaking roofs, draughty windows, perpetually peeling paper and crumbling plaster: in human terms, damp, cold, rheumatism, respiratory diseases and depression. The National Housing and Dwelling Survey in 1978 found that more than 7 per cent of households were overcrowded – occupied by more than one person per room. This was the third highest level in London, higher than any inner-city area outside London, and more than double the English average of 3·1 per cent. Many of the families I met were sleeping three or more to a bedroom, several of them two or more children to a bed, a number of them sleeping and living in one room. Over 19 per cent of Hackney households shared one or more than one amenity, lower than several traditional bed-sitter areas, but, again, higher than any district outside London and more than twice the average for England as a whole. In practical terms, this often means walking down one or more floors to toilet or bath, waiting around for other users to finish, and often, as responsibility for cleaning is confused, dirt and insanitation as well.

There are, too, other less commonly mentioned forms of housing deprivation. Most Hackney residents are denied the privacy and personal space which, in an era of increased egotism and reduced community solidarity, are essential to peace and sanity. Detached and semi-detached houses make up half the national housing stock: in Hackney they account for just over one-fiftieth. Only one in five dwellings, nationally, are flats, maisonettes or rented rooms. In Hackney, four out of five are, and in most cases they have no garden. In England as a whole, only 12 per cent of households do not have their feet on terra firma, with the lowest floor of their dwelling at ground level. In Hackney, no less than 55 per cent of household homes start on the first floor or higher, and 12 per cent on or above the twelfth floor.

Two final statistics give some idea of the level of discontent. In 1978, one household in four was dissatisfied with its accommodation, the second highest figure in the country (behind Tower Hamlets by the tip of a nose). And the numbers on the borough's waiting list for council homes, 15,000 in 1981, were equivalent to the sum of all the households in private rented accommodation and all households living as part of another household.

Refugees of the Welfare State

Homelessness is the most dramatic expression of housing stress. The intensity of that stress in Hackney can be judged from the fact that every year between 1,000 and 1,200 families – 5 or 6 per cent of all households with children – present themselves as statutorily homeless, that is, literally on the street or about to be put on to it. This is about ten times the national average. The proportion of families that have been through the trauma of homelessness at one time or another is probably five or ten times higher. And this is only a part of the problem, for it excludes all those whom the local authority has no legal responsibility to rehouse: the single, childless couples, or families with children who still have some kind of a roof over their heads, even if they are all sleeping on the floor in a friend's house.

The homeless who decide to seek public help for their plight gravitate to Hackney's Housing Emergency Section, housed behind a shop-front opposite the old Hackney Empire, once a famous music-hall, now a bingo hall. On a cold morning in December, an Asian family walks into the carpeted offices. The father, a tall thin man with tousled black hair and a military moustache, is carrying a one-year-old baby. Behind him a five-year-old son clutching a reading book, and a daughter of four, both in parkas, hoods up. At the rear his wife, in a dark-blue coat over flowered Asian trousers, carrying a two-month-old son in a quilted baby nest.

Two or three times a day a homeless family arrives here like this,

trailing children and assorted possessions. Mohammed Amir*
and his family had been evicted by his father in July. For five
months the six of them had been living in a single room of a friend's
flat, the children sleeping on the floor. During that time they could
not be helped, for they were not, statutorily speaking, homeless.
But today the friend's hospitality has come to an end and he needs
the room for a visiting brother.

Mohammed's parents hail from a small village in the Jhelum
district of Punjab state, Pakistan. His father, landless, joined the
army, then worked as a labourer in textile and cement factories.
Amir senior came to Britain in 1960, after his brother offered to
pay the air fare. Seven years later he brought over his wife and
children. With hard graft as a building labourer and a fitter
assembler, and with that astonishing capacity for saving that so
many Asian immigrants possess, he was able to buy his own house
in High Wycombe. He sold it to achieve the ambition of many
Asians: his own business. In 1975 he bought a grocer's shop in
Hackney, with accommodation on top.

Mohammed, now twenty-seven, remembers his first impres-
sions of England as a twelve-year-old: 'I was frightened by the
traffic. My village is a small village, only a few shops, the only
traffic there is horse-drawn cart.' He picked up English very
quickly and within a few years had two O-levels. His father had
grand ambitions that Mohammed should be a doctor, but his
grades were not good enough. Mohammed worked at Lesney's
making toy cars, then left to help his father in the shop. In 1976
he got married, and that was the beginning of his troubles.

'My father went to Pakistan to arrange a marriage. My wife
Khadija is my cousin, in my village her house is just there, across
the street from mine. I knew her when I was a boy. We got married
in Hackney town hall. But my mother doesn't like her, all the time
mother and wife fighting, mother saying you break this, you
shouldn't do cooking, you shouldn't go out of the house. My father
paid me nothing. We shared their food. Always there was trouble if
I wanted money to buy clothes. There were three bedrooms. My
family had one, my father and mother and my five brothers and

* Not his real name.

sisters the other two. My wife was getting very depressed. It was a small room, and all the time children were making noise, and sometimes she was beating the one and the other.' Back in Asia, this sort of tension would be contained indefinitely within the extended family. The daughter-in-law traditionally assumes the role of Cinderella of the household until her husband's mother dies. When he becomes the head of the household, she in turn assumes the role of matriarch and oppresses her own daughters-in-law. The moral pressures from members of the extended families of both spouses, members who have an interest in the survival of the marriage, combine to keep the young couple in place and to oblige them to internalize their anger. In Britain the pressure is absent, and the authoritarian style of the patriarchal family is in contradiction with everything the young couple can see around them. Living in Britain tends to explode the extended Asian family into its nuclear elements.

Things came to a head with the Amir family when Mohammed's father visited Pakistan again, with the idea of going back there to live and buying a business. Having spent his adolescence in Britain and formed his plans for adulthood here, Mohammed had no desire to go back. So he wrote to the Greater London Council and applied for a council house.

'But my father saw the letter and found out. He was angry; he said, if you plan to go, go now. He threw us out one night. When I went back to get our clothes, he talked with me and said I should stay. I thought maybe it was going to be all right, and so we went back. But after only one day the fighting with my mother and my sister began again. So we left home very early morning 6 a.m., because we didn't want to have argument. We stayed with my friend in Chingford, but he had no room. Then we went to my friend who is manager of Clapton mosque. We had left most of our clothes behind, I had to buy new ones. We had savings of £800 because all the time we had banked the family allowance. But that is nearly gone now, maybe £100 left. We try to do without luxury things, we use meat only once a week, we eat a lot of vegetables and chapatis. My wife's mother, when she heard of our troubles, wanted me to send her back to Pakistan. Her father loved her very much. He died four, five years ago in Saudi Arabia. He was changing the tyre of the lorry he was driving, but it was overheated. Someone threw water on it, and it exploded in his face.'

Thus the tragedies of a couple from a poor village in the Punjab are enacted half-way across the globe, twice over a victim of crisis, fleeing from poverty in Asia, straight into poverty in Britain. Along with his home, Mohammed also lost his job in his father's shop. Mohammed had been trying to look for a job, but without success. His wife's childbirth and the uncertainty of their situation had not helped: 'I am lost myself. I don't know where I am. Other times I came here, they could never give me nothing. I think they think I am lying. But if I have money, I never come to these people, believe me. I don't want to go to bed-and-breakfast place. I don't want to stay in council place. I want to start own business and maybe get accommodation on top. I need about £3,000 to start, then maybe I can borrow the rest from somebody. I can save fast, the way I plan to work. I don't drink and I don't go to cinema. I want to do minicab work. I bought car two weeks ago for £150. If you work hard, you can earn maybe £200 or £250 in a week. I have to save. If I can't save I get nowhere, just eat and sleep, no meaning of life. I want to make something of my life in this world.'

The Bed-and-Breakfast Belt

South of Finsbury Park is an area dominated by cheap hotels, of the modest kind where commercial travellers for small firms might put up for the night, in large, converted detached houses, or whole sections of terrace. This is the heartland for Hackney's homeless, and for many from neighbouring boroughs, putting up in places like the Maryland, Finsbury, Gresyl, Brownswood and Central Park. From outside there is little indication of the true function of these cold-climate refugee camps, except perhaps for a glimpse of an exotically dressed oriental lady and her three dark-eyed children gazing languidly out of an upper window. Inside the Central Park, the noise of televisions on in mid-afternoon, of children's feet running down long corridors with a drumming of floor-boards, and doors half open on to cramped bedrooms full of people and possessions reveal that this is a place of transition, a limbo for some of the lost souls of our society. Some were made homeless by flood or fire, most by man-made crises: out of every twenty, ten will be here because of disputes with parents or friends who had been putting them up, two because of broken marriages, and three because of eviction.

Family conflict was the reason for the presence of Rachel*, a self-possessed nineteen-year-old, with long black hair. She and her four-year-old son Michael* were housed in a single room in the annexe of the Central Park Hotel. Into a space about 3 metres by 2½ metres was crammed a wardrobe, a wash-basin, a fridge, a large television set and a double bed which she and Michael shared, leaving a space only 1 metre square in the middle to stand up in. She spent her days watching television from her bed or walking around Finsbury Park. For cooking, she used a small stove, in a room open only from 12 till 1 at midday and from 6 till 7 in the evening. If she misses these times or the stove is too busy, she goes across the road to the main hotel building and warms up a can of soup.

Rachel's first years of adulthood were not unlike those of many white working-class girls in Hackney: 'I had Michael when I was fifteen. We had a bit of sex education in school, but my mother taught me it was bad to have sex before marriage. I didn't think to go and ask anyone like a doctor for advice about contraceptives – I was afraid my mum would find out. So I went and got myself pregnant. I was too frightened to tell anyone, and I left it too late to have an abortion. My mother sent me away to a home in Brixton to have the baby, so the neighbours wouldn't know. Then she said I could only go back home if I let her adopt Michael. My mother is forty, but she's one of these women who likes to look young, you know, she's always asking people "How old d'you think I am?" She'd love to have a young boy so she could say he was her son. But I refused to sign anything. She let me come home anyway. It was all one happy family – except for me. She started fighting with me. She provoked me and provoked me. I just had to get out.'

She left Michael with her mother and moved in with her boy-friend's parents, but there were more arguments there too. From there they moved into a decrepit two-roomed furnished flat

* Not their real names.

in Amhurst Road, paying the princely rent of £27 a week. 'The cooker and the sink were on the landing. There was no bath or shower. We had to use the sink to wash in. The toilet was out in the back garden. We threw out all the furniture – it had fleas in it. The couch was full of mice droppings, I think they'd been nesting in there. There was no lock on the front door, and we had our stereo taken. I'd been on the council waiting-list for two years, but whenever I went there they said it was the same as everyone else, as long as I had a roof over my head, it didn't concern them.

'Then we got the chance of a flat in a block run by a charity. We didn't apply regular, we just bought the key and the rent book off a tenant who was moving out. We paid him £150. But the other people who lived there knew we shouldn't be there, and the caretaker complained. We had to leave after a few weeks. My boy-friend went back to his parents and I went back to my mum's. But she kept trying to take Michael off me. She had a black boy-friend, he would come with a bag of sweets and tell Michael to call him "dad". She split up with him, but he kept coming round to the house smashing the place up. Then my brother got into trouble with the police and they came round and searched everything. I just didn't think it was a good place for Michael to be brought up in. So I went to see the housing and said I had nowhere to go. That was how I got here. They said I might be here for seven months before they give me a flat.'

There are other groups of homeless who are harder to help. Most single homeless are no longer the traditional male down-and-outs in the latter half of their lives: they are getting younger and younger as the nuclear family shatters into its constituent particles. Young girls and boys leave home rather than put up with the bitter tensions of chaotic family lives. Hackney's Housing Advisory Centre sees as many as 2,000 single homeless in a year. Four out of every five are under twenty-five, and a large proportion of these are black.

There is little that can be done to help them. Bedsits make up only 6 per cent of Hackney's housing stock, though single people account for two-fifths of the waiting-list. There are agencies specializing in short-life tenancies – giving young people three or four months in a council-owned house unfit for normal habitation, waiting for funds to rehabilitate it. But the majority have to fend for themselves, and many young blacks end up sleeping on friends' floors or, in one case I heard of, in an airing cupboard.

Open homelessness, when people are literally on the street, is merely the tip of an iceberg of hidden need. There are around 2,000 families known mysteriously as 'concealed households', that is, living as part of another household, with friends, relatives, or usually parents. One in ten of all households with children in Hackney belongs to this category. It has always been common practice, in working-class households, for young couples to share with parents until they can get a home of their own: it reduces housing costs and increases the chances of getting a council house, because the overcrowding gives them higher points. But as expectations rise, and parental authority wanes, this arrangement is becoming less and less tolerable.

The Crumbling Private Sector

The past and present state of private-sector housing is the key to Hackney's destiny. For, although council housing has now taken over the role of providing accommodation to the majority, it is through the private sector that new arrivals to Hackney gain access to council housing. It is the rooming-house that acts as the inner city's recruiting officer. This is the first filter that ensures that most newcomers will be among the poorest and most disadvantaged families in London.

The private sector, which comprises property built overwhelmingly before 1919, and most of it between 1860 and 1890, is in the worst physical condition. As we saw in Chapter 2, that is not simply a matter of age. A great deal of Hackney's Victorian housing was built on unsuitable ground, with poor or skimped materials, by cowboy builders of the day who did not care if what they built started to fall apart after a few years. A lot of the worst housing has done just that, a lot more was destroyed by the Blitz and more went under the bulldozer after the war. Indeed the present large extent of council housing in Hackney, as in other inner cities, is partly a product of the appalling state of the slums which it replaced. Nevertheless, there are still 24,000 private dwellings in Hackney and they house 63,000 people. Two-thirds of this stock, in 1980, was either unfit or in need of substantial repairs. Two out of five of its units were unfit for human habitation, and many of these would involve demolition or extensive rebuilding. One in ten was fit but lacked basic amenities. Another one in six required repairs costing £3,000 or more. Within the private sector, it is the rented accommodation that is in the worst physical shape. In 1980 there were about 5,000 'houses in multiple occupation' (HMOs) in Hackney, containing more than one separate household. Almost half of these were the subject of enforcement orders from Hackney Council's environmental health department, requiring their landlords to remedy defects dangerous to life or health, to provide additional services, or to reduce overcrowding. In the Rectory Road Housing Action Area, only three out of 131 HMOs were considered to be in a satisfactory condition. In the Palatine Road Action Area, only one out of ninety-two required no action.

In addition, the private rented sector also offers the most degraded human environment. In 1981, 6,762 households (4 per cent of the borough total) were occupying *unfurnished* rented accommodation. Overcrowding was not too serious (6 per cent), but 23 per cent had no bath, 12 per cent had no inside toilet, 9 per cent had neither bath nor toilet. The *furnished* rented sector was the most overcrowded in Hackney – 12 per cent of the 5,400 households were occupied by more than one person per room. Few lacked bath or toilet, but almost half had to share these facilities with other households.

Badly built in the first place, Hackney's Victorian terraces were badly maintained thereafter. Like clapped-out old cars, they were cheap to buy but very expensive to keep going in decent shape. Then, as the people who buy cheap houses, whether to live in or to rent out, are often short on income or capital, the essential maintenance simply was not done. Neglect was added to sloppy construction.

The end result is visible even to the untrained eye, in luxurious proliferations of lichens, moulds and mosses that would offer a fertile ground for botanical study, and abstract collages of crumbled, cracked and flaking paint, plaster, pointing and stonework.

In many others, the underlying troubles are concealed behind a dash of paint or a slap of rendering. The extent of the problem has led local housing associations to press for a special 'Hackney factor' to be added on to the normal government cost limits for rehabilitation work. Many of the brick walls are only 9 inches (23 cm) thick and, instead of being bonded together like most 9-inch walls, consist of two entirely separate skins, each 4½ ins thick. The motive for this unorthodox method is to prevent the cheap and nasty second-hand bricks used for the inner skin from being seen on the outside. For the same reason, the front and rear elevations are often not bonded to internal walls or party walls, so they can move independently and bow out. Foundations are often inadequate, resulting in wall fractures, sloping floors, twisted roofs, back extensions pulling away from the main body of the house. Despite Hackney's high water table, damp-proof courses of any kind are virtually non-existent. The lowest metre of basement walls is frequently saturated and basement timbers rotted. Dry rot extends its cancerous white tentacles through many houses, digesting and cracking higher floors and ceilings. Roof slates suffer from 'nail sickness', a flaking around the nail.

The problem afflicts owner-occupied as well as rented property. Apart from the new gentry, most owner-occupiers are old people or first-generation immigrants who cannot begin to contemplate the costs, running into many thousands, of bringing their properties up to a decent standard and keeping them there. Most big landlords have now sold out to the council or to housing associations. The remaining landlords are small-timers, many of them immigrants, who rent out part of the house they live in, or own one or two houses besides their own – the exact parallel of those who invest their modest savings to start up, for example, a little clothing factory. Rents vary a great deal, but a large number are very modest by London standards – typical figures for 1981 would be £7 to £10 a week for a bedsit, £10 to £15 for two rooms, £20 for three rooms. The gross income from the three-storey house might often total only £25 to £50 per week – less, after deducting tax and expenses, than might be had from selling the place with vacant possession and investing the proceeds in a building-society account.

Titanic Terrace

A stone's throw from my old home in Rochdale is a terrace known as 'Titanic Row' because it is visibly pitching and sinking. It would be an apt name for numbers 87–99 Rectory Road, south-west of the junction with Brooke Road. The row of three-storey houses was built about a century ago. The site was a former clay-pit backfilled with public refuse – developers further down the road have had to dig down 6 metres to find subsoil solid enough to lay reasonable foundations on. The houses at each end of the terrace slope outwards. Some of the front walls have sunk, cracking window and door arches. At the rear are two-storey extensions which are breaking away and sinking.

Number 87 is a typical example. Deep fissures streak the entrance porch and several window-sills and lintels. One of the columns supporting the bay window has cracked and been patched up with cement. The front has not been painted for at least twenty years, the sills are peeled, down to the bare, crumbling stone.

A house is not merely a physical entity. It is the product of social relations, of builder and buyer, of landlord and tenant, of successive generations of inhabitants and owners with particular incomes. The occupants are an inseparable part of the story. Number 87 presently contains two households, an Asian landlord and his family occupying the upper two floors, and an ageing West Indian couple renting the ground floor.

Martin Hackshaw and his wife Catherine are both in their sixties. Hackshaw had a 1-hectare plot in the hills of St Vincent, in the Windward Islands off the coast of Venezuela, growing enough for his own meagre needs plus a little to sell. The Hackshaws came over in 1957, leaving behind their children, all old enough to fend for themselves. In those expansive days Martin found a job within three weeks of arriving, at a small machine-tool factory. He left after being refused compensation for an accident that nearly cost him his eyes: 'What going on in this country is, if you don't put it in court, you don't get nothing.' But he returned to the same factory in 1974. He was made redundant in May 1982. He gets £22·50 unemployment benefit (1982). His wife Catherine gets a pension of £23·65, plus £29 a week from a part-time job in a clothing factory.

The rent they pay, for three rooms, kitchen and toilet, is only £7·30 a week, but Hackshaw thinks that is too much. He showed me round. The front room, half filled with double-stacked trunks full of possessions, and with an embroidered map of St Vincent on the wall, is the only entirely habitable room in the place. The rear bedroom, adorned with Christian slogans and an enormous full-length portrait of the Queen, suffers from penetrating damp: rain enters through broken pointing and seeps down the wall at the rear, close by where Catherine's head rests when she sleeps. The french windows leaked for years until the former landlord sealed them with an unsightly sheet of zinc flashing nailed over the step and the bottom of the door in a typical Hackney repair job: don't get to the root of the problem, just cover it up.

But the worst part of the flat is the single-storey extension added on to the back, an extension of an extension, which houses the kitchen and toilet. The roof is corrugated asbestos sheet: rain leaks in between roof and wall, through the crest of each corrugation. The kitchen is about 2 metres square, and contains an antique gas stove, a porcelain sink 60 centimetres by 45 centimetres that would barely accommodate a single stack of dinner plates, and an ascot heater that doesn't work, so that kettles have to be boiled for hot water. At first sight there appears to be no bath, but it is hidden, here in the kitchen, under a hardboard work-top covered in flowered Fablon. The toilet is reached through a covered back entrance, open at the side. Its undulating floor has subsided to a depth of 15 centimetres in parts. All the roof plaster has fallen off, revealing the laths underneath.

'This house is all bad,' Catherine complains. 'This is the *worst* place. In winter all the walls, all the ceiling does be wet. We can't use the toilet and the kitchen when it rains. January the 14th this year, we couldn't sleep in here, we had to sleep with friends. I got nose bleeds. I got high blood pressure.' 'I tell you, friend,' Martin chips in, 'but for God's mercy we both be dead in here. And those council people say we don't have enough points for a council place. Where they get this idea of stupid points, when people is living in these conditions? They are too slothful. They will see a thing is bad, but they will wait till it go to nothing before they do something.'

The Hackshaws moved in in 1969, and complained repeatedly

to the former Jewish landlord. After getting no action, Martin complained to the council from 1974 on, and enforcement orders were made requiring the landlord to do repairs. But nothing was done. Faced with a massive repair bill he couldn't afford, the landlord solved his own problem by selling the place, in 1980, to its present owner, Kurha Singh.

Singh is a tall and handsome twenty-nine-year-old Sikh, sans turban or beard, though his two boys aged two and three wear little handkerchief-wrapped topknots, possibly on the insistence of their rosy-cheeked mother (now nursing a third baby son) whom Singh brought from India to marry. He hardly conforms to the traditional idea of the landlord. His own parents brought him to this country from Gwalior in India when he was small. He left school at sixteen, without qualifications, worked for a few years as a tailor, then got a job in a glass factory in New Cross, south of the river, sorting returned bottles. He works shifts and brings home £89 a week including overtime. In June 1982 he learned that the factory would close at the end of the year with the loss of several hundred jobs. Child benefit and the Hackshaws' rent push the family's net income up to £112 a week (1982).

Singh is more exploited than exploiting. He paid £11,500 for the house. That was probably somewhat over the going rate, as he could not afford to pay a surveyor who might have alerted him to some of the less obvious defects and brought the price down somewhat, or deterred him from buying. Nor could he get an ordinary mortgage – no building society would have made a loan secured on such a shaky property. He had saved £5,000 of the price from ten years of hard work and self-denial; £3,000 he borrowed from relatives, to be paid back in dribs and drabs whenever he had the money. The final £3,000 he borrowed from a finance company, repaying £30·90 a week, at an effective annual interest rate of around 30 per cent, more than double what a building society would have charged.

The local-authority rates amount to a massive £14·50 a week: the Hackshaws' rent barely covers half of that, let alone allowing for any repairs or maintenance. All that our 'landlord' has left after fares to work and housing costs (not counting repayments to relatives) is £60·60 a week for the five of them: that is £1·12 below the official poverty line as defined by supplementary benefits level. Singh cannot claim Family Income Supplement or the free school meals, free baby milk and other exemptions that go with it, as his income is too high.

Out of this subsistence income our landlord has to try to meet the massive expenses of repairing a house that is already, by official standards, unfit for human habitation, and that could well fall down entirely within the decade without drastic remedial measures. Singh has already spent more than £500 since he moved in, on rewiring (visibly a cowboy job – the wires hang away from the walls in many places), on patching the worst leaks in the roof, and on removing an enormous pile of rubble in the front garden. But many urgent jobs still remain, awaiting the day when Singh will have the spare cash to do them. The Singh family occupies only the top floor: the lounge, furnished with a cheap second-hand plastic-covered suite, is spacious. The whole family sleep in a single small bedroom about 3 metres square into which are crammed bunk-beds for the two older boys, a cot for the three-month-old baby, a double-bed for parents, and innumerable bags and cases full of clothing piled on top of two wardrobes. The kitchen is half a floor down, in the rear extension: as on the ground floor, the bath is here too, next to the cooker, covered with a work-top. The toilet is one floor down again. The landing ceiling sports gaping holes through to the roof. On one side are the marks of years of rainwater cascading down the wallpaper. On the wall of the landing that gives on to the rear, the plaster has crumbled away, revealing shoddy bricks with two long zigzag cracks, through which daylight is clearly visible. The first-floor flat is empty. Singh is gradually renovating the rooms for his own use and recently spent £240, plus materials, on having two rooms replastered. The previous tenant, tired no doubt of the noise of three small children, agreed to move out for a consideration of £300.

Relations between the Singhs and the Hackshaws are tense, as is inevitable between landlord and tenant. 'He is living in a better place than me,' Singh complains, 'and his wife is working and my wife is not. He complains all the time that he wants repairs doing. I would like to increase his rent, but my brother advised me not to, he said if I went to the [rent] tribunal they will tell me to repair the place, and I can't afford to. I asked Mr Hackshaw to help me clear the back garden, but he refused to help me.' When I asked to see the Hackshaws' flat, Singh rapped on their door.

'Who is it?' Catherine Hackshaw asked in a high-pitched voice.

'Me,' was the peremptory reply. Catherine allowed us in to see the bedroom, then Martin appeared, in outdoor trousers and pyjama top, and ordered us out. 'I didn't mean you,' he told me when Singh had left the room, 'but I ain't having *him* jumping in where I sleep at night.' He proceeded to list his complaints about Singh, which were a mirror image of Singh's complaints about him: 'When I first came here in 1969, they tell me this garden was for me. Now he wants his children to play there, and he ask me to help him to clean it up. Well I ain't going to. If he wants his children there, let him clean it. He asked me to pay more rent. I told him no, or I go to the town hall about that list of repairs he have to do.' He smiles knowingly, like someone who has their opponent over a barrel. Catherine speaks up, quite agitated: 'When them cooking up there it *stink*. And that hall there, they never take broom and sweep it. Those children, they tear my carpet in the hall.' Martin starts up again: 'He leave old things in that passage and block it up. And that doorbell, ringing, ringing all the time. It just ring seven times for him this morning and it don't ring once for us.'

It was a sorry drama: two families, both victims of colonialism and global inequalities, both at the bottom of the British heap; two men, one unemployed, the other about to become so – forced to feud by circumstances caused by their common poverty, over shared space, over rent, over the dreadful state of the house, which is a tribulation for all its occupants.

Number 87 Rectory Road embodies the destiny of Hackney's Victorian housing. Under the former absentee Jewish landlord, rents for the whole house were very low, not more than £800 a year in the mid-seventies, and repairs costing many thousands of pounds were required. The bad state of the property meant that rents could not be raised much without the risk of a rent tribunal lowering them below their previous levels: hence no capital could be generated to improve its state. Repairing the place was quite simply economically irrational: the interest on the investment needed would not only far exceed the expected *increase* in rents that could be charged, it would also exceed the *total* rents for the property. Indeed the whole business of owning such a place and renting it out was economically irrational: selling it and investing the proceeds in a building society would produce a higher net income, for far less effort and anxiety. As a result it was sold for owner-occupation. But the new owner is forced to rent out part of it to help repay his loans. He has a strong personal interest in repairing the house and makes strenuous efforts, but his income is so low that his entire programme of works to date is no more than a finger in the dyke. Thus the house is trapped in a vicious downward spiral of decay that had persisted for years and could only end in dereliction or the intervention of a *deus ex machina*.

The *deus* arrived in 1981 when the terrace was included in the Rectory Road Housing Action Area. HAA legislation empowers the local authority to compel house owners to improve their property, and to give them grants of 75 to 90 per cent towards the cost. The grant limit for a two-family house was £26,600, subject to the rule that the market value of the refurbished property must be greater than the cost of repairs. Two insoluble problems present themselves in the case of number 87. Singh cannot possibly afford the £3,000 to £9,000 that would be required of him as a contribution. Therefore, if rehabilitation was to go ahead, the house would have to be compulsorily bought off him. Second, the estimated cost of repairing the place to give it a thirty-year life expectancy would be £50,000 plus, way above the subsequent market value. It looked very much as if the houses of Titanic Row would end their sorry lives under the demolisher's hammer. Hackshaw would be re-housed by the council and finally realize the ambition that years of damp and degradation had not achieved. Singh would be compensated at the market value of the house; not much more, and possibly less, than he paid for it. Singh would, in all probability, move on to buy another decrepit house and continue the unhappy cycle, as destructive as death-watch beetle, of low incomes and housing decay.

The Ultimate Rooming-House

The private rented sector houses a constantly changing population, moving in and out as their destinies change, but never staying for long, because no one who could avoid it would stay in such conditions for a day or a minute longer than was necessary. Take one such house in Colvestone Crescent, parallel to Ridley Road market. It has three floors and a basement. In 1979, the occupancy was as follows: in the basement a twenty-three-year-old student and his wife in the front room and a twenty-one-year-old female accounts clerk in the back. On the ground floor, a twenty-one-year-old African student. On the first floor two African cousins, in their twenties, studying at Hornchurch and at Havering. On the top floor a twenty-seven-year-old machinist working in Hornsey and a twenty-nine-year-old accountant commuting to Cricklewood, plus his wife and small baby. Seven households in all, in a house limited by council order to three. A mere eighteen months later, all the occupants except those in the basement had left and were replaced by another motley collection of human beings, amounting to nine households, most of them on higher rents.

Successive Rent Acts have, in theory, provided private tenants with a high degree of security and protection against uncontrolled rent rises. One of the unintended results of that legislation has been the dramatic decrease in the number of properties available for private renting: Rent Acts had protected those with tenancies at the expense of those without, especially newly formed households, making it much more difficult for them to find a home.

In practice the law is widely avoided, evaded, ignored or blatantly flouted. The economic irrationality of renting at the prevalent rent-tribunal-fixed rents provides the stimulus. If the landlord is lucky, the tenants will not be aware of their legal rights and will not have recourse to the tribunal. Tribunal decisions, in any case, are not always respected.

Another commercial pressure on landlords, as gentrification spreads in Hackney, is the increasing inducement to sell for owner-occupation. A three-storey terraced house, in poor repair and full of tenants, would fetch only £7,000 or £8,000 in 1981. With vacant possession, it might command £20,000. The housing market put a bounty of £3,000 to £4,000 on the head of every evicted tenant.

Thus the economics of private renting or of speculative sale both push landlords, whether out of greed or out of need, into harassment of their tenants. Harassment is very widespread in Hackney. In the Palatine Road Housing Action Area, for example, there were no less than 101 reported cases of harassment from only 217 private rented dwellings in the five years from 1976. Each year, therefore, one tenant in eleven was harassed. The rate for the Rectory Road Housing Action Area was exactly the same. These are the known cases. Many are not reported: the tenant would simply leave, or pay the higher rent. The techniques of harassment are legion: the most common is a simple instruction to leave, without the necessary notice or legal procedure. Landlords also resort to turning off gas, electricity and water, locking up the bathroom and toilet, changing locks, threatening or using violence, pulling down walls and starting major repairs with the tenant in place. More subtle techniques are harder to pin down as harassment, especially if the landlord is resident: obstruction of entrances and passageways, noise, or the irritation of children, dogs, or constant argument about rent and repairs.

And the law still leaves several legal ways of denying tenants security of tenure or freedom from frequent arbitrary rent rises: the increase in 'holiday lets', the new short-term contracts introduced by the Thatcher government, or the ingenious expedient of calling your property a hotel or lodging-house and providing token meals.

Number 74 Colvestone Crescent carries no hotel sign and has no name. Outwardly it is indistinguishable from the rest of the terrace: semi-basement and three floors, average state of repair. With the council it is registered for use as a single-family dwelling. But inside it has been converted with considerable dexterity into no less than eighteen separate units. What was the old front room has been divided into two compartments, each enjoying half of the bay window. The large front room on the first floor has been segmented lengthwise into three units, and so on throughout, some of the rooms little more than cubicles, with makeshift plywood doors. Nor are the common facilities too attractive. The toilet on the ground floor stinks, the hardboard roof is collapsing and sodden with damp. There are two bathrooms. The one on the ground floor is passable, but the top bathroom has a gaping hole in the window through which breezes blow, so no one bathes there. In effect, eighteen households have to share one bath.

The residents are mostly single men, many of them unemployed, often with physical or mental health problems, some of them ex-offenders. Some are in work: a railwayman, a labourer in a whisky depot, a nightshift worker at Lesney's. The turnover is as rapid as that of piles of driftwood on the beach. The rooms cost anything from £30 to £50 a week (1981). So that the place can be described as a 'hotel', the services include a weekly change of sheets and two meals a day, at 12 noon and 5.30 p.m. These are served two or three hundred metres away, at a tiny café on Shacklewell Lane, with a few cramped Formica-topped tables. Because the place passes for a hotel, residents have no security of tenure and no protection against a rapid succession of rent rises. The total income from the house, when fully occupied, was well over £500 a week in 1981.

In one half of the old first-floor front room live seventeen-year-old Stephanie Kirk and her boy-friend Paul Burns, nineteen. They are newcomers to Hackney, driven there, like so many others, by housing and income stresses. Stephanie is pallid, her red hair falls over her eyes, her voice is a soft, melancholic croak, and she wears a dressing-gown though it is 2 in the afternoon. The room which is their home is about 2½ metres wide and 5 metres long. The red, flowered carpet is worn to a shiny black in parts. At the window end is a lumpy old double bed. The couple have lived here for five months. Stephanie is from Romford, Paul from Stratford, East London. They decided to live together when Stephanie was just sixteen. 'We couldn't live with my mum because Paul doesn't get on with my brothers, and we couldn't live with his mum because she only has two bedrooms and her and his dad have one each. So we went to live with his sister. She's been squatting for nine years. We stayed with her for eighteen months. We were at 74 Brougham Road, then at 69 Shrubland Road, then at 33 Amhurst Road, then at 22 Amhurst, then at 52 Brougham Road. [Brougham Road and Shrubland Road are close to the planning-blighted Broadway Market area, the only area of extensive squatting in Hackney.]

Paul's sister always squats in places belonging to the council or housing associations, because it takes them at least three months to get you out, but if it's private, they can get you out much faster.

'I was an office junior, I was bringing home £35 a week. Paul was doing odd labouring jobs, nothing permanent, because he can't read or write. We managed all right, we weren't going short, because we weren't paying any rent. But in June [1981] we had a bit of an argument with his sister and moved out. We went to the council, but they said we weren't their responsibility. To get on the waiting-list you've got to have lived in Hackney for a year, and with being squatters, we had no proof. They told us they'd have helped us if we'd had children. They gave us a list of bed-and-breakfast places we could try, and this was one of them. We had to give up our jobs to live here: it would be impossible to work and be able to live paying this rent, but now we don't work, the social security pay it for us. Sitting in this room all day makes you miserable, but we can't afford to go out. We just get miserable and then we start arguing over stupid little things. It looked worse than this when we moved in. We put up pictures. That chest of drawers is ours, the rug is ours. It's all second-hand. There was a little fire, but it didn't work. That fire is ours. We have asked for a new mattress – my boy-friend says this one is giving him a bad back. But the landlord said he'll be selling the place soon, it's not worth spending any money on it. He says the person who's going to buy it will make it into four flats. Then we won't have nowhere to live, we'll have to go to another bed-and-breakfast place. We could get a council flat if we had a baby, it would be quicker, but we want to be settled and have a home first before we have any kids.' I asked her how she hoped her life would look when she was, say, thirty. 'I suppose we will get a home, some day. I never look that far ahead. There's no point. We just live from day to day.'

The crisis in jobs and in housing had closed up her horizons, like a thick curtain of fog, reducing visibility to the next few weeks ahead. People with no future, drifting in time on the tiny raft of the present.

Improving the Private Stock

It is an unfortunate fact of life in Britain that political policies often produce the opposite effect to the one intended. It is partly the result of class warfare fought to a paralysing standstill, partly the result of pursuing reforms piecemeal with insufficient feedback and monitoring.

Hackney's Labour council decided in 1978 that the only sure way of removing exploitation and poor conditions in the private rented sector was to municipalize it. A massive programme of council purchase of terraced houses began. But hardly had this got under way, than the Tory government's deep cuts in public expenditure started, and the money to repair and rehabilitate these houses evaporated. The better ones were drawn into use for short-life schemes. But by March 1981, no fewer than 2,354 properties owned by Hackney Council were standing empty – almost 1,000 of them for over a year – their doors and windows bricked-up or tinned-up to keep out squatters and vandals. The sight of these empties was a perpetual irritant to those without proper homes of their own: everyone mentioned them. The lone Tory on Hackney council called for their sale, but this it was argued would simply bring in owner-occupiers and reduce the stock potentially available to meet Hackney's crushing housing need. The empties became a blasted no man's land in the battle between a monetarist government and socialist city councils. In addition, there were upwards of 2,000 private dwelling spaces vacant in April 1981, many of them kept vacant by landlords waiting for other tenants to move out so they could sell their houses with vacant possession.

The other major policy weapon for reversing the decay of the private Victorian stock was to declare a Housing Action Area. HAAs, as we have seen, have almost military powers to compel landlords to carry out the improvements that council surveyors deem to be necessary. But the end result is highly ambivalent. The physical state and life expectancy of the property is improved, as are the amenities for tenants. But there are undesirable social consequences. Rents are raised by 50 to 100 per cent, causing hardship for many tenants. Landlords sell out to owner-occupiers whenever they can. The total number of units to let is reduced, and the disadvantaged are supplanted by gentrifying professional couples.

The problem seems insoluble, and indeed it is, within the parameters of our present social structures. If inner-city housing is improved to acceptable standards, many inner-city residents are unable to afford economic rents for that improved housing, and will have to move elsewhere, creating another inner-city area wherever rents are cheapest. Only a truly massive injection of government funds can solve the problem of physical decay. Only radical reforms in income distribution and income support can enable inner-city residents to afford decent housing.

The problem is not confined to the inner city. Decaying housing can be found in scattered pockets everywhere – wherever occupants or landlords – public or private – cannot afford to maintain or improve their property. Recession and public-spending cuts have generalized the problem. Many more owner-occupiers with static or declining real incomes are no longer able to repair or rehabilitate their houses. The depression, compounded by the cuts, is deepening and spreading the kind of housing conditions that create the inner city, just as it is generalizing the economic decay that overshadows it.

11 Unfreedom of Choice: Council Housing

No one sweeps a common hall.
                    Chinese proverb

For a large proportion of Hackney's residents, the principal ambition is to get out of Hackney. Away to Romford or to Milton Keynes, to Enfield, Basingstoke – anywhere. Anywhere with little semis, and gardens, and countryside not too far away, and streets you can walk down without always looking behind you. It's not all that much to ask of life. Nevertheless, many of them know, deep in their hearts, that they will never achieve it. For most of those who do not already possess one, the major objective becomes the acquisition of a not-too-undesirable council house: for those who do, the acquisition of a less undesirable one than the one they have already.

The ideals of council housing that motivated Hackney's largely working-class councillors in the first three post-war decades were noble: to take families out of those overcrowded tenements, with shared or absent baths or toilets; to remove them from exploitation and insecurity; to provide decent, sound houses, each with their own bath, toilet and kitchen; to give tenants a humane and benevolent landlord without an interest in profit, offering secure tenures, rents they could afford, exemplary service. There may have been a time, in the 1950s perhaps, when these dreams were roughly approximated by reality. In the inner cities of the early 1980s, they ring extremely hollow. For many of yesterday's pristine estates have become today's slums, some of them fit only for demolition, many more requiring massive and expensive repairs and remodelling to make them anywhere near habitable. Powerlessness in the face of profiteering landlords has been supplanted by powerlessness against distant and often unresponsive bureaucracies. Social ghettoes in terraced Victorian streets have been reproduced, in more destructive form, in Elizabethan blocks. Private squalor in rented rooms has been replaced by public squalor in rented flats. The state of public housing, indeed, has become one of the central problems of the inner city. Slump and spending cuts have led to further deterioration and the delay of remedies.

Public Architecture: a Crime against Humanity

Poor construction and poor maintenance were, as we have seen, the central problems of Hackney's Victorian terraces. Ironically, the council estates built to replace them have suffered from precisely the same defects. The result is that estates less than forty years' old are already slums – indeed some estates took only a decade to become slums.

Out of Hackney's 46,000 council houses and flats,* some 4,000 (9 per cent) were unfit for human habitation in 1979 and a further 8,900 (19 per cent) needed substantial renovation or repairs, not counting those that required remodelling to make them come anywhere near modern expectations of a decent home. The cost of repair alone was estimated at £41 million in 1979. The cost of turning all of Hackney's estates into homes for human beings has not been estimated, but might easily be five to ten times higher.

Architecture, management and allocation all bear a share of the blame.

The architecture of public housing until the later seventies was a catalogue of disasters. The price of those errors is paid, not by those who made them, but by the unfortunate people who still live with them. Council-housing design, until quite recently, was the expression of middle-class ideas imposed on working-class communities with no power to influence what was provided. In the case of private housing, consumers have the power of money: what they

* In 1981, 18,000 of these belonged to the Greater London Council. Applicants obtained GLC dwellings by being nominated by Hackney Council. In April 1982, ownership of GLC properties was transferred to the borough councils. To simplify matters, discussion of council housing refers to 1981 Hackney properties. The principles, the social effects and the physical state are roughly the same.

don't like, they won't buy. With public housing, consumers have no choice, nor has there been until the last few years any effective channel through which architects could be informed of people's real and felt housing needs. Thus architects were liberated from responsibility to the consumer. They could realize their secret dream of being not simply glorified masons, but sculptors of space and designers of utopian communities. Government interference in cost limits, density requirements and backing for unwise technical experiments also played their unfortunate part.

The most visible outcome of these pressures is that most disastrous architectural invention of this century: the housing estate. The model is the college or monastery, where intimacy is made tolerable by and reinforces a common purpose. Families, however, require privacy as well as neighbourly contact. The estate thrusts them into a proximity that becomes increasingly intolerable as cultural diversity grows and social cohesion and control decay. Excessive intimacy, like an invasion of personal space, generates social isolation and hostility. Push two cats within a metre of each other, and they will fight.

Most of Hackney's estates fall into five main generations. There are still about twenty pre-war estates. These were soundly built, low-rise blocks, usually of four or five storeys, with access through internal staircases giving on to three or four doors per landing. Rising expectations, climbing energy prices, and changing domestic technologies have made these obsolete. They were built to very high densities – 615 people per hectare, or a space 4 metres square per person, inclusive of public spaces. As a result, rooms are small, kitchens too tiny to accommodate fridges and washing machines and freezers, electric sockets insufficient in all rooms. There is no central heating, insulation is poor and flats are often cold and draughty. Most flats are for families with children, producing a high density of children on each estate with unfortunate results for standards of behaviour. Open spaces are small and inadequate, often blocked up by unsightly electricity substations, stores, community halls, derelict laundries, defunct air-raid shelters and pram-sheds. A pram-shed, for the uninitiated, is a little hut, in a long row of other such huts, in which mothers can store their prams to save humping them up the stairs. In the age of vandalism, pram-sheds are no longer used for their original purpose, but as impromptu rubbish dumps, stashes for stolen goods, and sites for experimentation with sexuality or arson. The small areas that remain are fought over by cars, often abandoned or out of action (Hackney is like an elephants' graveyard for north London's cars – when they reach a certain stage of decrepitude and feel death approaching, they gravitate to Hackney) and by children: two diametrically opposed interest groups. The children damage the cars, and the cars damage the children, but the children usually lose in this unequal battle of metal versus flesh.

On the estates of the 1940s and 1950s, densities could be much lower – about 350 per hectare – because population had dropped and the Blitz had opened up new housing sites. In most estates of this era, access to individual flats is by external balconies, so that each flat has a door giving on to the world outside. Yet there is something indefinably ugly about these narrow alley-ways in the sky, serviced by absurd free-standing stair-wells – perhaps more than anything the result of the shortage of light, blocked out by the wall of the balcony and the overhanging floor of the one above. Rooms are larger in this second generation of estates, but most pre-war problems remain: high child density, inefficient heating and insulation, lack of car space and play space, unattractive grounds of tarmac or concrete with patches of unhealthy grass.

As the 1960s rolled on, architects became socially and technically bolder in creating the third generation. This was the era of tower blocks. The idea: stand the streets on end so as to liberate the open space and greenery that the city needs. The reality: malfunctioning lifts, vertigo, mothers terrified for children. In 1979, 14 per cent of Hackney families with children under sixteen were living above the fourth floor. This was also the age of industrialized building systems, when governments gave subsidies and incentives to local authorities to apply insufficiently tested methods on a wide scale, with disastrous results of which Holly Street (see Chapter 12) is a good example. System building on the tower blocks of Trowbridge estate in Hackney Wick has led to massive rain penetration which will cost an estimated £15 million to remedy.

The catalogue of blunders from the whole estate era, most of them arising from a failure to consult or consider eventual residents, is scandalous: total suppression of the well-tried concept that an Englishman's home is his castle; an excess of public space, featureless, underused, abused, belonging to no one and to which no one therefore feels they belong; a lack of private space; no gardens for kids to play safely; nowhere to dry washing, except on balconies and out of windows where it creates a shanty-town look; poor noise insulation, so that the sounds of all-night parties, violent family disputes and language of the foulest kind pass through party walls and echo round courtyards. (I shall never forget wandering through Stonebridge estate and seeing a woman locked out on a balcony by her own numerous offspring, their impish faces silhouetted at the window, and her shouting 'Open the fucking door, you fucking cunts' at the top of her voice.) And more: absurd collective refuse systems using chutes that are too small for the large plastic bags the council issues, and more exotic institutional objects known as 'paladins' and 'dumpsters'. The paladin is a very large cylindrical dustbin on wheels that will take as much as eight normal dustbins. The dumpster is a big metal skip similar to the kind builders use. Overall result: smells, refuse blowing everywhere, vermin, frequent arson. Inefficient and expensive centralized space and water heating systems, most of them completely outside the tenants' control, so that people are hot when they wish to be cool (and vice versa) and have no incentive to economize on energy and no freedom to determine the all-important levels of their own fuel bills. Boilers that break down, leaving whole estates cold for weeks at a time, often in the depths of winter. Warm-air ducts that transmit pests and possibly diseases. Most of these problems ought to have been foreseen and could have been forestalled, given a proper system of consulting tenants about their needs and aspirations, or indeed even of learning from past mistakes. The problems of delinquency were more unexpected, and had more to do with allocation policies and general social trends. Nevertheless, the design of most estates provided and still provides easy opportunities for crime and vandalism, with unsupervised spaces, passageways for quick escape, open access to outsiders, insecure doors and windows.

By the 1970s the lessons that should have been known all along had at last been learned: what the typical council tenant wants and needs is exactly the same as what the owner-occupier wants. A house, three storeys at most, with its own separate entrance from street level, its own garden, its own dustbin, its own central heating under the tenant's control, and with ample play space and car space in the vicinity. And so a number of smaller estates were built of attractive, coordinated houses, often in terraces, resembling conventional streets. Even then technical problems persisted. Party walls were still too permeable to noise. Damp – the curse of the old Victorian stock – was still a problem. Now rising damp had been replaced by condensation and rain penetration. Many of Hackney's outwardly attractive new estates are plagued with severe defects. A confidential 1980 report by the National Building Agency surveyed thirty-one smaller estates built since 1971. It discovered thin asphalt on balconies over inhabited rooms, untreated timbers in areas where insect and fungal attacks might be expected, unventilated roof voids, undersized permanent ventilation slots (often deliberately blocked up by residents), leaking roof-lights, draughty and sticking doors, cracking plaster.

With all this experience behind it, municipal architecture, by the beginning of the 1980s, had come full circle, back to the old traditional methods and designs. The approach of architects was unrecognizable. New estates and remodelling schemes for older estates were being planned in close consultation with potential users. Architecture had graduated from despotism to democracy. But the metamorphosis came at a bad time. Public house-building ground to a halt and the funds for remodelling dried up. In 1978/9 Hackney added no less than 1,023 new flats or houses to its housing stock. Four years later new additions totalled only 174, and in 1981/2 only 55 new dwellings were started. Hackney's cash limits for capital expenditure on housing were cut from a planned £37 million in 1979 to £14 million in 1982/3. The legacy of past mistakes remained: there are no more than a handful of estates in Hackney that do not suffer from major problems. The plans and programmes exist to remedy the problems: but there was no prospect of significant progress as long as a government committed to reducing public spending was in power.

Plastering Over the Cracks

Quite apart from their structural faults, many Hackney estates have a dirty, down-at-heel feel about them: a scattering of refuse across courtyard, murals of graffiti, and a battered, stained look about brick and concrete, wood and metal. These things, common to most inner-city areas, are the outward sign of a house that is not in order. The causes are multiple: poor design, bad management, worker–management conflicts in refuse and repair services, seven lean years of public-spending restraint, community and family collapse.

Maintenance of existing council properties has, in the past, taken a lower priority than new building. Moreover, the system for day-to-day repairs in operation until 1982 was a model of bureaucratic insensitivity and unresponsiveness. There are many institutions in Hackney that work together in unwitting harmony to drive its poorer residents to the brink of nervous breakdown: public transport, the National Health Service, social security. The council repair system is right up among the front runners: rarely have so many people had to waste so much time and energy to so little avail.

The sheer complexity of the system was responsible. The tenant had first to visit the office of the estate manager, open only in office hours when many people could not get to it. There an official would fill in a job ticket for the repair. This passed up the ladder of the housing department, and down the ladder of the quite separate Department of Technical and Contract Services which was responsible for carrying out the repair, and out to one of the many specialized depots like Gilpin Yard (Chapter 5). Here the job would, in theory, be pre-inspected by the depot foreman who would order the necessary supplies from a separate section of the department. The supplies could take days, weeks, sometimes months to arrive. When they did turn up, the job would be assigned to a workman, who would go along, sometimes on the day the tenant had proposed, when the tenant would be there to let him in, sometimes on another day, when he would not gain access and the tenant would have lost a day's pay and a day's patience for nothing. When access was eventually gained the workman would often find he lacked some of the materials needed to do the job, and have to go through the whole rigmarole again. Each point in this scheme represented a potential for failure of communication, loss of documentation, lack of coordination. It was a buck-passers' paradise, and the buck was passed, endlessly.

If you ask almost any Hackney council tenant what problems they have with their housing, repairs come out first or second on the list. It is yet another aspect of the powerlessness that infects most aspects of their lives. For Jean Clements, whom we met in Chapter 8, the repair system presents as many frustrations as social security. For the ten months before I met her, her bath had been taking two days to drain, so she stopped using it. For two years her wash-hand basin has sported a black, spidery hole in the centre of a cobweb of concentric cracks: it will not hold water. The family wash in the kitchen sink. For several years the frame of her bathroom window has been so rotten that she can't open it for ventilation. Two of her electric sockets are hanging dangerously away from the wall. She raises all these problems on average once a month with the estate manager's office: 'They say it's being done, but then you don't hear a word. A man came once, when I was out, and told the kids to tell mum to stay in the next day. I stayed in all day and he never came.' Geoff Tyrrell, chairman of Bannister House tenants' association, had his front door busted by a break-in a month before my visit, by which time it still was not mended. Another of his members has had no glass in her living-room window for two years, despite raising the matter twice a week at the estate office. 'It's a comic opera,' says Tyrrell. 'You've no chance of seeing them if you work. If you phone them up – if you can get through – it's like cat and mouse. They'll say, "It's in hand." When you have a go at them, they wriggle out of it. They play the left hand against the right hand. It's like talking to a brick wall.' Social workers complain that they cannot get priority repairs done for people with health problems or parents of children at risk. Even when jobs do get done, many tenants complain of bodging or of workmen causing further damage. One lady at Bannister House could hardly believe her luck when she succeeded in getting a new bath installed, but in the process the plumbers smashed the tiles and the bath panel and damaged the plaster: all the concern of other trades than theirs.

The problems of the system were aggravated when, in 1973, Hackney Council got rid of resident caretakers on its estates as an economy measure, replacing them with a mobile radio patrol. With no one at hand to deter vandals or to attend to minor repairs, the last vestige of local responsiveness was removed.

Vandalism and graffiti add the final touches to the painting. They are primarily the symptom of the decay of family discipline and of community control. But they are also, in part, a response to the environment, for an estate that is neglected by its landlords will not be much respected by its tenants. Perhaps the most graphic indication of this is the widespread use of public spaces as public toilets. On many estates residents complain not only of dogs, but of passers-through, drunks, children and youths urinating and even excreting on balconies, in lifts and in stair-wells. There could hardly be a more telling expression of how far social disintegration has progressed in the inner city.

By 1981, plans were afoot for a much more streamlined repair system in which services would be decentralized, depots would handle particular estates and carry permanent stocks of items of the right size and type for those estates, and local estate managers would be able to order repairs direct from their own depot. Estate offices began to open outside office hours and resident caretakers began to be reintroduced. It was a hopeful outlook, and a model for other services, a first step on the road to making bureaucrats more accountable to their clients.

The Two Nations of Housing

Britain is divided into two major housing classes: owner-occupiers and tenants, the great mass of the latter council tenants. The gulf between them is just as wide as the gulf between manual workers and non-manual workers, with which it often coincides. The line between the two is drawn by income and ability to save or inherit, and the system is heavily stacked against those on low incomes. In 1981 the cheapest two-bedroomed family flat in Hackney cost at least £20,000. The minimum weekly wage required to get a mortgage for that amount would be £160, and overtime and bonus pay, on which most manual workers rely to make up their earnings, might not be counted. The average male manual earnings per week in 1981 in Hackney were £121·90.

Owner-occupiers, within the limit of their finances, control their own housing destinies. They have a wide freedom of choice of property and location. They may view ten, twenty, fifty or a hundred houses before selecting the one they like best. They can choose their own heating system and alter or extend their home. They can arrange their own repairs. They can sell up and move out at any time they like. Inflation is their fairy godmother: as the years go by it ensures that their mortgage costs take up a smaller and smaller share of their income. It also allows them to accumulate very large amounts of unearned capital as the value of their property rises, and the kindly State itself helps them along by providing tax relief on their interest payments.

Contrast the position of tenants, who make up no less than 84 per cent of all households in Hackney and 47 per cent in England and Wales as a whole. Rents, for the vast majority of tenants, usually rise in line with inflation, and at times outpace it: the Conservative government, in an onslaught on council tenants as determined as the attack on the unions, forced council rents up artificially. In Hackney they rose by 76 per cent between 1979/80 and 1981/2, while the Retail Price Index rose by only 29 per cent. When mortgage interest rates fell rapidly, in 1982, owner-occupiers found themselves £10 or £20 a week better off, while council tenants faced further rent rises. Tenants can never accumulate unearned capital in the way the owner-occupier does, nor can they ever look forward to the day when they will be free from rent as the owner-occupier will be free from mortgage repayments. They are beholden to their landlord for repairs. They have no freedom to alter or extend their property, or, often, to choose the form of heating. In the private sector they face exploitation and harassment. In the public sector, they have no power to influence, by any rational action, the chances of their being offered a house, little or no meaningful choice of style or location and, once they are in a house, very little freedom to move. The condition of being a tenant in modern Britain is one of powerlessness, of severely curtailed liberty, of exclusion from the possibility of accumulating and bequeathing wealth. And it is worse: for we must ask the question, from where does the magic capital gain of the owner-occupier materialize? Not out of thin air, assuredly. It is a real transfer of wealth, of command over resources that can be inherited. From whom, then, is it transferred? The answer is: from all those who pay the cost of inflation without reaping the benefits, that is, from non-owner-occupiers. Inflation without taxation of capital gains in housing has, in fact, brought about a massive transfer of wealth to owner-occupiers, paid for out of the real incomes of tenants.

The council tenant's powerlessness is even more pronounced than that of the private tenant. There is nothing fair or positive that the waiting-list applicants can do to increase their chances of being offered a house, or, once in occupation, of being transferred. Patience will get them nowhere, for the principle of queueing has almost totally vanished in allocating council houses. As the latter are an increasingly scarce commodity, they have to be rationed according to need, on a complicated points system which varies from council to council. Hackney's own calculus of human misery works as follows: For each year you have been inscribed on the housing waiting list, you gain a mere two points. But for each room you lack, in your present accommodation, in relation to your needs, you are awarded twenty points; for smallness of rooms, up to twenty points; for sharing bathroom, kitchen or toilet, up to seventeen points; for badly placed amenities such as landing kitchens or outside toilets, up to twenty-three points; for medical conditions, up to twenty-five points; if the family is at present living separately, ten points; and there are ten discretionary points that the housing department can award.

Thus, applicants must submit to a degrading assessment of need, a sort of housing means test. Few of them fully understand the points system, even fewer know how to manipulate it. And it can, to some extent, be manipulated. For the applicant who is especially astute or articulate, or secures the help of an adviser like a social worker, expertise can add up to twenty or even forty points to the total.

But most applicants do not get such help. In the absence of positive power to influence their housing destinies, there are a number of negative things they can do. They can deliberately live separately from their spouse; purposely select the most over-crowded, unpleasant housing option open to them; conceive an additional, otherwise unwanted child. All these actions can easily backfire in the present climate of acute housing shortage. There is, however, one almost infallible method that families with children can use: that is, to persuade a landlord to evict them, or get parents to say they have had a row with them and can no longer tolerate their presence. The local authority then becomes responsible for rehousing them. Going deliberately homeless is the housing equivalent of social-security fraud: a desperate attempt to make an intolerable system work in one's favour. There has been a steep increase, nationally, in the numbers of families being declared 'intentionally homeless'. In Hackney the numbers rose from none in 1978 to seventeen in 1980. Some of them are caught, as the following extract from Hackney's register indicates:

Mr and Mrs A, two children aged two and one. Family initially approached as homeless in November 1978, giving false name. Investigations revealed true name and fact that family were currently GLC tenants in London SW2 and owing rent arrears of £93. The tenancy was available for the family to return to. Warned that if they gave up their GLC tenancy they would likely be treated as intentionally homeless. Subsequently returned March 1979 having given up GLC tenancy, therefore treated as intentionally homeless. June 1980 woman and children only reapproached claiming homelessness due to marital dispute, treated as fresh application and admitted into temporary accommodation. After some weeks husband joined wife in temporary accommodation and admitted was a ploy to be rehoused. Entire family still in temporary accommodation awaiting rehousing.

Mr and Mrs C, two daughters aged two and three. Relinquished self-contained private tenancy and stayed in grossly overcrowded accommodation with parents until private flat re-let. Then presented as homeless.

Most homeless families are, of course, genuinely homeless. But most fake homeless families generally get away with it. Out of 4,059 families accepted as homeless in Hackney between 1978 and 1981, only twenty-four were declared intentionally homeless, and nine of these were rehoused anyway.

Choice, for council waiting-list applicants, is no choice at all. In most cities, homeless families are given only one housing offer, while other people, after a longer or shorter wait, get three. In Hackney, there is no limit to the number of offers for most people, and from June 1982 the homeless had three offers. But this is not what most people normally understand by the word choice: it is not a simultaneous selection from which you can pick the best. It is a succession of single properties and the 'choice' with each one is: take it or leave it. If you leave it, there is a possibility, but no guarantee, that the next offer will be better. Applicants can, if they wish, specify the area or the estate where they wish to live, but this (by reducing the number of properties open to them) may extend their wait by any number of years. As Maureen Cooper put it: 'You got all these people deciding on your future. It ain't right. You got a right to say where you want to live.'

Nor is there any real freedom to move once you have your first tenancy. In the acute state of shortage that exists in Hackney, transfers are strictly limited to priority cases, people with strong medical or social grounds such as sufferers from heart conditions or racial attacks, and, if they are lucky, to people who have lived for ten years or more on the same estate. Again, even when the lucky break comes, there is no real choice, only a succession of take-it-or-leave-it offers. Tenants can try for a voluntary exchange, but if their flat or estate is unpleasant, they haven't a hope of finding someone gullible enough to swap them something better for it. The more desperate and determined, provided they have children, get into deliberate rent arrears in the hope of getting evicted and rehoused in a slightly more attractive circle of hell. The most desperate go as far as setting fire to their flat.

The Waiting Game

It is not easy, for someone not personally subjected to it, to imagine the sense of impotence, frustration and suppressed rage that council-house applicants feel while waiting to be allocated a place. For most people, aspirations for a home are the most important in their lives. To be unable to influence the choice or the timing; to be forced to wait impatiently for months, more often years, and in many cases decades; to be offered nothing, or to be offered places that you have seen, not in your dreams, but in your nightmares: it is the nearest thing to torture that the welfare state can offer.

The Davies family* have long experience of the tribulations involved. Doris Davies is a school cleaner in her fifties, her husband George a telephone engineer. For the first years of the marriage, they lived with Doris's parents, in one bedroom. By 1955 there were five of them, and after seven years on the waiting list, they were offered the three-bedroomed maisonette on Geffrye Court estate where they still live. It was then just the right size for the five of them, but more children began to arrive, and overcrowd-ing started again. By 1968 there were eleven of them in the flat: four boys in one bedroom, four girls in another, Doris and George in the third with their youngest son Cary.

Since then they have thinned out, but several of her children have started their own families in Doris's home while awaiting council flats. At one point daughter Pam* (see Chapter 13) and her first child were sharing a bedroom with another daughter, Pat,* and two of her children, along with Doris's youngest daughter Ellen. Big sons Mike* (see Chapter 17) and Johnny* shared another. Cary was still in his parents' bedroom when he was thirteen, and still couldn't tie his shoelaces.

Most of Doris's five married children now have council homes of their own – four of them very close by, so family links have survived longer than usual for the inner city. But three of them had to 'go homeless' before they got an offer. And Pat James,* an attractive twenty-six-year-old with auburn hair and the Davieses' turned-up nose, couldn't bring herself to do that. She has been married ten years and has three children, but has never had a home of her own or even an offer of one. She put her name down on the council waiting list in 1971. When she was living at Doris's house with the two children, the family had seventy-three housing points and could have expected an offer before long. But she couldn't take the waiting, the overcrowding, and the continued separation from her husband Douglas. So in 1977 they all moved in with Douglas's mother, who was living alone in a two-bedroomed flat in a Greater London Council block a stone's throw from Doris's place. Because

* See page 441. All names in the Davies family have been changed.

the flat was less crowded, the couple's housing points dropped to fifty-three. At the same time the number of points needed for rehousing was rising, so they were further than ever away from a council tenancy.

Apart from her housing problem, Pat is one of Doris's better-off children. Her husband is a builder. 'I don't know how much he earns, he doesn't tell me, but I think it's about £20 or £25 a day, and he works six or seven days a week. He gives me £95 [1981] in housekeeping, and puts the rest in the bank for when we need furniture or clothes. On top of that there's the child benefit of £14·25. But I still often have to borrow £10 or £20 off my mum on Friday morning and pay her back Saturday morning.'

For the first three years with Douglas's mother, Pat and Douglas had the luxury of a bedroom to themselves. Their two daughters, Tracy and Terry, shared a bedroom with their grandmother. But the arrangement soon began to break down.

'His mother kept complaining she had no privacy. And she was coming home drunk every night and I didn't like the kids to see her drunk. She used to make a lot of noise coming in, and wake them, and argue with them about silly little things. So when we had Toni, our third, we moved the other girls in with us. We have a double bed. The girls sleep in a single bed head to toe, one at each end. Toni's cot is in a corner under the window, so she's always getting colds. The damp is terrible in the winter, you get all that furry stuff, what d'you call it, mould, all down the windows. Water pours off the windows down the walls by the cot. Then there's a wardrobe and a chest of drawers for all our things. There's only about two feet in between the beds. It makes it really hard for your private life, the kids have got to be well asleep, and then you never know when they're going to wake up.

'We're always having stand-up rows with Douglas's mum. She's never threatened to put us out, but she's always throwing it in your face that it's her flat. When we moved in there was nothing in the way of furniture, just an old three-piece suite out of the ark, and nets at the windows, no curtains. Everything in there is mine, but when we get something new and say "Do you like it?" she starts saying to Douglas, "You never went out and bought anything like that for me." He says, "Well I'm not married to you, am I?"

'His mum pays the rent, that's about £20, and I pay all the bills and feed her. She's got £27 a week to spend on herself. I'd like to have that much pocket-money just for myself. She gets her pension on Mondays, but she's often spent it all by Wednesday and starts feeling sorry for herself 'cause she can't go out. Come Thursday night she'll borrow £5 off me. We've had lots of rows over rent we thought she'd paid and she hadn't. She just got a letter saying she owed £170.

'She drinks a lot. She goes out about 1 o'clock every day, betting and drinking. She comes back about 8 o'clock. If she comes in drunk I won't talk to her. She talks to the kids like pigs. But it's not my place to tell her what to do and what not to do. She'll come in and sit in the living-room when we're trying to watch the telly, and she'll keep on talking. My husband says, "Now look, mum, we're watching this." She says, "You got to remember this is my flat and if I want to talk I'll talk."

'She had four kids. Douglas was her youngest, her only boy. She's jealous 'cause I took her little boy off her. She likes to try and boss me, but when he's there, she don't. She'll help me out while he's there, but when he's out, she won't do a thing. She likes to make you feel uncomfortable. She'll go and sit in her bedroom sometimes, and sometimes she'll threaten to go in an old people's home. She doesn't want to really, she just says it to make you feel guilty.'

In ten years of virtual homelessness, of unrelieved overcrowding and total lack of personal privacy, Pat James has not had a single offer of a council house. Nor have her encounters with housing officials been pleasant ones. As with social security and health, it is the old story of lower-middle-class bureaucrats confronting working-class petitioners, rules and regulations meeting simple human need, scarce supply in the face of overwhelming demand. The result is a class conflict of another dimension: the conflict between public servants who control the allocation of crucial resources, and the poor who are more or less powerless to influence the outcome. 'I phone up the housing about once every two weeks,' Pat explains. 'But it's a waste of time. They always say the same thing: "As soon as something comes up we'll send you an offer." They give you an appointment time to go there, but you wait for an hour, and when you complain, they say they're short-staffed. Well if they know that why don't they allow for it? Why do they have to give you appointments at the wrong time? Then when you get to see them, all they say is half a dozen words. They don't give you no encouragement. The first thing they say is, "What you come down for?" Then you say, "I come to discuss me housing", and they say, "Well, if we'd had anything we'd have let you know." When I had my Toni I went up there. The man told me I'd get two extra points for that. I asked him would it be soon when I got an offer. He said, "No, it could be a long, long time." I done me nut. I said what should I do then, go and have half a dozen babies and paint myself black and come back? He said don't be nasty now. I said, "You're the one that's being nasty."'

The Allocation Lottery

The housing market of the city as a whole acts as a funnel channelling its most disadvantaged people into its least desirable areas – adding environmental deprivation to all the other deprivations of their lives. The council-house allocation system, in its turn, channels a large proportion of the disadvantaged into council estates, and unintentionally but inevitably sifts the most disadvantaged of all into the most unattractive estates.

The focus of the housing hopes and aspirations of four-fifths of Hackney's households is the housing allocation department. The office is on the first floor of Hackney's housing department in Mare Street, lined with tall grey cabinets through which, at some point, files on virtually every family in the borough have passed. This is the mysterious place where applicants and properties are matched. It is an immense raffle, in which the prizes, from the *bijou* residence to the unspeakable slum, are ranged on one side, and the ticket-holders on the other, all of them waiting with baited breath for the result. Most people would give an eye-tooth to get inside and tilt the outcome in their favour. Perhaps that is why a locked door separates the allocation office (and the rest of the housing department) from the public. The need still filters through. The files brim with pleading letters, brief notes, complaints, invectives, cries of despair, missives loaded with every relevant and irrelevant fact the supplicants can think of to support their cause. Handwriting from copperplate to scrawled illegibility, language eloquent or totally incomprehensible, tones submissive or demanding. Some rise to humour: 'Please don't offer me anything on a high floor. One of my boys thinks he's Spiderman, the other thinks he's the Incredible Hulk.' But the tone of most is more like the following, from an Asian living with his wife and child in the attic of a multi-occupied house in Dalston.

Dear Sir,

Further in support of my previous application I would like to bring it to your notice that since my last letter the conditions here have deteriorated very much, viz:

1. There are no proper facilities for the preparation of the child's feed, as the kitchenette is very small and all the wallpaper is falling apart. The wall dividing our kitchen from our neighbours has a hole and this provides free access for the rats between the two rooms. All this has been brought to the attention of the landlord without much help.

2. We share the bath and toilet with three other families and since writing you a neighbour on the same floor as us has acquired a rabbit, hen, cat which are now sharing the bath and toilet with us and they also intrude into our rooms when the doors are open to let fresh air in, since as you already know our ventilation is poor.

3. Each time a car passes the whole house shakes particularly the floor, and we have since observed that each time this happens it frights the baby and it wakes up hence lack of proper sleep.

The ceiling is falling down and this has been repaired more often and still continues to fall, any time the ceiling can fall down and we are afraid that it might fall on the baby.

Yours faithfully, L. T. S.

Applicants live in hope. They are persistent, aggressive, vigilant. They spot vacant properties and write in asking if they can have them; they notice neighbours who got on the waiting list after them, but have been rehoused before them, or who have had better offers. They have little understanding of how the system operates and, like hunter-gatherers in the face of the forces of nature, assume that malevolent forces must be at work when they do not succeed. Or they presume that you need 'pull' or 'bottle', inside influence, to get what you want. The more resourceful visit councillors or MPs in the vain hope that they can somehow be lifted over the heads of the queue, as so many of them live in such bad conditions that they are convinced theirs must be the highest-priority cases in Hackney. The allocators themselves can be reached by phone and they are the targets of endless accusations like 'You only help whites', or, just as frequently, 'You only help blacks'.

At the time of my visit there were just three senior allocators for the whole of Hackney's estates: one concentrates on two-bedroom properties; one on larger; and one on smaller places. Christine Skinner is in charge of three-bedroomed places and above. Every day an average of six record cards plop on to her desk, each one with the particulars of a property ready to let. A few are newly built, most are recently vacated or have just been offered and turned down. She also has on her desk two boxes full of cards with the salient details of the most pressing two or three hundred priority applicants. The task – an infinitely delicate one, fraught with individual and social consequences – is to find the best-fitting match between property card and client card. The match has to be as carefully done as an arranged marriage, for every time the fit is poor and an offer is turned down, a flat stays vacant for several weeks more. Added up right across the borough, that means the equivalent of hundreds of properties effectively unavailable to meet the growing queue of applicants. One of the aims of allocators, then, has to be to maximize the proportion of offers that are accepted first or second time.

The contents and order of entries in Christine's box of client cards reflect the realities in the race for a council house. The box for three-bedroom applicants is about 60 centimetres deep. Right at the front, getting first consideration, are the 'decants', people the council has a legal obligation to rehouse because of redevelopment or rehabilitation. Because the council often wants them out speedily, they get a far better quality of offer than most, so they snap up almost all new properties along with the best of the rest. Next in priority come medical and social priority cases – people requiring adapted dwellings or low floors because of handicap or heart trouble, along with the more extreme cases of family violence, racial attacks or serious mental breakdowns.

These first two groups take up about 5 centimetres of the box.

The second 5 centimetres are occupied by homeless families presently housed in hostels or hotels. The council has an incentive to rehouse them as quickly as possible to keep down the high cost of temporary accommodation.

Next comes the largest category in the box, about 50 centimetres of cards of people seeking transfers. They get fourth priority, because their move will free another property for letting. In time of heavy stress, even transfers slow to a trickle because the vacated properties take several weeks or months to prepare for a new tenant. Finally, at the very back of the box, are a mere handful, perhaps about a centimetre thick, of the 15,000 waiting-list applicants, those with the very highest level of points.

The matching procedure works as follows. Christine notes the number of rooms and the location of the property card she is dealing with, then works through the box of client cards, starting at the front, until she finds a client seeking the same size and location, or not bothered about location (this is why those who are least specific about where they want to live get rehoused most quickly). If she gets as far as transfer cases, to avoid giving unfair advantage to those whose names begin with the first letters of the alphabet, she sifts out all the cards that fit the bill and juggles them around, assessing ages, sexes, room requirements, incomes in relation to rent and rates, date of joining the waiting list – until she finds the match that leaves her with the fewest second thoughts.

In the depth of the housing crisis, she very rarely got as far as the back of her box of clients. Only about one offer in fifteen was going to an applicant from the waiting list. 'Only in desperation,' she says. By 1982, the situation was so bad that the average applicant, even in high need, could expect to wait for decades before being offered a council flat, if the pattern of that year continued. Those in the most critical difficulty might get housed immediately: most of the rest would be dead before they got an offer. The reason was the acute shortage of lettings available, caused by the drastic cut in council-house building and rehabilitation. The total number of lettings halved between 1977–8 and 1981–2, from 3,000 to 1,500, but the number of priority cases did not diminish by anything like the same proportion – hence the share of lettings that had to go to them rose from 42 per cent to 71 per cent over this period. The brunt of the cut in lettings hit the waiting-list cases. In 1977, no fewer than 1,143 people from the waiting list were given council dwellings, implying an average wait, for people in high need, of only three or four years (which in itself is bad enough). In 1979 only 403 people were rehoused from the waiting list, implying an average wait of eleven years for high-need cases. In 1982, about two hundred flats were let to waiting-list applicants, and the total numbers in high need were more than 8,000. Hence the number of points required to stand the slightest chance of an offer soared. In 1978 you needed thirty-two points for a one-bedroomed flat – in 1981, fifty-four points. For a two-bedroomed flat, the requirement rose from forty-seven points to eighty-eight over the same period. And where you might get a three-bedroomed place with a mere fifteen points in 1978, you needed eighty in 1981.

Before long a computer will assist in the anxious task of matching properties with applicants: but the results will be no more satisfactory. Given a great mass of needy people, and a smaller mass of mostly undesirable housing, there is simply no way of doing the job right. The system has always seemed like a lottery to those outside the allocators' office, and for all the intelligence and care devoted to allocation that is largely what it still is. But as the number of prizes shrinks, the bitterness over apparent injustices grows and the desperation of waiting in bad and worsening conditions deepens, taking its toll on family health and family stability. The housing crisis of the second slump is almost as profound and as damaging as the jobs and incomes crisis.

12 The Inner City's Inner City: The Dump Estates

> There, sighs, laments and loud wailings resounded through the starless air
> . . . Strange tongues, horrible cries, groans of pain, cries of anger, shrill
> and hoarse voices, and the sound of beatings, made a tumult, circling in
> the eternal darkness, like sand eddying in a whirlwind.
>
> *Dante*, Inferno, *iii, 22–30*

Through its low rents, the inner city ingathers the disadvantaged from a wide area. Through various channels – slum clearance, homelessness, the points system – council housing in turn attracts a large proportion of the disadvantaged. The institution of the estate thus concentrates the social problems of the inner city in an even smaller and more intimate space, where they can interact more destructively. Within the council sector, the allocation game creates pockets of even greater deprivation: the dump estates. If the inner city is like a chemistry lab full of dangerous social reagents, the dump estate is the test-tube where they are most corrosively combined. These are the least attractive, worst sited, worst provided with amenities. Usually they are unmodernized estates of pre-war flats, but sometimes more modern estates, more deeply flawed than usual with architectural blunders. They are the inner city's inner city.

Disadvantaged people tend to get very much worse council housing than the norm: older rather than newer; flats rather than houses; higher floors rather than lower. Studies like the Greater London Council Lettings Survey of 1974–5 showed that certain social groups fared badly: the homeless, the unemployed and blacks worst of all, with female single parents and unskilled workers not far behind. The public sector seems unable to allocate desirable and undesirable housing any more fairly than the private.

225

How does this state of affairs come about? One answer is that housing allocators have only recently become as socially sensitive as they now are, but their past actions bore a large measure of responsibility for the inequities. As we have seen, the principal aim is to make fullest use of the housing stock and to reduce the number of vacant properties by making sure the maximum number of properties are accepted on the first offer. The estates of older flats, or the newer but flawed estates, are what housing officers call 'hard to let': one Hackney property in five comes into this category. These properties have to be offered four or five times, sometimes up to nine times, before anyone desperate enough to accept them comes along. Allocators used to solve part of the hard-to-let problem by offering flats on the worst estates to those who got only a single offer and had no choice: the homeless. The homeless, inevitably, contain a higher proportion of disadvantaged and unstable families, evicted for rent arrears or split up by family disputes. A new political sensitivity about the homeless in Hackney put an end to the practice of offering them only the dump estates. But the legacy of the past is still imprinted on the present of each estate, as many tenants are still in place.

Even among those with a supposedly free choice, there is a subtle self-selection process at work. Rent levels are one element here. The higher rents and rates of more desirable properties deter those on low incomes, and deter allocators from offering them to the low-paid. Rent and rate rebates have helped to alleviate this, but they refund only about 60p in the pound of higher rents and rates. Supplementary benefit pays the whole of the rent and rates: but most people have not yet reached the stage where they expect to be on the dole for the rest of their lives, and have to take their eventual earnings into account. Hence the poorest tend to be pushed into less attractive, low-rent housing. Then there is a factor one might call 'staying power': the determination to hold out on the waiting list, turning down the earlier offers until something better turns up, to avoid moving into a dump. Staying power is obviously less among those who are most anxious to escape their present accommodation, because of overcrowding, bad repair, shared amenities or family conflicts. Once again, these people tend to be among the poorest and most unstable families, for whom even a hard-to-let estate may seem preferable to what they have at the moment. Finally there are elements of a culture of silence among society's most unfortunate victims: a tendency to be unaware of rights, to have little confidence in their ability to control their own destiny, and – at the lowest levels – to be so demoralized or so habituated to a squalid environment as to be almost indifferent to their surroundings.

Once an estate acquires more than a certain proportion of disadvantaged tenants – perhaps, say, one-fifth or one-quarter – it can find itself trapped in a descending spiral which may continue until it is demolished or massively rehabilitated. The preponderance of single-parent families and families with conflicts caused by low income or unemployment weakens parental discipline, so vandalism and crime are more prevalent. The atmosphere of demoralization and the culture of silence make it harder to form effective tenants' organizations to press for maintenance, or for individual tenants to get their own repairs done. The 'better' tenants, with higher incomes, savings or skills, or more persistence over getting a transfer, move out and are replaced by more disadvantaged people. The estate acquires a reputation, usually worse than the reality, which discourages those with any hopes for their own future from even viewing a flat there. It is exactly the same sifting process, in miniature, as that which creates and maintains the inner city as a whole.

The Ecology of Inferno

In a place with so many bad estates, it is not easy to determine which ones are dumps and which are not. No records are kept of their social make-up. Each estate is an institution of infinite complexity, the product of architecture, allocation, management, residents' behaviour, and the interaction of all of these. Nor is an estate a static thing. It changes over time, it has its own historical destiny, its own dynamics.

The story of Holly Street estate, which changed from a showcase into a sink within five years of opening typifies the expensive problems that past errors have left for present generations to suffer and resolve. You would not guess, from an outward glance, that it is one of the hardest to let in the whole of Hackney. True, it has four gargantuan nineteen-storey tower blocks, perched on a pedestal of unused pram-sheds in the middle of a windy patch of open grassland, close by a vast underground car park that because of vandalism has never been used since the estate was built in 1971. But the tower blocks are not hard to let. The core of the problem are the 500 or so flats in the nine low-rise five-storey blocks, poetically named Rosewood, Jasmine, Columbine, Pine, Cypress, Lilac, Aspen and so on, ranged in quadrangles around grassy, landscaped courts.

They must have looked beautiful as architect's drawings, and at the time of construction they must have seemed a considerable technical achievement. They managed a high density – 336 persons per hectare – without a look of overcrowding. Innovative ideas were used to imaginative effect to keep costs low. The low-rise blocks are five storeys high. On the ground floor are lock-up garages on some blocks, maisonettes on others. On the second floor are one-bedroom flats, many of them for pensioners, with access from long external balconies. The top three floors are given over to two- and three-bedroomed family maisonettes, the front doors of which all open on to a single internal corridor in the heart of the fourth floor, winding its way through the nine blocks – a long, covered street in the sky for pedestrians only. The maisonettes form a scissors pattern: all have living-room and kitchen at fourth-floor level. On one side of the corridor the bedrooms are above, on the fifth floor, and on the other they are below, on the third floor. The long corridor provided large savings on stairs, balconies and fire escapes. The estate was let briskly and, according to district housing manager Vic Sales, four out of five tenants were 'good type' households and only one in five 'bad type', mainly decant cases from a redevelopment area of poor terraced housing.

The flaws in the design, which we shall examine below, soon became apparent. They enabled the 20 per cent of 'bad type' tenants to make life hell for the rest. When I first visited the estate in 1975, to write an article on juvenile delinquency, the process had already started and children's behaviour was at the root of it. Children could be divided, and indeed divided themselves, into 'good' children and 'bad' children. One group of goodies I spoke to voiced a deluge of complaints: 'The bad boys light the dustbins and the rubbish chutes . . . They put bangers in cars and blow them up . . . They beat old ladies up . . . They nick people's toys 'cause they've got none of their own to play with.' They all agreed heartily when one of them said pensively: 'I'd rather be dead than live round here.'

Concern about other children's behaviour and its effect on their own drove many of the 'good type' families out as fast as they could go. Those who were offered the resulting vacancies viewed, not an empty show-case, but a fully occupied estate whose defects were all too obvious. Applicants with any options tended to turn down offers on Holly Street, while those with none accepted. The proportion of disadvantaged tenants, particularly blacks and single parents, rose, the exodus of better-off and white tenants accelerated, the problems intensified. The change can be seen dramatically in the pattern of allocations: between 1970 and 1975, when the problems were less apparent, 63 per cent of allocations were to whites. But between 1977 and 1980, no less than 77 per cent went to blacks, so that by 1981 the estate was 46 per cent black, three times the council average. Holly Street gained a reputation which compounded the letting problem. On average, each low-rise flat is now viewed by five applicants before it is accepted, two and a half times the Hackney average. As a result, an average of fifty flats are empty at any one time, some of them squatted. That means not only fifty dwellings less for the waiting list, but also an annual loss of rent and rates of £80,000 a year.

The reasons for the rapid decline were built into the design. Walk along the endless internal corridor and you will see why. No natural light, no fresh air filters through here. Cooking smells from the fourth floor kitchens creep along it: sponge cake, goulash, curry, hamburger, onions, chicken and rice. In the daytime they can be distinguished, in the evenings the odours of the world's cuisines, the scents of exotic spices, the smell of poor meat and fried fish mingle into a sickly stench that seeps into every flat. Worse perhaps is the transmission of noise, aggravated by thin and cracked party walls between flats. Do-it-yourself hammering, industrial sewing-machines, all-night parties, bitter family rows, ablutions, all reverberate vertically and horizontally. The bed-rooms on the third floor suffer especially, as they are directly below the corridor. As tenants' leader Betty Shanks puts it: 'I can lie in my bed and hear other people's sex lives and going to the toilet, like a bucket of water emptying over your head.'

The corridor is a thieves' highway: no one questions the passage of strangers, who may be residents of a distant block taking a sheltered short cut. At the corners where blocks join are dark passages, blind alleys, gloomy staircases. It is easy to get lost in these labyrinths, and easy for robbers to lurk or to lose their pursuers. The fear of muggings is so widespread that people, if they have to venture out at night, stick to the lit areas and walk hurriedly. Burglaries occur more frequently than in the richest leafy avenues of Hampstead Garden Suburb. In a single week in 1980 there were twenty-one break-ins on the estate. The front doors on the fourth floor are made of glass and flimsy wood and break open at a kick.

Bad design creates the opportunities for crime: bad allocation creates the mix of social ingredients out of which crime arises: not only poverty, unemployment and family instability, but a simple numerical factor like the density of children. Thirty per cent of the total population is considered the threshold above which destruc-tive processes gather their own momentum. Children and adolesc-ents begin to outnumber restraining adults in public spaces, the influence of a few examples of outlandish behaviour spreads more rapidly. On Holly Street's low-rise blocks, the child density was 36 per cent in 1978. On the upper floors it might approach 50 per cent or more. Place this weight of children in a scale that is pitifully small in play facilities, and the balance collapses. Holly Street has two or three small wire-surrounded enclosures (known as 'cages', another exotic feature of estate landscape). Three small groups playing football are enough to fill them, leaving the others to roam in search of opportunities for excitement.

The signs of vandalism are everywhere. In the early days the estate had forty 3-metre outdoor lamps with umbrella tops. Every one had to be repaired an average of eight times, at a total cost of over £5,000, before they were replaced by eight tall vandal-proof highway lamps. Along the corridors, squares of lino have been cut out, chewing-gum stamped in, holes gouged in the walls, initials burned on to the roof with cigarette lighters. Then there are the graffiti: on some staircases every single brick carries an inscription, and few of them would pass the censor: *Suck my ten-inch dick*; *Spunk my hole*; *I will pay for sexual pleasure*; *I like to feel young boys*; *If you want a fucking laugh, ring this mad woman* (phone number provided). All this in full view of prim old ladies and innocent children who have no chance of staying innocent for long and adolescents for whom the old idea of romantic love is increasingly outweighed by the most cynical and crude egotism.

The system for refuse disposal has had the effect of turning the whole estate into a garbage heap at times. On the upper floors there are chutes at the end of each stretch of corridor. Rubbish was supposed to be emptied here and funnelled down to dumpsters in chambers below. But the hole at the top was, as usual, too small for the regulation black plastic bags. Much rubbish was spilled while emptying the sack down the chute, while the lazy simply dumped their sacks in the chute area. Taking the rubbish is a child's chore in many families – you see kids staggering around with sacks bigger than themselves, strewing waste in a trail behind them. Some children were too small to reach up to the chute door. Piles of sacks accumulated in the chute recess, so even the willing could not get through and dumped their sacks too. At the weekends, when the estate cleaners were off duty, mountains of garbage would accumulate, with the stench rolling down the corridors. 'One weekend the whole of one recess and the lift had been bunged up with sacks,' Betty Shanks told me. 'They even had maggots breeding in them.' But the most serious problem was that children would set fire to the rubbish, sending thick smoke billowing down the corridors. At one point the fire brigade was being called out several times a day.

So the chutes were closed and the recesses wired off. Henceforth people had to take their rubbish even further, down to the dumpsters on the ground floor, which had to be pulled out of their neat recesses to give people access. This aggravated the distance problem. Many people now put their sacks outside their front door, removing the smell from their own home but stinking out their neighbours. Children had further to totter with sacks, spilling rubbish over a larger area. Some people on upper floors now throw rubbish out of their window – bottles, tins, paper, even sanitary towels. Full sacks of rubbish have been flung out of the fifth-floor windows sometimes into the gardens of those on the ground floor, perhaps as a sort of protest and revenge against those lucky enough to have gardens and entrances from the street. The estate cleaners knock off at 3 p.m. on Fridays and do not start again until 8 a.m. on Monday. All weekend the rubbish accumulates, until every courtyard is scattered with litter, the dumpsters are overflowing on to the pavements and sacks are piled up around them.

Holly Street is cursed with a visitation of plagues as numerous as those that smote the ancient Egyptians. As well as crime, vandalism, noise, smells and garbage, there are five principal species of pests.

Pigeons, guaranteed a basic food supply from the refuse, drift in flights across the courtyards and brood on the grassy banks. They perch on window-ledges, whitewashing the walls below. The old ladies of Spruce Court encourage them and feed them – one leaves her window open so they can go inside – but for most people they are a nuisance, fouling windows, laundry, cars, hair and clothing, and occasionally drowning in water tanks.

Dogs are the seventh plague. Hackney people keep dogs on a wide scale, to deter burglars. For that purpose the noisier and more aggressive they are, the better. Their barking annoys neighbours, but worse – and this happens in working-class areas throughout North England and Wales – they are left to walk themselves, and team up with strays, roaming the estate in hunting packs, reverting to wolf, fouling paths and play areas and not infrequently attacking adults and children.

Then there are mice and cockroaches, feeding off the refuse. But the tenth plague is the most exotic of them all, and straight from Egypt: pharaoh ants, a tropical species of tiny brown insect that thrives and spreads through the warm-air ducts of Holly Street's centralized heating system. They also afflict Nightingale Estate. They appear to be virtually ineradicable. In 1979, at great expense, every flat on the estate was sprayed with long-acting insecticide and the ants seemed to have disappeared. By 1981 they were back again.

Life on Holly Street is not pleasant for anyone of any age or any race. Many have applied for a transfer, but find themselves virtual prisoners because they have not lived on the estate for ten years, or are in rent arrears. Debbie Sims is an eighteen-year-old black single mother. She lives with her mother and two teenage brothers in a three-bedroomed maisonette spanning the third and fourth floors. Descending to the bedrooms, down a dark and narrow internal stairway, is like going down into the hold of a ship. The background heating (cost: £9 a week, winter and summer) is on the fourth floor and rises. The lower bedrooms are icy-cold in winter. Until two years ago Debbie slept on the sofa. Her mother had one room, her two brothers another. Her sister Beverley had the third, along with her husband and baby. Beverley was offered a flat on Stonebridge estate, an even more notorious dump than Holly Street. Debbie, by then pregnant herself, moved into Beverley's room. It measures 4 metres by 2 metres. There is a double bed at one end and a single one at the other. A large wardrobe and two chests of drawers take up all the remaining space. A paraffin heater is squeezed in between the two beds. 'This heater stinks,' Debbie complains. 'I can't let Fabian [her boy, now one and a half] near it. You supposed to have a bucket of water next to it, but I can't, he'll kick it over. I hate it in here. My brothers take liberties with me. They don't knock to come in, they just barge in. I don't turn my back for three minutes and they nick my TV. We used to live near London Fields, then this white man knocked my mother down, and she asked for a transfer. She doesn't like it here. She's black, but she says there's too many black people here. And the noise: we're next to the stairs here, we hear them trampling up and down. And the lady upstairs, I can hear her sewing-machine all evening. We all want to get out. But my mum's been told the only way she can get a transfer is if I'm out of here. I been on the waiting list two years, I got seventy-five points. They told me I'd probably have to wait till he's at least five. I did go homeless once, last year, I went in a hostel, but I came out of there after three weeks, I couldn't take it. I'll have to wait. But I won't take a dump, I don't want to bring my boy up in a dump.'

But the group that finds life on Holly Street most intolerable is the old. It must have seemed a nice idea, when the plans were laid

233

in the mid-sixties, to mix old and young, so the young could keep a watchful eye on the old, cheer them up and run errands for them. But the smashing of the extended family, the collapse of discipline and the rise of the 'me' generation made the age mixing a source of torment. The young no longer offer consolation to the old in the inner city, but are the bane of their lives.

Rose lives in a one-bedroomed flat on the first floor. Rose is not her real name – she is afraid of the consequences if she is identified, and that, in itself, says a lot about the estate. She is sixty-six, though she looks much older, small and frail, her thin, pallid face deeply lined. When she sits down she holds her legs out straight, like wooden limbs, because of arthritis. Her flat is like most old women's, neat and clean, though she refuses to ask for a home help. She was distrustful at first, but relieved, when anonymity was promised, to unburden herself of her woes. Parts of her story sound as if they could be the figments of an old spinster's imagination, but I have confirmed with other neighbours those details that could be checked, and am satisfied that none of it is imaginary. It is a sad reflection on the inner city that real life so often sounds like a paranoid's nightmare.

'Our family used to have a little terraced house, but we got bombed out in the war. Then my mother and me had rooms in a garret. When my mother died I was left all alone in that house. It was due for demolition and there were two empties on either side and no lights downstairs, but I wasn't half so afraid as I am here. I was told these flats were all for pensioners, and I was only fifty-six at the time. But the housing lady said, because I'd been in hospital and had two operations on my legs, she said, "I think we'll let you have one of them, for your health."

'I was so happy when I first came. The place looked lovely, and I thought, I'm going to have my own street door again. But I've only had six months' peace here in ten years, the first six months, before the place was fully let. My health has never been worse than since I came here. I didn't realize there was going to be family maisonettes on top. The children upstairs jump up and down all evening, and all day long at weekends. We're persecuted day in and day out. They use the balcony like a playground, roller-skates, skateboards, and if you go out to them, they say "Eff off you old bag", and all the other foul language they sling at you. They spit at my windows. And they write on my front. Now it says, well I might as well say it, it says "Fuck off". I used to clean it, but this time I thought, oh, leave it there, it goes for you too.

'I've had ants in here. The drawers were alive with them. I've got camphor squares in there now, they don't like them. Being personal, I couldn't use my toilet for three months when we had the worst of them. The seat was covered with them. I'm not spotless clean myself, but you still get them whether you're clean or not. They're called pharaoh ants. I say, well the pharaoh can have them. Quite honestly, I think they've come over in these foreign foods. Then there's the filth of those bins, I don't think they're ever disinfected out. I've been run alive by mice – three mice have been killed in this flat. They come in through the pipes, they can squeeze through the grilles. And along this block we get upsurges from the toilets. It comes right over the top and swamps the living-room, and it's all filth, real filth. We've had twelve since I've been here. To be fair, I don't think it's only the drains, there's people upstairs that put things down the toilets that they shouldn't.

'I still say that Hackney borough council are traitors, because they brought in people they should never have. The flat next door has been the last straw for me. I've not had one good neighbour since I moved in. The first tenants were a man and wife. They were always quarrelling. Then there was a coloured man. He was quiet, but he was very sick, and he was dirty. He'd just got himself a home help when he was found dead in there. After that there was a couple where the woman was neurotic, a terrible life I had with her. She'd be raving out on the little balcony at the back.

'The worst for me are those girls that are in there now. I won't say what I think they're up to, but their life-style is so different to mine, you see. There's loads of men go in, huge great black men. They play loud music, they've got a pool table in there, you can here the balls pinging, they've even got a red light in there. I've had nights and nights with no sleep whatever, in and out of bed all night. It's really brought me down. I've led a good clean life all my life. I never, ever, thought I'd be brought down to living like this, having to hear all the goings-on in there. I've never been married, and to be brought to this. I feel contaminated. I even moved my bed away from the wall. I won't walk past there – I walk all round the court if I have to go in that direction.

'I feel frightened to complain. There's such a lot of men go in there. I would complain, let them stick a knife in my back if they like, I wouldn't mind if they did and they finished me off. But what if they didn't finish me off, that's what worries me, because I don't want to be a cabbage. That's why this information has to be confidential. We're not in our own country now, I mean, they're in complete control, they've lowered the tone, they've brought us down to their level. I know you shouldn't have prejudices.

'It's altered my disposition living here. I always used to be concerned if a kid fell down, I'd go to help. Now I don't care what happens to them. It's changed me. I've lost my faith, I've lost my religion. I think to myself: I've had misfortunes all my life, I'm not the only one, I know, but I look back on my life and I can't see what I've done in the past to deserve this, though I do admire people who keep their faith.

'I'm on my own, I never married, I've no family. I had one dear friend of forty-five years' standing, all during my illness she was a brick wall for me, but she's dead now. I do have some distant cousins in Kent. I only hear from them once a year, at Christmas, but they would see to me if anything happened to me. That's been planned for years. I carry a card round with me with their address, and there's one there on that table. One thing that gets me is, there's no one who ever asks: how are you getting on there now? I never talk to my neighbours, because I feel they don't want to know. I never talk to anyone about all this, I bottle it all up. When you've gone now, I shall probably have a good cry.'

Rose has asked others to back her up in her complaints about the girls next door, so she couldn't be victimized. But the atmosphere of fear and indifference on the estate is such that no one will speak out. The very ecology of the place divides tenants up and creates a mass of conflicts and cleavages: young versus old; delinquents against the law-abiding; victims against the parents of perpetrators; top-level maisonettes against middle-level maisonettes; those on upper floors against those on the ground floor; those who are concerned about cleanliness and those who are not; the quiet against the noisy; pigeon-feeders against pigeon-haters; dog-owners against non-owners. To these we can add more generalized divisions that arouse deep emotions: rent-payers against squatters; tax-payers against claimants; black against white; not to mention political, moral, religious, sexual or class cleavages.

There are a score or more possible divisions, and most of them cut criss-cross through each other, creating a multi-dimensional matrix with more than a million possible compartments, whose inhabitants will be set against the rest on at least one divisive issue. The community is atomized, ground into fragments like sand on the beach. The stresses of poverty and uncomfortable proximity intensify the conflicts. The architect of Dante's hell economizes in places by using the souls of the damned to torment each other. The inner city achieves the same effect, setting the victims of our society against each other so they cannot effectively organize to change the causes of their predicament.

Change and Stagnation: People's Participation under Monetarism

In 1979 a patch of blue sky appeared in the clouds over Holly Street. Endless pressure from tenants, interminable management problems with letting, refuse, arson, pests and vandalism finally got the estate, only eight years after it was first let, on to Hackney's list for priority rehabilitation, otherwise reserved only for pre-war estates.

Experiments on other hard-to-let estates like Wenlock Barn in Shoreditch had pointed to some general solutions to a problem that was found in every inner-city area. The package of changes needed included measures to improve security and amenities, such as stronger doors and windows, entry-phones; elimination of blind spots and muggers' escape routes; better landscaping; individual and communal gardens and allotments; provision of more play facilities designed and run in consultation with parents and children; management changes to ensure a more responsive service, with locally based senior managers and repair teams and resident caretakers; and social changes to create a sense of community, especially the formal involvement of tenants in decisions affecting the estate's future, tenants' participation in helping to make some improvements, and the voting of sums of money the use of which would be under the control of the tenants' association.

A process of close consultation between tenants and architects – who opened an office on the estate so residents could pop in with suggestions – produced the outline of a set of solutions for Holly Street's problems. In the short term, staircases were to be painted and better lit, and compactor units installed for refuse. In the medium term, infill housing would be built on part of the site to allow tenants to be decanted while rehabilitation proceeded. Three blocks would be converted to sheltered housing for the old people of the estate, with wardens and alarm bells. The windswept plain around the tower blocks would be landscaped to provide 'privacy and a sense of belonging', in so far as such a sentiment is ever possible in a place like Hackney. In the longer term the boiler house would be demolished and all the low-rise dwellings provided with tenant-controlled central heating. Noise insulation, lighting, lifts and drainage would be improved, and entry-phones provided to keep out intruders. The most ambitious part of the programme involved breaking up the low-rise blocks, doing away with the hated internal corridor, and taking out a number of flats along its length to provide new staircases up from ground level. The bottom two or three floors would become large family units, the upper floors small family units.

The redesign plan reversed all the drawbacks of the original. Both the overall density and the child density would be reduced. The destructive mixing of old and young would be ended. It represented the new spirit pervading the more progressive council architects' departments: a greater humility, a genuine desire to learn from people what they wanted. The architect ceases to be a benevolent despot, decreeing out of superior wisdom what kind of houses and settlements people will live in, and becomes a democratic facilitator, taking their needs and aspirations as guide and enshrining them in economically and technically sound designs.

Unfortunately, just as this new spirit was emerging, the cash with which to do anything about it was drying up. The total plan for Holly Street was very expensive: £16 million at 1980 prices, most of that for the low-rise blocks, and far more than it cost to build the estate in the first place. The monetarist attack on local-government spending destroyed all hope of obtaining even a tenth of that before 1984. In 1980/81 nothing was spent. For 1981/2 a mere £65,000 was allocated. By the end of 1981 all that had been done was cosmetic. The stair-wells had been painted with murals by unemployed youths on a Youth Opportunities scheme, and the ground-floor garages painted in attractive bright colours. An abortive attempt had been made to exterminate the curse of the pharaohs. And on one block the dumpster had been replaced by an experimental high-technology shiny green compactor unit, which the big black plastic bags wouldn't fit into.

Consultation between the officers involved in the estate redesign and tenants' representatives continued, but, with hardly any money to spend, there was not much of great importance to discuss. Hopes raised in 1979 had been dashed, spreading cynicism and despair. Hence the reality of tenants' participation was much more modest than the ideal. Whether out of bitter disillusion, apathy, laziness, infirmity, fear or the burdens of shiftwork and child care, the vast majority of tenants do not come to even the most important meetings. The representatives who do attend regularly have no systematic channels, in many cases no channels at all, for consulting the wishes of those whom they are supposed to represent. They are riven by rivalries and personality clashes. And the experts who are there, in theory, to be accountable to the people, in practice are able to direct most affairs in the direction they wish. All this is entirely typical of people's participation in unequal societies anywhere in the world.

I attended a meeting of the steering committee in November 1981, which illustrated some of the real problems that face grass-roots organizations in poor areas. Only four tenants were present, but six officials. Also present was Anne Blaber, from the Department of the Environment's Priority Estates Project, who kicked off the proceedings with proposals based on experience at Wenlock Barn.

(*Anne Blaber*) 'You've got to make some physical improvements, so tenants start to believe the council will do something. Given the scarcity of resources, it may be better to concentrate on a couple of

239

blocks rather than spreading it thinly over the whole estate and having nothing to show for it.'

(*Betty Shanks, former tenants' chairwoman*) 'The problem is, if the money runs out and the rest of the tenants get nothing. If we spend it on just three blocks, the rest wouldn't be very pleased. That's the way I look at it anyway.'

(*Gordon Theobald, present chairman*) 'They wouldn't be pleased anyway, because it would be spread out too far. If people saw one block done up they'd get together and demand action for their blocks. But the work we get done has a negative side too. The council can say the estate has improved so much that we don't need any more money.'

(*Blaber*) 'But politicians are influenced by pressure, don't they say? So the estates which are going to get the money spent on them are those that shout the loudest. If you can build up tenants' interest, then you're in a much stronger position to get what you're after.'

(*Mr Webb, the only black tenant present*) 'The original plans got a lot of response. The tenants were overjoyed, but now it's been over a year and there's been nothing. When I tell people I'm coming to a meeting, they say to me, "What you going there for? They just take your plans and throw them away."' (A few alternative modest items are tossed around: improving lighting, providing more secure front doors, painting the corridors, with tenants painting the area outside their own front doors. The progress of the compactor unit is discussed.)

(*Betty Shanks*) 'We had a meeting about it. (*Ironic*) The turnout was fantastic. We couldn't get into the hall, we had to fight our way in through the crowd: one person. We knocked on every door, and no one came.'

(*Marlene Christian, tenant, invalidity pensioner*) 'To be honest, tenants haven't got a lot of confidence. They've been promised so much in the past. It's been promises, promises, promises, and then nothing.'

(*Cathy Kell, area team leader*) 'Well how *do* we get their reactions? Could you put it in the newsletter, Gordon?'

(*Gordon*) 'I haven't had time to do one lately.'

(*Mike Ward, tenants' liaison officer*) 'We could put up a notice saying, "Only put small green plastic bags in the compactor." But how could we put up a notice that no-one could rip down?'

As the meeting wears on, the personal interactions become clearer and one begins to see another sort of reason why council tenants don't turn out to meetings. Chairman Gordon Theobald is energetic and articulate and puts in a lot of work. But he tends to dominate the tenants' side of the meeting, and the officials reinforce that domination. They all address their comments to him, the district manager shows the plans for a new estate office to him alone and does not pass it round. Gordon talks the same language as the officers, he understands the big words. His presence saves the officers the difficult task of learning to express themselves in the language of the manual working class, to rephrase intellectualized or Latinate remarks into concrete Anglo-Saxon. The language, the length of time taken, the lack of opportunity for most people to say much, the remote prospects of more than marginal change, all conspire to deter most tenants from attending meetings.

The other tenants present make only brief comments. They seem slightly overfaced, carried along by middle-class expertise and evidence. There is a certain reluctance to bring conflict out into the open. But it is there, close beneath the surface. When Marlene objects to the idea of the tenants' liaison officer sharing an office with the estate manager, Betty becomes agitated: she sees the setting up of the managers' office on the estate itself as one of the most important improvements, and feels (as she told me later) that Marlene is trying to sink it, but she is, quite simply, too angry to say what she thinks. 'I'm going, it's a waste of time,' she mutters, and fidgets nervously until a gap arises in the proceedings and she leaves.

The final agenda item of the evening arrives: fences and gates. Ground-floor tenants in several blocks have high wooden fences back and front. Money was available to paint these, and a survey was made of tenants' preferences as to colour. The result was a jumble of shades that would have made the courts look like a Brazilian shanty-town. Therefore the tenants' wishes had to be overriden in the interest of aesthetics. The architect, the liaison officer and Gordon Theobald met to decide exactly how. The most common choice was teak on one block, blue on the other, so the whole of one fence would be teak, the other blue, with the tenants' original choice used for their gate.

(*Marlene, looking skyward like a martyr*) 'I don't think we really want that.'

(*Gordon*) 'It's too late to change.'

(*Mike Ward*) 'I think the main thing is to get this started, so the committee can go to people and say, "Look we've achieved something." I can assure you that we considered every other possibility at great length.'

(*Marlene sighs.*)

(*Gordon, impatient*) 'Well what else are you going to do? (*No response.*) There you are, well shut up then, hahahaha, or we could go on discussing this hour after hour.'

(*Marlene*) 'Have I opened my mouth?'

(*Cathy Kell*) 'I thought it would be a good idea if tenants could tell people in advance.'

(*Gordon*) 'OK, Marlene can go round.'

(*Marlene*) 'You're joking. You hang everything round my neck.'

The experts' choice is railroaded through so that the contractors can start work the following week. People's participation degenerates into representative democracy, which in turn becomes chairman's action, with technocrats calling many of the tunes. Cathy Kell rounds off the meeting: 'Well, you may not have realized it, but you've made quite a few decisions tonight.'

It was a considerable improvement on the traditional paternalistic approach or the blunter 'You'll get what you're given' of some old-style officials. But it was still a far cry from meaningful democracy. As things stand, most Holly Street residents, like most Hackney residents, stake their hopes, not on changing their environment, but on getting out of it, not on collective action, but on individual escape. That attitude is one of the strongest obstacles to change.

Certainly the lot of the dump estates, and of Hackney's older estates, can be improved with a few quite cheap changes. But significant improvements will require significant sums of money for remodelling, improving insulation, providing tenant-controlled central heating and so on. No real advance could be expected under a monetarist government committed to keeping the lid on public spending. And even with high levels of spending, some of the most intractable problems of estates will remain. For the source of the most depressing experiences on Holly Street is other residents and their children: hell is other people. Fill the prestigious Barbican estate in the City of London with the social mix of a typical Hackney dump estate, and the problems would be the same. It is the social architecture, not just the physical, that is to blame.

Improving the social make-up of individual estates is an almost impossible task in the catchment area of the inner city. Child density can be reduced, but only by increasing it on another estate, or by denying housing to families with children on the waiting list. Other factors in the social balance – the proportions of single parents, immigrants, unemployed, unskilled – cannot be changed dramatically as long as applicants have a free choice, although advice services can help, as can positive assistance to disadvantaged groups such as immigrants, single parents, the unemployed and low-paid, with racial and social monitoring schemes to ensure that they are getting a fair share of good first offers. More generally, the dump estates are an inevitable product of the inequalities in housing provision, incomes, power and education within the inner city, just as the inner city as a whole is the inevitable product of similar inequalities in the wider society. Only by removing those inequalities can the creation of dump estates and of inner cities be prevented.

13 From Cure to Crisis Intervention: Social Services and Health

A poor epileptic had fallen face down in a street puddle and was drowning. The onlookers did nothing to help. My cabby shouted 'Turn him over', meaning 'Roll him on his back so he doesn't drown.' That 'Turn him over' is all the pity one Englishman will ever show for another.

Anecdote on London from the Goncourt diaries, 1882

Outside the area social-services office in a Shoreditch back street, a Maltese man waits for the doors to open. He has just been made redundant and his wife has thrown him out. He has nowhere to live and nothing to live on till his first giro cheque arrives.

Inside, intake team leader Peter Cole talks over a few of the day's new cases with his social workers. An eighty-one-year-old woman who is anaemic and relies on a neighbour to help her in and out of the bath has been threatened with disconnection of her gas within the month for a debt of £129. She is not on supplementary benefit, and cannot afford it. Are there any charities that could help? The only one that springs to mind is one for widows of the Boer War, for which she is too young. Another call. Can the office pay £15 a week for a child-minder, for a sixteen-year-old mother with a very small baby. She has no feelings for the child. The husband, an unemployed ex-drug addict, has to look after it, and that prevents him from looking for work. Another of the insoluble dilemmas that social workers deal with every day: for if they do pay, wouldn't they be weakening the mother–child bond even further? Or should they perhaps give up the fight to get the mother to love it, and take the child into care?

Like an entomologist's light-trap, social-service offices attract most of the multifarious species of need that swarm and intermingle in their vicinity. And they swarm in the inner city far more densely than in most areas. Hackney tops the list of many social problems in London, as we saw in Chapter 1: it abounds with single-parent families, handicapped people, mentally ill, unemployed, homeless, low-paid. Social services have the task of attempting to alleviate some of this mass of suffering. It is an utterly impossible job, like trying to drink the ocean dry. In an ideal world social workers would play a preventive role, helping out at an early stage with families' personal and financial problems, to prevent family breakdown; providing the physically and mentally handicapped and ill, and the old, with personal and material support to help them lead fuller lives and avoid institutionalization; acting as a catalyst for community self-help organizations. This approach, of course, could only be effective if social workers were able to call upon effective back-up from agencies dealing with those factors that have the greatest impact on welfare: providing jobs, adequate income support and housing.

In Britain the emphasis in social services, as in health, has always been on cure rather than on prevention. We have no systematic early-warning systems to locate people in need. The usual practice is to wait for someone to present themselves with an acute condition before treating it. At that stage the medicine is often unpleasant, ineffective, or has undesirable side-effects. In this, social services are typical of almost all British institutions. The monetarist-managed recession moved us further and further away from the preventive ideal. The pressure of problems generated by falling incomes and poorer housing, rising crime rates, and unemployment, and the effect of all these on family stability and physical and mental health brought a massive increase in demands for help. At the same time the capacity to offer help was deliberately slashed by the Thatcher government's assault on 'overspending'.

In Hackney, social-services manpower had to be held down: just over 11 per cent of posts were kept unfilled in 1981. The hours of home help provided to the old and the handicapped were cut. The impact of these cuts was much worsened by the policy of the National and Local Government Officers' Association of not covering the work of vacant posts. Social-services teams left without secretarial help refused to take on new cases. Places in nurseries and children's homes had to be cut back. Emergency moneys, given out to families to help prevent children being taken into care, dropped at a time when the need for them was rising: payment of fuel bills fell by one-fifth from 1979/80 to 1980/81, while disconnections were soaring; money for clothing was cut by a half in the same year that clothing grants from social security were withdrawn; help towards holidays fell by a third. There were fewer telephones, televisions, aids and home adaptations for the old and disabled, essential to make their lives safer and more tolerable.

The cuts bit deep into plans for improvements too. Plans for new teams of workers for disturbed adolescents and juvenile criminals were shelved at precisely the moment when the problems posed by these groups reached crisis proportions. Such cuts cannot provide any real savings: they simply delay dealing with problems while they are still manageable, allowing them to build up until much more expensive courses – prison, children's homes – are unavoidable.

Social work in the slump became more and more a matter not just of trying to cure problems, but of dealing only with the worst crises. Nursery places became unavailable to any except cases of the highest priority need. Social workers cut out almost all their preventive and discretionary work. The task of keeping a watchful eye on the elderly and the handicapped was dropped. Cases that were already being handled by other agencies were not touched, even though the other agencies were often the source of the problem. Social workers were increasingly dealing only with those cases where their legal responsibilities were unavoidable: people unable to look after themselves, and children in care.

Abandoned by the Welfare State

Sarah Jones* was just one of the unnumbered poor, abandoned without effective help and crushed by the specific handicaps of being female in a society that, for all its laws against sexual discrimination, is still loaded against women. She is thirty-eight. Her straight blonde-rinsed hair frames a face that life in Hackney has hardened. Mathias House, where she lives, is one of Hackney's worst estates, a five-storey block with external balconies. As usual,

---

* The names in the family have been changed.

there is nowhere for children to play but down on the concrete courtyard, around derelict cars with jagged, rusty bodywork and shattered windscreens, old mattresses and pram-sheds with their broken doors lying on the floor. The stair-well to Mathias House is scattered with broken glass, decorated with burn marks, imprints of tiny paint-covered hands, and graffiti: *Marshal woz ere the skin, Jennifer is a cunt*. It stinks of urine. On its roof is an impromptu still-life: an empty can of Heineken lager; a child's sandal; a Moroccan purse; the dropped handlebars of a racing bike; and a pigeon dead for weeks. Sarah lives on an upper floor. Her washing dangles from a line stretched from the balcony rail to the walkway leading to the free-standing lift-shaft. The view from here is of other estates like this, terraced streets, and beyond, the giant towers of Nightingale estate.

Sarah married at eighteen and had five children in as many years, two of them twins. Her first husband was an alcoholic. After ten years of violence she left him, and left the children with him, but later got custody of them through the courts. After a spell on her own, she found a boy-friend, who moved in with her. They married when she became pregnant with her sixth child. In April 1979, soon after the seventh was born, her second husband left her. All seven children still live with her in her cramped four-bedroomed flat. One bedroom is unusable because of a gaping hole in the wall to the stair-well, which years of visits to the estate office have not succeeded in getting remedied. Her eldest daughter, eighteen-year-old Marie, sleeps in one bedroom. One of the seventeen-year-old twins, Martha, sleeps in another with her four-year-old half-brother Martin; Sarah herself sleeps in the third with Margaret (fourteen) and Meg (two). The other twin, Molly, sleeps with the family next door. Both twins have been unemployed since they left school. Mark, sixteen, an apprentice in the dying trade of french polishing, sleeps on the sofa in the lounge.

Sarah's problems came to a head in 1979: 'I used to pay all our bills, but I'm one of those people who, if I have the money, I don't pay a debt, I spend it. Some people have got vices, smoking, drinking. My vice is my kids. If I've got it, I'll spend it on them. As we were getting behind with the bills, we agreed that my husband should pay them. He gave me less housekeeping to cover them. But he wasn't paying them either. I knew he wasn't paying the electric, because we thought there was something wrong with the meter. Every time the bills came in they would be £160, £190. We had special meter men and wiring men round, but they couldn't find out what was wrong. One of them said, "I can't understand this, you wouldn't pay bills like that for a penthouse."

'I'd just come out of hospital from having Meg when my husband left me. He just walked out, I've never known why from that day to this. After he'd gone I found out that he owed the electricity board £1,173, and £580 in rent, and £900 on hire purchase. I had to carry the can for all his debts. I found out where he was living earlier this year. I've given them all the evidence, so how come they don't approach him for the debts?'

It was debt, added to low income, handicap and overcrowding, that proved the straw that broke Sarah's broad back. Her case is not exceptional: time and again public bodies hold unwaged or low-paid women responsible for the debts of their deserting husbands, with disastrous effects on the whole family.

'They cut my electric off in April 1979, just after my husband left. I'd only been out of hospital for three weeks. They came and said we've got to turn you off. I had a fight with them at the door. Did they injure me? No, I injured them. My baby was four weeks old. It wasn't warm weather. I had to give her four-hourly feeds with no cooker, no light, no nothing. Social services gave me a two-cylinder gas cooker and that was all, but calor gas is £5·50 a bottle and then you've got the fumes, so I didn't use it. You know, no one has come knocking on my door since to see if we've got any heating, or if I'm dead on the floor. We were without electric for two years. We cooked our meals in a friend's house, or we used to go to cafés if I had a bit of money. We had candles, and then I got one of those miner's lamps. We had no TV, we just sat around like zombies getting on each other's nerves. At night when it was cold my babies slept in my friend's house.

'I lost four stones in the first three months with worry. The furniture was repossessed. I sold all my home to keep going, I was taking the mirrors off the wall to get £4, I sold my eternity ring for £4. The place was empty. Then I exchanged my gold wed-ding-ring for a second-hand sofa and a sideboard. The ring was nothing to me, but it takes all your pride away. I ain't got none left.

'To stay in this place I had to agree to pay off £3·30 a week towards the rent. I'm still paying that. Then I came to an agreememt with the electric to pay off £2 a week and they put the electric back on again, but I was only on for a month or so, then they cut me off again, don't ask me why. But there's no way I can let my kids stay without light again. I can't leave them in with candles. You've seen my little boy, he's a sod. And if there's a fire, you can never get them back again, can you? So I put the fuse-box back in down the landing and connected myself up again. If someone grasses me up, I don't care. What they gonna do, put me away? Let them put me away.

'I've had no social worker since my Marie left special school [for the mentally handicapped]. They say they've blacked new cases in this area. These official people just don't care. Why have I been left like this? All I ever got off any of them is "I don't know, I'll see, maybe, perhaps". Everyone who comes to my door officially, it's no, everyone says, or yes, Mrs Jones, then nothing. What use is all the stuff they write down? I'd rather they said we can't help you, sod off. When they see you've got through so many years, they think you're going to get over it. But there's always a point where it gets too much. What I need is someone who'll back me up and help me find the person I've been looking for for years, but they always seem to pass it on to a person you can never find. I never come under this scheme or that scheme. Well what scheme do I come under? It's as if I don't exist, I've been cut off. I've had twenty years of bullshit off housing, social security, social services. They've given me so much bullshit they can't give me any more.

'Well take the housing. I want to get off this estate, it's deplorable. I been here eleven years. The council's attitude is, leave it, because it's old. When I came out of hospital with the baby, the dustmen had been on strike and they'd left all the mess. Babies were out there, and there were maggots and rats. I said to two of my friends, come on, let's clear it up. We put some in the estate office, through the letter-box. The next day the council was here, cleaning it all up. I want to transfer out of here, but they say I can't till I've cleared my rent arrears [normal policy is to allow transfers only to people whose rent books have been clear of arrears for at least three months, thus denying transfers to the poorest]. I had the housing man round here to see what it was like. I told him, "How would you like to be sitting in the bath and a girl of sixteen wants to go to the toilet?" He said, "Oh, I've never thought about that." I got girls in their womanhood and a boy who's a man. They want to bring their boy-friends and girl-friends here, and supposing I find a man friend, which I'm entitled to, what privacy have I got even to sit and talk? What is stopping them rehousing me? I've told them I'll take one of these boarded-up places, they do the sanitary work and I'll wallpaper and redecorate, and they could still keep this £3·30 a week going that I pay towards the arrears. What have they to lose?

'Social security is no better. Whenever I want some money off them, they say, "We can't find your file." But they soon find it if they want me. They stand there and take the mickey out of you. They sent me two books with the wrong payment days stamped on them. I went up to the office and said, could you just alter this? The girl took them off me and ripped them, and said, "It's got to go to Newcastle, we'll send your money out next week." What are you supposed to live off in the meantime? When my baby was born, the head office in Newcastle was on strike. It took seven months before I got my family allowance through for her, and when I complained they told me, "Go to Newcastle and collect your book yourself." I've just been eight weeks without milk tokens, and I never get a refund. I've tried being nice, I've tried being understanding, I've tried every way, but then you just lose your top. I've had so many rows up there, I daren't show my face any more.

'Even the social services have messed me about. One social worker I had she came one day and said, "I've been in touch with the electricity, if they don't get £250 by Wednesday, they'll cut you off and the council will have to take your kids away." I said, "What about the baby I'm carrying?" She said, "We'll have to take the baby when it's born." At Christmas time she came up one day. I had a big tree, she said, "What have you got a tree for when you owe all that money?" She said, "Don't let me come in here and see these kids have got any toys for Christmas, a tin with marbles in it is good enough." The next time she came I hid the tree in the bathroom. She said, "I've got a nice present for every one of your children. It's only small." You know what it was? Fifteen pounds'-worth of electric stamps, in a book. What use was that to me when I owed a thousand pounds? Then Martha said something cheeky to me and I smacked her. The social worker said, "I saw you do that, don't do that." She's brought us shoes from charity that were all black and worn, like you'd find shoes in the street. Then when I was having the baby she said, "Don't let me see you coming out of hospital without being sterilized," and she wanted my eldest daughter sterilizing because she's mentally handicapped. It's easy to tell someone what to do. But no one tells me what to do with my life, unless they're offering to make my life better.'

Life is a matter of surviving from one week to the next, one day to the next. Sarah gets £17·25 in family allowance for the three youngest children, including £3 extra for being a single parent, plus £7 a week in maintenance from her first husband, but neither of the additions do her the slightest bit of good because they are simply deducted from her social-security benefit, from which she gets only £19·35 (£3·30 is deducted at source, along with the rent and rates). Total net income for herself and three children: £43·50 a week (1981), or £1·55 a day each. This is higher than for many other poor families because Sarah pays nothing for electricity: her illegal reconnection helps to make up for her inadequate benefit. Without that, there would be no more than £1·16 a day left for each of them. Her three eldest daughters pay her £8 a week each and her son gives her £10, but these sums are barely enough to cover the cost of their food.

'I get my social security on Monday and my family allowance plus the girls' money on Tuesday. That lasts me till Wednesday night. Then I'm skint till Friday evening when the boy gives me his £10. He throws it at me. He won't tell me how much he earns. By then it's so late that all the shops are shut so we have to go to the fish-and-chip shop, which costs more. Then what have you got on a Monday morning? You haven't got a tea-bag, and there's no one will help you. We never had a proper baked dinner since my husband left, we never bought a proper piece of meat. I just had to buy my son a pair of shoes for £9·99. I was buying him trainers every fortnight, he's such a little sod he wears them out. You can't get a grant for·clothes any more. They say you're supposed to manage on what they give you each week, but how can you?

'My family is a funny thing. They're all unsettled, like me. My eighteen-year-old is mentally handicapped. At six months she was saying ma and dad, then she stopped, suddenly. I think it might have been the injections. I won't let the others have any. The fourteen-year-old has eczema from nerves, the four-year-old's got eczema on his feet. He was fretting for his father when he left, and he clings to me. With all the arguing in this place, we all get on each other's nerves. I got so fed up I put two of them in a home for eight weeks. They're fed up with me – I've always got the hump. And I'm fed up with them. They're big, the older ones. Not one of my kids takes any notice of me. I'm the kid in here. I'm the lodger. I get told to get to bed if they want me out of the way.

'It's hard when you haven't got a man. You've got to be hard and fight for what you need, you've got to be a man and a woman. But you can only take so much. I'm a human person, I'm not an animal. When you're left on your own your two shoulders don't seem to balance any more. Who do you go to for help? If those who are supposed to help don't want to know, who'll help you? Who can I ask to help me? Who can I ask, a stranger in the road? They call it a welfare state. Never! It's not a welfare state no more. You ain't got a chance. No one's said, "We know she's a one-parent family, let's give her a new start." I've never been given a chance.

'No one knows what's in here [she points to her head]. I manage to laugh and joke, but really I can't see anything to laugh about. I can't see nothing funny in the world any more. It's a good job I know how to get it out of my system. I'll just go and smash something up. I'm known for shouting. I don't care any more. They can only kill me once.

'I can't see no light at the end of the tunnel. What's the good of my living, every day and every night? It's not a life, it's not a life. I just live day by day. I hardly go outside this house. I get up, I do a bit of housework, I go to bed at eight. You tell me, is that natural? When I get up I think, Christ, I've got to get through till 8 o'clock tonight. If I had tablets here, I'd have taken the lot. But then I look at the two babies.'

Humpty-Dumpty

The inner city is a precarious, shaky wall and most of its inhabitants and families are fragile Humpty-Dumptys. It is the entire complex of pressures acting on them that leads to their downfall. Social services and other helping agencies can only pick up the pieces and try to fit them together again. But they can only succeed on a lasting basis if the factors that led to the initial collapse are changed: if incomes, employment and housing are improved. If a patch-up job is done and the victim is propped up on the same unstable wall, he will certainly fall and break time after time.

The inner city, with its squalid housing, its atmosphere of decay, its endless conflicts, its threat of crime, is the worst conceivable environment for the mentally unstable. And yet the inner city attracts them and creates them and becomes, to some extent, a vast informal mental hospital, about as humane and caring as Bedlam, which in its infamous heyday was sited within a stone's throw of modern Hackney. A 1973 study by the Hackney-based Psychiatric Rehabilitation Association found that, out of nineteen constituencies in north-east London and Sheffield, Hackney North and Hackney Central had, respectively, the second and the third highest hospital discharge rates for schizophrenia. The North Hackney rate was 19·5 per 10,000 in 1968, almost double the national average. The study found that the discharge rate was very closely related to aspects of poverty, especially the unemployment rate, the proportion of unskilled workers, and the percentage of overcrowded and one-parent households. Hackney North and Hackney Central scored respectively second and third highest on a composite index of these factors.

There are two main theories to account for the connection between mental illness and poverty. The drift theory holds that those with a tendency towards mental instability will have a poor work record, pushing them gradually towards unskilled, insecure jobs. The stress theory suggests that the conditions of life in poor families generate mental illness. Almost certainly both are partly valid and work together to produce a concentration of mental disorder in the inner city. For the low income of unskilled workers pushes them to move into low-rent areas, while the multiple stresses of life in the inner city produce more mental problems, both of the more florid varieties and of the less visible kinds, such as depression, anxiety, nervous tension (all fully realistic in the circumstances) and phobias, obsessions and persecution complexes, which again frequently have a very real basis in the inner city. Recession intensifies the risks of most of these.

Thus the principal aims of mental-health care – prevention and sustained rehabilitation – are quite impossible to achieve for most people in the inner city and even more so in a slump.

Immigrants are often even more susceptible to mental problems because of diets lacking in essential nutrients and the added stress of cultural conflict and discrimination. Douglas Prehaye is a short, bearded West Indian of thirty-four, trying his best to get back to mental health after a breakdown that shattered his family. He now lives in a single room, about 2 metres by 5 metres, in a lodging-house, for which he pays the princely sum of £35 a week inclusive of two meals a day. When I visited him, he had on a donkey jacket and a woolly hat indoors, to keep warm, and had drawn the curtains to keep out the cold of a winter's day. The head of his bed was pulled half-way down the room, away from the draughty windows, and on the wall next to where his head would rest was a large patch of damp condensed from his breath in the night. Shopping-bags full of laundry and litter leaned against the walls, and on the chest of drawers was a row of bottles of drugs.

'I used to drive a bus till three years ago, but my nerves went. I just couldn't keep up. It was the bills that did it. The electric. Over £100, and you couldn't see how you used it. I went into hospital. While I was in there, my wife's wages was only just enough to buy food and pay the bills. She couldn't keep up with the rent and she got notice to quit. When I came out of hospital she'd gone. She lives in the country now, somewhere. Since then I been in and out of hospital. I take a lot of pills. I spend my time just as you see me here, writing to my mum back home [he has a fat sheaf of paper in front of him, twelve or fifteen pages long]. Or I walk the streets looking in the shop windows. I go to the park, sit on the bench. Weekends when the police is out more, I keep out of their way. I come and sit in that chair you are sitting in and sleep. It's like a cave in here. You just lock yourself in. I put 40p in the meter, if the heater is on low, that lasts me from 6 p.m. to maybe 3 in the morning. Then if I'm cold I wake up and put more money in. Right now, God, it's so cold you can't sleep.

'I'm trying my best to get back where I was, to get a job. I try everything, even cleaning. But what getting me upset is, they take you on and they keep you maybe three weeks, and then they come up with some little excuse, or maybe no reason at all, and tell you to go. I just pray to God someone will take me on permanent, and bear with me for a little while till I get back on my feet. I just hope a miracle would happen and I would get a job like before all this trouble happened you could. I reached a blank. I don't want to think about the way this country is. I don't buy the paper any more. It's the same thing in there as I am going through in here. I just don't want to know.'

Prehaye has no chance of regaining his self-respect and self-confidence in a slump. His housing is unimaginably depressing – little larger, and much colder, than a prison cell. His chances of a job are poorer even than average: recession has knocked all the charity out of employers. His social worker provides occasional sympathy, his drugs suppress the worst of his anxiety. But they are dealing only with the symptoms. The causes remain.

Health: The Inverse-Care Law

All the inequalities of society, inequalities of power, status, income, conditions of work and housing, take their toll on the body as well as the mind. The general mechanism of stress has a potent effect: in nature it is adaptive, leading to either fight or flight. In human society, convention inhibits these natural responses, diverting them into redirected aggression and even into self-destruction. The body turns against itself, just as a rat that is involuntarily confined to the territory of another rat can die from stress. All the environmental sources of illness are stronger in poor areas, and even more so in the inner city: smoking is more prevalent, especially among women; diets contain more sugar, starch and fats because foods high in protein, minerals and vitamins are more expensive; damp and cold give rise to chest complaints and rheumatism; nervous tensions, air pollution, moulds from damp, all contribute to allergies, asthma, eczema; low birth weights are common because of poor maternal diet and smoking during pregnancy; there are more accidents in the home and on the street, from the use of paraffin heaters, lack of safe toys, absence of safe play facilities; injuries from family or street violence, and from work, are more common; there are health risks arising from poor refuse-disposal systems, shared toilets, ducted air heating; exhaustion from overwork and the effort of coping with stress leads to reduced resistance to other diseases. The inner city incubates illness, and attracts to itself those whose earning capacity is limited by long-standing illness.

Recession intensifies all the factors precipitating illness, by reducing incomes, and increasing malnutrition, damp and stress. A 1983 survey of pregnant mothers in Hackney found that they had an average intake of between 1,600 and 1,700 calories a day – 500–700 calories less than the recommended minimum, and less than the average consumption in Ethiopia, the most malnourished country in the world. Between half and three-quarters of the mothers were also short of most essential vitamins and minerals.

Personal health is one of the most telling and tragic indicators of the degree of inequality in Britain, and of its consequences. Comparing our lowest social group with our highest, we find that unskilled manual workers have three times the rate of limiting long-standing illness as professional and managerial types; four times the rate of mental illness; six times the rate of accidents at work; double the incidence of deafness; three times the incidence of total tooth loss; infant mortality two and a half times as high and stillbirth rates twice as high. Thus is inequality incised into the very flesh of the poor. And where the need is greatest, the inverse-care law sees to it that the provision, generally, is poorest.

Primary health care in Hackney is no exception to the rule. It is not an area that would attract most doctors. There is a shortage of suitable premises, and the prospects of supplementing earnings from private practice are negligible. General practitioners have lists smaller than average, but that is more than made up for by the number of health complaints per person. Hackney GPs are older than average – one in four is over sixty – and half of them work alone rather than in health centres. Their surgeries are often behind dingy shop-fronts or on one floor of a terraced house. Many surgeries are open only fourteen hours a week, at times that do not suit working people (manual workers who take time off to see doctors usually lose pay). Many do not work an appointments system, so patients begin queueing out on the street, long before opening time, even on cold winter mornings. One in five patients waits for more than an hour, in rooms that are often unheated and without toilet facilities.

I spoke to a Hackney women's group about their experience of the health service. They complained of brusque, offhand treatment from GPs of a kind that it is difficult to imagine being meted out with impunity to middle-class patients.

(*Ruth*) 'There are three doctors at the surgery I go to. It's a flat, really, and you've got to walk through one doctor's room to get to the others. You can see people being examined, and there are no screens. He was examining me once, I said, "What if someone comes through?" He said, "Don't be stupid, you're all here because you're ill, it's all the same."'

(*Jacqui*) 'They want to get you in and get you out. You never have time to sit there and tell them what's the matter with you. And they don't bother to explain anything, you've got to ask them what's the matter with you. Plenty of times I've come home and my husband has said, "What's wrong with you", and I've said, "I don't know, he wouldn't tell me."'

The patient becomes a mere swallower of pills, a passive spectator in her own treatment. Her own view of what is wrong with her is not taken seriously.

(*Ruth*) 'I told him once I had tonsillitis. He said, "I'll tell you when you've got a sore throat, not the other way round."'

(*Sandra*) 'They don't seem to take your view seriously on what might be wrong with your kid, even though it's you what's living with them.'

Two-thirds of Hackney's GPs live outside the area. Hence getting hold of a doctor out of hours is more than usually difficult. The first problem is the phone. The phone is an essential but usually ignored element of our health system, taken for granted by the middle classes. But for the less affluent, who do not possess one, it is a constant tribulation, very much worsened by vandalism, and a nightmare in an emergency.

(*Doris*) 'There might be enough phones around here, if they were all working. But half of them are out of order for days on end. There's always six or seven people waiting.'

(*Iris, who has an epileptic sister*) 'You can never find one that's free or working. You just keep running and running till you find one, then if there's a queue, you never know whether it's worth waiting or if you should run on and find another.'

(*Irene*) 'When I've asked for a home visit for my kid, they've never taken less than three hours to get here. One Sunday we phoned up at 10, they got to us at 4.30. Another time we waited four and a half hours, then my husband went out and phoned again. They said they had no record of the first call. It took another three hours after that.'

Nor are the problems over once the doctor is seen, for prescriptions have to be taken to chemists and medicines collected. Pharmacists are a second element of the health system that is largely left to chance. Hackney has fewer chemists than a better-off area would have, and hardly any open after 7 p.m. When they are all closed people have to embark on distressing and expensive voyages around London to find others that are open.

(*Ruth*) 'My baby had been in hospital for six months. When they let her out they gave me a prescription, but it was 8 at night and all the chemists were shut. I had to get a taxi to one at King's Cross. I got there at 10.25, just before it closed.'

(*Irene*) 'Our baby had croup. I got out of the doctor's at 7.15 and there were no chemists open. My husband had to borrow his mate's van and drove all around London. He went to Piccadilly, but they've closed that one down. He asked policemen but they didn't know. Finally he was over in Earls Court and asked the police station. They said the only one open all night was in Willesden. He didn't get back till about 3 o'clock in the morning.'

In most deprived areas, hospital services would not make up for the deficiencies in primary health care. Hackney, because it is close to the centre of London, is well provided and benefits from specialized and teaching hospitals like the Queen Elizabeth Hospital for Children and Bart's. But a disproportionate share of the City and Hackney health district budget – 91 per cent in 1979–80 –

was taken up by hospital services. A mere 6 per cent went on community health care, to provide health visitors, district nurses, child-health clinics, family-planning services and health centres. The hospital service itself was becoming more and more centralized, partly because of budget restrictions, partly because of a misguided drive to rationalization. In future, services will be even more heavily centralized at a new general hospital in Homerton and at Bart's. Centralization makes life easier for doctors and nurses, but more and more difficult for poor people in an area so badly provided with public and private transport as Hackney. For transport is the third unseen element of the health system and is the source of enormous distress and cost in time and money for the poor, taking its toll of patients, and making supportive family visits that much more difficult. This has a particularly disastrous effect on antenatal care. Many mothers have their babies delivered at Bart's, and are expected to have their monthly and fortnightly check-ups there: but the journey there and back takes them at least two hours, often more, without including the long wait to be seen.

(*Sandra*) 'Everyone gets given the same time. You get an appointment for 9.30 and you find seventy other people have been given an appointment for 9.30. They take you in the order you turn up. I was there for six hours once. But if you can't make it for 9.30 because you've got another child to take to school, they have a go at you, they say, "Well, you'll have to find someone else to take it, because 9.30 is the time of the appointment." They're really insensitive to you as an individual. You go there in spite of them.'

(*Ruth*) 'I gave up going. I was there all day once, and they say you're not allowed to take any sandwiches, but if you go to the canteen, they might call your name while you're out. They keep you waiting there all the hours that God sends, and in the end you just can't be bothered.'

Patients are kept waiting for hours without the slightest thought as to the enormous social cost in stress, inconvenience, loss of pay – costs which are proportionately far greater for the poor.

259

Who Controls Fertility?

Family planning is a particularly crucial factor in the welfare of poor families. Manual workers tend to have larger families than non-manual workers. Illegitimate births and shotgun weddings are more common. Use of effective family-planning methods is less. There is a greater reluctance to use family-planning methods. Girls are deterred by parents and doctors from raising the subject. Myths about the dangers of contraceptives abound, pill side-effects are aggravated by stress and poor diets, method failure is more frequent, and male machismo often more pronounced.

Family-planning methods requiring hospital treatment pose a particular problem. Sterilizations on the National Health Service are often refused until people are in their late twenties, but many working-class women have had as many children as they want or can cope with by their early twenties. In the case of abortions, the first hospital appointment may be as late as twelve to fourteen weeks into the pregnancy, by which time refusals on the grounds of danger to health are more likely. With ill-informed and less articulate clients, doctors and consultants can more easily impose their own medical view of the situation on the woman, regardless of her social problems, and she will rarely have the necessary information or funds to get treatment charitably or privately. The resulting unwanted pregnancies are a very serious matter for the poor, involving additional housing and income stresses.

I met several women whose own wishes and social needs had been overridden by health professionals. Elaine W., whom we shall meet in Chapter 16, was refused sterilization and abortion.

Pam Johnson, Doris Davies's* fourth daughter, was also denied the right to control her fertility. She is a rosy-cheeked twenty-four-year-old with the family's snub nose, married to a metal-polisher who has been unemployed for two years. She has strong and valid reasons for wishing to limit the size of her family. Her three children Steve (eight), Carla (three) and Gaynor (one) share one small bedroom 3 metres square with a lodger whom the Johnsons put up because they need the money. The family income is £72·25

---

* See page 441. All names in the Davies family have been changed.

(1981), less £22 for rent, rates and hot water and an average of £9 a week for fuel. 'Personal weaknesses' consume another £8: £2·50 for colour television, £3·50 for cigarettes for Pam, £2 pocket-money for husband Jim. Remainder for food, clothing, household goods etc for five people: £33·25 a week, 95p per day each, enough for one Big Mac hamburger. Pam gets her own clothes second-hand. Her youngest children have so few clothes that they have to stand around naked on wash day. The Johnsons' three-piece suite was bought second-hand from Pam's sister Pat James by handing over the child-benefit book for six weeks.

Their straitened circumstances inevitably lead to frequent rows.

'Sometimes he'll complain about the food, if he's got egg and chips he'll say, "Is that all I got for dinner?" I tell him to go out and get food on my money. Now I'm giving him sausage and chips, we've gone up one rung. And we row a lot about a lot of silly little things. Like any little bit of dirt he sees on the floor he'll say, "Hoover it up." But it seems to me like he's not helping out enough. He sits around indoors and watches telly all the time. It gets on my nerves.

'I know it's not his fault. He wants a proper job that's paying the money. Social security call him up for interview every now and then. They get him in a little room and say, "Why ain't you got a job?" He says, "There's none I want." They say, "Have you looked in the *Hackney* [*Gazette*]?" He's took the *Hackney* up there and stuck it under their noses. A couple of months back they threatened to take him to court for not maintaining his family. [This persecution of the allegedly work-shy by unemployment review officers persisted even when there were 3 million unemployed and more, with the aim, or at least the potential effect, of driving them into competition for jobs and pushing wage rates down.] They've had a go at me too. They've been here and pointed at my telly and said, "You ain't supposed to have that," and my fridge, they say, "That's a luxury." If they're coming round I've got to hide most of my nice things or they'll say I'm not supposed to have them.

'We want to get out of this place. I been waiting for a transfer for two years. We asked them to nominate us to the GLC waiting-list because we wanted to go to Enfield – Jim's got family out there –

but they wouldn't. They won't even let us out of Hackney now. I said, "Innit good, when you're gonna tell us where we're supposed to live."

'I don't want any more kids. I couldn't cope with any more. They get on top of me sometimes, in here all the time, under my feet. There's nowhere for them to play round here, because you got all the roads, and the playground has had all the equipment taken out of it.

'I have used the pill, but I forget to take it. I'd need to have it tied round my neck really, and I fall [get pregnant] easily. I had my first abortion when I was seventeen. Steve was only nine months old when I fell again, I wasn't using anything at the time. I couldn't cope with being pregnant again so soon. By the time I saw the hospital, they said I was too far gone, I was four months. But I got it done at a charity for nothing. Then about two years later I got pregnant again. I was living at my mum's at the time, sharing a bedroom with Pat and her two kids, because we couldn't get a council place of our own. It was two and a half months before I saw the doctor to ask for an abortion, and it was another month before I saw the hospital. They said an abortion would be dangerous, but I started getting premature labour pains, so they gave me one in the end.

'After that I had these two [Carla and Gaynor]. A few months ago I went to the doctor and asked if I could get sterilized. He said, "No, you're too young." I said, "I don't see why, I've got three kids and I've already had two abortions." He said, "You could have it done and in another couple of years you'd want another one." But I don't want to go being a bleedin' rabbit all my life. I should have argued more, but I'm one of these that sits back and listens. The doctor said, go and have the coil fitted. But you can still fall on the coil. A friend of mine had it and she fell.

'After that, everything got too much for me, the kids, the house, not getting a transfer, me and Jim was rowing all the time. The doctor gave me sixty pills to calm my nerves. I swallowed the lot. My sister-in-law Sheila found me. She made me sick them up. Mum took me back home and I was dozed up for a couple of days. I don't think I'd do it again. I'll have to manage, somehow.'

As bad luck would have it, a few weeks after I interviewed her,

Pam 'fell' again. In April 1982 she gave birth to twins and became the mother of five, when three were already enough to push her into attempted suicide. But the pregnancy finally forced the council's hand. Two weeks before the babies were due, Pam and Jim were offered, and accepted, a three-bedroomed town house in Dalston, where they would still be as overcrowded as they were in their two-bedroomed Shoreditch flat.

14   Hard Times to Grow Old in

Men will dishonour parents, who grow old too quickly. Wretched and
godless, they will cheat their aged parents of their due.
                        Hesiod, Works and Days *(tr. D. Wender)*

No generation of old people has lived through such traumatic
changes as today's. Two world wars, the Blitz, the Great Depression. The physical environment they knew has been transformed
beyond recognition. Social change has left them even more dis-
oriented, for they have seen a revolution in personal values and
habits, in technology and communications and tastes, and now, in
the evening of their lives, the dark times of the second slump.

No generation of old people has been so marginalized as today's.
The accelerating pace of change has deprived them of their role of
elders and found no new role for them to fill. Their wisdom is rated
as worthless. Respect from the young has been replaced by indifference or ridicule, consideration by neglect or even predation.
Family responsibility and neighbourly concern have receded,
giving way to isolation and institutionalization. Talk of these
trends in the fifties was premature, as Peter Townsend's *The Family
Life of Old People* showed. Twenty-five years on, in the spreading
inner city, they represent the reality for a growing proportion of old
people.

No group of old people is more deprived than the old of the inner
city. Nowhere has the physical and social fabric altered so dramatically: with massive slum clearance and redevelopment; the destruction of old communities; the out-migration of their children
and grandchildren to greener pastures and the in-migration of
people of different races and cultures; the pervasive fear of street
crime and violence. Nowhere are old people more isolated than in
the inner city. The proportion of old people living alone in

264

Hackney was about 35 per cent in 1981, equal to the inner London average, but much higher than in outer London, where only 28 per cent live alone. But this figures expresses only a part of their isolation. For in more stable areas an old person living alone will have relatives living near by who can visit regularly and provide help when needed. Many of Hackney's able-bodied young between the ages of twenty-five and forty-five have moved out, to Essex, Hertfordshire, or new towns in other areas, leaving their old behind. Even when they have remained, housing pressures may have forced them to accept a flat some way from their parents. The lack of phones or cars among the poor, and the state of public transport, make a few kilometres in Hackney equivalent to fifty or a hundred kilometres for a car-owning family. And the local community helps the old in the inner city less than anywhere else. Good neighbourliness has dissolved, giving way to the insolence of infants, the menace of youth, and the indifference of adults with more problems of their own than they can cope with. What the community cannot offer the state and local authorities should provide, but public-spending cuts have stopped and reversed progress here. The health service was increasingly short of long-stay beds for the old. Social workers no longer kept an eye on the still mobile old. The hours of home help were cut.

While pensions have kept better pace with inflation than unemployment benefit and supplementary benefit, rents and fuel-price rises have outpaced them. Despite the emotive priority always given to pensioners, their poverty is not as acute, nor so far-reaching in its consequences, as the poverty of families with children. But it is still true that the last years of a life of privation are, by and large, also spent in privation.

The old of Hackney cope with their tribulations, for the most part, with admirable stoicism. Perhaps that is because they are no strangers to lives full of problems. Past and present are both disagreeable in divergent ways. Deeper memories are mixed, of poverty far beyond the worst you can find today, but also of a warm, living community that now is virtually dead.

Company for Lunch

The more spritely of the old compensate by keeping each other company at lunch clubs, where they can also get a very cheap, fairly nutritious (if often overcooked) meal. The clubs are curiously segregated places. There is rarely a black face to be seen, even in areas where blacks dominate, and the sexes, for the most part, also gravitate to their own kind. Hoxton Hall lunch club meets in a gym, using trestle-tables. Lunch is stodgy traditional fare, meat and two veg, fish on Fridays, sponges and pies and custard for pudding, all in little foil trays. People serve each other: one collects the dessert for the whole table, another fills all the cups with tea.

Here I met Ted Harrison, a well-preserved seventy-nine-year-old, very smartly turned out in gold-rimmed glasses, brown tweed sports jacket, light brown herring-bone trousers and brown cardigan. Every item of clothing was bought at jumble sales. 'I haven't bought any new clothes for eleven years. It was hard, in the beginning, going to jumble sales. You went in like this, hiding your head with your hand and looking down, in case anyone saw you. But you get used to it. You can get a nice overcoat for £2, shirts for 50p, shoes for 50p. [All at a tenth or less of lowest shop prices.] The only new things I have are socks and underwear. I make sure I get given them for Christmas.'

Ted's pension, with supplementary benefit, amounts to £36 a week (1981), and he gets a railwayman's pension of £8 a week, inflation-proofed into the bargain. This, like most of the modest savings of the aged poor, is counted against him. 'You look forward to the letter around Christmas time saying your railway pension has gone up, but then a cold doubt creeps into your mind, and you remember that every time it goes up, the same amount is taken off your supplementary benefit. You can't win. I realize now that what I should have done earlier is not pay towards an extra pension for my old age, I should have spent it all. The only savings I've got now I'm keeping so that when the time comes, my children won't have to pay to bury me. I don't want them to have to start collecting to put the old man under.'

He has never borrowed or loaned money in his life, he says, as if having your children pay for your funeral was a kind of debt which, being dead, you could never redeem. His rent and rates come to £17 a week, fuel on average to about £8 – so heat and housing take up 57 per cent of his income, leaving only £19 for everything else. That is precious little, but it is double the per-capita sum available to many of the families with children I met. I asked him if his pension was sufficient.

'It is, but's that because I cut my cloth to suit my purse. I don't go in for luxuries. I can't even go out and buy myself a nice tie. You pick up a tin of sardines off the shelf, last week it was 18p, this week it's 24p, so you put it back again. The only time I can afford a bit of luxury is in November each year, when the state pension goes up. Then I buy myself a portion of cherry cake, or a bar of chocolate, which I'm not able to at other times. I've not had a holiday for fourteen years. I did apply for a council holiday a while back. I filled in the form, but I didn't like it, they ask too many questions about what you're earning. After a couple of years waiting, they told me I could go on a holiday in another two years, so I thought, sod it.'

Ted Harrison has lived alone for ten years, since his wife died: 'At the time I felt like doing myself in, I didn't think I was going to get over it. But the kids said, "You've got to look after yourself because of the grandchildren." I'm thoroughly domesticated now, I can clean, sew, wash and cook. I don't need a home help – if I had one I might start getting a bit amorous with her.' Ted had four children, and now has five grandchildren and three great grand-children. None of them lives anywhere near Hackney – his children moved to Essex and Basingstoke, some because they couldn't stand the waiting for a Hackney council house, some because the firm they worked for moved out. But he does manage to see at least one of them each week.

I asked him if he thought things were worse now than when he was young. I expected the answer to be that they were worse but several of the fitter old men I spoke to said they were better. Most of the old women, by contrast, said they were worse. The crucial difference is that the women are much more susceptible to the fear of crime.

'It's a lot better today,' said Ted, who grew up in Shoreditch. 'When I was a kid, in the years before the First World War, we used to go to school without shoes on. You could buy shoes off the school for two pence a week, but they were marked so the pawn-broker wouldn't take them. Some days we would have only one slice of bread for dinner. My mother used to send me up to the market to get three pennyworth of bits, bits of sausage-meat leftovers, chops that weren't fresh. You'd buy things in tiny little paper packets, or a pennyworth of jam in a saucer, or a farthing-worth of condensed milk in a tea cup, that would be about three teaspoonsful. I used to go round the dumps picking up rags and bones and getting three farthings for them. There were no pen-sions, no unemployment benefit. My granny got relief – I used to be sent up to the bunhouse [a nickname for the national assistance office] to get her rations. She used to get a quartern loaf a fortnight – that's about the size of two ordinary loaves. And each alternate week I would take the biggest jug in the house – the one that belonged to the toilet set – to get it filled up with her ration of milk. There were no fridges then, so we'd share out the milk around all the family and drink it the same day, and the rest of the time we'd give her some of our milk.'

Nightingale lunch club is housed in the community centre in the middle of the giant estate. Outside there are seats intended for pensioners' use: all the wood has been stolen and only the concrete frames remain. Inside, a vandalized window is boarded up and there is no piped music, because the wall-mounted speakers have been stolen for the umpteenth time. Several of the club's forty-six members have been mugged, several live high up in the nineteen-storey towers.

'They should never have built all these big estates,' Lydia Best sighs. She has a face like Harpo Marx, ringed with tight, light-brown curls. She is eighty-two, her husband died four years ago, her brother and sister are dead and she had no children.

'When my husband died I asked them for a sheltered flat with a warden, because I'm partially blind, I can't see for more than a couple of feet, even with strong glasses. But they put me here on Nightingale. There's filth everywhere. The children come skating along the balcony and nearly knock you over. I never see a soul hardly, not even my neighbours. I've been robbed three times in three years since I came here, though thank God they've never hurt me. But I never go out after dark. It's very hard for me to clean my flat without help. I can't see to use the hoover, so I have to go down on my hands and knees with a brush and duster. I did apply for a home help: three times they told me someone would start coming, but no one came. I went round the social-services office again last month, but they said they'd had to cut down a lot on home helps, and they didn't hold out much hope. I wish I'd never come here. We used to live in cottages down on the River Lea. They were all pulled down – we had mice, cockroaches, beetles. The toilets were outside, and there was no bath – we used to have our baths in a copper, in the washhouse. But we were happy down there.'

Albert Perrin, seventy-nine, echoes her feelings: 'Hackney's not a patch on what it was. You walk around, you feel lost, you don't see any shop you know. All the famous theatres and cinemas are gone. All the sweet-shops are owned by Pakistanis. In the old days somebody might move their piano out on the street for a singsong, but nobody wants to know you these days. People don't care. Bus-drivers couldn't care less about old people, they always seem to jerk off when you're getting on. I've seen old people thrown from one end of the bus to the other. And this inflation: why should things go up? Why shouldn't carrots be the same price? They come out of the same ground.'

Perrin was nicknamed gunpowder in his youth, in honour of the method his mother used to try to prevent his birth. He has no savings at all to show for a long life of intermittent unemployment and employment as milkman, piano fitter, electrician's labourer, plasterer's labourer, aircraft gunner, furniture warehouseman, removal man and many other vocations. His children all moved out, to Enfield, Harlow, and Canvey in Essex. His wife died in November 1980. 'The only company I got now is a little canary.' But he still has active links. He spends weekends with his daughter in Enfield, and his grandson comes to see him twice a week. 'I look at him and I wonder, what's it going to be like for him? I can't see any way out. I just hope they got more sense than to use the atom bomb.'

The Orphans of the Storm

Our welfare state is not a caring state. It provides, increasingly sparingly, for those who come knocking on its door. It frequently neglects those who suffer quietly. No effort is made to identify need before it becomes urgent. Few stories in Hackney better illustrate this point than the saga of Buccleuch House, built in 1951 in one of the finest settings in Hackney, overlooking the tree-lined pond of Clapton Common, and close to Springfield Park. It was a bold innovation in its day, and opened with a fanfare of press coverage: a block of bedsit flats entirely reserved for respectable working spinsters over the age of thirty-five. It had its own restaurant, in the basement, its own launderette, two porters and a resident caretaker.

What no one seems to have anticipated at the time, or noticed until it was far too late and many unnecessary tragedies had occurred, was that these ladies would one day retire, and gradually grow older and weaker in flats that were designed for fit women, and quite unsuited for frail old ladies, and a few old men who were assigned a flat. As the years passed, the facilities that made life comfortable for them in their prime were withdrawn one by one as the need for them increased. The restaurant closed within a few years for lack of custom. The launderette was shut down some time in the late sixties because children had started vandalizing the machines and robbing the coins from them. From then on (for there was no room in their tiny kitchens for washing machines) the ladies had to walk half a mile across a busy road to the nearest launderette. The porters and the caretaker were pulled out one by one in progressive rationalizations, economy drives and centralizations, so the ladies had to make their way to the nearest estate manager's office for the slightest of repairs, and with no better a success rate than any other type of council tenant, so that repeated journeys were necessary.

As the ladies became septuagenarians and octogenarians, they were left stranded. As one of them put it, 'We were like the orphans of the storm.' And the environment round them was changing. Some of the nearby estates like Fawcett and Lea View had become dumping-grounds for homeless, low-income and immigrant families. Vandalism, burglary, fraud and mugging became an every-day occurrence, and the ladies had to walk through an area that, in the briefing room at Stoke Newington police station, is stuck thick with coloured pins, each one signifying a street robbery.

By 1982 all but seven of the eighty-five residents were pensioners. At the beginning of that year the tenants' association chairman, Mr Carmichael, drew up the following list of the frailest residents:

Flat 13, hospital 1 January, heart trouble, one hundred and two years old (subsequently died).
Flat 16, arthritis hands and legs, age seventy-seven years.
Flat 18, partially blind, age seventy-seven years.
Flat 23, arthritic hip, diabetic, heart trouble, age seventy-three years.
Flat 25, severe arthritis, falls, weak heart.
Flat 26, heart attacks, hallucinations, age eighty-seven years.
Flat 27, has black-outs, falls, age eighty-eight years.
Flat 29, heart condition, age seventy-eight years.
Flat 39, severe stroke, house-bound.
Flat 42, house-bound, daughter feeds, dresses etc, age, eighties.
Flat 43, house-bound, under hospital, age seventy-nine years, 1 January fell, broke hip, lying on floor eighteen hours.
Flat 45, very absent-minded, age ninety years.
Flat 55, loses memory, does not know where she lives, goes back to old flat, age, eighties.
Flat 58, epileptic fits and convulsions.
Flat 62, chronic asthma, age seventy-seven years.
Flat 66, hip operation, fell New Year, broke arm, age seventy years.
Flat 67, cripple, always falling.
Flat 72, broke wrist November, had a stroke Christmas, taken to hospital, age seventy years.
Flat 74, only one leg, arthritic arm.
Flat 78, had stroke in November, age seventy-six years.
Flat 85, found dead Christmas, lying one week before found, eighty-four years.

Eighty-one-year-old Mary Hurwitz is among the milder cases on the list. She is only 150 cm tall and weighs 35 kilos, but she has a youthful mind and the manner of a bright young thing of the 1920s. She has no close relatives within reach, only a nephew and a niece in north-west London, who visit her three or four times a year.

Mary's left leg has been in a brace since her youth, from polio. In February 1980 she slipped on ice on the tiny balcony where she grows flowers in little boxes, and broke her right hip. The break was slow to heal, and two years on she was still walking, very slowly and deliberately, with two sticks, and going to hospital once a week for treatment. 'Since then things have just got worse, I had diarrhoea last year for a month, I was afraid of going to bed for fear of dirtying it. I'm getting rather worried now, I've never been like this before. I sometimes laugh at myself, I feel so damned helpless.'

Her flat, a cramped bed-sitter, has become an obstacle course around chairs and occasional tables. Her kitchen, unaltered since 1951, presents a growing hazard as her agility decreases. 'The top cupboards are so high you can't reach them from the ground, but you've got to use them, there's not enough storage space otherwise. What I do is climb on the small steps I have, and then I stand on the work-top and hang on to the shelves with one hand and reach up with the other [an operation that would be hazardous even for a fit person]. The bath – well, I do have several little gadgets to hold on to, but it's still very difficult. Getting in, I gradually lift one leg and put it in, and then follow with the other. Getting out is a bit harder, but I put a little wooden stool on the floor and put a bathmat on it and get on to that first [the stool is tiny, only about 30 cm by 20 cm, raised about 10 cm above the ground]. I've not fallen yet, but I've always got my fingers crossed. [She did fall, about a fortnight after I visited her, but fortunately only got bad bruises.] I have a home help for four hours a week. One day she does some cleaning, the other she goes to the shop or the launderette. But there's still such a lot to do for myself. The home helps are not allowed to climb on anything, so I have to get up on a ladder myself to clean my windows or change my curtains. They're not allowed to turn your mattress, or to kneel down to do anything, so I have to crawl about and dust under my cupboards myself. I get the list for the shopping together the day before, but there's always something I forget, and I often have to go to the little supermarket across the road, but that's difficult, because I can't use both my sticks you see, I have to have a hand free to carry the shopping. I've not been mugged at all: I'm not a nervous person, I'd face the devil himself, but sometimes the children call me names like "bandylegs", and once a rather nasty man called me names for being Jewish, because I spoke to him about parking his car in front of our entrance. It takes me ages to get to the shops, I get so exhausted that I can't do anything for myself for a whole day afterwards. Another problem I have now is the doctor. My doctor crossed me off his list recently. I asked for two home visits – I'd never asked for one before. He was rather shirty about coming and I gave him a piece of my mind, then I got a letter saying he was crossing me off his list. I've found another doctor, but it's about a mile away and I can't walk there, I have to get a taxi.'

Mary lives on her basic state pension and on her savings. These amount to more than £2,000, so she does not qualify for supplementary benefit, which would pay her rent and rates plus a heating allowance and a long-term addition. This arbitrary cut-off threshold leaves many old people who have worked hard to save for their retirement, and accumulated more than £2,000 but less than £6,000 or £7,000, worse off than those who have saved nothing at all. 'I'm not sorry I saved, saving is part of my nature – I always remember my mother's surprise when I bought a doll that cost sixpence, and my pocket-money was only a halfpenny a week. I'd saved it all up. She didn't know what an economical little daughter she had. I don't want supplementary benefit and I don't need it. But I will say this, the people in here who are on full supplementary benefit have more left over than I have when they've paid the rent.'

In the absence of a caretaker or a full-time warden, tenants' leader Mr Carmichael and his wife, both a lot younger than the average, have found themselves dragooned into service in the many small and large emergencies that occur in Buccleuch House. 'I moved in here with my wife five years ago,' Carmichael told me. 'We thought we'd be coming to a nice quiet place, without any children. We never imagined all these tragedies that happen and don't have to happen. There's no one checking on these ladies. No one's got a list of phone numbers and addresses of relatives. Sometimes they're discharged out of hospital without anyone checking on whether their flat is all right for them to come back to.

'We've had so many tragedies. At Christmas we had a little

party, the man at the top was supposed to come, but he didn't show up. We found out that his neighbour hadn't seen him for a week. We broke the door down and found him dead, he'd committed suicide. He'd been without heating for three weeks because his radiator was broken, and he'd been going down to the estate office every day in the snow. I'm not saying that's what killed him, but it certainly didn't help. In the nights, many times I've got out of bed to hear someone moaning and banging. One night I heard someone at 3 a.m., well you can't knock at their doors at that time, and the mobile patrol knock off at midnight. We got in the next morning and found her leg all swollen and infected. Another lady had just come out of hospital after an operation because she'd fallen and broken her hip. I took a parcel up to her flat. She said, "I can't get to the door just now, come back tomorrow." The next day the mobile patrol let themselves in with a key. The pin had come out of her hip and she'd been lying on the floor all night. One lady called the ambulance, but she couldn't get up to press the button for the entry-phone to let them in. She had to drag herself all down the passageway and down the stone steps to reach the front door. Another lady with bad legs and sores on them was trapped in the lift and had to clamber up a ladder to get out. Every few months there's a death. We had five ambulances in here in one day at Christmas.

'This is a rough area around here. Some of the old ladies have been mugged. Others have been taken in. People have offered to carry their bags and come in with them, then they've asked for all their money. One girl said she'd come to visit her auntie and she wasn't in, so the lady at number 72 said come in and have a cup of tea and wait, and she was robbed. We only got entry-phones put in here a couple of years ago – until then anyone could just walk in. We just had a letter pinned to the door telling them to get ready for fighting in the Falklands and to get extra food in. That kind of thing scares them stiff. Sometimes they'll be looking out of the window and they'll see a mugging on the common, but they won't phone the police, because they say they'd want their names. No one goes out of here after 5 p.m., and you wouldn't be let in after dark. One day I saw a black man standing at the door waving a piece of paper, but I wasn't opening that door. He wouldn't go away, he kept on waving his paper. Then another lady came along who knew him. It turned out he was a doctor come to see one of the tenants.

'We get used as unpaid caretakers. Everyone comes to us for little things, like if their light bulb's gone or if there's a coin jammed in the electric meter. To be quite honest, we've got a bit impatient. We'd be having our dinner and we'd hear bang, bang, bang on the door and we'd open it and they'd say, "You've got to come at once."'

Buccleuch House was neglected for so long because it lacked a forceful tenants' association – the neighbouring Summit estate, built more recently than Buccleuch House, fought for and got new kitchen units through concerted pressure, while in Buccleuch House kitchens were only renewed when flats were vacated, or, as one old lady put it: 'The only time I'll get a new kitchen is when I'm dead.' The more the old ladies needed resources and help, the less able were they to exert pressure to get them. It is an inverse equation that we shall meet again in Chapter 20.

The presence of the Carmichaels transformed the situation. Finding themselves acting as unpaid wardens and forced to cope with many of the ladies' chronic problems, Carmichael formed a new tenants' association, and began to shower the council with petitions and proposals for changes, at first with little effect, but then, as tragedy followed tragedy, progressively approaching a much better state of affairs. Entry-phones were installed, the ground-floor windows permanently locked. A gate was pierced through a very long wall that the ladies had to walk right around to get across Clapton Common. Finally in 1982, after a terrible winter in which the whole block's heating system was out of action for days on end, a winter with a death, a suicide, two strokes and several crippling falls, Carmichael secured agreement that warning bells would be installed in every flat, with long pull ropes reaching to the floor, and that a full-time warden would be appointed when finances allowed. In the meantime Carmichael himself would be paid a modest allowance for his existing work as acting voluntary warden.

The Buccleuch House story is, of course, dramatic and exceptional. But it is unusual only in the sense that so many neglected old people were concentrated in so small a space. Elsewhere they are just as neglected, but more scattered and less visible. The individual tragedies that were enacted at Buccleuch are commonplace in the inner city and, for that matter, anywhere in the UK. Problems that could be prevented with vigilance and material help only come to light and are dealt with when they become acute. For several decades we have been in the transition between a gradually dying family and informal neighbourly care and a gradually improving state and organized community care. In the slump the first process continues and accelerates, while the growth of the second is halted and reversed.

15 Schooling for Failure

There are those who use their minds, and there are those who use their muscles. The former rule, the latter are ruled.

Mencius (tr. D. C. Lau)

Hackney has an unfortunate tendency to come top of all the wrong tables and bottom of all the right ones. Educational attainment in Hackney, on almost every score, is by far the lowest in Inner London. Inner London as a whole itself came second worst among the largest urban authorities in England, in 1978, for the proportion of school-leavers with no grades or low grades in O-level General Certificate of Education or Certificate of Secondary Education, and second lowest in the proportion of school-leavers going on to full-time education.

After housing and the local economy, education is the third of the key links in the chain that binds the inner city and its children to their destiny. As we have seen, cheap housing attracts people on low incomes, with low skills, or poor educational qualifications. There is thus a local shortage of skilled or certificated manpower which deters employers from starting enterprises in the area. That shortage is endemic and persists over long periods of time. The small proportion of local children who do do well in the school system tend to move out of Hackney. But the high-flyers are a minority, for by and large the children of people with low incomes and poor educational attainments also fare badly at school. In an unequal and hierarchical society, educational failure is all too often hereditary, just as success is hereditary. This occurs not through any genetic transmission, but because the parents' circumstances provide the environment in which the child grows up: environment is hereditary. The school system obligingly certificates failure, in a way that largely determines the subsequent career and class of the

victim. Instead of compensating for disadvantage, British education reinforces it and perpetuates it.

Failure begins to show at an early age. Pupils' ability is first
thoroughly measured at transfer to secondary school. Hackney's
children regularly perform worst of any of the ten divisions of the
Inner London Education Authority. In 1979, their average score in
English was 96·6, against an ILEA average of 101. In mathemat-
ics, where the average was 96·7, Hackney's children scored 93·2. In
verbal reasoning their score was 95·7 against an average of 99·1.
On each of these three measures, Hackney was bottom of the
league. Taking an average of all three scores, Hackney stood out as
exceptional, 4·7 points below the ILEA average. All the other
divisions ranged between 1·2 points below and 2·3 points above
average.

While it may have been true a couple of decades ago that
Hackney's children got a rough deal in educational provision there
is no evidence that by the end of the seventies Hackney's schools
offered anything worse, in terms of staff-pupil ratios, adequacy of
school buildings or staff turnover, than the average for Inner
London. The reasons for her poor performance lie primarily in the
poor home background of pupils. In 1980, 69 per cent of Hackney
pupils had unskilled or semi-skilled parents or guardians (ILEA
average: 59·5 per cent); 33·5 per cent were poor enough to qualify
for free school dinners (ILEA average: 22·3 per cent); 27·4 per cent
came from large families (average 22 per cent); 28 per cent came
from one-parent families (average 26·5 per cent) and for 18 per cent
of pupils English was not the first language (average 12·6 per cent).
Hackney did not top the league on any of these individual
measures, but she had the highest *average* position. And she had
the highest proportion of children from families with New Commonwealth heads.

Family background affects schooling in two major ways. The
first is through educational performance. The typical Hackney
home, the typical inner-city home, the typical semi-skilled or
unskilled worker's home, offers fewer toys and books; fewer outings
and holidays; shortage of personal space for play or study; and
shortage of attention from parents because of larger, less widely
spaced families, unsocial working hours or preoccupation with

persistent housing and income problems. The actual realities of many schoolchildren's lives in the inner city go way beyond these well-known platitudes about deprivation. Take the Willis family: Jamaican parents and five children living in a cramped three-bedroomed flat on Northwold estate. Mother and father have one bedroom. The second bedroom is shared by three adult girls, top to tail in one double bed. One of them, sixteen-year-old Sharon, is doing O-levels at college. The lounge is reserved for the family's best furniture and frills and is used only when visitors come. So the family eat and watch television in the third bedroom. Towards midnight they move out, and fifteen-year-old Raymond and his thirteen-year-old sister Yvonne unpack a put-you-up double bed. Their clothes are in plastic sacks in a corner, their school-books balanced on the window-ledge. In many other families, children sleep on sofas, on mattresses put down on the floor for the night. Some sleep with relatives or neighbours for lack of bed space at home.

The other main impact of family life on schooling is made through pupils' behaviour. The inner-city child, as we shall see in the next chapter, is more anarchic and indisciplined than average. Many children come from families where arguments, disruption and instability, often involving violence, are everyday occurrences. Added to these are the perennial attractions of truancy, delinquency and street life, and the intractable problems of discipline of many families, especially those with single parents. All these influences are reflected in school in attention-seeking, insolence, and inability to concentrate.

The overall outcome of these factors is a proportion of backward pupils in Hackney – 32·3 per cent in 1980 – that is by far the highest in Inner London, where the average is 23·4 per cent.

In addition, an average of 27 per cent of Hackney's pupils exhibited disturbed behaviour in the years 1976–80, when the ILEA average was 21·5 per cent. At this high level, disturbed behaviour not only affects the performance of the individual child, but also disrupts the work of his or her classmates.

Teething Problems

Gayhurst Infant School is housed in a gaunt Victorian building close to London Fields and to Holly Street estate, which sends many of its children here. Its social make-up is deprived even by Hackney standards. Two-thirds of the 170 children get free school dinners. Two-thirds are from one-parent families. Well over half are of immigrant origin. Even before the school day begins, you can discern some of the problems just by watching children in the playground (about 150 square metres of tarmac, providing less than one square metre per child). The general character of play is heavily influenced by television: even at this tender age karate chops and kung fu kicks are attempted, with all their potential for accidental pain and deliberate injury in retaliation. Two black boys are fighting: one of them is holding a smaller boy by the scruff of his neck against the wall of the toilet. The taller boy is shouting, his face contorted with hatred, the smaller is crying. In another stretch of yard, two white boys are wrenching a parka off a smaller white boy and karate chopping him on the back of the neck, quite hard. Meanwhile a small Asian boy with short, jet black hair walks up and down, by the wall, alone. No one talks to him or asks him to play.

Already two problem groups are evident on the edges of a relatively normal, if somewhat unruly majority: a fair number of children are abnormally rowdy and violent, while another group is abnormally quiet and withdrawn. The division is related to one we shall see in the next chapter, between the 'street' kids and those who are kept safely at home, the neglected and the overprotected.

Gayhurst assembly, by contrast, is a surprisingly orderly affair, no doubt because of the firm but caring attitude of the head, burly, bearded Mike Mulvaney, who strums a guitar as the children sing, in a semicircle, a rainbow of shades from white to dark brown. The assembly tries to smooth over conflicts and create a homely, encouraging environment. There is an opportunity for every child, once a month or so, to show off, so that even those who do not do well at classwork feel there is something they are valued for. Katrina,* whose own mother is illiterate, reads out the very first

* All children's names in this chapter have been changed.

story she has ever written, an autobiographical tale entitled 'There's a Robber in My House'. Blond, booted Mickie Stone is applauded for being the third-ranking junior BMX bike racer in the country. A few months later the *Hackney Gazette* reported that he'd been pulled off his saddle in the street and his £300 bike stolen – the fate of many young bike owners in Hackney. Next, three children who've done very neat work parade around holding their books open at the page. Finally a little girl who is bursting with pride over her shiny new purple shoes is allowed to stand on a chair and show them off.

Classroom arrangements are designed to bring the best out of each individual child: no desks aligned to face the blackboard, but tables grouped in fours, chairs facing each other. Children work in groups, each group, often each individual, doing a different task geared to its own abilities. The teacher moves among them, checking, explaining, helping. In this way every child can proceed at its own pace: it will not be held back by blackboard work aimed at the inevitably low average level, nor need the backward be virtually abandoned, as could so easily happen with the old methods. But the potential of this approach is seriously reduced when staffing levels are cut, and continually jeopardized by the risk of disruption, ever present in the inner-city school.

In the class I sat with, a single teacher, Anna Dutta, had to cope with twenty-eight children. There were three relatively ordered groups. In the reading corner six-year-old Amanda was giving reading practice to six other children, holding up little cards and asking what they said. Another clutch of six was doing maths, each child a different problem – fractions, adding up, colouring in shapes. Three girls were waiting patiently to read to the teacher. Around the fringes of these groups is a fluttering of individualists. Mehmet, a dark-haired Turkish boy, was writing a story by himself in a corner. Two small Gujarati brothers explore various cupboards and trays full of paper coins: they have only just arrived in the country and neither speaks a word of English. Another new boy, John, hovers around suspiciously, observing the others without joining in.

A single disruptive individual, Jimmie, succeeded in transforming mild disorder into something approaching chaos. Jimmie is a thin white boy with spiky blonde hair. He has spent four of his seven years in care. Now he is back with his mother, but she is facing eviction for rent arrears. Like many inner-city schoolchildren, Jimmie has a very short span of attention, whether because he is hyped up by too much television and too many domestic arguments, or because his thoughts are continually pulled from their course by worries about personal security and belonging at home. He cannot stick at one task: he will try it for no more than a couple of minutes, then he will leap up and roam about the room in search of distraction. Even when he is only asking other children for help with his work, he interrupts their learning. But he also provokes fights that cause wider disturbances. In the couple of hours I was there, he spanked one girl on the bottom and attempted to strangle another. He bit John, who ran out of the classroom and stared in through the door, frightened and distrustful like a wounded deer. He knocked the tray of paper coins out of the Gujarati boys' hands and spilled them on the floor. They patiently collected them all up, then Jimmie spilled them again. 'Jimmie is very aggressive,' Anna Dutta complains, 'and very moody. Everything has to be just as he wants it. Whatever I asked of him this morning, he refused. His good side comes out when I can give him the time, if the helper is here, but if I am on my own in the classroom, like today, I can only give him attention at the cost of the other children.'

It is all too often the Jimmies of Hackney, at primary and secondary level, who set the tone for the whole class, indeed sometimes for the whole school, in collaboration with the many others of their kind. Their behaviour is dramatic and highly visible. It attracts attention from all present. It creates a general atmosphere of disorder. Such pupils can easily pre-empt the teacher's time and attention. By interrupting other pupils, they impose their own short attention span on everyone else, and make it impossible to develop habits of concentration. Their aggressiveness provokes retaliation and spreads lawless behaviour.

The other sizeable educational problem group is the quiet, withdrawn types. They may be overprotected at home, or mildly handicapped. Because they do not demand teacher's attention while others do, they may pass unnoticed and neglected for long periods. The disruptive children can instil in them a fear and dislike of school, which can affect performance and attendance. Dean is one of the quiet kind at Gayhurst, shy and slow to learn, and recently diagnosed as partly deaf. I met his mother Joan when she came to pick him up. 'He's not got the confidence,' she told me. 'I think it's because I don't let him play out. The courtyard in our block has been taken over for car parking – the council has drawn lines and rents them out at 45p a space, and some of the cars drive through at fifty miles an hour. I daren't let him out, but he's going mental through being locked up all the time. He's been playing with matches, lighting fires in the bedroom recently. We asked to have ramps put in to slow the cars down, but the estate manager said no, it might encourage motor bikes to do stunts. You can't get anything done. If you try to get anything done, you always seem to come up against a block.'

Given the enormous impact of home environments, the inner-city school cannot afford to regard itself as a purely educational institution. The dividing lines between school and society have to be overcome. Gayhurst has done a lot to cross the conventional boundaries. One teacher, Dinah Morley, was spending five afternoons a week trying to solve some of the parents' social problems that were interfering with children's learning. Some of her recent cases show the kind of thing the children are up against: helping a mother, who had walked out on her husband and children after a severe beating, to return home; advising an unemployed Asian man, too proud to claim social security or free school meals, and whose family was living off child benefit and his wife's modest part-time earnings; giving moral support to a family with three young children at the school, facing prosecution for trading in stolen child-benefit books and illegally reconnecting their electricity; helping a battered mother to get an injunction to stop her husband from harassing her, and to get the tenancy transferred to her name; putting an illiterate, mentally subnormal mother in touch with a literacy class and washing her daughter's clothes when she forgets, so the child will not be stigmatized. And the more straightforward consequences of poverty also affect schooling: Gayhurst children are not infrequently kept home from school because they have no shoes or winter coats. Every year Gayhurst sends off fifty or sixty children on free or subsidized holidays. The list of required clothing is deliberately kept to a minimum, but some parents still admit they can't take up the offer because the child has no wellingtons or rainwear.

Gayhurst has also been among the first in Hackney to try to enlist the parents as helpers in their children's education. Every night each child takes home a little plastic folder with a reading book to read aloud to its parents, and a card telling the parent how much help the child will need with it. With this system, which spread rapidly among Hackney schools in the early 1980s, the actual time each child gets for reading practice can double, or more than double, and their attitude to books and school changes: they are no longer something alien from the home. Thus the working-class home can take on some of the educational characteristics of the middle-class home, and help to narrow the gap in opportunities. The parent is no longer the marginal spectator of her or his child's education, but takes a rightful place as educator alongside the professionals. This, at any rate, is the theory, but it tends to become reality in the less-disadvantaged homes: in the poorest families, with multiple problems, parents may be less likely to be willing or able to read with their children, because of illiteracy, unsocial hours, the demands of other children or the pressures of poverty and family conflict.

Because it raised its funds directly from Inner London boroughs, the Inner London Education Authority had been spared – at the time of this writing – the kind of cuts that damaged education in other areas. Even so, Mulvaney had been forced to cut the afternoons devoted to social work from five to one. Further man-power losses, of the kind the Tories were talking about, would force him to cut remedial, nurture and English as a second language teaching, and to increase class size to the point where group teaching was no longer possible. The final logic of cuts would be a return to the old style of face-the-blackboard classroom, which in the inner city would be quite simply unworkable.

Towards Terminal Failure

It is at secondary level that poor performance and poor behaviour at school become more dramatic and more critical for the long-term future of pupils. For most graduates of inner city schools, underqualified and undisciplined, are poor prospects for employers, especially in times of recession and rapid technological change.

The school system in the inner city becomes a franking machine to stamp the words 'certified failure' on most of its output. In 1978, in Hackney, no less than 28 per cent of fifth-formers came out of school with no certificate of any kind, more than twice the national average of 13 per cent. Another 42 per cent in Hackney passed out with low grades in the Certificate of Secondary Education, or with fail grades in the General Certificate of Education O-level (here the national average was 35 per cent). Thus no less than seven out of ten Hackney children left school unambiguously labelled as failures – as, indeed, did 47 per cent of children nationally. Only one in twenty received the clear stamp of success of five or more good O-levels or CSE grade ones – half the national and London averages.

As at primary level, there is no evidence that educational provision is worse in Hackney's secondary schools than elsewhere. Space per pupil in buildings and playgrounds is better than the London average, the proportion of older schools is less, and of split sites equal to the average. Once again, home backgrounds emerge as the dominant factor, and they are, on average, a good deal worse than at primary level, because a lot of parents who will, if reluctantly, send their child to a Hackney primary school will make every effort to get it placed elsewhere at the more crucial secondary level. Thus Hackney leads London in the proportion of secondary-school pupils from large families (36 per cent in 1980; London average, 30·4 per cent); and from single-parent families (31 per cent; average 28 per cent). And it comes second in the proportion getting free school meals (32·3 per cent; average 26·5 per cent) and having English as a second language (13·6 per cent to the average of 8·2 per cent). Home deprivation influences educational outcomes in the clearest fashion. On a score combining all the factors of educational deprivation, Hackney tops the table, just as it tops the failure table. Tower Hamlets is second in the deprivation league and second in the poor educational performance league. No less than six of ILEA's ten divisions have exactly the same position in the two tables, and the other four differ by only one or two places.

Hackney's secondary schools have the worst intake, in terms of ability, in inner London. Children transferring to secondary schools are given a test of verbal reasoning and divided into three broad bands of ability designed so that, on average over the whole of ILEA, a quarter of all children come into band one (above average) one half in band two (average) and another quarter in band three, below average. The purpose of this banding system is to try to even out ability between schools, but because ILEA gives parents some freedom of choice of secondary school, it does not work out that way. Hackney's results on these tests are regularly the worst in London. Only 16·6 per cent of pupils were in band one in 1979, while 31·5 per cent were in band three. Instead of being equal, as was intended, low-ability children outnumbered high-ability children by two to one in Hackney. The next worst result, Tower Hamlets, was very much lower: there the band threes outnumbered the band ones by only 1·35 to one. Over the river in Greenwich the situation was reversed: the above-average children had it over the below average by 1·6 to one.

Inside each division, individual schools are supposed to balance their intake so that it approximates to the average for their division: the idea is to prevent the emergence, under the guise of comprehensive education, of élite schools, patronized heavily by the middle class, and dump schools for the children of the poor. In practice, as we shall see later, this is precisely what happens. Even if it did not, Hackney's problem is that the average level of ability and behaviour is so poor that every school, in terms of its intake, is a dump school compared with a suburban comprehensive.

The underlying cause, of course, is the same phenomenon that causes the inner city as a whole: the marked geographical segregation of social classes in Britain according to the desirability of housing. Because of the powerful influence of home background, schools with largely working-class catchment areas have a much lower standard of intake than schools in middle-class areas. With fewer pupils taking exams, smaller sixth forms, and a powerful anti-academic ethos among pupils, children in largely working-class schools do not enjoy equal educational opportunities. It is the central unresolved problem of comprehensive education in Britain.

The Blackboard Circus

I went to two secondary schools in Hackney to observe the problem at close quarters: Hackney Downs, an all-boys school that was once a respected grammar school and still achieves the best academic results in Hackney; and Clissold Park, mixed, once the most notorious dump school in the borough but recently on the mend after the arrival of a new head.

The remedial class at Clissold Park takes children with acute learning problems for five periods a week. I sat with one group of five second-year pupils, some of them bigger than the teacher, petite, curly haired Trisha Jaffe. Only one of the five, James, had a relatively normal home background. William is epileptic, one of four children of a black single parent. John, who wears a peaked cap to the lesson, has a mother who sanctions his regular absenteeism. David is a big fat white boy, son of over-anxious and over-protective elderly parents whose high expectations of him at school may, paradoxically, have contributed to his failure: he came up from primary school unable to read a single word. Denroy, a diminutive black boy in a pullover with Al Capone written all over it, is one of eleven children living with their single mother in a three-bedroomed flat. He used to disrupt his own class, and if sent out would wander aimlessly into other classes and disrupt them, too. When he joined the remedial class, he could read only five words, which gave him a nominal reading age of seven.

Now Denroy can read fifty or sixty words. For the remedial class gets results. It has a very high teacher–pupil ratio – one to six. All work programmes are individually tailored – Trisha works one and a half hours at home every night producing worksheets for the next day. The children choose their own projects, almost always subjects like sport, cars, space, fashion, pop music and the like, far more interesting than normal school fare. Self-chosen projects awaken commitment in a way an imposed curriculum can never do. Denroy's soccer-scrapbook cover has a superbly executed painting of a match in progress and, inside, carefully researched workcards on top teams and star players.

Teacher–pupil relations here are more personalized, more affectionate and more tolerant than in most normal classes, and as part of that a high level of disturbance is accepted without sanctions. Half-way through the period David yowls with pain. 'Miss, Denroy stabbed me in the arm.' He exhibits a red mark lined with black where a pencil point has clearly been jabbed with some force. 'Could I get lead poisoning?' 'You will if I do it again,' Denroy threatens. Trisha warns him in a playful manner: 'If you do it again, you'll feel a pain up your bottom.' Denroy glares at her under his eyebrows. 'You do that and I'll *kill* you.' He stresses the word kill with the sinister voice of someone who is not bluffing. Later, when Denroy's alert guard has lowered, David stabs him pretty hard in the back with his pencil, and both chase loudly round the room.

The class expresses, in extreme form, the essential problems and possibilities of the inner-city secondary school. Deprived and unstable home backgrounds lead to behavioural and learning problems. The school is forced to relax its methods and standards of discipline, and to adapt what is taught and how it is taught to the pupils' needs and interests. The outcome, from one point of view, can be seen as a modest success: the outbreak of absolute anarchy is avoided and the incidence of total illiteracy reduced. But from another point of view it remains a failure, though not through the school's fault: achievement, though improved, is still too low to make much difference in a competitive world. Behaviour, though stopping short of the criminal, is still creating habits which most employers will be unable to tolerate for long. The job prospects for the likes of David and Denroy would not be rosy in an economic boom. In a recession they are nil.

As at primary school, problems at home intrude destructively into the school: many teachers notice how children are more disturbed on Monday mornings, after weekends of domestic conflict. But at secondary school further pressures intrude from the pupils' own social lives, as adolescence proceeds and adult life approaches. The closer school-leaving age looms, the more does the outside world make itself felt inside the school. There is the world of awakening sexuality. In 1981 two third-year girls at Clissold Park and one fourth-year girl got pregnant. All three chose to keep their children.

There is the world of work. Many of the fourth- and fifth-year pupils, who should be devoting increasing amounts of home time to study, have part-time jobs, many of them working twenty hours a week in shops, supermarkets, small factories, to bring in the kind of money they need (but which parents cannot provide) to buy clothes and records, and to go to discos and clubs. Ironically, most of them will lose these part-time jobs when they leave school, and many will be unable to find other work. Because of this danger, in the fifth year, a fair number of boys start full-time work prematurely: one Clissold boy serves on a stall in Ridley Road market, another has a job loading and unloading vans, and two Turkish boys have left to start work in their families' clothing firms.

Truancy is a progressive cancer that eats deeper as the years progress. Attendance in the first year at Hackney Downs averages 90 per cent. By the fifth year it is down to 70 per cent, on some days as low as 50 per cent. Truants play video games in cafes, sniff glue, wander the streets and, not infrequently, break the law. The world of street life invades the school. 'Hackney kids bring into school the style of surviving on the street,' says John Kemp, head of Hackney Downs. Vandalism at his school is moderate – ten or so classroom door panels have to be replaced each week, and the classroom ceilings have holes poked in them. More serious is the continuous gleaning action of petty theft, common to all Hackney schools, and committed by pupils and by insiders walking in. Anything of value that is left lying around – handbags, keys, calculators, dinner money, laboratory equipment – is certain to be stolen. Extortion rackets – extracting pocket-money with menaces – are often uncovered. In some schools knife fights have become noticeable.

Serious violence at Hackney Downs, against teachers or other pupils, is rare, but only because the school has radically changed its approach to discipline. John Kemp explains: 'Our kids tend to be more brusque, more suspicious of authority, more precociously self-reliant than kids from suburban areas. In the early seventies, shortly after we went comprehensive, we tried to clamp down on disorder, but the result was a number of very dramatic confrontations. You can't screw these kids down. You have to talk through and defuse tensions, so you don't get explosions. But that means, inevitably, that we have to accept a less orderly and demure, more rough and ready atmosphere than you might expect to find in the suburbs.'

This is noticeable in and around Hackney Downs. Inside the building, one boy is strangling another on the stairs below the head's room. Another pair have each other in half-nelsons in the entrance. Teachers pass by without reacting. In the playground, boys push in front of teachers, trample over the shrubberies, and in whatever direction you look, there are half a dozen fights going on, of every degree of seriousness from horseplay to vicious sadism. At Clissold Park, the atmosphere is more restrained – the presence of girls exerts a moderating influence. Even so, on the day of my visit, boys stand permanent guard on the toilet, while inside it stinks of cigarette smoke; four boys are playing a banned card game inside a store-room; another group play the old trick, on a master, of balancing a bucket of water on the door; and a hard-packed ice ball clangs against a classroom window. Inside most classes, the blackboard jungle has been replaced by the blackboard circus. To avoid a gaolhouse-riot atmosphere, most inner-city teachers tolerate, with varying degrees of complicity, a routine level of noise, jokes, chat, backchat and downright impudence any one element of which would have earned the cane in a 1950s grammar school.

A tall teacher with a day's beard, nervous and somehow abstracted from what goes on around him, is a target for fun as his class queue for an injection. One black boy feels the teacher's biceps: 'Sir, look at that, you ain't got no muscle. Hit you like *that* and you'd double up.' The boy mimes a blow to the stomach, stopping only two centimetres short. No action is taken. The teacher seems part amused, part indifferent. Over in the home-economics room, a second-form is making stuffed cushions and draught-excluders. A white boy moulds a wad of kapok into the shape of a wig and walks round in it. Later the same boy spends some time doubled up inside a low cupboard, and when he gets out he is mock strangled with his own draught-excluder by an Asian boy. Another white boy takes his shoes off and thrusts one foot under the teacher's nose: 'Look at that, miss, I got foot and mouth. People can get it, a friend of mine had it.'

The blackboard circus helps to make school a less alien environment, but it cannot be said that it is conducive to learning or to habits of application and respect for authority – all values which employers, rightly or wrongly, still overwhelmingly demand. In that sense it helps to foster those attitudes that help many inner-city youths to get the sack again and again for insolence and indiscipline at work. The school, to some extent, cultivates unemployability. But it is not the school's fault: it has had to adapt itself to the home and street environment of the inner city in order to survive. Schools that do not adapt – and there are some – may impose an artificial order for much of the time, but pay for it in higher levels of violent disruption and truancy. It is, like so many inner-city dilemmas, a no-win situation.

The Alienating Curriculum

The British secondary-education system is largely an irrelevance to the needs either of society and the economy as a whole, or of its individual members as human beings. Its major effective function is to provide valuable certificates to a minority which can be traded against more secure jobs, better conditions and higher incomes, while the majority leave with either worthless certificates or none at all.

Again it is not the individual schools that are to blame – most inner-city schools would revolutionize education given a free hand – but the system of constraints and parental expectations in which they operate. Most employers attach importance – increasingly so in recession – to paper certificates. Most parents are aware of this and expect school to help their children obtain the most attractive of these pieces of paper that their children are capable of. The General Certificate of Education still dominates the scene, and even at ordinary level it is still geared to the requirements of university entry. Over-academic, over-specialized, dry or literary, it represents higher middle-class Norman-Latin culture, far distanced from the realities of working-class life, and even further from the real-life drama of the inner city. Thus GCE O-level alienates the working-class child by its content.

The Certificate of Secondary Education was introduced to remedy this situation. Especially in the Mode Three version, which is set by individual schools, it is often as relevant as one could wish, practical, lively, focused on real-life needs and the study of local realities. The trouble is that most smaller employers do not recognize a good CSE result as equivalent to an O-level pass, nor will they ever do so as long as the two certificates, one of them explicitly designed for the less able, exist side by side. Hence the CSE – potentially exciting for its content – alienates the working-class child because of its lack of wider recognition as an entry into better-paid employment.

Alienation is also produced, of course, by the external imposition of learning, by the examination system, by the requirements for home study, and by the poor performance which most pupils in the inner city expect of themselves. They are going to do badly anyway, so what's the point of trying?

There are additional pressures pushing towards failure. There is the pupils' subculture – present in all schools – which creates an alternative system of values, rewards and punishments, working in diametric opposition to the school's formal values. This alternative system awards praise and acclaim precisely for maximum deviance from the formal values: for mucking about in class, delinquency, neglect of work, as well as for out-of-school values such as sexual experience and street wisdom. Those who do well academically can easily find themselves facing the sanctions of the pupil subculture: ostracism, ridicule and sometimes worse. Lawrence Robbins's children (we met him in Chapter 6) performed well when they first arrived at Woodberry Down School in Hackney. But they were bullied and victimized because of it. 'My son John,' Robbins remembers, 'he was beaten, prodded, kicked and even spat on by gangs of boys, black and white. They used to be called "clever clogs". John came home one night and said, "Dad, I know now how Jesus Christ must have felt, being kicked and pushed." He was scared to go to school. I went to see the head and I was given an assurance that the class teacher would take him under his wing. But that only made things worse, because he ran to the teacher and was teacher's pet. Then my boys were gradually coming down in school, and as they came down they were getting more popular and coming home with less complaints about trouble.' Thus the gifted pupil in the inner-city area often resolves the conflict between the school's formal-value system and the informal pupil subculture by deliberately underperforming.

Teachers, too, are under constant pressure from pupils to reduce their expectations and demands, particularly over homework. Home study is extremely difficult for the majority who do not have bedrooms of their own. And it is often hard to find the time for homework when you are heavily into far more interesting pursuits such as part-time jobs, street life, night life, or sex life. Take just one example: Tom, a fifteen-year-old-boy at Hackney Downs. His mother is a cleaner, his father an unemployed carpenter. He shares a bedroom with his younger brother and does homework (when he can be bothered, which isn't often) on the kitchen table while his mother does the cooking. Every evening he puts in two hours' hard labour at a bakery, making doughnuts and cream cakes, plus another ten hours on Saturday, and earns a handsome £20 a week – more than his sixteen- and seventeen-year-old friends get on the dole, and far more than his parents have to spend on themselves. The bulk of Tom's earnings go towards his major pastime, motorcycle scrambling. He has a £600 motorbike, and spends most of every Sunday tearing across Hackney Marshes on it. An additional source of distraction for Tom, as for many inner-city children, is dealing with police and courts, in his case for fairly harmless matters: 'They've done me for practically every type of motoring offence there is. No tax, no insurance, you name it. I've been nicked God knows how many times just for pushing my bike down the road.' Only in December of his last year at school, a few weeks before the mock exams that would decide whether he would be entered for CSE or GCE exams, did Tom finally get the wind up and start to work seriously, far too late to change his educational fate more than marginally.

Whenever teachers propose setting homework there is frequently an uproar: groans of protest, pleas for mercy, collective and individual excuses, most of them spurious. Inner-city teachers, with no ultimate power to enforce their will, are all too

293

often tempted to throw in the towel. The sheer pressure of pupil resistance can easily turn them into the unwilling accomplices of children's low expectations, midwives of educational failure.

Adapting School to Society

Most inner-city secondary schools have been forced, by their location, to adapt to social change more rapidly than any other group of schools. Elements of the primary-school approach of group teaching in mixed-ability classes are creeping in: there is more individually tailored work. But it is not just elements that need changing: the whole structure of the school has to be modified to achieve results. One of the most thoroughgoing educational experiments in Hackney is under way at Clissold Park.* The school's labyrinth of modern buildings stands opposite a row of decayed Victorian houses with columned entrances that now house radical squatter groups. Clissold Park's natural catchment area includes some of the worst private rented accommodation in Hackney.

Before 1978, the school had a reputation for vandalism, and violence. It was the educational equivalent of a 'dump' estate: the place where the children of those with the least freedom of choice ended up. In theory, Clissold could have taken up to 14 or 16 per cent of Band One, above-average children. In practice it could not attract them. Parents of above-average children who had failed to get in the schools of their choice, and who had been allocated a place at Clissold, would often refuse to take it up. They would hold out right through the summer holidays, in the hope that a vacancy would arise at a more desirable school, often aiming for a place at Islington schools like Highbury Grove or Islington Green – and often, because people move a lot in London, striking lucky. Others would move out of Hackney to ensure a better secondary education for their child, or pay for private education. All these mechanisms depended on either a good knowledge of parental rights and possibilities, or possession of funds, and hence were used almost

* Owing to falling rolls, Clissold Park was amalgamated with Woodberry Down in 1982, and became Stoke Newington School.

exclusively by middle-class parents. In this way, Clissold's already small quota of above-average children was whittled down. The disadvantaged, who didn't know enough about the secondary transfer system or have enough cash or personal mobility, would be unable to manipulate it to their child's advantage and would accept their places at Clissold, while the places vacated by the above-average would be taken by children of newly arrived immigrants, and by children expelled by other schools. Thus Clissold Park's poor reputation and its intake chased each other down a descending spiral.

Just how far it got can be judged from the 1981 fifth-year, many of whom came to the school in 1976. Only 4 per cent were in the above-average category – one-sixth of the Inner London average – and 48 per cent were in the below-average category, who thus outnumbered the high-flyers by twelve to one, six times worse than the Hackney average, which was itself the worst in London. The effect of this intake shows up clearly in the 1981 exam results: 31 per cent didn't sit an exam or got no grades, and another 51 per cent got low grades. Only nineteen pupils out of 217 got even one O-level – many of them Turkish children taking O-level in Turkish – and only two pupils, one boy, one girl, obtained five or more good CSEs or O-levels. Eight out of ten were certified 'failures', one in a hundred stamped 'successes'.

Robin Chambers came in as head in 1978, determined to reverse the school's fortunes. With the help of the staff, he quickly set about introducing a revolutionary set of innovations, encouraging an ethos of equality, fairness and participation, but with very businesslike managerial systems to reduce class disruptions and increase the amount of school work done. To ensure that work is taken more seriously by children and parents, each pupil carries a ring-file containing all current school work and homework. At the back of the file is a homework diary, with spaces for teachers and parents to correspond. To avoid serious disruption, teachers can refer children to 'Extension 41', manned by year heads and other senior teachers. So that the whole class will not lose learning time, the disruptive child is collected and taken to a small room on the ground floor where it gets a chance to explain its own version of what happened and the year heads put the other side of the case:

'When a kid has a chance to express its grievances, and pupils and teachers treat one another fairly, much of the need for violence, abuse and anger goes,' Chambers explains. The really hard nuts, who could not even be cracked by this system, were suspended or expelled.

The content of what is taught was also transformed: 'The inner city puts the school under pressure to offer what is appropriate,' says Chambers. 'If you don't, the kids will take your place apart.' The curriculum for the first three years now includes child care, family planning, nutrition, health, sex education, moral and political education. There are even lessons in sex-assertiveness training: teaching girls to be less shy and retiring and boys to be more gentle and considerate.

The Clissold reform package has not had long enough to show up much in exam results, but it has already turned round the school's reputation which has begun to attract a far-better-balanced intake. In the 1981 first year, the share of above-average pupils was up to 13 per cent and that of below-average pupils down to 42 per cent. The Band Ones were still outnumbered, but only by three to one instead of twelve to one. The 1982 examinees, with four years of the new regime, performed twice as well as the class of 1981.

But the school is not an island: and what it can deliver is severely limited by the realities of the surrounding community and the constraints of the national educational system. The worst of the violence has gone, and vandalism is only trivial. Serious classroom disturbances are quickly removed from the classroom. But the normal level of noise, which interferes with the transmission of learning, is still high: many teachers refer children to Extension 41 only *in extremis*, for it is, in part, an admission of weakness on their part (nor are the discussions in the little downstairs room always as elevating or as equal as is envisaged).

Clissold Park's curriculum reforms – like those of Hackney Downs and every adventurous secondary school – have been severely hampered by the national educational context. Most parents of able children insist on their having a chance to do GCE O-levels: thus the most intelligent children in the inner city are subjected to the most irrelevant, over-specialized and dry material.

The middle range of ability do the regionally set CSE exams, which are still a little dry and theoretical. One of the best courses that Clissold offers is the Mode Three CSE (set by the school) in community studies: it covers child development, family planning, money management, how to find accommodation, welfare benefits and how to claim them, how to apply for a job and handle an interview, how to cope with unemployment, plus surveys of local social problems and two weeks of work experience. But the course is taken only by the lowest half of the ability range. Thus the most relevant education, the best preparation for adult life and work, is reserved for those without any hope of conventional success. Perhaps because they know this, or perhaps simply because it is *taught* rather than being sought out of the motivation of personal need, much of the course is received with the usual glazed eyes. Dave Masters, head of social studies at Clissold, reports that pupils don't seem any more interested in how to claim supplementary benefit than in history.

Nor is it easy to train inner-city children, many of whom come from families where problems are not verbalized and there is no involvement in the community, to participate articulately in discussions. Every class has one or two spokespersons, usually male, but getting opinions out of the majority is like trying to squeeze blood out of a stone. I sat with one fifth-form group as they 'discussed' a television programme they'd just watched about public schools.

Ivan, a black boy, had the entire British social system well sussed out: 'People like them only look at society from the middle class upwards. It's going to ruin the lives of people like us.' The others are more reticent; they have to be prodded to respond, and even then they do it reluctantly, to get it over with. Especially the girls. They keep looking at each other and tittering. Whenever one of them opens her mouth, the others laugh, as if it is silly to join in a discussion like this. A redhead helps a girl in a cap to pull her gloves on.

(*Teacher*) 'Would you like to go to public school?'
(*Redhead*) 'I'd like to go to a cleaner school. This school's filthy.'
(*Girl in cap*) 'It's boring.' (*Titters.*)
(*Teacher*) 'Do you think public school would be less boring?'

(*Girl in cap*) 'Do I what?'

(*Teacher*) 'Do you think public school would be less boring?'

(*Girl in cap*) 'It'd be worse.'

(*Ivan*) 'In a comprehensive you get a broader view of society. In a private school you'd only get one view.'

(*Teacher*) 'D'you agree with that, Michelle?'

(*Michelle nods.*)

(*Teacher*) 'What did he say?'

(*Michelle*) 'I don't know.'

(*Teacher repeats Ivan's comment.*) 'Do you agree?'

(*Michelle*) 'Yeah.'

There is obviously a long way to go towards creating the articulate, well-informed community in the inner city that is capable of organizing and fighting for its rights and due resources. But the limits of what any school can do are set by the context in which it works. Unless the context is changed, the inner-city school, and the neighbourhood school in other working-class areas, can improve things modestly, at the cost of immense efforts, but will never be able to offer their pupils equality of opportunity, and most pupils from disadvantaged homes will fall far short of their potential. For whatever the school does, it can never be the major educational influence in its pupils' lives. Most children spend the crucial early years at home. By the time those from poor homes start primary school, irreparable damage will have been done to their potential through poor nutrition, lack of stimulation and verbalization, and emotional disturbance. The family is a more potent influence than the primary school, the street is more potent than secondary school, television is more potent than either level.

The poor neighbourhood is itself the principal school for its children, its inhabitants are the chief instructors. It is a disastrous environment for learning or discipline.

Part Three

Tensions and Conflicts

Brother shall strike brother and both fall.
Evil shall be on earth, an age of whoredom,
of sharp sword play and shields clashing,
a wind age, a wolf age, till the world ruins.

The Elder Edda (tr. P. B. Taylor and W. H. Auden),
on Ragnarok, the twilight of the gods

The Divisiveness of Deprivation

Low incomes and poor services, private squalor compounded by public squalor, are not the only tribulations of deprived areas. For poverty can also weaken the bonds between human beings and generate conflict within the family, between neighbours, and between races.

When resources are scarcer, competition for them, between groups and within groups, is more intense. In poor areas, family and community resources are usually insufficient to meet everyone's needs. But political awareness and activism is usually too weak for the poor to unite against the sources of their common problems – those institutions and structures that ensure that they receive an inadequate share of total resources. Instead, the disadvantaged more commonly turn against one another. Each individual, each family, each ethnic group attempts to gain a larger personal share of the small slice of cake available. Within the family, competition occurs over personal space in overcrowded homes, and over personal shares of limited incomes. Where better-off families can usually accommodate multiple demands out of more ample funds, poor families often find themselves in a situation where one person's need for shoes can be met only at the expense of another's need for a winter coat, or a man's desire for a drink and a gamble can only be satisfied at the expense of his family's food or fuel.

There are generalized pressures towards family breakdown in modern, media-dominated societies: unrealistic expectations of personal happiness, an increased desire for sexual liberty without the corresponding reduction in possessiveness needed to accommodate it. Added to these, the sources of conflict in poor families are legion: disputes over spending priorities, items of luxury or of waste, unpaid bills, strategies for increasing income. Unemployment stimulates rows over responsibilities, sex roles, standards of housekeeping. Bad housing generates arguments over who is to blame and how it can be remedied, over space for hobbies, homework, washing, noise. And every argument is loaded with an excess charge generated by a more diffuse tension, anxiety and insecurity. Thus all the inequalities of society, weighing down on the lowest strata, turn the family into a battleground. Husband and wife, parent and child are transformed into the sharp edges of conflicting social pressures, cutting and grinding into one another with a violence proportionate to the external stresses applied. Thus the poor family is more likely to be divided against itself, more likely to split up, less likely to be capable of successfully socializing its children.

In the neighbourhood, competition occurs for space and freedom. Space creates freedom: with detached houses, and large gardens, the liberties of neighbouring families rarely conflict. In crowded areas, one man's freedom becomes another's restriction, one person's pleasure can become another's torment. The noise of parties conflicts with the need for peace, car-parks with play space, laundry and lumber with free movement on the balconies.

There is also competition for sources of income and for housing. In its most basic form, this expresses itself through street crime and burglary: one deprived person secures more resources by simply taking them from another. And as resources diminish in relation to social needs, crime increases. Crime stirs up expanding waves of conflict, bringing in its wake heavy policing and the danger of group conflict between youth and police. Most people are content to compete for jobs and housing on an individual level. But many are tempted to see racialism as a way of winning the competition by excluding other racial groups. And the inner city, where black immigrants and their children are concentrated together with the most deprived whites, becomes the focus of the most explosive tensions.

Conflict in poor families and neighbourhoods is also intensified by redirected aggression. Individuals in the lower reaches of any dominance hierarchy or pecking order, when attacked by a superior, tend to seek out the nearest inferior or equal on whom to vent their aggressive feelings. Aggression in human societies more often takes symbolic rather than physical forms: but it still awakens aggressive urges in the recipient. Britain is still a pronouncedly hierarchical society, with clear relations of power and status between managers and workers, bureaucrats and public and so on. Lower-ranking individuals in these hierarchies – junior officials, foremen and the like – all too often vent on inferiors the aggressive feelings awakened in them by their superiors. Thus people in the lowest reaches of the various hierarchies become an 'aggression sink', subject to frequent humiliations, arbitrary orders, interrogations, insults, and reminders of their powerlessness and low status. Unable to direct their aggression at its source, the disadvantaged seek out scapegoats – spouses, children, neighbours and people of other races. But at this lowest level people often pass beyond symbolic aggression, which the poorest have no power to assert, into actual physical violence. In more settled areas, these conflicts are resolved or mitigated by community solidarity. In the inner city, redevelopment, emigration and immigration loosen community bonds and destroy the mechanisms of social control, so that it becomes a theatre of violence of all kinds and all degrees.

All the sources of conflict were intensified by recession and monetarism. When resources are increasing – as when family incomes and public spending are rising – competition is less acute. It is possible for one person to gain from the *growth* in resources, without diminishing the resources available to another. Recession and monetarism, however, have led to stagnant and sometimes declining resources for family and community: lower real incomes, fewer homes and fewer jobs, and reduced local spending. Competition then becomes a zero-sum game, where one person can gain only if another loses, and hence an altogether more embittered affair. With increased work-loads, slower pay growth and greater insecurity, the humiliations of work have increased, as have the indignities of claiming from overworked social-security offices, and the spurnings of housing departments. Lowered real incomes have arrived at a time of unprecedented expansion in social expectations, in adults and in children, with a flood of new 'essential' household durables, toys and games based on the new microchip technologies. There is thus a heavier load of symbolic aggression, of insecurity, of frustrated desires, weighing on the poor, resulting inevitably in a greater incidence of hostility and open violence against children, against spouses, against property, against the random victims of crime, and against other races.

At other times, in other places, Britain's situation of the early eighties might have led to revolution, or to fascism. Economic crisis tends to heighten political extremism at both ends of the spectrum, and extremes feed off each other. Mass protests have often been sparked by sudden falls in real incomes after periods of rising standards and expectations. The growth of revolutionary parties has often been the result of blockages to employment and promotion created by recession.

While these processes, certainly, radicalized the grass-roots of the Labour Party as never before, they did not radicalize the electorate as a whole: the growing vanguard found itself without much of an army behind it.

Those who were hurt by slump and government policies could, in theory, have channelled their aggression towards its real causes. Crisis could have mobilized them into protest, demonstration or conventional political action. In practice several influences worked against this. The poor and the disadvantaged, drained of morale and self-confidence, are the hardest of any group to mobilize. Television anaesthetized the distress of the slump, much as coca-chewing stills the hunger pains of Andean Indians. More significant perhaps was the widespread lack of class-consciousness and of awareness of the root causes of exploitation and inequality and their intensification, partly due to the absence of radical critiques and documentation in the dominant mass media. Against this chorus, the efforts of the Left at political education were practically inaudible.

Thus it was that, instead of becoming a creative force for change, aggression remained bottled up inside poor families and poor districts. The slump led, not to organized protests, let alone revolution, but to an increase in chaotic conflict within poor areas, dividing the disadvantaged against themselves, weakening them further, and adding to their deprivations.

16   Growing Up Nasty

Zeus will destroy this race of mortal men, when babies shall be born with greying hair. Father will have no common bond with son.

> *Hesiod*, Works and Days (*tr. D. Wender*)

Nowhere is childhood less like the best days of your life than among the poor, and in the inner city. The child who, in more comfortable circumstances, would be a source of pleasure and an object of love, all too easily becomes an irritant and a focus of resentment. The family, which should provide the foundation for learning, cooperation and self-control, becomes instead a school for failure, conflict and crime. The neighbourhood, which should provide a secure environment for play, exploration and adventure, bristles with physical and moral dangers.

How Little Darlings Become Little Sods

The frequency of negative contacts between children and parents in poor and overcrowded homes is very noticeable, and the causes are often purely ecological. Bernadette Tsokallis, whom we met in Chapter 6, has all the makings of a good mother, warm, decent and conscientious. But the strain of dealing with two very small children, in a small flat, on a small income, poses heavy demands. Nine-month-old George had just begun crawling. The lounge is so cramped that he cannot move more than a metre in a straight line without trouble. While Mum is making tea, he bangs his head on the steel frame of the coffee-table and howls. There is near panic as he touches the white powder on the air ducts: it is insecticide, put there to kill pharaoh ants and cockroaches. Meanwhile Peter, only a year older, falls over a tricycle on to his face and later totters out of the kitchen with a carving knife in his hand. Bernadette shouts at him. She is forever controlling, checking, forever on edge, forever in danger of losing her own self-control. Only that afternoon, while she was in the supermarket, she'd had to tell Peter off. He had snatched a packet of cream cakes from the shelf and bitten into it, so she had to pay for it. On her tight budget, 6op wasted on cakes, which she normally never buys, is a major setback for the week. Her own nervousness and anxiety, created entirely by the stresses of low pay and bad housing, turns up the tension in every incident.

As children grow older, the potential for open conflict grows, and the climate of the times does not help. Even toddlers wear long trousers, and get holes in the knees. The soles of cheap trainers peel off within a month or two. Meanwhile television constantly raises children's expectations. When I was in Sarah Jones's house (Chapter 13) the television – always switched on, to keep the children quiet – was playing tea-time adverts for electronic racing-car circuits, robots, space games, all costing from £10 upwards. With hardly a toy in the house, the little ones are always improvising their own from household objects, often dangerous or fragile: more cause for conflict. Meg, a pretty little blonde girl of two, starts to unscrew the electric-fire guard with a knife. Four-year-old Martin, in an army jacket and short-cropped hair, digs into the lounge door with a paint scraper. 'You can see what a little sod he is,' Sarah comments. It is an expression I heard many parents in the inner city use of their children.

In many families children are resented, sometimes even hated, because of their incessant demands on the limited space and resources of a poor home and the limited time and energy of their parents. The child becomes, not the fulfilment of the parents' existence, but an obstacle to the parents' idea of self-fulfilment, to relaxation and entertainment and the achievement of social ambitions. This feeling is most pronounced among women, especially single mothers – most fathers simply do not allow the children to limit their own autonomy and slope off, gaining their own freedom at the expense of the mother's.

Elaine W. (not her real name) makes no attempt whatsoever to conceal her attitude to the six children she has had to raise alone. 'I had too many children,' she says. 'They spoil everything for me.' She came over to Britain in 1968, from Montserrat, to join her husband, already working here as a train-driver. She got a job packing sweets, then gave up work to have her first three children, John, eleven, Rosa, ten, and Marianne, aged nine. Her marriage was already breaking up and she wanted no more children. 'When I was having Marianne I begged them to stop [sterilize] me. I couldn't take the pill, it gave me headaches, I used to get depressed and upset with everybody. But the doctor said I was too young. I kept on asking, they kept on saying the same thing.'

Her husband left her. Four years on she met her current boy-friend and got pregnant again. Maria, now four, was the result. Two years later Elaine was in the family way again. It was by now apparent that her boy-friend would not marry her or support her, and she did not want another child. She asked for an abortion: 'I was ten weeks when I went to see the doctor, but I was getting really big and fat. The gynaecologist said I must be fourteen weeks gone, and an abortion would be too risky. She said "Make this your last" and she mentioned that my boy-friend wanted to have another kid with me, as if it was him and not me that was going to bring them up. Well, when I saw the scan and saw they were twins, I was frightened, and with the father wanting them as well I thought to myself: just forget about it and have them.'

She was finally sterilized after the birth of the twins, two boys, now enormous two-year-olds. Elaine lives in an attractive three-storeyed terraced council house, but with only three bedrooms, and with the parsimony of social security it is cramped and badly furnished. Elaine sleeps in the first-floor bedroom with one of the twins. From there on up, there are no carpets, only bare planks that give the children splinters when they walk barefoot. At the back is the girls' room, with two beds each 75 cm wide. Marianne sleeps in one, Rosa and Maria head to toe in the other. In the bedroom opposite, eleven-year-old John, and the other twin, sleep in a single bed. There is no other furniture in the room, and their clothes are jumbled in an enormous heap on the floor. Neither bedroom has any curtains.

Elaine's income from social security sounds high – at £94·48 it is a good deal more than many manual workers take home – but when rent, fuel and weekly payments to a credit catalogue are deducted, she has only £61 in summer and £51 in winter for all other needs of seven of them, that is, £1·24 each and £1·04 a day each respectively. As the father of her children still sees her and often stays the night, she also faces the intrusive investigations of her private life that single mothers are often subjected to. 'After the twins born, they called me up there [to the social-security office] and took me into a little room and asked me, when did I meet my boy-friend, how often did we have sex, was it at my place? I said what does it matter? When I got home I thought it over and said to myself, this is ridiculous. A few months ago the lady next door said two men knocked at her door and asked if she knew if I was living with a man. I think they must have been from social security as well.'

Elaine's problems stem from the irresponsibility of men, the power of health professionals, the lack of adequate income and support for single mothers. But all these causes are distant, or beyond her reach to influence. The children are there, inescapably, every day and every night. She cannot help seeing them as the root of her problems and, often unconsciously, taking it out on them.

'I'd love to get a job,' Elaine complains, 'but who will employ me with so many children? I can't even go out during the day, sometimes I can't push the twins because they are so heavy, I can only go out when the older children come home from school. It worries me, sitting here all day, I get so bored. I haven't got many friends, sometimes I'm dying for someone to come and knock at the door. I tried to get a place in a nursery for the small ones, but I can't get one. Sometimes I haven't got the strength to deal with them. I think of putting them in a home. But that wouldn't be nice. I'm grateful when they sleep, because when they are up, I can't manage.'

Our conversation was brought to an end by the noise of crying from the room where the twins had been napping. 'They're up, oh my God!' she says in a tone of desperation, almost of horror. She goes up to see. They are big, active, loud boys. One has his hair soaked in milk. The other's buttocks are smeared with diarrhoea. Elaine shouts at the boys and tells ten-year-old Rosa to wash up the mess and rinse the clothes. It is an impatient order, not a request, and Rosa jumps to it. But Elaine has no control at all over her biggest boy, John. As she sees me out, he is putting together bits of bicycle, a hobby for which he has taken over the entire store-room. She gives him a message that he has to meet someone somewhere. 'I ain't going there, why should I? Let him come here,' he says, with an almost venomous contempt in his voice. 'He's so cheeky,' Elaine comments. 'He is mending bikes at midnight with the radio full on, keeping all of us awake. He gets into fights at school, he takes liberties with me. He's been like that ever since his father left when he was four. I haven't got the energy to shout at him or to hit him.'

I ask her how she sees the future: 'My only hope now is to go back to Montserrat, or maybe I could get to Canada. I need a new way of life. Otherwise I'll just have to wait till these are older, and I'll try to get a job.'

Space Games

Overcrowding, lack of toys, domestic tensions, all conspire to drive the inner-city child out from under its parents' feet and out of the home. Very few families have gardens for safe, supervised play. Thus the child is forced on to the concrete balcony, on to the stairs and the lift-shafts, on to the courtyards and the streets.

The need for outside play facilities is much greater in a poor inner-city area, but the provision is often less, because of lack of open spaces (the public park movement did not begin until the southern half of Hackney was built over), the density of housing, the lack of local-authority funds and manpower, and vandalism. The poverty of play space in Hackney has to be seen to be believed. Every estate carries signs on its walls, *No ball games*, yet on many there is no play area at all, only concrete and tarmac where children compete and collide with parked cars, abandoned cars, unsafe cars often past the end of their useful life, stolen cars or souped-up cars driven at chase speed.

Where play space is provided, it is usually too small for the demand, or the equipment has been vandalized or removed for safety reasons. Bannister House is unusually well provided by Hackney standards, with three tarmac areas, surrounded by high wire nets like prisoner-of-war compounds. Two of them were playgrounds, but in 1979, after a boy fell off a high slide and knocked himself unconscious, workmen removed almost all the equipment, and it was never replaced. In one enclosure, only five tyre swings remain. In the other are a long yellow iron rocking-horse that has rusted rigid and five unusable baby-swings, every one with its safety frame busted. The children do not play football in the enclosures, because they say the surface bursts their balls. So they play on the narrow grass verges, running for cover like pheasants when the council's mobile patrol comes hunting.

A 1981 report from the Hackney Play Association looked at a typical selection of playgrounds:

Somerford Gardens: A dismal little playground that local parents find too dangerous for their children to use.
Clissold Park: umbrella immobilized since April, see-saw chained up since July, playground unchanged since Victorian days. If dangerous equipment is removed little remains.
Springfield Park: paddling-pool empty for a year; sandpit fouled by cats and dogs; swings chained up; never seems to be open.
Millfields: roundabout has exposed nails and rotten board seats; sand has broken glass in it.
Hackney Downs: rocking-horse removed; slide irreparable, must be removed immediately; dogs a problem.

Complaints common to nearly all playgrounds were: unsafe equipment, poor maintenance and repair, dirt, and irregular or infrequent opening hours due to staff shortages.

Prisoners in the Tower

Where formal facilities are lacking, children inevitably create their own playthings and play spaces out of objects and areas that are not intended for play. Vandalism and conflict with adults become inevitable, in the same way that elephants when confined to an artificially small range will turn it into a desert. Nightingale estate has a population larger than the Falkland Islands, yet the only formal provision for the hundreds of children who live here is one small playground, with two slides, a climbing-frame and tyre swings; and one small cage for ball games. Many use the enormous concrete platform over the underground car-park, above which the tower blocks rise. It is approached by sloping ramps ideal for dangerous stunts on chopper bikes. It is as big as a soccer pitch, and conveniently floodlit at night from lamps mounted at the summit of the towers: on summer nights, ignoring the *No ball games* signs, large gangs of black youths play football till midnight or later. The underground garages, which only the brave or the foolhardy still park their cars in, serve wider purposes. Several bays have been burnt out, others have their doors torn off and are used as love-nests by teenagers, while a couple of rusting cars, wrecked by joy-riders, block the passageway.

There is a polarization: the roughnecks rule (and ruin) the public spaces, with the most daring acting as examples and guides to the rest. Children whose parents can still control them, and who still care enough about their welfare, don't let them out to play.

Shirley Weymouth, a well-built forty-four-year-old with curly blond hair, has raised five children in her three-bedroomed flat more than forty metres up on the twelfth floor of one of the tower blocks. 'We were living with my mother-in-law, five in a bedroom, before, and we'd been on the waiting list for sixteen years. Quite frankly we'd have taken anything they'd offered us. But to be honest, I thought this place was lovely when I first saw it.' She soon discovered the truth. Her three youngest boys, eleven-year-old redhead Darren and two nine-year-old twins Mark and Paul, their black hair in basin cuts, grew up surrounded by restrictions. The window openings were wide enough for a baby to fall through, and easy to reach from a chair. 'I was anxious the whole time they were small, always checking up where they were. If we noticed one was missing we'd panic – oh, where they gone? where they missing to?'

But as the boys grew older the restrictions did not relax. Listening to the Weymouths talk is an introduction to a child's world as distant as Mars from the suburban or rural child's prospect.

(*Shirley*) 'I don't let the boys down to play. I'm frightened for them. The cars are supposed to go at five miles an hour, but they come flying through. I feel if they had an accident down there, they could be bleeding and I wouldn't be able to get down to them in time. Mark had concussion the other week.'

(*Mark*) 'One of the other boys pulled on his back brake and he swerved into me on my bike.'

(*Shirley*) 'They want to go down but I just can't let them. There's a lot of dirty old men down there, tramps, down the garages.'

(*Darren, dramatically*) 'There's *murderers*.'

(*Paul*) 'I was in school and a bloke came up to me and said I'm a detective, would you mind coming with me?'

(*Shirley*) 'There was this gentleman going round pretending to be a policeman. Luckily Paul knows what a police warrant looks like, his uncle's a policeman. There's toilets on the ground floor, supposed to be for the kids to use, but they've had to be permanently locked because dirty old men were going in there. Tramps sleep on the stairs in the end blocks in winter – you can see their motions on the stairs – and there's gangs of girls and boys up the top, glue-sniffing.'

(*Me*) 'Which places are you most scared of going to?'

(*Paul*) 'I wouldn't go in the playground. A car came crashing through there on fire, from the garages. If we'd been playing there we'd be finished.'

(*Darren*) 'Down the swing park [on Hackney Downs] they shoot airguns. They fire darts, sharp, like nails they are.'

(*Paul*) 'They try to hit tin cans with them. One kid over in that block got shot in the knee. They was firing at me, too, but I ducked too quick for them.'

(*Shirley*) 'Their dad won't let them go on the balcony of the flat. And they're not allowed to go in the lift unless they're all together.'

(*Paul*) 'I been trapped three times in the lift. The kids pull the door open at the bottom and that sticks the lift wherever it happens to be.'

(*Shirley*) 'I'll only let them play out down there on a Sunday morning, just below my kitchen window, where I can keep an eye on them. Otherwise they play in here, with me, they play with their Lego, their trains, their racing-cars, or we watch children's TV programmes.'

The Weymouth boys are well parented, but seriously deprived nevertheless: deprived of the experiences of exploration, excitement, interaction with their peers, which are the need, the norm and the right of children. Those who do play out face greater hazards. The rural or even suburban child can enjoy adventure without much real risk, catapult a bird, swing on an old branch till it breaks, explore an unknown copse. But the flora and fauna of the inner urban landscape is infinitely more menacing, a jungle of glass, metal, concrete, electric wires, clogged canals, derelict houses and factories; inhabited by cars, heavy lorries, fast trains, stray dogs, and sometimes dangerous people. However the inner-city child chooses to express its need for play, it is usually illegal, dangerous, or both. There are few places it can turn its adventurous or destructive urges to without hurting or offending someone, breaking someone's property or falling foul of the law. The competition for breathing space sets kids at odds with adults. Residents often complain, and sometimes raise petitions to the council to get playgrounds closed, or slot-machine licences withdrawn from cafés. Children have a constant source of aggression to redirect into vandalism.

Danger has its own irresistible and sometimes fatal lure. Near Stonebridge estate is a railway viaduct where some of the local boys have a den, with cushions and candles, in a store-room under a trapdoor next to the live electric rails. Several boys have had shocks, one was killed there. Death by misadventure is common enough to terrify concerned parents. In 1981 there were three deaths from play in Hackney. An eleven-year-old boy was killed by a fall through the roof of a Shoreditch warehouse where he'd been playing at camping. A girl of eleven died of cerebral contusion after she fell while sliding down the banisters in a block of flats in Finsbury Park. Paul Rowe, fourteen, who had been riding on the roof of a lift on Kingshold estate near Victoria Park, was crushed to death against a metal bar.

Play Street

Anton Street is a dingy backwater off Amhurst Road, in Stoke Newington, passing between a clothing-factory and a row of run-down houses. At one end are railway arches with small workshops, at the other a small open space left by the demolition of the end house of a terrace. The corrugated tin fencing around this lot has been pulled down and the site used as a rubbish dump for old tyres, beer-cans, oil-cans, paint-cans, and dozens of broken television sets.

Opposite is a row of vandalized garages. Inside one of these, a gang of four young white children have made a den out of old car seats, a mattress, an old television console and a sideboard. The kids are aged eight to eleven, two boys and two girls. They complain that there's nowhere to play closer than the over-used play-park on Hackney Downs, a mile from their homes. In the den, they have fitted out their own play area, but it is surrounded with hazards. Busy Amhurst Road is only a few yards away – eleven-year-old Elaine, on roller-skates, was knocked down by a car last year. There is a large skein of barbed wire, relic of a failed attempt to keep the kids out of the garages. There is broken glass from the television tubes everywhere. And the children climb on the thin asbestos of the garage roofs – only the week before, ten-year-old Paul fell off and cut his arm badly. He shows me the scar, and another, on the bridge of his nose right between the eyes, where he was hit with a slug when his brother shot a loaded slug gun at him. Paul's brother Mark, in a green army-style sweater, was beaten up the night before. 'All the big ones beat up us little ones,' he complains. His assailants were black youths who use the self-same den after dark, fit up corrugated iron sheets to the door, turn their radios on full blast, and smoke.

As I leave the group, Elaine and her eight-year-old cousin Kerry skate down the side entrance of the factory, while the boys take turns at cycling stunts. A piece of chipboard, balanced on a half brick in the centre of the street, serves as a ramp. They take a run-up from way down the street and pedal furiously at the ramp, flying a metre into the air. On Paul's second run the chipboard snaps in two and he goes crashing to the ground: another bad graze to his arm.

There are two abandoned cars in the street, number-plates missing, windows shattered into a thousand mosaic fragments. Two black boys are sitting in the front seat – the driver rattling the gears and making revving noises. Darren is thirteen, short and slim, with an Artful Dodger look, and a forehead scarred from a fight. His friend Malcolm is twelve, plump, with Rasta hair under a high peaked cap. Both still have the looks of children, but the premature experience of young adults. I ask them if they have problems finding places to play. Darren does the talking: 'We ain't into playing, our playing days are over, that's really just for children. We just walk around. We like travelling – we're just going to Mile End now. The furthest we been is Brighton, on our bikes, but they broke so we had to come back on the train. Fridays and Saturdays we stay out all night, that's when we go raving, you know, parties and clubs, pulling birds. But I don't like the girls round here, because they're what I call slags, they're anybody's for a quick one. Usually people don't start raving till they're fourteen or fifteen, but we started young. We can afford it. We work at that garage down there every Saturday for £5. We play disco for parties, we get £15 a time, more if it's far away. I don't go mugging, but I do thiefing, if I see something I can thief. We spend £50 a weekend sometimes, on drink and joints [marijuana], you can easily smoke fifteen joints in a night and it costs £3 for a lot, that will make five joints. We don't drink beer, we drink shorts, Bacardi and coke. Some people say we're too young to drink but we're not, 'cause we know what we're doing.'

Both boys live with their mothers, but see their fathers regularly. I asked Darren if his mother ever objected to his wanderings. 'She did at first, but now she doesn't worry 'cause she knows I'm all right. We live at my sister's house. My mum has her own room with her boy-friend, and I got my own room. My sister cooks my dinner for me, 'cause my mum's a waitress, she's out from 3 till about 9 or 10 at night. So what I do is really up to me, 'cause I don't really live with my mum. The police came to our flat last year – they said my mum had an argument with a neighbour, but she hadn't, so she shut the door on them and they kicked it down. They started hitting her so I stabbed one of them in the leg with a knife.' Darren's braggadocio is hung around a basic framework of fact: in Chapter 18 we shall meet the policeman he stabbed in the leg.

The Collapse of Social Control

The inner-city street is a school for scoundrels. In an area that ingathers social casualties from all over north London, the street is the habitat not only for children, but for thieves, pushers, prostitutes in certain areas, tramps, winos, mental patients enacting their elaborate fantasies in public. Not that Hackney is crawling with such people, but they are all common enough sights that children see. Quite apart from these bad examples, the mere fact of being forced to play with things not meant for play brings dangers. The line between legal and illegal is a fine one, and easily crossed. Hence the inner-city child encounters the police at an early age, and is hectored, lectured, labelled and sometimes arrested. The child acquires a negative image of the police – and the police acquire a negative image of him.

The community that surrounds the street no longer controls what happens on the street, for it is no longer, in any meaningful sense, a community. The automobile slices it in two. Redevelopment scattered the inhabitants of individual streets to the winds, gathering them together again arbitrarily, as groups of strangers, in estates whose architecture divided them against each other. The emigration of the fit and able split extended families, while immigrants to the area – white or black – had already split their own extended family to come here. Discontent with housing and with the area fuels a continual movement of people in and out, preventing a stable community from re-emerging.

Adults no longer stand together in controlling children's behaviour outside the home. If a neighbour complains about a child's behaviour, to the parent, the parent no longer backs the neighbour against the child, but more often backs the child against the neighbour. Therefore each individual adult stands alone against a crowd of children and youths. Time and again one hears the same tales from different areas: people telling children off and being told to fuck off, or complaining to parents and being met with abuse or even, on occasions, a meat axe. Racial tensions complicate the picture: it is virtually impossible for white adults to tell black children off, or vice versa.

But the child is often out of control before reaching the street. All those features that research shows contribute to delinquency are more common in poor urban homes: discipline is far more likely to be excessive or inconsistent. Corporal punishment is more common, yet at the same time parents disagree more often about standards of strictness and interfere with each other's actions. Fathers are frequently distant or absent figures, out working overtime or shifts, down the pub or betting office, or catatonic in front of the television. Many mothers work unsocial hours, cleaning from 6 till 9 evenings or mornings, in catering, or nursing on shifts. Children are then left in the care of their eldest female sibling, and often play out, in the dark, till late at night. Beat officer PC Dave Perrier once found a six-year-old out at 11 p.m., without shoes. Her mother worked at Ford's in Dagenham, leaving home at 6 p.m. and getting back home again at 10 a.m. the next day, leaving a girl of nine in charge of her younger brothers and sisters.

Conflict inside the family is liable to aggravate the inconsistency of discipline. Conflict, as we have seen, is more likely among poor and manual working-class homes. Early marriages and unplanned pregnancies are more common.

Children are used as allies or as ammunition in the battles that the circumstances of poverty provoke. Parents compete for love and undermine each other's discipline. When parents separate, single mothers often have neither the physical strength nor the emotional energy to control their children. In many homes television has taken over the role of parent, but it is no longer the Reithian educator of the masses. The middle-class assumption that parents will control their children's viewing is not applicable here. The programme planners' 9 o'clock cut-off line for material unsuitable for children has no meaning: even primary-school children often watch till midnight. In my wife's primary class of eight-year-olds, one in three stayed up to watch the bloody carnage and terror of *Alien*. Thus in the name of free speech (but it is the free speech of the advertising men and the middle-class intelligentsia) a generation is brutalized, hyped up, and prematurely geared to the expectations of adulthood.

The Disintegration of Cultural Control

There is no group on whom these influences have had a more destructive impact than West Indians and their children.

Perhaps half the families in the West Indies are affected by the cultural pattern of mobile males and mother-focused families – deriving partly from African polygamy, reinforced and totally destabilized by slave-owners for their own profitable ends. The pattern is kept viable in the West Indies by the key agents of grandmothers and the extended family of neighbouring relatives. Maintenance arrangements in the mother-focused families are informal and unreliable, so the mother often goes out to work to ensure a stable income for her children, while grandmother acts as child-minder. Discipline is harsh, and the ultimate sanction is to throw the child out for a while, knowing full well he (for it is usually a he) will cool his heels in a relative's house and come back sobered and unharmed.

Migration to Britain destroyed, for many families, this system of social control, for the linchpin, the grandmother, was usually left behind in the islands, creating a serious child-care vacuum which Britain's inadequate public provision filled only for a lucky few. The sanctions of a supportive community were absent, and the traditional methods of corporal punishment were discouraged, indeed often totally undermined, by social-services departments. Unable to discipline her children, unable to call on grandmothers and uncles to help, the single West Indian mother (and about one-third of mothers of West Indian origin in Hackney are single) found herself alone and unable to cope, forced to work in lowly jobs with unsocial hours, with her children, especially her male children, almost totally outside her control. Twenty years on, there are now grandmothers and relatives on the scene, but the housing situation often puts them out of easy reach, and the damaging examples of the first generation remain to influence younger ones.

Mothers of West Indian origin, when they reach the end of their tether, often turn to outside agencies for help, to replace the role of grannie and uncle.

The police are one resort. I met eleven-year-old Derek (not his real name) at Stoke Newington police station. His mother, a factory machinist, had brought him in for a talking-to. She is neatly dressed in a fawn raincoat and scarf; he has on a smart cord jacket and a flat cap. She explains the problem to PC Dave Perrier, one of the very few Hackney policemen who actually live in the borough, and a beat officer for the Springfield area: 'He is out till midnight, sometimes till 2 o'clock every night. When it gets past 11 I get scared. When I worry everything shakes in my hands. I have been out at 1 in the morning looking for him in the street, but I'm frightened [the street where she lives is an emergent red-light district where there were three murders in 1981]. He stays the night at friends. If he rings me he never says which friend he's at, or if I ask the address he says he doesn't remember it. When he should be at school he takes the bus to Brixton, or he rides his bike, all over the place, to Epping Forest, to my mother's in Walthamstow. I tried to organize for him to go to a club, but he prefer to go exploring anywhere where I won't know about.

'I do try to discipline him, but my husband and me separated, he lives downstairs in the same house, and whenever I tell Derek off he runs down to his dad and tells him a different story, so I can't punish him the way I would have liked. And when he does this terrible staying out, I don't punish him when he comes back because I'm so grateful to see him. He's been bad since my marriage broke up in 1978, but it's getting worse now. This last year he's been very restless. I missed a lot of work because of the ups and downs of his troubleness.'

Derek gets a grave and authoritative ear-bending from PC Perrier, who points out that his mother might have to sign a form saying Derek was out of her control so he might have to be taken into care. Derek refuses to say a single word, answers every question with an ambiguous sigh, and stares at his mother accusingly, as if to say, 'How could you bring me here?' Towards the end, when there is talk of putting him in a home, his eyes moisten. Perhaps the visit would have a temporary effect on him, but the omens were unfavourable: in a year or two he would be so big his mother daren't touch him, and well along the path that leads to more serious delinquency.

Another agency that fills part of the vacuum is the social-services department – but often with a destabilizing effect that runs directly contrary to what should be its primary aim of keeping families together. Repeated and highly publicized cases of deaths of battered children have made social workers play extra safe – perhaps too safe. In cases of harsh discipline they may take the child into care (even where the methods of discipline were simply those in common use in this country a generation ago), thus imposing white middle-class mores on black (and often white) working-class families. Short of that, they frequently interview families in cases reported by teachers or neighbours (often based on nothing more than a bruise or the noise of persistent crying) to investigate suspected cruelty. This has created a widespread misconception among black parents that it is against British law to hit your children. The children themselves also believe this and threaten to report their parents to the police.

Both parents and children often use social-service departments as a threat against each other. A growing number of black children, from twelve and thirteen onwards, seek refuge in the community homes when parental discipline is too strict for their taste. Similarly, some parents resort to council care, in the hope (usually vain) that the homes will teach their children a lesson.

Home from Home

The overall proportion of children in care in Hackney is quite staggering – about one child in forty in 1981, three times higher than the national average. Among black children, the rate may be as high as one in every fifteen or twenty. That is only the score in one particular month. As children are constantly coming into and going out of care, the proportion of Hackney's children who have, at some time in their childhood, been in care, could easily be as high as one in ten. Juvenile crime is the most common reason for care, with 'unsatisfactory home conditions' second.

Mathias House, one of Hackney's community homes, merges discreetly into a row of council houses off Newington Green. Sixteen children live here at any one time – eight less than capacity, because of staff shortages imposed by government cuts. To re-create a more familial atmosphere, the children divide into two houses, each with its own dining-room and lounge and regular staff. For dinner on the day of my visit, there is chicken and rice with blackeye beans. Around the table are some of the most unfortunate victims of the inner city. Four-year-old Marie* was abandoned by her young mother because she is backward. Her father says he is willing to have her, but he lives in a rooming-house where children are not allowed and is demanding a council house before he will take her on. Joyce, thirteen, and her twin brother

* All names in this section have been changed.

Michael, came into care only a month after their black father left home: Joyce, a big girl, beat her white mother up when she wasn't allowed to stay out late. Helena, a white girl of fifteen, has been in care for seven years, along with her five brothers and sisters, ever since her parents split up and her mother couldn't cope with them.

Fourteen-year-old Andrew's white mother left home when he was three. He started a career of petty crime when his Jamaican father remarried four years ago. 'I don't believe in a second mother,' he says. He was first taken into care aged ten, for acting as a look-out for an older friend who was housebreaking. Since then, there has been a succession of petty thefts, paralleled by trouble at school – he was expelled for punching a teacher – culminating in the latest care order, for stealing from cars. Why did he do it? 'It's just Hackney. It's the atmosphere. I never did it cause I needed money. I just did it because it was there,' he explains, like a mountain-climber.

His friend Tony, a black boy of fourteen, has been in and out of the homes since he was two, when his parents separated. Far from setting him on the right track, some of the homes unintentionally provided a schooling in toughness and criminal technique. Some of the children clammed up when sensitive areas were touched on, but Tony tells his tale with a detached coolness: 'My mother was young when I was first put into care. She was working and she was studying at night school, and she was going to have another baby. She couldn't cope. I remember she took me and my sister to Liverpool Street station, I remember falling asleep on the train. When I got to the home, I went to sleep.

'I started thieving when I was four or five. I started with drinks, sweets, I learned it off the older kids at the home, they encouraged the little kids to thieve. And they used to beat us up, really hard. Then my mum got married to my stepdad and she brought me back home when I was nine. But I still did thieving. I never broke into houses, because our flat got broken into three times so I know what it feels like. I did shops, they got plenty of money. And I got into trouble at school. My friend pinched me on the leg hard, so I stood up. The teacher said sit down, and I said I ain't gonna sit down, so she hit me round the head with a book, so I hit her in the face with my hand.

'My mum can't take it when I'm in trouble. She throws me out when she finds out. I used to go and sleep at my dad's house, and I been in and out of homes thousands of times. My mum beats me, but she can't really hurt me, and my stepdad beats me, he's a really big man, sometimes he uses a stick or a wire. But it never stopped me because I was used to it. I grew up in tough company, the big children in the homes toughened me up.

'How I came in here this last time, my friend broke into a shoe shop and his mother rang the police about him. They took him in and he grassed me up, but they couldn't prove anything against me and they let me go. My mum didn't want me to sleep at home then, but my real dad said he couldn't take me in any more, he's only got two bedrooms, and he's got three children and my grandad living there.'

Tony is determined that this will be his last time in care. 'I've given up thieving now, I'm positive. I promised my dad I won't get into trouble again. I won't go round with those kids who get into trouble any more.'

It will be a hard resolution to stick to in Hackney.

17 Criminals and Their Victims

The people will not have constant hearts if they do not have constant means.

Mencius (tr. D. C. Lau)

More terrible than the crimes themselves was the fear they aroused, every man as in war hourly expecting death.

Josephus, The Jewish War *(tr. G. A. Williamson)*

Hackney's local newspaper, the *Hackney Gazette*, regularly rivals from its small catchment area the sensations of the national *News of the World*. Its front page is often a roll call of disasters, inscribed in gory headlines: TEENAGERS STABBED BOY TO DEATH FOR 10P; OLD LADY FOUND IN A CUPBOARD – BOUND, GAGGED, BATTERED, AND DEAD; MURDER HUNT LAUNCHED AS TORTURED GIRL DIES; HOMERTON MAN LEFT VICE GIRL IN POOL OF BLOOD; DOG WALKER STRUCK DOWN – MURDER WITHOUT A MOTIVE. All these are just a selection from 1981.

For those who can take its twice weekly dose of gloom, the *Hackney*, as locals call the paper, can add a peculiar quality of anxiety to the routine depression of many people's lives: the impression that they are bobbing on a stormy sea surrounded by unseen reefs and mines and monsters. Rather as, in the Middle Ages, poor peasants suffered not only the bodily tribulations of poverty, but mental terror at the temptations and torments of demons into the bargain. Yet the *Hackney*'s tales are no figments: even if they select, they also reflect the realities. For in 1981 there were no less than sixteen homicides in Hackney, the Metropolitan Police G district. Thus one London murder in every seven was committed in Hackney, though it contains only one-fortieth of the Met area population, and Hackney's murder rate was ten times the national average.

In 1981, there were more than 23,000 serious crimes in Hackney – one for every three households in the borough. The equivalent of one person in every hundred was mugged, one dwelling in sixteen was burgled, and one car in every four stolen, or stolen from. These figures refer to reported crimes only: the experience of the General Household Survey suggests that the true incidence will be anything from 60 per cent to 100 per cent higher.

The level of crime is one of the key features that distinguishes the inner city from other kinds of area. It casts a shadow over life, and the poorer the family and the neighbourhood, the deeper is that shadow. And as the inner city's economic fortunes worsen relative to the national norm, the crime rate worsens in tandem. Back in 1971, when Hackney's unemployment was no worse than the national average, the crime rate of 50 indictable offences per 1,000 population was only 50 per cent above the England and Wales average. By 1981, when unemployment was very much worse than the national picture, the crime rate had risen to 132 offences per 1,000 population, 120 per cent higher than the average for England and Wales, and 50 per cent higher than the overall rate for the Metropolitan Police. Hackney's robbery rate was no less than twelve and a half times the national average.

The Steady Toll

Crime exerts a continual, random attrition in the inner city, like waves eroding the base of a cliff. Judge the frequency from just ten days of the most serious incidents reported in the *Hackney Gazette* in January 1982 (remembering that Hackney is only nineteen square kilometres in extent):

9 January 1982: Two youths armed with hand-guns entered the off-licence of the Crooked Billet pub in Upper Clapton Road, punched the manageress in the mouth and took £45 from the till.

12 January: A raider with a sawn-off shot-gun took £250 from the A. R. Dennis betting-shop in Kingsland Road.

14 January: Fifty-five-year-old building-society clerk Harry Linden was stabbed to death with a carving knife while walking his dog in the Finsbury Park area (this, incidentally, is a separate murder from the headline quoted above).

15 January: A busy day. A knifeman snatched £2,500 in wages from Haggerston business man George Georgiou as he was taking the wages to his firm. A petrol bomb was thrown through the window of the London Apprentice pub in Shoreditch, but it did not go off. And shop owner Dinash Patel was shot in the stomach when he refused to hand over money to three youths who burst into his chemist's shop in Hackney Road. Reported in the *Gazette* on the same day, the trials for two earlier offences that reveal the tortuous depravity that also lurks in the darker corners of the inner city: a seventy-two-year-old Stoke Newington man was charged with raping a girl of five; and a sixty-seven-year-old pensioner and his forty-four-year-old son were charged with incestuous indecent assault on the younger man's two daughters, aged twelve and fifteen.

16 January: Edna Quirk was murdered on Chatsworth estate.

18 January: Two armed bandits threatened to kill security guards delivering money to a post office in Woodberry Grove, and ran off with £1,300.

A much more realistic idea of the daily cost of crime can be got from police record books. I asked to look at a single day, Friday, 20 November 1981, chosen at random from the records of crime at Stoke Newington police station, which is just one of G district's three main stations. They are logged in four separate books.

First the 'serious crimes' books:

11.30 a.m., Portland Avenue, Stamford Hill, an IC3 (identity category three – Afro-Caribbean) male approaches IC1 (white) female from behind, hits victim in back, forcing her to the ground, stealing handbag, value £60, then decamping.

12.30 p.m., Queen's Drive, Finsbury Park, two IC3 males aged 22/25 and 18/19 approaching victim, an IC1 female aged 25 years, from behind, snatching handbag, then decamping, value £90.

4.00 p.m., Stoke Newington Road, by a group of IC3 males, all aged 14/16 years, entering shop, hitting victim, an IC2 (Asian) male aged 50 years, stealing money from till, then decamping.

4.50 p.m., Stoke Newington Church Street, by persons arrested, entering shop just as it was closing, punching victim, an IC1 female aged 55, in the face, stealing cash from till, then decamping.

5.30 p.m., Craven Walk (off Clapton Common), by IC3 male aged 25 years, approaching victim, an IC1 female aged 34 years, from behind, grabbing her about the throat, stealing handbag, then decamping, value £20.

A second book records major crimes other than robbery: on that Friday there were eleven burglaries involving six flats, two houses, a factory, a shop and a school, of cash and valuables ranging in value from £8·60 to £4,850; three attempted break-ins; one theft of petrol from a garage; one handling of stolen video and camera equipment; plus two assaults where charges were dropped because the victims did not wish to prefer them – one a serious attack in which a husband hit his wife with a shoe and she needed stitches, and one a minor assault on a woman by her ex-husband.

Now turn to the 'beat crimes' book for less serious matters. The following are recorded for that Friday: theft of wine from street stall; theft of £120 off shop counter; theft of cycle from outside Woolworths; assault involving kicks to the head; punching; theft of a compressor; theft from a gas meter.

The final book records auto crime: six cars stolen, three of them recovered (cars are often taken for joy-rides or by people without money for bus or late-night cab fares); nine cases of theft from vehicles, including theft of number plate, road fund licence, two batteries, clothing, cassette recorders and tapes; and one case of criminal damage to a motor-car.

It was, according to Detective Chief Inspector David Reed, a quiet day, as Fridays go.

Crime, Poverty and Unemployment in the Inner City

Just as Britain's economic and social structure gives rise to inner cities, so the inner city generates crime with the inevitability of a purpose-built production line. We have already considered some of the factors that contribute to juvenile delinquency: the gradual breakdown of the family and the community; the collapse of social control; educational failure leading to truancy and the search for alternative roads to status; lack of legitimate play facilities inside or outside the home; housing-allocation policies producing high densities of children and high concentrations of disadvantaged families on individual estates. To these must be added the factors pushing adults towards crime: low and fluctuating wages; inadequate and sometimes erratic social-security payments; unemployment. More generally, there is also the glaring contrast between low incomes, many of which were becoming scarcely sufficient for survival, and a still rising level of social expectations generated by the mass media and advertising.

Crime emerges from this whole complex of causes, not from any one factor in isolation. Recent recessions have undoubtedly stimulated crime, just as the brief recovery of 1978–9 reduced crime. But it may be misleading to blame the rise in crime entirely on the rise in unemployment. As we have seen, there are many other factors that are aggravated by recession and public-spending cuts: slowed, stagnant or declining real incomes of those in work; increasing inefficiency of the social-security offices because of increased workload; darkening housing prospects; and the effect of all of these on family stability. Last but not least the destructive effect on social consensus and social responsibility of a government that quite brazenly fed the rich and robbed the poor.

Nevertheless, unemployment itself is one of the strongest of the complex of factors that act together on the individual. The reason is simple and obvious. The unemployed have both stronger motives for crime and greater opportunities for it. Their incomes are usually even more inadequate to meet their expectations than when employed, and they are idle for most of the day and time weighs on their shoulders like a cloak of lead.

Changes in some categories of crime in Hackney, such as assault without theft and shoplifting, have borne little relation to the economic cycle of recession and recovery. But two categories of crime do seem to move in harmony with the level of unemployment. Burglary shows some correlation (0·86); violent theft a very close correlation (0·94). Between 1971 and 1973 when unemployment in Hackney dropped from 3·2 per cent to 2·4 per cent (a 25 per cent drop), the number of violent thefts declined by 31 per cent. By 1977 unemployment had risen in Hackney to 7·8 per cent (a 225 per cent increase over 1973). Violent theft rose by 443 per cent. By 1979 unemployment had dropped again, to 6·7 per cent, a fall of 14 per cent, and muggings, too, fell, by 24 per cent. By 1981, registered unemployment had soared to 17 per cent (up by

155 per cent over 1979). Violent theft also climbed, by 72 per cent.

Burglary and mugging are both, significantly, crimes committed overwhelmingly by males, with the sole aim of obtaining funds, and they are easier for the unemployed to commit than the employed. Unfortunately, they are also precisely those crimes that generate the most widespread fear and suffering among the public: recession enhances terror as well as poverty and misery.

Further confirmation of the connection between crime and unemployment comes from a quick survey of four separate months, between April 1981 and March 1982, of the pages of brief court reports that feature twice-weekly in the *Hackney Gazette*. The employment status of the offender was given in 591 cases. Unemployed people – averaging 20 per cent of the workforce over the period – accounted for no less than 48 per cent of the charges. Thus the unemployed were two and a half times more likely to commit crimes than the average – and nearly four times more likely than the employed.

The relationship is, of course, not a one-way street. For crime also causes unemployment. Employee crimes figure frequently in the *Gazette*'s columns and, when detected, invariably result in dismissal. Other crimes, especially those that result in the accused being remanded in custody or given a custodial sentence, also lead to job loss. A past record of criminality, if discovered, can make it easier for an employee to lose a job and harder for him to find a new one in the present climate. Thus the crime-prone are over-represented among the unemployed, just as the unemployed are over-represented among criminals.

Sheer poverty, too, can act as a potent stimulus to crime. A growing amount of crime, in the dark days of the early eighties, was arising out of straightforward need, in an increasingly Dickensian way. Thus a forty-year-old unemployed bricklayer who was caught with his head and shoulders inside a warehouse told the arresting policeman he needed to steal because Christmas was less than a week away. Two unemployed teenage brothers stole a plant worth 60p to take as a present to their mother in hospital. A Well Street father of young children illegally reconnected the gas so that his children could have a bath. A thirty-year-old mother of three boys under the age of ten, with her gas and electricity cut off, was convicted of stealing gas worth £4. Then there are the tell-tale cases where people are convicted of shoplifting the most modest essentials. A twenty-five-year-old unemployed Greek Cypriot and his wife, living in Stoke Newington, were caught stealing one pair of shoes and six pairs of socks from Littlewoods in Oxford Street. The couple were getting only £56·25 a week in social-security benefits and had £12·50 a week to pay out in hire-purchase debts.

There are more indications that social-security cuts and inefficiencies generate crime. A thirty-five-year-old mother, given an emergency cheque for £15 for a week, altered it to read £45. The magistrate commented: 'This was an act of mercy for your children's sake.' A mother of a child of five, convicted of soliciting in Queen's Drive, said she had been living off child benefit of £5·25 a week because of delays in her assessment.

Pressing need, too, awakens old habits, old tricks learned in youth and long forgotten. Recession has precipitated recidivism. Probation officers at Edridge Chambers, Stoke Newington, noticed a sharp increase between 1979 and 1981 in the number of re-offences after long periods of going straight – as well as a rise in first offences among older people, usually far less prone to crime. The economic situation made the probation officers' job of rehabilitation and reform impossible in many cases. As Sylvia Roberts says: 'I feel so stupid sitting there telling someone with no job and no money not to do it again, when I'm on a good salary with holidays.' 'It's a joke,' says Andy Bernhardt. 'I have two experienced jewel thieves on my books, and all I can offer them is a job cleaning a store for £40 a week.' 'Where did you find that?' the other officers chip in with earnest, eager curiosity.

Getting Pound Notes: The Hoxton Creeper

In the real world, all these influences flow together in individual criminals who, for the most part, are under the pressure of two or more at least of the factors that contribute to crime. Individuals like Mike Davies,* Doris Davies's* third son, an athletic twenty-

* See page 441. All names in the Davies family are pseudonyms.

one-year-old with rough good looks. He is at an age when people should begin to outgrow their teenage transgressions, but unemployment and low income make it almost impossible for him to start going straight. Mike comes from the heart of white Cockney Hoxton, Britain's longest-standing traditional high-crime area with a reputation that dates back for centuries. An area where the Old Bill (police) are regarded with respectful hostility, where fences tout from door to door offering anything from dresses to vacuum-cleaners or forged luncheon vouchers, and where criminal records are often hereditary to the third and fourth generation. And an area where many young white boys have their own distinctive subculture in which vandalism, petty crime, gang warfare and an often ugly racialism play a part.

Mike's career of lawless behaviour began when he was only nine, helping older friends to break into shops and lock-up garages. It was related, from the first, to educational failure. Failure on Mike's part to do well, failure on the school's part to hold his interest: 'I used to run out of primary school. The head of my house at secondary school said, "We can't do nothing with Michael", so they let me pick my own lessons. I only did four hours a week, cookery, motor engineering, and PE. The rest of the time I bunked off.' He belonged to a gang that prided itself on being the toughest in Hackney, and that was responsible for more than its share of racial violence: 'Most of the gangs would keep their own plot, but we used to go on to their territory and bash them up. We had a big fight with the spades up at Hackney Town Hall. That was quite good, it got into the *Evening News*. And we used to go beating up the Pakis down Brick Lane. I still don't like Pakis, I couldn't work with one, they're loners: but I can see their point of view a bit more now I'm older.'

For eight years Mike was the baby of the family and shared a bedroom with his parents, then he moved in with his elder brothers. He never used to get much pocket-money – with nine children to keep on low incomes, there was no chance of that. And there was (and still is) virtually nowhere to play in the whole of Hoxton. 'All we used to do was go and play on the dump and that was it.' He left school at sixteen, hardly having attended it, with poor reports and no qualifications, and with great difficulties in reading and writing. It was not surprising, then, that instability at work followed the pattern of his school experiences: three months on the dole (that was in 1976), then a job-creation scheme sprucing up Abney Park cemetery, followed by three long years out of work. In 1980 came his great chance to get back on the rails: he got a job as a bacon hand in Smithfields Market, cutting up meat, humping it about, serving butchers. The hours were 5 a.m. till 1 p.m., the take home pay £61 a week, including five hours overtime. Around the same time, Mike also got married, to Sheila, the girl he'd been going steady with for five years. Irrepressibly macho, he waited till she had given birth before taking her to the registry office: 'I wanted to see if it was a boy or a girl before marrying her. If it had been a girl, I might not have bothered.'

But the Smithfields job didn't last long. 'I didn't like the owner. He was always talking out of his earholes, he always wanted to know where you were taking everything. He'd be sitting there writing and keep one eye on you like a hawk, he was the horriblest geezer I know, grotty he was. We used to get half an hour break, and the hardest work was between 11 and 12. Well the old geezers used to take their breaks at that time and they'd be sitting upstairs and having tea and laughing at you working. I told the gaffer this was wrong, but he said this is your hours. He sacked me in the end because a lot of meat was going missing, but he came unstuck because he sacked the wrong man: it was the other guy.'

Housing was a problem for the newly-weds and their baby. There was no room at Doris's, and they went homeless, but they couldn't stand the bed-and-breakfast hotel and left. 'We had to split up – I was with my mum and Sheila was with her mum in Loughton. But we were lucky, we got the offer of this place about three months later.' It was a two-bedroomed flat on a run-down hard-to-let GLC estate in the dead centre of concrete Hoxton, five storeys with external balconies.

'I felt sick when I saw it, really sick, I was gutted. You should have seen the state of it. We had to live here for days with no windows in. It was dirty, filthy, and we had to clean it up ourselves. The wallpaper was peeling off. I copped hold of this housing geezer, I said to him, this ain't fit for a dog to live in. These are problem flats, too. You got some rough characters here. You can hear all their rows. I think it's funny half the time, but it gets my wife down.'

It is the economics of the Davieses' life that leads them inexorably to crime, as well as to recurrent marital troubles. The family income from social security and child benefit is £61·85 (1981). Mike's friend, who lodges with them, pays them £15 a week, though he was in gaol when I met Mike. But it is over the division of that income and its inadequacy to finance a normal life-style that the rows arise. A full £6·10 is deducted at source for an old electricity debt. Mike insists on taking off £8 for himself out of the social-security money. This, in itself understandable, poses a major problem as it amounts to one-fifth of the weekly amount available for food and clothing. Thus women and children are often poorer than husbands, and inequality inside the family compounds inequality in the society. Sheila is left with only £62·75. Out of that she has to pay rent and rates of £19·95 a week, rental of colour television at £2·20, hire-purchase payments on the cooker of £1·42 a week, and put something aside for electric bills that average £7·50 a week. All that remains is £31·68 a week, to cover food for three adults and one child, not to mention clothes, nappies and other essentials: £7·92 per week each, or £1·13 per day, the price at the time of three tins of cat food.

Balanced against this are the couple's quite modest expectations, as outlined by Mike: 'You've got to wear something, and you've got to have a little bit of luxury in life, like a colour telly. The sosh [social security] don't give you nothing for luxuries, they don't even give you a black-and-white telly, not even for educational programmes for the kids. This is the bastard thing about that old shitbag Thatcher. They used to give you £60 or £70 every now and again to get clothes, but because of these cutbacks you can't now, you got to walk around like an old wick on a paraffin lamp, with holes in your jacket and shoes. I'd need about £75 or £80 a week just to live a little bit comfortable. You pay nearly £15 now for a pair of jeans, or £30 if you want a nice pair of shoes. I ain't had a nice bit of steak for years. We live on pork strips.'

The painful gap between needs and resources leads to interminable rows. The pair were separated when I met them – Sheila was staying with Mike's sister Pam. And money is almost always the cause of their troubles. Mike gets at Sheila. 'She won't pay the bills,' he complains. 'We ain't paid the telly for four months, we ain't paid the cooker for three months. They'll be coming to take them back any minute.' Sheila explains the background: 'He gets paid his money on Thursday mornings, but the rent's £20 and I usually owe £20, so all my money's gone by Thursday night. Then he'll tell me I've spent too much on shopping.'

But Sheila also gets at Mike. 'She wants all my money off me,' says Mike, 'but I say no, bollocks, you're not having it all. I got to have something for myself. Then she has a go at me about getting a job. She wants me to get a job on the side, without cards [i.e., while continuing to claim social security]. If I did that I could give the bird a oner [£100]. But you got to get the job first. She winds me up, she says I've got to sort myself out. Then I tell her, "You go out and find me the fucking job then." Then she'll start throwing things at me and I throw her out. She goes over to my old woman, but I tell her, "Piss off, ma, it's got fuck all to do with you." Or her old man comes here and tries to sort me out. I can't stand her family. Their attitude is, "I'm it and you're shit."' Sheila puts her side of the case: 'I can't stand it in that flat, and I can't have what I want to make it nice, because you can't do nothing on the money I get. I think to myself: if he had a job, I could get what I wanted.'

The net result of present pressures and past backgrounds is that both of them – conjointly and separately – are pushed into a whole range of illegalities. Sheila does her share. Before she married Mike, she lived with her baby at her parents' house in Loughton and claimed social security as a single mother. After they married, she went on claiming, with Mike claiming for all three of them as well. That brings in an extra £24·35 a week, but it still isn't enough. When I met Sheila she was up on two charges for shoplifting and 'kiting' – passing stolen cheques – for which she got probation.

Mike's activities are much more serious. He has a long string of offences behind him: TDA (taking and driving away); 'allowed to be carried' (in a vehicle knowing it to be stolen, uninsured etc); GBH (grievous bodily harm); burglary; theft; malicious wounding. 'I don't like anybody taking liberties,' he explains. 'I get aggressive.'

He has taken thorough precautions to ensure that his electricity bill does not pass modest proportions again: 'That's where the money goes, on the electric, so you got to stop it.' He showed me how. He had broken the wire through the seal on his meter and removed the cover, then given the top left-hand screw a slight turn to the left until the spinning disc slowed and halted. Then he put the cover back on and slotted the wire back into the seal. If the meter reader calls when he's in he doesn't answer the door. They pop a card through, and he fills it in himself. The secret of the whole operation is not to be too greedy: Mike lets the meter run for three or four weeks a quarter to allay suspicions.

This helps to reduce expenditure. To increase his income, Mike goes out thieving from time to time with his mate. 'You've got to thieve. I got to go out and earn myself a few pounds, I go creeping. That means, you walk into little firms, one of you asks for a job and keeps the gaffer talking, the other sneaks around and grabs the cash box. I've had anything from £40 to £3,000. But I'm not greedy. If I've got £40, I'll stay in till that's gone. When the dough's there, I don't go out. When it's run out, that's when I have to go out again.'

It's all small-time stuff, strictly out of need, or unwillingness to suffer deprivation impotently. For even with all their fiddles the couple are still desperately poor, deep in debt, with very little in the way of furniture or clothing. Life for Mike is unutterably drab: 'I'm pissed off, bored. I've got absolutely nothing to do. I walk about like a zombie all day long. I go and see my sisters, or I go down Hoxton, or if I've got a pound I'll sit in a pub and make a pint last for three hours. When my mate comes out [of gaol], I'll be out creeping again. Then I got my mind occupied, getting pound notes.'

'I've got to the stage now where I just don't care. I make out. When I'm short of money my ma will say, there's a few pork chops, here's a bit of bread, here's a pint of milk. She'll always help. She's terrific, my old woman. Or I can ask my sisters.

'I got no plans, I just take it as it comes. What's the worth of thinking ahead? If you make plans you'd only be disappointed, they wouldn't work out anyway. The only time you can think ahead is when you got money. You got to take it how it comes, 'cause you ain't gonna change it. Life to me is one joke, I got no religion, I think it's all balls. If God's about, he's no good any-way.'

Jumping Down a Hole: Stoke Newington Street Thieves

The whole of Hackney breeds crime, but the other distinctive subculture besides that of Cockney Hoxton is the one that has developed in the major area of West Indian settlement, across the centre of Hackney, embracing the worst private housing and some of the worst council estates.

We have seen the potent pressures that fragment the family of West Indian origin and destroy its capacity for discipline. Most West Indians over thirty-five are law-abiding, hard-working, God-fearing people, as indeed are many of the children. But a minority of this group has created a subculture that exerts additional pressures towards crime. One of the focal elements in it is the all-night party, where reggae music blares from speakers so big they are known as wardrobes, alcohol and cannabis are consumed freely, and there are displays of male finery worthy of birds of paradise. The tea-cosy hat and the bomber jacket are signs of plodding poverty: the style that the fashion setters have adopted is not Rasta, but straight from the pages of *The Tatler*, gold-buttoned, double-breasted blazers, silk shirts, camel-hair coats, Burberries. There are distinctive exotic elements too: broad-brimmed leather hats, tall peaked caps in pure-wool tweed, gold bracelets and pendants, and a whole status hierarchy of shoes in which sneakers are the bottom rung, leather is looked down on, and reptile skin is the rage: lizard, crocodile and ostrich-skin shoes costing up to £250 for a handmade pair. Other possessions are essential equipment too: portable stereos the size of small suitcases; fast cars, again in a hierarchy, from souped-up bangers to the most expensive coupés. It is a subculture of conspicuous consumption: no radical rejection of capitalism, but a caricature of conformity to its values. Full participation in it requires money – at least £50 or £60 a week on top of other basic needs. That kind of money is not readily available to most black youths in Hackney, hence crime is a standing temptation to those wanting to participate fully in the subculture, but short of cash because they are in school, on the dole, or in dead-end jobs. Everyone knows someone who is into crime and, given the low detection rate, it does pay, allowing a life-style that very few young blacks could ever hope to achieve by legitimate means.

Ian (not his real name) is an eighteen-year-old who has not worked since he left school, except for an abortive three weeks as a junior clerk. He goes to clubs or parties several nights a week, and spends £10 or £15 inside, plus £10 or £15 a week on clothes. 'I like to look good,' he explains. 'Clothes are important to me, it's like a battle with other individuals, keeping up with the Jones in the way you dress.' Total expenditure: £50 to £100 a week. Total income from social security: £17·05 a week (he is living with his parents). Result: not, as for Micawber, misery, but crime. Ian started housebreaking when he was fourteen, often while truanting from school. He now goes housebreaking a couple of times a week. 'We try not to do black people's houses,' he says. He also steals purses and handbags. 'Sometimes you get a run [chase]. At first you're scared, but then it's fun, it's something to do.' Ian is not strong on conscience, or on compassion. He does not relate the effects of his own actions to the risk of his own family suffering from the actions of others. I asked him how he would feel if someone burgled his parents' house. 'I'd go mad. I'd probably go out and do a burglary.' Did it worry him if he hurt people? 'It can't be helped. If you ain't got no money, what you supposed to do? I never think about the people I do.' What would he do if someone mugged his mother? 'I'd kill them,' he says, and means it.

The majority of black youths resist the lures of the subculture. But far too many are drawn into a temporary but often disastrous dalliance. Macaulay Jones (not his real name) is a tall twenty-year-old, one of seven children of an upright Jamaican couple. Macaulay is at the bottom of all the heaps: he is black, homeless, unemployed, and handicapped. He has been epileptic since he was ten. The epilepsy led to strains with his parents, who regarded it as a form of madness. He had an excessively strait-laced upbringing, in comparison with his friends. 'Even when I was fifteen I had to be in by midnight, when my friends were just ready to go to a party.'

He blames his involvement in crime on the influence of his elder brother, Delroy, who has just served a four-year sentence for robbery. Delroy, in turn, was misled by mixing with the wrong crowd. Macaulay had just come out of a special school for epileptics, only to find that his brother was in gaol. 'I was mad at that, and because nobody told me, and that was when I started doing stupid things.' He stole two platinum rings from a house he was decorating, and got two years probation. Then he took a clock out of a van that had been left open, and was given twenty-four hours at an attendance centre – two hours a week every Saturday.

'While I was going there I got caught for mugging a lady. I had no money at the time. I was on social security, but my mum was taking it all so I had nothing left, and I really wanted to rave [go dancing] that night. It happened just round the corner from my house. I saw this lady and I came up behind her and hit her with a stick, but she must have had some strong head because she didn't fall down and she wouldn't let go of her bag. I was tugging at it till she let go. I didn't know her but she knows two of my brothers and she called out the name, but I kept on running. I ran into a little alley-way, what they call jump down into a hole, and looked in the bag and dumped it. All that was in there was £1·50. I felt bad, you always feel bad afterwards the first time. I went home, got changed and went out to Cubie's. The group that was playing was Shaka, but I didn't like it, I couldn't stand it for long. When I got back the police had picked up my brother, but he had an alibi, he was working when it happened. He must have said it was me, because the next morning they knocked the door at 7 and took me to the station. They kept saying I done it and nagging me till I couldn't take no more, and I gave in and gave them, what d'you call that, a statement.'

After this incident, Macaulay was remanded on bail, and started to go straight. He got a Youth Opportunities job serving at a garage, but he had an epileptic fit on the forecourt and woke up in hospital (as he often does) to find himself out of a job. He then got a place at a training workshop. The mugging was a distant memory by the time the case came up, eighteen months after the offence, at the Old Bailey. Such delays are common, and in the meantime the offender's life suffers from a kind of trial-blight, for any progress he makes may well be totally wiped out by the sentence. 'I only had ten or fifteen minutes with the solicitor. I didn't really bother with what they said in court, I didn't understand half of it.' Another aspect of the British cultural dichotomy between Norman-Latin and Anglo-Saxon: spend a day in any inner-city magistrates' court, and you will see dozens of defendants staring round the room while their destiny is debated, in terms incomprehensible to them, between the lawyer and the justices. Macaulay got borstal, and spent nine months inside. 'I didn't misbehave in there, I was acting like a goodie-goodie, like a good little child. I had a few fights: if you show you can fight, they don't bother you after that. Half the boys in there were black, and some of the screws [prison officers] were nasty, they'd call you "Wog", they'd say, "You, nigger, come here." But I just swallowed it. What got me most was that my mother didn't come to see me once, she didn't even write. And when I came out, she didn't want me to live with her.'

Macaulay's probation officer put him in contact with a short-life housing group, and he got a single room, in a semi-derelict house, with no hot water. After three months the council was ready to rehabilitate the place for letting to its waiting-list, and the short-life users had to move out. Macaulay moved to a room in another short-life house in Clapton. He returned to his place in the training workshop, but then got a better-paid job at a spectacle maker's, cutting glass (a highly dangerous job for an epileptic to do). He had a fit and cut all his clothing up, and left the job of his own accord two weeks before I met him. In that time he'd had no money out of social security and had not eaten a proper meal. He was still waiting for social security to pay for dental treatment to replace his four top front teeth, knocked out in another fit three months earlier.

His criminal record, his epilepsy, his existence on the fringe of the Dalston subculture, all raise enormous problems for going straight in stable employment. 'I'm supposed to be getting £31·25 a week social security [1982], but it won't be enough. My rent is £8 a week. It costs me £20 or £30 for a night out – £15 for drinks, £6 for weed [cannabis], that makes me feel better and think more positive, and £3 or more for a cab home. I don't have any clothes except these I'm wearing, I made them myself at the training workshop. I got an order in for a wool suit for £80, but I can't save the money for it. I'm not interested in really expensive things.

When I see these guys with eight-ounce gold bracelets on their wrists, really weighing their hands down, I just laugh. Those things cost £800. And the black girls expect gold things like that. If they know they can't get it they don't stay with the guy. And those people with ostrich-skin shoes costing £300, I laugh at them: if you step on their shoes they pull a knife on you. If you go to a shebeen [drinking den] these days most of the people there would be carrying a knife. You've got to. Whenever there's a fight there's always weapons. When I was thirteen we used to fight with our bare hands. But today even the little boys got knives in their pockets. They think they're such big, big men, they got cuts and slashes all over their arms.

'For my future, I really can't see nothing. When I was working I used to feel better. Now I just get up, eat, walk, come back and sleep. My dad's gone back to Jamaica: he got made redundant two years ago, and he used the money to build a house back home. My mum's going back in two months. I'd like to go to Jamaica to see what it's like, but I don't want to stay. I think of myself as English.'

Victimology

Crime is sometimes the product of thoughtless brutality or sheer greed. But often it is the product of the powerlessness of lives in the lower ranks of society: powerlessness to create an acceptable destiny for oneself by legitimate means. It is at times a redirection of aggressive feelings aroused by social hierarchies that are beyond retaliation, at times a personal redress for deprivation, a refusal to accept the lot society has allocated, a rebellion against inequality.

But it is a grossly misdirected rebellion. It does not demonstrate against the causes of hierarchy, inequality and poverty. Indeed, it divides the community against itself, fuels racialism, and reduces solidarity between tenants or workers. It temporarily increases the power of the criminal, at the cost of intensifying the powerlessness of those who do not resort to crime. It may be a protest against injustice: but it is itself a source of further injustice.

For the great majority of Hackney's criminals are no Robin Hoods. They do not head for the big banks in the City of London or the palatial residences of Hampstead Garden Suburb. The days of honour among thieves, of reserving one's depredations for members of the more fortunate classes, are gone. Hackney's thieves rob on their own doorsteps. Indeed, the poorer the area, the more likely are its inhabitants to become the victims of crime, and repeatedly. Theft in Hackney most commonly amounts to robbing the poor to feed the poor. It is a chaotic form of redistribution of income in among the lowest classes.

To the victim, crime is often an additional deprivation added to the other deprivations of inner-city life: for the victims are often poorer than their attackers. In January 1982 pensioner Mary Hogg, who lives on the ground floor (always the easiest target) of Stonebridge estate, reported her ninth break-in in four years. The burglars also left a calling card – a pile of excrement wrapped in a newspaper. In the same month twenty-three-year-old Juliet Willis complained that she had successively lost her cooker, fridge, television set, and carpets, and had her toilet bowl and new beds smashed and wallpaper pulled down. She had to move out of her Queensbridge Road flat in fear. To a poor person, the theft of a week's wages or social-security money, or the theft of coins from their meter, for which they are then liable, can be a crippling blow, for the poor are usually uninsured.

There is a chilling heartlessness about many crimes. In May 1981 a blind lady, walking in Springfield Park with a friend, was robbed of her own cash and of two collecting-boxes for the blind. In October 1981, a mentally retarded sixty-year-old was walking past Fawcett estate in Upper Clapton when he was knocked and kicked in the head, as a result of which he lost the sight of an eye. The thieves got away with the princely sum of £12 and a bus pass.

The impact of violent crime lasts far longer than the shock of the incident itself. Apart from financial loss, physical injuries and the hassle of medical treatment and house repairs, there are deeper psychological disturbances which can undermine mental and physical health, especially among women and children.

On a warm afternoon in April 1981 a community worker who does not wish her name to be revealed, and whom I shall call Mary, was strolling across Hackney Downs with her two children, eleven-year-old Peter and Anne, aged seven. She noticed three tall young men, two black, one white, walking some distance behind her, but thought nothing of it as it was broad daylight, in a wide open space, with plenty of people about. Suddenly she felt herself being knocked down from behind, and fell on top of her bag. One of the three kicked her in the face to try to turn her over, but she couldn't because another was sitting on her back trying to twist her off it. 'The stupid thing is, if they'd stood there and said give me the money I would have given it. But they kicked hell out of me. The kids were beaten up, because they tried to fight with the men to get them off me. Nobody came to help, although there were people within twenty yards of me. When they ran off, I got up and ran after them shouting. Blood was pouring from my face, I had a white coat on and there was blood all over it. You can imagine what I looked like. I stood in the middle of the road to try and stop a car, not for me, but to help my son who'd run into some flats after the men. But the cars drove past. That was one of the worst things. All your life you spend your time helping people, and when it's your turn to need help, they turn their backs on you. All I wanted myself was to knock the hell out of those men. I felt such an overwhelming hatred. It's a terrible blow to someone brought up as a Christian to see there's such a depth of feeling.

'I had cracked ribs, bruises everywhere, broken teeth and a dislocated jaw. Three days later a lump appeared on my breast and I had to have it removed. Because of the state I was in I was afraid to have a general anaesthetic and had the operation under local. I could see everything, like on one of those TV programmes. The men had damaged my womb and I had to have another operation to prevent thrombosis. Now I'm on warfarin, the rat poison: it's an anti-coagulant. At first, I had to run up and down to hospital every day to get my blood checked, and for dental treatment for my teeth. Now it's only once a week. But the treatment makes me tired, it's hard to cope with a full-time job.'

The psychological effects have been equally disturbing and long-lasting. 'At first I lost my memory. I had fainting attacks and black-outs. I didn't go near Hackney Downs for six months, until November the 5th, bonfire night, but even then I couldn't take the strain, I blacked out. I used to feel physically sick whenever there were youths walking behind me. It's a year later now, but I still avoid times when school kids are about on the street. I very rarely go to a place I know will be crowded.

'I still have nightmares, I wake up hitting out at my husband in bed. My son Peter has been affected. He's very suspicious of people, now. He has nightmares too, you can hear him screaming "Mummy help me", and you know what he's dreaming about. He always wanted to go into science, to help people, but his attitude has changed, now it's number one first. He couldn't care less about other people, he seems to have become terribly callous about people suffering, like when he sees pictures of people who've been hurt by bombs, on television.

'I wrote off to the criminal injuries compensation board. It took them two months to send me a form to fill in. Then in January, that was nine months after the robbery, they asked me for receipts for all the clothes that were damaged, even my tights, and for my son's clothes. I still hadn't heard in April, a year later, so I rang them. The man who was dealing with it said, "Well, you have rather complicated matters for us haven't you? You're claiming you're still ill. If you said all the effects were cleared up, then we could settle it straight away. But if you continue to claim you're still ill, it could take a number of years." I broke down crying, and he couldn't understand why he'd upset me.'

The Wider Ripples

Crime, when it is widespread, does not only affect its victims. It has created an oppressive atmosphere of fear in Hackney. Those who are less exposed to risks talk of this fear being 'exaggerated', so it is worth examining the realities. As we have seen, on reported figures there was a risk of one in a hundred of being mugged in Hackney in 1981. Allowing for under-reporting, and deducting groups like small children and big men who are unlikely to be targets, the risk is probably one in fifty. This risk is very much higher for certain groups – such as women carrying handbags – and in certain places. A survey of tenants on Nightingale estate found that one in eight said they had been assaulted in the previous year. Contrary to stereotypes, pensioners were less likely to get attacked, but that was undoubtedly because they are far more cautious and go out less than younger people.

The predominant method of mugging is a sudden attack from behind, to knock the victims down so that they cannot retaliate and find it harder to identify the attacker. The favoured housebreaking technique is no more sophisticated: kicking the front door in. Given these methods, and these levels of risk, there is simply no level of fear that is 'realistic'. The desire to avoid injury is instinctive. In those of a nervous disposition, of which there are many in the inner city, it can become obsessive. The danger that is unknown and unseen before it strikes can assume the proportions of a nightmare. For many, especially the elderly and women, fear is the major factor that colours inner-city life in such grim shades. To avoid the relatively small risk of an attack, major changes in life-style are made. No one with any sense walks alone after dark in Hackney. There are many old people who virtually never go out, even in the daytime. Many of those who do venture out are as nervous as a field-mouse when there's a hawk about. The neighbourhood is no longer an extension of home, but alien territory, where, if you are attacked, you can expect little help from others.

Many live in fear even inside their own homes, like eighty-year-old Mary Andrews. She looks much younger than her age, but she is almost blind: beyond a few centimetres she can see only vague shapes. Another pensioner, petite, curly haired Anne Bryndle, acts as her guide around Hoxton where both live. Anne herself was mugged in 1978 by three white boys. They followed her home from the post office, where she'd just picked up her pension: 'I thought, I'd better not go indoors, because they'd just push their way past me and steal a lot more. As I walked along the landing one of them asked me the time, and then grabbed at my bag. I told him, you're not getting it, I held tight. He dragged me down the stairs by the handle, but I didn't let go. Then they gave up and ran off. I definitely wasn't going to let them have it. It was my pension, I need it to live on.' The poorer the victims are, the less they can afford to lose money, and the more likely they are to resist theft – and the more they resist, the more likely they are to get injured.

Mary's daughter, too, has been mugged. She herself has been

burgled once, while she was out, and except for the times when she is with Anne, when they go shopping or spend an afternoon in the Marie Lloyd pensioners' club playing bingo, Mary's entire life is dominated by the fear of crime. She lives on the sixth floor of a block of flats in Ivy Street. At least once a week she has to tramp up the stairs, often with shopping, when the lifts are out of order. Once she was stuck in a lift for half an hour, petrified that it might fall, and had to be freed by firemen. But she accepted a high-floor flat because she was convinced she was safer up there from burglars, who prefer targets where a quick getaway from the scene is possible.

'I don't go out at all in the evenings,' Mary explains. 'I watch TV, but I just listen to the voices, I can't see the faces. I've had my windows nailed up. But I'm nervous of bolting the door, in case anything happens to me and the neighbours can't get in. I get frightened if anyone knocks at the door. Some of my friends say, don't open your door at all to anyone, but you've got to, you don't know who it might be. I get nervous even if it's a policeman, because I did hear they were dressing up as policemen.' She uses the word 'they' as if there were an army of con-men and burglars constantly on the prowl. 'After my last break-in I had a special chain and alarm bell fitted, but I still think about burglars all the time. I lie in bed at night and worry. I think, what if they got in? If my alarm bell went off at night, I'd die of fright. My son set it off once by mistake, I nearly had a heart attack.

'It was never like this. We used to go out and leave our doors tied with a string for the kids to come in after school. We used to go out to music-hall and come back late, and all I was ever afraid of was if a rat ran across my path. During the Second World War, I used to work on the Underground, and I'd come home in the early hours. When the Blitz was on we'd be running down streets with bombs dropping and burning timbers falling, but I was never scared as I am now. You were out in it then, you could see what was happening, everybody was in it together.'

What is different in today's inner city is that the threat is diffuse and invisible and the individual stands alone in the face of it, unprotected by the community.

The Community Cost

The victims of crime are not only individuals: the community as a whole is diminished by it. Crime reduces the profitability of local shops and businesses, increasing their insurance premiums and often making them uninsurable. It is an added pressure on firms to move out of Hackney, a tax or tribute levied on local employment, and a further disincentive to investment. It handicaps all efforts to improve services and the environment. Every school, every public amenity, every community premise, faces a continual wearing down by major and minor theft and damage.

In June 1981 De Beauvoir junior school's fondest creation, a fibre-glass-bottomed pond with water plants, tadpoles, frogs and snails – the children's own bit of nature in an area without a sizeable park for more than a mile in any direction – was ripped out of the ground and stolen and the plants and animals trampled on. In August an old red double-decker bus used by Gayhurst primary school's parent–teacher association for outings was stolen. In November the Comet day nursery in Hoxton was broken into, windows smashed, food and water hurled around, and the children's pets – mice, hamsters, goldfish – were killed. Every school in Hackney is subject to continual thefts, often of valuable audio-visual equipment.

It does not seem to make the slightest difference whether the facility is for the benefit of individuals or of the whole community or part of it, nor whether it is provided paternalistically by the authorities or created with the active participation of local people. The level of participation in the inner city is so low that the participants, in any case, are never more than a minority, often a tiny one. Kingsmead Estate tenants' association does its best, socially and politically, to make life a little more tolerable on one of London's bleakest settlements. Yet, in June 1981, an old people's party had to be cancelled because the food and drink had been stolen. In August the social club had to close for a time after two burglaries had cleaned them out of bar stock worth £300. And in January 1982 the disco equipment was stolen from the community centre – for the second time.

Even facilities provided specifically for young people, to give them something to do and keep them out of trouble, become targets for the kind of behaviour they try to prevent. A youth club in a flat on Haggerston estate was broken into, records stolen and the juke-box smashed. A play group on Stonebridge estate bought a slide and a swing with a small grant from the council: the slide was stolen and the swing busted. Holly Street's adventure playground was closed for a year after some boys smashed all the windows and fittings in the hut.

But it is not just the facilities that suffer: it is the solidarity of the community itself. Redevelopment, migration and the rapid turn-over of people seeking better accommodation mean there is precious little of that to start with. But crime dissolves it even further. The climate of fear engenders a defensive egotism of survival, in which everyone looks after themselves. A new code of ethics emerges: that thy days may be long, thou shalt not question strangers on the stairs; thou shalt not look if thou hearest screams or shattering glass; thou shalt not admonish youths for vandalism; thou shalt not admit to witnessing a crime; thou shalt not help the victim of an attack. Crime itself, when it passes a certain threshold, helps to break down even further all the social mechanisms that used to control it. Like a parasitic life form, crime fosters the very conditions for its own survival.

It becomes one of the most potent factors in community disin-tegration, weakening all efforts at community organization, turn-ing neighbour against neighbour, young against old, white against black. The collapse of community control leads, of necessity, to a heavy presence of police in the inner city and this, with equal inevitability, has sparked off even wider outbreaks of disorder and violence.

18 The Roughest Beat: Policing the Inner City

The peacemaker gets two-thirds of the blows.

He who lights a fire should not ask to be protected from the flames.

Arab proverbs

In 1981 a Conservative government that had promised a strong approach to law and order presided over one of the most serious breakdowns in law and order in mainland Britain of this century.

On 10 April, the first Brixton riots erupted. On 3 July came disturbances in Southall, followed in rapid succession by major troubles at Toxteth in Liverpool, Moss Side in Manchester, and again in Brixton. There were smaller-scale disorders in Bristol, Southampton, Leicester, Nottingham, Derby, Birmingham, Wolverhampton, Bradford, Halifax, Leeds, Huddersfield, Blackburn, Preston and Teesside, and across London from Acton to Walthamstow and from Haringey to Clapham. The list was a catalogue of Britain's inner cities, finally forcing themselves dramatically into the nation's consciousness.

Hackney, too, had its say. The year had already seen the earlier emergence of an ominous phenomenon of law-breaking by large groups of black youths. On 20 April, towards the end of a bank-holiday fair at Finsbury Park, hundreds of youths went on the rampage with sticks and bars, smashing up stalls and mugging people. On the night of Tuesday, 5 May, about a hundred youths, most of whom had just come out of Cubie's, the popular Afro-Caribbean disco off Dalston Lane, gathered round while some of them ripped out a jeweller's window and stole jewellery worth £500. The retreating crowd threw bottles at the police. In the early hours of Wednesday, 24 June, gangs of youths roaming the streets, again after chucking-out time at Cubie's, smashed the windows of a travel agency and a fish-and-chip shop, grabbed the till of Kentucky Fried Chicken on Kingsland Road, and mugged three

347

pedestrians. Part of the problem was that London Transport bus crews, fearful of trouble, had been refusing to pick up passengers from Cubie's for some months, thus leaving large gangs of black youths to walk home, along streets lined with shops, in a mood of anger and frustration.

It was not until Wednesday, 8 July, that the first attacks on police occurred. That night two officers on patrol in Stoke Newington were stoned and towards midnight four police cars were damaged by missiles. The next evening, police were out in force, on foot, in the Dalston area, keeping a couple of hundred youths on the move. Five shop windows were smashed and one policeman injured by missiles.

The worst disturbances occurred on 10 July. The location: the junction of Sandringham Road and Kingsland High Street. There was a certain inevitability about the site. Sandringham Road leads down into the heart of some of the worst private rented housing and the densest settlement of people of West Indian origin in Hackney. At the top, on the left, the Argos showroom windows gleam with consumer products. On the right, Johnson's café, a haunt favoured by young blacks, the scene of frequent drug busts and raids in pursuit of 'dips' (pickpockets) escaping from their favourite hunting-ground of Ridley Road Market (a quiet back alley, Birkbeck Road, leads between Ridley and Sandringham). At the junction of Sandringham and Kingsland, there are permanent pedestrian barriers lining the road, offering support and, if necessary, shelter against attack.

The trouble that day began around 5 p.m. when a group of youths robbed a jewellers' shop in Kingsland High Street. The police closed down Johnson's café and moved on groups that formed outside: a few bricks and bottles were thrown. Then larger groups of blacks began to congregate. At around 7.30 p.m. two fire-bombs were thrown: one at the Argos showrooms, followed by looting; and one at a policeman in Arcola Street, site of the main social-security office in Stoke Newington. The police charged down Sandringham Road, but were pushed back by the youths for a distance of about 40 metres before making a successful counter-charge. Just before midnight bricks were thrown at the police stationed at the mouth of Sandringham Road, from the barrier railings outside the Rio cinema, opposite. Under attack, exhausted from working days of fourteen and sixteen hours around London's riot areas, some officers lost their cool. A unit of helmeted police charged across the road, truncheons drawn, and used them to 'disperse' the crowd at the railings. One girl suffered a head wound and was rushed to hospital.

I arrived on the scene just after midnight. There was an atmosphere of Sweeney and Starsky and Hutch. It was just after the stoning incident, and police Rovers, Escorts and blue-and-white vans packed with men were using Kingsland Road as a race-track, hooters wailing and lights flashing, in pursuit of the suspected assailants. For the meanwhile, the protection of property took a back seat, and I watched for half an hour as menswear shop, Mr H, was looted down to the last button and buckle. The window smashed a few seconds after I had walked past it: there was no one in sight but a young black boy of about thirteen, looking a picture of innocence. A few minutes later five or ten youths, black and white, began to arrive, clambering over the railings from the road, then leaning against them and looking around themselves with great caution before acting. One boy set the example, snatching a white sweat-shirt and stuffing it down the front of his jacket. The others helped themselves, each one walking away in a relaxed manner calculated to allay suspicion. Mr H's alarm was ringing noisily: but so were many others. After a lull more wardrobe hunters arrived, and some of the first wave returned for second helpings. The first time they'd snatched anything that came to hand. This time they were more discriminating, checking sizes and colours and discarding unsuitable ones.

Three whites in their late twenties stood opposite, smiling benevolently and shouting 'Police', with the accent on the first syllable, whenever men in blue came near. A skinhead in a long Edwardian jacket, attracted by the Victoria Wine off-licence next door to Mr H, wrapped a brick in a paper bag and hurled it at the window with all his might. It bounced off. A boy slipped on the glass outside Mr H, and cut himself badly, and the others gathered round to help. The looting proceeded, while at the back, thieves were smashing their way through security bars and looting the racks inside. Some of the earliest looters had the opportunity to saunter by five or six times, while the skinhead persisted in his increasingly desperate attempts to smash the off-licence window, the only effect being to leave a dusting of brick powder on the glass. At about 1 a.m. a big black bearded youth in a long leather raincoat took out a pair of model legs from the window and threw them into the middle of the road. Police vehicles had passed the scene at least forty or fifty times, but this act finally attracted their attention. A van screeched to a halt, a dozen officers leapt out, and one of them stayed behind to stand guard over what, by now, was a totally empty window.

The whole evening had been, by the standards of Brixton, Toxteth and Moss Side, a mere affray, but it was a disturbing pointer to what could happen when police attention was diverted and the thin veneer of ice that caps Hackney's troubled waters was cracked. In all forty premises were damaged that night and sixty arrests were made. The score of injuries was even: twenty-three police, twenty-three members of the public.

High Noon in Dalston

The following day, Saturday, 11 July, far worse was expected. Shoppers stayed away from the High Street and the Wimpy Bar owner complained of his worst Saturday for business in twenty years. But the shopkeepers had their minds preoccupied in other ways. From Dalston Junction to Stamford Hill, they were measuring and sawing, drilling and screwing, fitting and hammering. According to means, great panels of corrugated iron, wood, plywood, chipboard, hardboard and cardboard were being battened up by those who did not already have armour-plated glass, grilles and shutters. Builders' merchants were running out of supplies, security firms doing more business than they could cope with, employees and friends and relatives were dragooned into a frenetic race against time to put up their protective walls before the expected confrontation of the late afternoon and evening.

The media came sniffing for trouble. One camera crew arrived and interviewed people on the street. Another crew filmed a festival at London Fields where trouble had been predicted. People threw darts at images of Thatcher, drum majorettes twirled, and the Marlborough pub heavies won the tug-of-war match. But there was not a stir of trouble. When one of the organizers phoned the television company to ask why the festival had not been televised, she was told it was because 'nothing happened'.

Up at the end of Sandringham Road, the atmosphere was *High Noon*. The police were scattered, in twos and threes, all down the High Street. About fifty black youths, with the merest scattering of whites, were sitting along the railings and on the wooden fence of the petrol station and crowding outside Johnson's cafe. I talked to many of them and the grievances bubbled out, against unemployment, racialism, but above all against the police.

A pretty girl of seventeen, with four grade ones in the Certificate of Secondary Education, out of work for ten months, said: 'I go down the temp agency every morning. There's only been two jobs going there all week. Since Thatcher's come in, everything's just fallen. She needs a knife through her heart.'

Her nineteen-year-old friend continues: 'I got three O-levels and that's done me no good at all. A lot of my friends are having babies. If you haven't got a job, you might as well have a baby.'

Vengeance for colonialism and slavery, rebellion against discrimination, redress for police abuses, all mingled together as a group of boys pitched in. They were angry, agitated.

'You can't win,' said a tall youth worker. 'If a black person drive a nice car, the police say, where you get the money to drive that? You wear a gold chain, they say, where you thief that? We like to gather in a little place and have a drink and music, so what the police do? They like to close it down, so we all on the street instead. And what happen when they get hold of you? They fling you in the van, they say, come on you bunnies [short for 'jungle bunnies']. They play find the black man's balls. They treat us like animals, man, they treat their dogs better than they treat us. They kick the shit out of us and put us inside to rot. They think they are OK in their uniforms. But if that one there was to walk over here naked now, we'd kick the hell out of him. Somebody said, black people will never know themselves till their back is against the wall, well, now our backs is against the wall. I'm gonna sit right here, and I ain't gonna move.'

A boy of eighteen in a flat corduroy cap said: 'I was driving down from Tottenham to Hackney once, I got stopped seven times on the way. Four years ago, they came to my house searching for stolen goods and asked me to provide a receipt for everything in my house. We've been humiliated. It's time we show them that we want to be left alone.'

'We're fighting for our forefathers,' said the seventeen-year-old secretary. 'We've been watching *Roots* [the film series on American slavery]. They used us here for twenty years, now they got no use for us, they want us out.'

An eighteen-year-old boy in a green, red and black tea-cosy hat went on: 'The police can call you a fucking cunt, but if you say one word at them they'll take you down. They don't even like you to smile at them. You try to fight them at court: you can't fight them, because black man don't have no rights at all in this country.' There was a lot of military talk, for this was not seen as a challenge to law, but a matter of group honour: the police, as a clan, had humiliated young blacks, as a clan, and clan revenge had to be exacted.

'Since they got these riot shields,' said a boy of twenty, 'they think they're it. We can't stand for that. Tonight we have to *kill* one of them, and now there's a crowd of us, we're gonna do it. If they bring in the army we'll bring in more reinforcements and kill them.'

One boy in sun-glasses, sixteen at the oldest, launched into a lecture on guerrilla tactics. 'If you come one night and they make you run, then the next night you bring enough stones, bottles and bombs that they can't make you run: you don't run, *they* run.' He smirks, as if he has just stormed their lines single-handed. 'But look at everyone here. They're all empty-handed. Last night they were wasting their petrol-bombs, throwing them on the street. It's no use throwing one without a specific target. Look at that police bus: one bomb at the front, one at the back, and that would be thirty-two or sixty-four police less. You got to have organization, like they got.'

There were moments of humour, too. One drunken man in a leather jacket was straining to have a go at the police.

'What can you do?' his girl-friend asked him, holding him back by the jacket.

'I can at least fuck up two of them. I can take the consequences. They ain't gonna kill me.'

'They will kick the *shit* out of you,' says his girl-friend.

She pacifies him for the moment, but he eludes her and stands, slouched on one elbow, against the railings, awaiting his moment of glory. Levering himself up he staggers half-way across the road towards the main police gathering, shouting, 'You're all a load of fucking wankers.' Before he has got five metres he is arrested by the district commander in person.

In the end, the brave talk remained talk. At 6 p.m. the police decided to clear the crowds that had assembled. They moved on the group on the petrol-station fence, pushing them down Sandringham Road. At the same time another cordon of police began to walk up Sandringham Road from the other end. An escape route was deliberately left open – the alley of Birkbeck Road – and the cordons let through most of those who wanted to get by. But many of the youths believed the police had trapped them in a pincer with the intention of beating them up. Several of them started to break down the wall next to Johnson's café to use the bricks. As one young boy explained: 'When they come smashing you over the head with a baton one night, the next time you know you've got to get something to defend yourself with.' But this misinterpretation of police intentions itself brought on the attack it was intended to prevent. The police closed in to forestall the brick-throwers, there were scuffles, one policeman was injured, and five arrests were made.

And that was it. The expected explosion did not occur. The proceedings ended not with a bang but with a whimper. It is perhaps typical of Hackney that, although more deprived than Lambeth and most of the other scenes of disturbance, it couldn't get together a full-blooded riot. The reason lies in Hackney's fragmentation: it has no single core like Brixton has, where blacks predominate and congregate, no ghettos without their admixture of poor whites, Asians and Mediterraneans. The sheer numbers required to start a large-scale disturbance never came together. Police tactics, too, were flexible and effective: with the experience of Brixton to learn from, they did not offer a static, concentrated defensive line that was a sitting target for missiles. And they split up the opposition into smaller groups and kept them moving down separate side roads, preventing any larger crowds from forming.

Nevertheless, there was rioting and there was looting and there was violence. It is important to understand why. These were not the first skirmishes in the revolution, nor were they an organized protest against monetarism or mass unemployment. Many of the rioters were at school, some had jobs. The conscious motivation of those who were not just in it for the looting was, quite simply and straightforwardly, hatred of the police among the young and the desire to hit back at them for humiliations received. Monetarism and recession were, however, powerful indirect causes. The strains produced by loss of hope and faith in a society that seemed to have lost all charity certainly provided emotional fuel for the troubles. More specifically, recent recessions, each one deeper than the last, pushed up levels of violent theft and burglary, and therefore led to a greatly increased pressure of policing in the inner city, bringing police into unpleasant contact with increasing numbers of whites and blacks, guilty and innocent alike.

The Charges Against

Hatred of the police among young blacks is deep and bitter, and is based on three main allegations: that the police harass them because of their race; that they intimidate them and beat them up; and that they subject them to racial abuse.

Tales of harassment are legion. Maurice, a serious and sober sixteen-year-old doing GCE O-levels at Hackney Downs School, told me that once he was standing outside his own house rummaging in his pockets for his keys. A policeman came up and asked him what he was doing, and when Maurice rooted out his keys and showed they would open the door, the officer suggested that Maurice might have found them or got them from a stolen bag. Maurice was also facing a threatening behaviour charge: 'I was at a football match with my friends, when the police came along. When my friends see police, they always start to run, so they won't be questioned: that's just the way they are. Well, I just walked and I shouted my friend's name after him. One of the police grabbed me and said I was shouting at the Sunderland supporters, trying to provoke them.'

More serious are the allegations of police violence at the points of arrest and interrogation. These charges are widely believed by many of the more respectable elements in Hackney, including teachers, community workers, probation officers, left-wing politicians and leaders of ethnic groups. Andy Bernhardt, probation officer, comments: 'The quantity and consistency of the stories about violence and racial abuse is such that you'd have to be a bigot not to believe that it goes on.' Another officer, Sue Campbell, remarks: 'Some people stagger into court with black eyes and blood on their faces, and no one pays any attention or asks if they've just been beaten up.' The best-documented case was that of David and Lucille White, a middle-aged West Indian couple who, in 1982, received aggravated and exemplary damages of £51,392 in the High Court for assault, wrongful arrest and malicious prosecution. One September night in 1976, two police officers watching a house in Lordship Lane, Stoke Newington, saw three black youths coming out of the front door at 12.45 a.m. Suspecting a burglary, they radioed for assistance and were joined by fifteen other officers. The judge, Justice Mars-Jones, accepted the Whites' version of what happened next. This was that no search warrant was produced, so that the family had every right to resist entry. Their son Dennis was knocked unconscious with a truncheon blow to the head. Mother Lucille was truncheoned on the head when she came downstairs in her dressing-gown. Her husband David, in pyjamas, was so badly injured that he had to take nine weeks off work. The family were taken away in their night-clothes, leaving three young daughters unattended at home, and kept for four or five hours at the police station. Then they were charged with assaulting police officers – and acquitted after a Crown Court trial. Justice Mars-Jones called the police action 'monstrous, wicked and shameful'. The police appealed against the decision.

There are a number of such tales floating around Hackney at any one time, creating a complex mythology, partly based on fact, which many people accept because they tie in with their own disagreeable experiences of being stopped and questioned or searched on the street. Blacks believe that such incidents occur for no other reason than that they are black, and conclude that the police are racialist.

The first step towards a more sober perspective is to recognize that, while many Asians complain that police do not come quickly when they call, and are not entirely happy with the level of protection the police afford them against racial attacks, they do not often make allegations of harassment, racial abuse or violence. Nor do Turks. The second step is to realize that many white youths, too, hate the police and feel they are picked on for no other reason than that they are young, or live in a rough area, or have been in trouble once or twice before. Listen to Doris Davies, her son Mike, and friend Ellie Riley,* all from Hoxton.

(*Doris*) 'My other son Johnny, he was a bit of a villain when he was sixteen or seventeen. He might have nicked a dress or two. He had his collar felt a few times. But once they know you they're on to you all the time. He was nicked for a burglary in Knightsbridge when he was in Germany at the time. He got off, but he spent a week in Brixton [remand centre] first.'

(*Ellie*) 'Once their faces are known they can't walk up Kingsland High Street without getting flung up against a wall and searched. This sus law that the coloureds say they're always getting picked up on, that's been going on for years. My nephew was talking to his mate with his hand leaning on a car: he got six months for sus and he'd never been in trouble all his life.'

(*Mike*) 'The police are only doing their job in one sense but in another sense they're animals. They broke my foot just before Christmas. My brother-in-law was driving paralytic drunk the wrong way down a one-way street with no light on, and the police stopped us and breathalysed us. I said, "Shut up, he ain't done nothing serious," so this Old Bill he got his leg down and stamped on my foot. At the station I said, "My foot's killing me," it was coming up like a balloon. Five hours later they dragged me to hospital. They was laughing. When we left they said, "D'you want to press charges against the officer?" I said, "You're taking the piss, what chance have I got?" They've done me over a few times.

* See page 441. Not their real names.

They slap you here, they give you a dig in the ribs there, but they won't leave a mark on you.'

The Case For

Having heard a barrage of such tales, I was almost convinced, when I arranged to spend several days with Hackney police, G District of the Met, that I was about to enter a lions' den. I cannot speak for earlier periods, but from what I saw and heard, I came to the conclusion that, while there are obviously far too many individual cases of misconduct, for the majority of the allegations there are more innocuous and more credible explanations than the charge of systematic racism and brutality among the police.

Take the matter of racial harassment. 'To harass' according to the dictionary, means 'to worry and impede by repeated raids; to annoy persistently'. Now it is certainly true that the police do harass known criminals. As Superintendent Mike Jeffers admits: 'If people are criminals, I will harass them, that is my job, and I will harass them to the ends of the earth if necessary.' It may be unfair, it may not give the leopards much of a chance to change their spots, but it has its rationale for crime detection and prevention in a situation where there are often few leads to go on other than previous form. Most of the white villains of Shoreditch reluctantly accept this as part of the risks of the game. But many of the black villains of Stoke Newington violently resent it, and regard it as a scandalous injustice if they are frisked when they are clean.

The term 'harassment' is used rather loosely in the inner city. The usual dictionary requirement of persistent, repeated annoyance is often dropped. Some people say they have been harassed if they have been stopped and questioned or searched while going about their normal business, even if this has only happened a handful of times or less in a number of years. This kind of incident involving innocent people arises frequently in the normal course of routine policing, and all the more frequently in an area of high and rising crime rates.

Three encounters I witnessed in the area car will illustrate this. Golf Four had been called to a house burglary in Mount Pleasant. Scotland Yard radioed the description of two men seen climbing out of the back window, both IC3 (identity category three – Afro-Caribbean) one a young man in green overalls, the other a mature man in a dark jacket carrying a white plastic bag. Tearing along Upper Clapton Road towards the scene of the crime, driver Colin Dryden (who has the rare skill of being able to drive fast and safe *and* scan around for suspects) notices a man fitting the second bill, swerves round, screeches to a halt, jumps out, runs across the road and asks to look in the man's bag. It is his weekend shopping. Golf Three had cruised through the area of the burglary just before the call came through, and afterwards recalled that two men exactly fitting the radioed description had walked along behind them, up Warwick Grove, slowly and casually. They had seen nothing suspicious, and had not stopped them.

In the second incident, Scotland Yard broadcast the colour and number of a Ford Escort stolen in the Hackney area. One of the area cars spotted an Escort with a number that was very close. The driver would not stop when flagged down and a chase ensued, with no less than three police cars pursuing the luckless individual. At this point his colour was not apparent, for it was after dark. He was finally penned in and halted, and happened to be black. His papers were checked and cleared. The officers explained the reason for the chase, but the man drove off in very high dudgeon. On the third occasion, two car thieves had abandoned their stolen vehicle and taken to their heels in the Green Lanes area. There was no precise location, no description other than their colour. Inevitably, when two other black youths were spotted running down Green Lanes, they were stopped and questioned.

Stops of these types usually have a good reason. Some officers do not always explain the reason, and that invariably causes offence. Golf Four driver Colin Dryden, correct on every occasion, made a point of politeness and explained to each individual the reason for the stop. But three out of the four still took deep offence. In each case they might well go home and tell their friends they had been 'harassed'. There are many such encounters every single night in Hackney. The frequency with which the person stopped is black is a straightforward function of the frequency with which suspects of serious crimes are identified by witnesses or victims as black.

Down in Shoreditch, by contrast, you would find that white youths would be stopped far more frequently than Asians, and for exactly parallel reasons.

There are, however, other occasions when police stop people without a report of a crime that has been committed, that curious category of incidents when they see people behaving 'suspiciously'. What is considered suspicious is, inevitably, a subjective matter, but police officers develop certain rules and instincts that limit their suspicions to a manageable proportion of people. What would make them stop someone?

(*PC Rod Bateman*) 'Anything out of the ordinary. It's a sixth sense you pick up.'

(*Colin Dryden*) 'They say the hairs on the back of your neck stick up. I'd stop someone acting suspiciously in house doorways, near cars, or at bus-stops.'

(*PC Paul Wilson*) 'Any younger blacks in a Jewish street, that would draw my attention.'

(*PC Simon Herrema*) 'In the early hours of the morning, we'd stop almost anyone walking the streets doing anything out of the ordinary. If we see a couple of young lads, white or black, driving a car at 2 in the morning, it's always worth while stopping them.'

It is an unfortunate fact of cultural diversity that many young Afro-Caribbeans, innocent or otherwise, behave in a way that makes those hairs stand up on white policemen's necks. They tend to hang around in the street more. More of them are out partying in the small hours. Many run away on principle when they see a police officer – which most police also take as a prima-facie sign of guilt, as they cannot understand why any law-abiding person could possibly wish to avoid meeting them. But this is not simply a matter of cultural misinterpretation. For while in many cases these signs are innocent, they are also, often, the places, the times and the patterns of behaviour that do, regardless of race, fit in with actual or imminent crime.

Police themselves are often the recipients of unprovoked racial abuse. Every police officer on the beat faces it: 'raasclaat', 'pig', 'fuck off, Babylon'. The less mature officer can easily be drawn by the taunting into an unnecessary confrontation that can end up in an equally pointless arrest. The young recruits are now trained to walk away. PC Rod Bateman says: 'They try and wind you up, but if you don't take the bait, that's a victory for you.' It is a refreshing new concept of manliness which one hopes will spread. District Commander George Howlett makes a point of teaching all his recruits to be impeccably polite and to treat others as they would wish to be treated themselves. Senior officers respect this code with admirable self-control, but a proportion of younger officers have an abrasive, domineering manner with whites and blacks alike that can become threatening when they are challenged – and young blacks often do challenge them, as a point of honour. Often it is a case of two groups of young males, each intensely loyal to its own members, each socially isolated and easily provoked, pushed into destructive conflict by the social pressures towards crime and the demands of crime control.

The most serious of the charges is that of police racial violence. The belief in this is widespread, indeed almost universal among people of Afro-Caribbean origin: one Hackney policeman, lecturing in a primary school, was approached by a six-year-old who said: 'You're the people who beat people up, aren't you?' The orthodox police explanation, which certainly accounts for some of the cases, is that many of the accusations are purely fictitious. A person who confesses in the heat of the moment, and regrets it later, can only plead innocent at court if he claims that the confession was extracted by force or threat. A routine complaint against the police is then lodged, and is withdrawn as soon as the trial is over, or persisted with as a vendetta. No less than 55 per cent of complaints against the Metropolitan Police in 1981 were withdrawn or not proceeded with.

This explanation cannot, however, account for the injuries which many Afro-Caribbeans claim to receive, and which others witness them to have. There is, however, an explanation which accounts for these facts: there is indeed a great deal of police violence in the inner city. Some of it may be excessive, but most of it is used in self-defence, in preventing injury to others, and in securing arrests against violent resistance. When the police are called in to stop family violence, they often become the target for violence themselves. When it comes to an arrest, many blacks resist, often desperately, whether as a point of honour, or because they have come to believe all those stories of police brutality and imagine they will be tortured if they are taken in. Superintendent Mike Jeffers says: 'If you want to make an arrest you'd often need eight officers, two for each arm and leg, and when they got here there'd be blood all over them and blood all over the officers.' And it is not just the arrestee who resists. Detective Sergeant Graham Golder adds: 'A lot of the families don't listen to reason, they don't believe their son or brother could be responsible for a crime. They shout and scream, and other black people near by come around. We always go to an arrest at least six-handed.'

And there is another, largely untold side to the 'police violence' story. Most officers at Stoke Newington police station have been punched or kicked or bitten in the course of their duty. Many have been seriously injured. Golder had to book a whole family once when making an arrest, and was stabbed in the thigh by a twelve-year-old boy. Colin Dryden has been wounded several times: 'In my first year here, I got my neck ripped open in Wigan House. A Cypriot was beating up his sixteen-year-old daughter. He stuck his long thumb-nail in my windpipe. And when I came out of hospital *he* had filed a complaint against *me* for assaulting him. When the trial came up, there were two detectives from A10 [the Met department that used to deal with complaints] sitting at the back of the court. The complaint didn't stick, but it's there in my record if I'm up for promotion. Since then I've been bottled outside the Four Aces, bitten right through the tunic, and battered with stiletto heels. The last bad injury I had was from a guy I had to get down from a roof. He'd been drinking and smoking ganja, and he had a pitchfork in his hand. He said, "Don't come near me or I'll jab you." I did go near him and he jabbed me. I ducked, but he got me in the back of the neck. To be honest, I've often felt like bashing someone myself, like when they've made you have a long car chase, but I want to keep my job, so I don't do it.'

Resistance does not stop after the arrest is made, but can continue into the station and down to the cells. The degree of resistance routinely encountered means that police make sure they arrive at many scenes in massive numbers. To onlookers this can look like brutal bullying. During the July riots, one youth told me that he had just seen a dozen officers 'beating hell' out of a man lying on the floor. I had witnessed the same incident from much closer. The man in question was screaming and struggling like seventeen devils. The officers were kneeling on his limbs to hold him down, while a senior officer was leaning over him, reasoning with him and trying to calm him down. There is a tendency among police officers – based on previous experience – to expect trouble when arresting or questioning Afro-Caribbeans, and to be prepared for it, just as Afro-Caribbeans, again from experience, expect trouble from the police. These mutual expectations create tense situations in which gestures are easily misinterpreted and rapid escalation to high levels of violence is facilitated.

There remains, however, a small residue of genuine cases of excessive or unwarranted violence. Police working in the inner city are under constant stress of a degree that would drive most people to the verge of nervous breakdown. Inevitably, there are occasions when they over-react. Finally there are the bad apples, nature's bullies, and genuine racialists, who might indulge their tastes when senior officers are not around to watch: a very small number of individuals of this type, interacting daily with ten or more people, can quickly give a whole force a bad name.

The Unbridged Gulf

I modified my own views on the police after seeing things from the inside. Most inner-city community leaders did not have this opportunity, indeed relations had soured to such a point that many might well turn down an invitation to do so, for fear of losing credibility in the eyes of their supporters. At the time of writing (1982), the Hackney Council for Racial Equality was refusing formal liaison with the police; the Labour council set up a new committee to monitor police behaviour; and the Hackney Teachers' Association voted that police speakers should no longer be invited to talk to schoolchildren.

There was, thus, an immense gap in confidence and communication between the police and the most vocal sections of the local community. The charges against the police circulated publicly – and they were never answered publicly. The following is a typical example. On a cloudy Wednesday in December 1981 a demonstration about sixty strong, including left-wing councillors, some ethnic leaders and even the chief community-relations officer, wound their way from Hackney town hall, carrying posters saying 'Sack the thugs', 'Child battery', 'We have nothing better to do than to harass you', with pictures of pigs in police helmets. They stopped in the road outside Stoke Newington police station and shouted: 'Racist police, out, out! Criminal police, out, out, out!' They moved on to Stoke Newington Green where one speaker described the police as 'a bunch of thugs using their uniforms as a front to attack black people'. Ian Haig, of the Hackney Commission for Racial Equality, complained: 'It's clear that many police feel they can do whatever they like. Again and again we are hearing of people being assaulted.'

The subject of this demonstration was a West Indian lady and her three daughters. The demonstrators handed out a leaflet claiming that she had called the police in to report a burglary. Instead of investigating her claim that the family downstairs were responsible, the police had kicked and hit her in the face and subjected her to racialist abuse. She was taken to the station and forced to sign a statement, the leaflet went on, and then charged with assaulting the police. A few days later, after she had made an official complaint, she was further charged with grievous bodily harm.

The police version of the same events was not made public at the time. It could not be, because the case was still *sub judice*. The police evidence was first presented publicly at the trial eight months later. The lady was found not guilty on three charges of bodily harm. On two others, of assault, the jury could not agree. Whatever the true facts of the case were, there were two sides to the story, and the public at the demonstration came away with only one. And it is the same with every such incident, and every personal tale of police brutality. Only the alleged victim's account circulates in the community: the police never tell their side.

The police complaints system in force at the time did nothing to ease this communications problem. Complaints were investigated by the police themselves, often by officers of the same force. Their confidential report was submitted to the Director of Public Prosecutions, who then decided whether there was sufficient evidence for criminal proceedings. Because of the high standard of evidence required for a conviction ('beyond any reasonable doubt'), and the fact that in most cases it was one person's word against another, the overwhelming majority of complaints – 92 per cent of those proceeded with in the Met in 1981 – were rejected as unsubstantiated. And no disciplinary action was taken, on the grounds that an officer should not be placed in double jeopardy. Hackney's community relations officer Ian Haig took a dim view of the procedure: 'Not a single complaint we have helped to submit has been substantiated. The whole thing just vanishes into thin air.'

In fact, most police officers I spoke to dreaded having complaints filed against them. PC Paul Wilson: 'The prisoners here are treated better than we are. Anyone can ring up and complain anonymously, and every call will be followed up.' PC Martin Morgan: 'A complaint will stay on your record, even if it's not substantiated. The stain will always be there.' Once again, outsiders do not know this. The police officer's answer to the complaint is never published. Justice may be done, but it is not seen to be done. Thus outsiders easily gain the impression that the complaints procedure is a farce, that the police protect their own, and that the enforcers of the law are themselves above the law.

The volume of complaints that they hear, and to which they never hear any specific reply, has made many left-wing politicians, activists and ethnic leaders into outspoken critics of the police. The police, in their turn, feel very bitter that their critics never speak out forcefully to condemn crime, and that a single instance of alleged police misconduct provokes a public outcry, while the daily toll of street theft and burglary continues to spread terror and suffering without attracting any adverse comment except from local Conservatives. The gulf between community leaders and the police should be bridged by a much more open and independent complaints procedure, and by a greater measure of democratic accountability of the police. In response, there should be a greater readiness among local leaders to speak out in condemnation of crime and to help to take measures to control it.

But it is the gulf between police and young blacks that is the most menacing and most intractable. Though the summer of 1982 passed without major rioting, conflict erupted again in Hackney in

January 1983. The stimulus was the death of a twenty-one-year-old black, Colin Roach, in the unattended foyer of Stoke Newington police station, from a shot-gun blast in the mouth. Roach was an unemployed cloth-cutter who had recently been released from a Christmas spell in prison for stealing a wallet. Police were convinced from forensic evidence that it was a case of suicide. Roach's family found that hard to accept, and complained of failure to investigate the possibility of murder, and of rude and insensitive treatment by police. Black people's groups, trade-union, Labour Party branches and the Commission for Racial Equality called for a Home Office inquiry. Hackney Central Labour Party set up a 'response unit' to help youths who were stopped and searched or beaten up by the police, while a Dalston youth centre set up a 'security and defence force' for young blacks. In the three months after Roach's death on 12 January, eighty-four people were arrested, after repeated scuffles with massive forces of police during marches and demonstrations.

Though blacks and radicals tended to view the police as the enemy, it was the economic situation that set them against each other, in a vicious spiral of worsening relations.

As massive unemployment and discrimination in jobs tempts more young black males into crime, increasing numbers are brought into unpleasant contact with the police – remembering that for every guilty party found, several innocent people may be stopped and questioned or searched. The more blacks distrust the police, the more likely they are to resist arrest and to help others to resist arrest. This resistance, in turn, compels the police to use greater numbers and greater force, and this, in its turn, increases the blacks' hatred of the police. Some of the same considerations apply to Hoxton whites: but with blacks the racial dimension adds an extra emotional charge. For Hackney's police force are 99 per cent white – only five officers out of 450 were non-white in November 1981. In view of the history of colonialism, slavery and discrimination, blacks are very understandably sensitive about white assaults on their dignity.

The tension frustrates all attempts to defuse it. Thus strenuous police efforts to recruit blacks have had very little success because those who are recruited lose their friends and face an even more hostile barrage of abuse and threats when patrolling the streets. Other measures to reduce tensions have been taken both before and after the riots of July 1981 and the Scarman report. Hackney police are no longer involved in taking legal action over party noise: Hackney's environmental health officers deal with that. While they do not ignore drug offences if they see them, detectives do not spend much time pursuing soft-drug users. Police avoid making arrests close to the two main clubs for Afro-Caribbean youth in Hackney. They also started to withdraw from situations which looked as if serious confrontations might develop. Some officers found this policy hard to stomach. PC Paul Wilson was used to taking a tough line with white roughnecks in South Shields: 'We'd have thousands, not hundreds of officers on the streets at chucking out time. You knew you had to call help fast, or you'd be kicked unconscious. But down here they know we'll withdraw. That gives them an incentive to mob us. But we're the last line, and if we withdraw, what happens then?'

What happens, inevitably, is that some arrests are lost, and some crimes are not prevented or dealt with. And however accommodating the police become, there will always be arrests so important, and crimes so grave, that they cannot withdraw without abdicating their function. Given the right time, place and numbers any one of these situations could spark off a riot or a near riot, as indeed could any demonstration about real or imagined police brutality or failure to investigate crimes against blacks. In the inner city today, there is no way of policing crime that does not involve some risk of civil disorder on some scale, and few ways of policing it less strongly that do not involve the risk of an increase in crime. The only way of minimizing the risk of civil disorder is to prevent crime. The only way to prevent crime is to remove its economic and social causes.

The Tough Patch

Policing the inner city has always been a harrowing experience. 'If you transplanted Chichester police force and put them in here,' says Superintendent Mike Jeffers, 'they'd all be crying in the toilets. I'm a Londoner myself, but I never fail to be shocked by the Dickensian sights you see round here. You get a mother topping herself and her kids at Christmas, or a twelve-year-old girl pregnant and with VD. You realize what a terribly sick society we are living in. Hackney is a bloody awful place, a stinking cesspit.'

Even from a purely professional point of view, policing is harder here. Crime is far more common than elsewhere – and far more difficult to detect. People often don't know their neighbours. Victims find it hard to identify suspects of other races. People don't question strangers in blocks of flats, and stay inside if they hear the splintering of a door frame. Shouts for help are ignored: the din of domestic rows is so common that the screams of victims of wounding or even murder have been known to pass unnoticed. Witnesses to crimes do not come forward. Even the victims themselves often refuse to give evidence, for fear of retaliation. The first line of policing in any area is the community itself: when the community will not help itself, the police can only fill in part of the vacuum. Factors such as these account for the appallingly low detection rate in the Metropolitan Police – only 16 per cent of crimes were cleared up in 1981, less than half the England and Wales average.

But as the recession deepened, the task of the police became more thankless than ever: a tidal wave of crime, a rising level of complaints, showers of insults on the streets, a barrage of political criticisms without any balancing condemnation of criminals. Even physically, the police seemed isolated and beleaguered. Stoke Newington nick is like a fortress. Only 5 per cent of G district officers live in the community they serve. Young recruits live in the tower block of flats overlooking the courtyard, the garage, the steaming stables. Married officers have their semis in the suburbs. From their centralized headquarters, the police sally forth like commandos, equipped with all the latest technology, into enemy-held territory. The speed of response to calls is remarkable – but because of its speed, it is often out of proportion to the situation. At one incident near Clissold Park, four vehicles with a total of perhaps twenty officers were on the spot within five minutes of the radio message from Scotland Yard, and all piled into the house on the trot – only to find that the disturbance was nothing more than a heated argument between a tenant and a landlord, both of them African. Everything happens so fast that there is no time for a calculated decision on how to match the response to the real needs of the situation. Bystanders gain the impression of a heavy, high-profile presence engaging in overkill.

Maintaining this centralized capacity to respond quickly means, conversely, that the continuing police presence in the community is extraordinarily weak. In November 1981, there were just thirty-one home-beat officers in G district, only 7 per cent of the total strength of 450. Many more police, of course, go on routine foot patrols, but for safety they must often move in pairs in the inner city, so that the area they can cover is effectively halved.

What is needed is a move away from crisis intervention towards crime prevention: by neighbourhood watch schemes on streets and estates – though in a fragmented and racially divided place like Hackney, these are less likely to succeed; by a stronger, continuous police presence on the streets and around the estates; and by liaison with residents' and tenants' groups and with planners and architects on preventive measures – entry-phones, reinforced doors and windows, improvement of lighting, elimination of dark corners and escape routes, provision of adequate play facilities. (Some of these measures were initiated, in January 1983, by the new Metropolitan Commissioner of Police, Sir Kenneth Newman.) But they all involve spending money, and are impossible, without other sacrifices, under a regime of public-spending parsimony. Such localized solutions would help to slow the rise in crime by reducing *opportunities* for crime. But national measures are needed to alter the factors that provide the *motivation* for crime: tighter control of television violence; a new educational deal for the less academically gifted; improvements in housing; an attack on family poverty; and a massive reduction in unemployment.

As things stand, we have, in Hackney as in other inner-city areas, a police force that is largely isolated from the majority of people it serves, with a low detection rate and therefore a low deterrent effect; a police force whose very efforts to control the high level of crime have led almost inexorably to more serious disorders. The police face the virtually impossible task of keeping the lid on the explosive mixture of ingredients that the dynamics of British society have assembled in the inner city. This mixture, heated by recession and high unemployment, inevitably generates a high level of crime. This necessitates, in turn, a far more numerous and ubiquitous police presence than in other kinds of area, far more frequent unpleasant contact with the public as potential suspects, and far greater opportunities for police misjudgement or abuse.

And the poor are caught in the cross-fire. For the most disadvantaged groups in society also suffer the worst incidence of crime, the heaviest police presence, and the gravest risk of violent confrontations on their streets. They are more likely to be stopped and searched by police, to have their house invaded, and (as mistakes do occur) to be arrested or detained or even convicted by mistake. Also, much more seriously, they have lost the freedom to walk the streets of their own neighbourhood without fear, the right to enjoy their property, their health and their life without fear. Thus, added to economic and social deprivations, the poor of the inner city also suffer a grave loss of human rights and civil liberties.

As housing decline and industrial decline spread, and unemployment and inequality deepen, so too will the problem of crime spread and intensify, and with it the intensified police measures needed to control it. Futher riots may, or may not, be avoided or muted by improved police methods or equipment. But there will be a steady rise in the climate of fear and the society of barricaded self-defence, and a steady erosion of civil liberties. Of all the warnings that the inner city has to offer for the direction British society is taking, this is perhaps the most sinister.

19   Brother Shall Strike Brother: Race and Class

Me and my brother against my cousin; me and my cousin against the foreigner.

Arab proverb

In 1736 William Goswell, the enterprising builder of St Leonard's Church at Shoreditch, decided to dismiss his English labourers and hire Irish at half or two-thirds of the wages. 'On Monday night last,' wrote Sir Robert Walpole on 29 July, 'there was an appearance of numbers being assembled in a very disorderly manner at Shoreditch. Their cry and complaint was of being underworked and starved by the Irish.' The next day some 2,000 men assembled and attacked an Irish pub and the houses of master weavers who were employing Irish workers. The Riot Act was read, fifty guardsmen drafted in and the militia of Tower Hamlets marched. The troubles died down within the week, for Goswell had recanted and rehired his English labourers.

Immigration and racialism both have long pedigrees in Hackney. Huguenot refugees joined the weavers of Shoreditch, more Irish labourers came in large numbers to build London docks in the early nineteenth century, and Jews, driven out by pogroms in Russia and Eastern Europe, flooded in from the 1880s, first settling close to the docks where they arrived, then as they made good moving gradually northwards, through Hackney to Stamford Hill.

In 1951, in the then metropolitan borough of Hackney alone, the foreign-born population was only 6·5 per cent of the total, and was overwhelmingly European. There were a mere 466 residents born in New Commonwealth countries. During the 1950s the West Indian migration got under way. Many settled in Hackney, and not only because there were plenty of rooms to let at low rents: Hackney was one of the few places where discrimination against black tenants was less pronounced. The mainly Jewish landlords, having been themselves the victims of discrimination, were not concerned about the colour of their tenants. Thus an area that had accepted previous waves of immigration became a focus for subsequent waves. So by 1961, there were already 10,282 West Indians in Hackney and Stoke Newington, and the Cypriot and Asian migrations had begun, with 2,300 from Cyprus and 1,600 from India and Pakistan. New Commonwealth-born citizens made up only 6·3 per cent of the population in these two areas. Shoreditch, at that time, had so few New Commonwealth immigrants that the figure was not recorded.

All three main groups continued to grow over the sixties. By the time of the 1971 census, there were 14,000 Caribbean-born residents, 4,000 Cypriots, 3,000 Indians and Pakistanis and 3,000 Africans, though together they still accounted for only 11·5 per cent of the population of what was now the London Borough of Hackney. The total number of those born in the New Commonwealth did not change much over the next ten years: the size of the Caribbean and Cypriot groups stayed roughly the same, Africans increased to 4,800, while the Asians decreased slightly. But the greatest ethnic change was the exodus of the white population, accounting for almost all the drop of 40,000 in Hackney's population over the seventies.

It was an ethnic sifting closely paralleling the social sifting: the inner city was becoming a racial semi-ghetto as well as a social ghetto. Thus, by 1981, no less than 26 per cent of Hackney's population was born outside the United Kingdom, and, as most of them had had children, a full 42 per cent of the population lived in households with foreign-born heads. Some 27 per cent lived in families with New Commonwealth heads – the third highest total in Greater London, after Brent and Haringey.

Hackney's browns and blacks are not uniformly scattered throughout the borough: they are most heavily concentrated over the central saddle, across the worst of Hackney's Victorian housing and the bleakest of council estates. In each ward in this belt, upwards of one-third of the residents are of New Commonwealth origin. This central band of colour shades off steeply at its margins, so that in the wards lining the northern and southern boundaries, less than one person in four is of New Commonwealth origin. The four northern wards are more than a quarter Jewish, while the southern five are overwhelmingly white and Cockney.

Outside Shoreditch, parts of which still retain a distinctive culture, ethnic and national groupings are so thoroughly blended that no single culture gives its dominant stamp to any particular area in the.way that, say, Afro-Caribbeans have in Notting Hill or Brixton and Asians in Southall. A Jewish religious foundation and an all-black youth club face each other across Stamford Hill. On Stoke Newington Road, Turkish and West Indian night-clubs stand a stone's throw apart, close to Asian grocers and newsagents. Hackney could probably go a long way to mustering at least one representative for each member of the United Nations, but here they are far from united. Each major grouping is further subdivided: Turkish and Greek Cypriots, Pakistanis and Indians, Muslims and Hindus, small islanders and big islanders, orthodox and reformed Jewish. The result to the chic radical may look like a rich diversity of colourful cultures: but I suspect that to immigrants it feels more like a curiously faceless, characterless place in which their cultures are undermined and uprooted, and moral values and family solidarity are eroded.

The dynamics of British imperialism accounts for their presence here: for, after having conquered and exploited half the world and created artificial states, economically and culturally dependent on her, Britain graciously granted them independence without having invested in their future, abandoning them to underdevelopment and conflict. In the post-war economic upswing, British employers facing a labour shortage at home, instead of upgrading technology, training and pay rates, imported ready-formed workers to serve as low-paid, low-skilled labour. Discrimination in the labour market pushed even the well-qualified among immigrants into lowly jobs. Discrimination in the housing market concentrated them in pockets, usually in areas inhabited by low-paid, disadvantaged whites. Thus employers pocketed the profits of immigrant labour while working-class areas in the inner cities paid the social costs.

As the great upswing began to flatten around 1966, and later to turn downwards into slump, immigrants and their children became increasingly unwanted. Descendants of the victims of empire, they became the victims of expanding capitalism and their children the abandoned victims of contracting capitalism. Meanwhile the downturn was also deeply affecting the semi-skilled and unskilled whites, reducing their job and pay prospects and their hopes of decent housing. The inner city became the prime location of increasing racial tensions in Britain.

Pressure and Prejudice

If we define racism as the belief in the genetic superiority of one's own race over others, and racial discrimination as the favouring of the dominant race over others in the allocation of resources, then most whites in Hackney are too intelligent or too humble to be racist, and too powerless to exert racial discrimination. Nevertheless, most of them suffer to some degree from racial prejudice: the application to all members of certain races of unfavourable stereotypes derived from myth or limited acquaintance.

Listen to our old friend Doris Davies* and her neighbour Ellie Riley, both from Hoxton, talking about immigrants.

(*Ellie*) 'If you go to another country, you got to live as they live. They come here, they should live as we live. Look at those Ugandan Asians. They had all new houses given them when we couldn't get them for ourselves.'

(*Doris*) 'Every shop you go in now you've got a Pakistan [*sic*] there. Every post office round here has got a Pakistan in. They'll talk to you as they want to, but you can't talk to them as you want to. It reminds me of years ago, the Jews, when they come in here. They had all the businesses 'cause the likes of us didn't have the money. Where do they get the money from, I'd like to know?'

(*Ellie*) 'This country has never been like this, everybody fighting one another. A lot of this violence what's coming up is a lot to do with the race relations board. By law, a white man has to take on a coloured worker, but a coloured man don't have to take on a white, does he? There's a flat upstairs in this block, it's one lot of Nigerians out, another lot in. They're selling the key to each other. Now if that was a white person you'd get slung out. My grandmother applied for a ground-floor flat, they said no she could have

* See page 441. Not their real names.

first floor. She went up the housing office and she sat down, and she died there, in the housing. That got me, so I said to the estate manager, three times I pulled him up about those Nigerians, he said, no, they're not changing, it's the same people.'

(*Doris*) 'It's not their colour, a person can't help their colour, it's their attitude. Five of them jostled me up the stairs and frightened me, and I'm supposed to like them. The coloured kids have come round here, and called up, white prostitutes, white whores. I told one of their mums, can't you tell your kid to stop calling us names, and she came out with a meat chopper.'

(*Ellie*) 'The coloureds *demand* things, they don't ask and walk away like the English do.'

(*Doris*) 'Look at these all-night parties, they go on all night and half-way through the next day as well. If you have a row with them, they say you're prejudiced against them. It's always us is prejudiced against them, but I think the coloureds is prejudiced against us.'

Here we have almost the full range of white working-class attitudes and prejudices, some based on selective facts, some based on misconceptions. We must view them against the background of the speakers' lives. Both women are cleaners. Both rise at 5 a.m. every weekday, Ellie to look after a toilet in a City bank, Doris to clean a school. Doris and her children, as we saw in Chapter 11, have had the most appalling housing problems, long waits for council flats, dense overcrowding. They do not understand the complex housing-allocation system based on need: they believe instinctively in the queueing principle, and they know that they have had a rough deal while some immigrants who have been here twenty years or less have been allocated better housing, faster. Doris has two sons, Mike and Johnny, and two sons-in-law – Pam's and Maureen's husbands – who are unemployed. They do not understand the dynamics of the world economy or the economics of monetarism: all they know is that they don't have jobs, while some immigrants do. They know nothing about Keynes or Brandt, or the alternative economic strategy. The simple conclusion that springs to their minds is: keep out or kick out the blacks, and there will be more jobs and houses for us. Race-equality laws are like red rags to a bull for them: they do not know that blacks still get the roughest deal, they only know that they have a damned rough deal, too, and no one is setting up a 'Working-class equality commission' to help them out.

The worries about jobs and houses relate primarily to Afro-Caribbeans, who are more direct competitors in the employment and housing markets. The resentment of Jews and Asians is of a different order. Doris and Ellie see Asians who arrived less than two decades ago swiftly become landlords, shop owners and small-business men, just like the Jews before them, able to extract profits and rents from their customers, employees and tenants. They do not understand the years of working round the clock and of self-denial that lie behind the saving potential of these two groups. All they know is that after a lifetime of drudgery they themselves have not a penny of capital, and do not even own the house they live in. They resent the extraction of incomes not earned by 'elbow grease', and are convinced that some sort of dishonesty must lie behind the rapid accumulation of capital.

Thus is racial prejudice generated by deprivation: by lack of access to decent housing, to secure, decently paid employment, and to the capital necessary for self-employment or the employment of others. The most disadvantaged whites, at the bottom of the white British heap and openly treated as such by employers and bureaucrats, naturally look around for someone even lower in the pecking order on whom they can vent, verbally or physically, the anger aroused in them by the British class system.

Among most poor whites, these attitudes find no effective expression except through the enactment of restrictive immigration laws and grousing among themselves. There is none the less, as with any belief, a minority among whom racial prejudice assumes a pernicious and pathological character. London's East End has long been a stronghold of hard-core racism – and of resistance to racism. It was a fertile recruiting-ground for Sir Oswald Mosley's blackshirts as well as for the socialists who opposed them. Both traditions are still alive and kicking.

Today the fight against racism has the higher profile, and most organized groups, from teachers to trade unionists, take an outspoken anti-racist stance. In 1982 Hackney Council began to implement employment policies amounting to positive discrimination and elected Hackney's first black mayor, Sam Springer.

Overtly racist groups lead a more shadowy existence, formally limited to distributing literature, some of it to secondary schools, and standing in local elections, though informally sympathizers are involved in racial threats and attacks. Electoral support for the National Front reached disturbing proportions in Hackney in the mid-seventies. In the 1974 general election, when the Front gained only 0·4 per cent of the vote nationally, it won 3·7 per cent in North Hackney, and 9·4 per cent in Shoreditch. In the 1978 borough-council elections, the National Front gained more votes than the Communists in every ward where both were standing, and in seven wards they outvoted the liberals. In the four southernmost wards, they won more than 20 per cent of the vote, and came second to Labour in three of them. The strength of their vote in each ward varied inversely to the proportion of blacks present, possibly because the extent of racist support in Shoreditch – though still a minority – was strong enough to deter black families from accepting council houses there.

One small encouraging sign more recently was the dramatic slump in the racist vote in the 1982 borough elections. Candidates were put forward in only two wards, where they scored only one-seventh of their 1978 performance. I do not believe, however, that their electoral collapse was a sign of a retreat in racial prejudice in Shoreditch. Part of it was due to the fact that increasingly tough government action was being taken against coloured immigration. Part of it was due to the disintegration of the National Front into factions. And a major part, too, stemmed from the emergence of a strong local alternative, in the form of the Liberal Focus Team. Ever since it was absorbed into Hackney in 1963, Shoreditch has been casting protest votes against its neglect, choosing the most credible rival party for its support. In 1982 the Liberals won seats in the same four wards where, in 1978, the National Front had polled highest.

Racial Attacks

Recession and monetarism intensified precisely those factors that fuel racial disharmony, worsening access to jobs, housing and capital among whites and black alike and leading to a growth in racial conflicts of all kinds and on all scales in the inner city.

The most disturbing omen is the rising toll of racial attacks. In Hackney those reported to the police rose from fifteen in 1978 to sixty-six in 1981, with the rate of increase accelerating each year. It is not easy to assess the true extent of the problem. There is a tendency to call many attacks by white persons on black persons a 'racial attack' even when the prime reason may be a neighbours' quarrel or a robbery. Conversely, it is much rarer for an attack of a black on a white to be called a 'racial attack', even when it is clearly so. The only unambiguous type is an unprovoked threat or attack of a white person against a member of another ethnic group or their property, accompanied by racist abuse or graffiti. Such attacks, terrifying for the immediate victims, have a much wider impact, spreading fear among immigrants, fuelling racial tensions, and provoking retaliation. The most widely publicized of these in Hackney was on the Singh family in Martello Street, London Fields. In November 1980, burning rags soaked in petrol were pushed through the Singhs' letter-box and much of their flat was burned out, forcing them to live in one room for months while the local authorities haggled over rehousing them.

In December 1980, West Indian and Asian traders in Ridley Road market suffered a spate of burglaries and daubings of racist slogans and swastikas. The gravest attack – if race was the motive – occurred on Kingsland estate, near Dalston, in July 1982. Norma Cunningham, aged twenty-seven, and her nine-year-old daughter, Samantha, were stabbed to death, and seven-year-old Syreeta Cunningham was drowned in the bath. The initials of the National Front party had been scrawled on the door of the flat. The murder remained unsolved at the time of writing.

Contrary to stereotypes the victims are not always Asian. Orthodox Jews in Stoke Newington continue to be plagued, couples in mixed marriages in the Shoreditch area are vulnerable, and white radicals who sympathize with blacks receive threats. Just in December 1981, for example, two Jewish homes in Stoke Newington had swastika-painted bricks thrown through their front windows with notes attached: 'Fuck off Jude', and 'Hitler rules OK, Himmler'. The Hackney Council for Racial Equality got a recorded message on their telephone-answering machine saying that a campaign of bombings would be started against blacks in schools and estates in revenge for muggings of old people. And Ernie Roberts, left-wing MP for North Hackney, got a Christmas card that read: 'Black greetings and evil wishes. May those who will benefit from your death receive their inheritance early in 1982.' Neither of the last two threats materialized. But many others did.

Some of the most blatant cases were on council housing estates, especially in Hoxton and Shoreditch. In October 1981 Hackney Council set up one of the country's first racial-harassment monitoring systems, to record and act on reports of attacks on council estates. In its first six months twenty-one allegations of racial harassment were reported, ten of them involving damage to property and eight physical assault. In the summer of 1981 white teenagers moved in near a West Indian couple and started baiting them, shouting abuse, banging on the door and running away. When the woman came out to complain she was assaulted, and her husband pulled her indoors to safety – but the neighbours came out and joined the youths, banging on the doors and smashing the windows. In November 1981 a Turkish Cypriot with an English wife and child was attacked in the street by a gang of white youths. When he returned from hospital he found his door had been spray-painted 'NF Turkish cunts'. Four days later his wife was chased in the street by three whites calling her 'Turkish lover', one of them brandishing a razor and threatening to cut her baby up. A neighbour intervened to prevent anything more serious. The following day the couple came home from an evening out to see fire-engines on the estate. Petrol had been poured through their letter-box and the door set on fire. The family would not stay on the estate and went to sleep on a relative's floor until they were rehoused.

The aim of these attacks is often to keep estates and neighbourhoods white, and to some extent they have succeeded. Terrorized families are often transferred elsewhere. Housing allocators are reluctant to offer flats on certain estates to coloured families, knowing they would be exposing them to risk. Black families viewing flats may see racist graffiti and hear racist abuse, and turn offers down.

The responses of officials and police were, until recently, not overhelpful to victims. Racist graffiti were left in place until routine cleaning or redecoration. Requests for transfer were met with reluctance – understandably, since to move people out was to concede victory to their attackers. There is a widespread feeling, among Asians, that the police do not do enough to prevent attacks or to prosecute attackers. Official responses are improving. Racist graffiti are now removed as soon as they are noticed. Tenancy agreements with Hackney Council include an understanding that the tenant may be evicted if found to be involved in racial harassment. Police now record racial attacks separately from other forms of assault and may make follow-up visits not usual in most assault cases. But genuine problems still remain, for police manpower does not stretch to providing protection from even the most bloodthirsty threats, and prosecution generally depends on the victim preferring charges. That goes for family violence, too, not just racial violence.

Love Thy Neighbour as Thyself

But this kind of racial attack is merely the visible tip of an immense iceberg of minor and daily disputes and conflicts, in which ethnic minorities are often capable of giving as good as they get. It is often hard to say whether they are personal quarrels with racial abuse thrown in for good measure, or racial animosities seeking any minor excuse to burst forth. Either way, it is the specific ecology of the inner city that provides the matter for dispute, its social geography that conjoins the poor of diverse cultures, and the stress of multiple deprivation that supplies the nervous energy.

The number of causes for conflict are legion: the behaviour of children forced, for lack of play space, to get under adults' feet; troubles over disposal of refuse; washing-lines on balconies; and, most commonly, over noise. Noise conducted through thin party walls and flimsy doors, in jerry-built Victorian terraces and cost-cutting modern estates; noise echoing round courtyards and balconies and rising to the pinnacles of tower blocks; noises of loud children, of dogs kept for their bark, of industrial sewing-machines, of rusting car exhausts, of foul-mouthed family rows.

But perhaps the most racially divisive noise is the sound of music. The playing of loud music is, of course, a widespread phenomenon, but all-night reggae parties with their high-powered speakers are a source of particular annoyance. Many blacks view white neighbours' complaints as a manifestation of racial intolerance, but this is often not the case. The fact is that most Hackney residents of whatever colour are not long on tolerance of noise at night: tranquillity is a rare gift, sleep a precious release from stress that most of them cannot afford to lose after a day's hard work or dealing with children. Arguments over loud music are intractable. Neighbourly relations are soured whatever the outcome.

A typical example comes from a wet Saturday night in January, on Smalley Road estate, newish terraced houses with poor noise insulation. The complainants are a black family. The next-door white neighbours have thrown a brick at their back window. The splintered dent is clear evidence. The older sister explains to the police officer: 'Whenever my brother is left on his own in the house, the people next door start on him. It's always when he's on his own.' The boy, about seventeen, is slouched across an armchair, smiling. Is it a vicious racial attack? We go next door. The tenants are a white couple with a four-month-old baby. The husband, around thirty, thin and long-haired, admits he did it. His slightly younger wife, pallid and angular, explains: 'It's the noise. Whenever his old man goes out next door, the son has the stereo on. Often I've only just got the baby off to sleep. If we bang on the wall, he just turns it up louder. We've called the police before and he turns it down while they're there, then turns it up again as soon as they've left. My nerves are like that.' She holds out a hand that is genuinely trembling like a leaf in a breeze. The husband smiles sardonically: 'If you can't get any satisfaction you go and do something stupid. I should have used a bigger brick.' The officer advises the man he could face a charge of criminal damage unless they can sort something out with the neighbours: 'You've got to live with them.' The wife sighs: 'We could never live with them.'

It would be a mistake to go away with the idea that only whites exhibit intolerance or racial prejudice. The failing, unfortunately, is widely distributed throughout the human race and is found in intensified form wherever two or more distinct cultural groupings are competing for the same scarce resources. As blacks in Hackney are subject to the same pressures as whites, as well as being subject to racial discrimination, it would be surprising if they did not respond with some racial prejudices of their own.

Afro-Caribbeans are placed in a similar position to that of white working-class people over jobs and houses, and exhibit many of the same attitudes to Asians. Listen to two black single mothers, neither of them with jobs or places in nurseries, echo the sentiments of Cockney Hoxton:

(*Beverley*) 'Look at the people come over from that country, where was it, Vietnam, and they gave them lovely houses. We're not the ones what's overpopulating this country, it's them, and the Pakis.'

(*Me*) 'Don't you like Asians?'

(*Carmen*) 'Why should we like the Pakis? If you go for a job and a Paki bloke interview you, you don't get it 'cause they think they're white, 'cause they got straight hair.'

(*Beverley*) 'At the post office, the Paki serving told me to wait while he filled in his books. I said I didn't realize he was busy. He said fuck off, go on, fuck off out of here. Are they allowed to say things like that?'

(*Carmen*) 'But if there was a skinhead walked in there, they'd treat him like Prince Charles.'

The feelings start young. In Hackney primary schools, white children call blacks 'wogs' and 'monkeys'. Blacks call whites 'ice cream' and 'white monkeys'. 'African' is a term of abuse among West Indians. Whites and blacks ostracize or victimize Asian children. Games are played like 'last one to touch the railings is a Paki'. One primary-school headmistress lamented that the only time her diverse racial groups presented a united front was against Hasidic Jewish children in their skull-caps and ringlets, who often had to walk past a volley of stones and epithets like 'Jewbug'.

Children and youths of different races sometimes segregate themselves. In Hackney some playgrounds are dominated by one racial group to the exclusion of others. The main Afro-Caribbean night-clubs are virtually all black, with only the occasional white girl to be seen. In 1979 Stamford Hill youth club was half black and half white, but rising unemployment, endless police pressure and racial attacks made the blacks increasingly defensive and hostile to whites. By 1981 the club had become all black.

A lot of the violence is mutual, a lot of it in revenge for previous violence. But violence only breeds more violence. Group solidarity is hardened, racial pride is at stake. The following are a few of the examples that have come to my notice. A black woman in her forties is walking with shopping across London Fields when a white man turns on her, knocks her to the ground and kicks her, shouting: 'That's for my wife.' His wife had recently been assaulted by black youths. Worse: Two white youths are robbed by blacks and hit on the head with a staff. They notice a respectable Ghanaian solicitor's clerk buying a takeaway meal on Kingsland High Street. As he gets into his car they stab him in the arm. He meets them again in Hackney Hospital, where they too have retired to get their wounds dressed.

Worst of all was the frightening and indiscriminate racial warfare that occurred on Holly Street estate on 19 March 1982. Every other Saturday, the tenants' association holds a disco for young people, which has gradually become almost exclusively black, attracting hundreds of black youths from all over Hackney. Two white brothers living on the estate, smarting perhaps from some previous encounter, took it into their heads to wait outside the disco and stab the first three blacks they saw, two girls and a boy. Those inside the disco immediately ran out and chased the attackers back to their flat, where they had barricaded themselves in. The police arrived before the blacks could force an entry. They arrested the two white boys, but while they were leading them to the police car through angry files of black youths, one of them was stabbed by someone in the crowd. When the police had gone, the blacks returned to the white youths' flat, broke into it, and smashed everything in it to pieces. The white boys' parents returned home from a night out to find their home destroyed, then raged up and down the corridors banging on coloured families' doors and shouting racial abuse. That same evening six black youths fell upon three white boys coming home to Holly Street from a scout meeting and stabbed one of them for revenge. A few days later another group of black youths mugged two whites in Dalston, saying they were doing it 'because of Holly Street'.

The mentality of the blood feud, of medieval Iceland or nomadic Bedouin, is at work here. Revenge for an attack on the group may be exacted indiscriminately on *any* member of the opposing group. But then they, too, must have their revenge for the revenge. Blood feuds are self-perpetuating and self-spreading. The implications for the future of race relations under recession and monetarism are nothing short of terrifying.

Race Bias – or Class Bias?

By almost all indicators, New Commonwealth immigrants and their children fare worse than whites in every sphere that determines the overall quality of life. They have a far higher proportion of semi-skilled and unskilled manual workers in Hackney: 34 per cent of West Indians and Asians in 1978, against 28 per cent for whites. They are much less successful in obtaining secure employment.

In 1980, Hackney Council, provider of some of the most secure and desirable jobs in the borough, began monitoring its own performance as an equal-opportunities employer, and uncovered some disturbing facts. Although 27 per cent of the borough's population lived in households with a New Commonwealth head, only 12 per cent of the council's employees in June 1981 were of non-white origin. The further up the ladder of promotion and high pay, the less room at the inn was there for non-whites. Among manual workers, 20 per cent were non-white, but only 3 per cent of the higher-officer grades. And there appeared to be a closed shop among the council's seventy-five dustmen, every single one of whom was white.

Unemployment affected immigrants more seriously than whites. In a 1978 survey their unemployment rate was about double that of whites, and in the following years it rose more steeply.

Housing conditions were worse for immigrants. More of them did own their own homes – half the Asians and a quarter of West Indians, against only one white in eight – but the proportion who were overcrowded among households with a New Commonwealth head was, at 48 per cent, more than five times the average level. The proportions who were renting furnished accommodation and sharing bath or toilet were two or three times higher. Even in the council sector, immigrants were likely to live in the worst housing. The Greater London Council allocation survey in the mid-1970s found that whites were three times more likely to be allocated a house (rather than a flat) than blacks, and blacks were more than twice as likely as whites to be living on the eleventh floor or higher. Four times as many whites than blacks were in the best-quality housing (on an index measuring age, type and floor of the property) and three times as many blacks as whites were in the worst quality of housing. Social differences explained much of the discrepancy, but within every social and economic category the average quality of housing obtained by blacks was lower than that of whites. A similar pattern of results emerged when the Commission for Racial Equality studied allocations to Hackney's council houses in 1978 and 1979. Whites on the waiting list were three and a half times more likely to get houses than blacks, and 1·6 times more likely to get maisonettes, and they were no less than eight times more likely to get post-1975 housing than blacks.

Nor did the education system appear to serve blacks well, particularly those of West Indian origin. A depressingly low proportion acquire worthwhile educational qualifications. The Committee of Inquiry into the Education of Children from Ethnic Minorities surveyed six major local education authorities in 1981 and found that only 3 per cent of children of West Indian origin got five or more higher grades at GCE O-level or CSE – against 18 per cent of Asian and 16 per cent of other leavers. The picture at A-level was very similar.

Each of these individual handicaps adds up to a sum far greater than its parts. The overall impact is an average level of disadvantage and a quality of life far worse in every aspect than those of whites.

Some of this disadvantage is due to deliberate and conscious racial discrimination in individual employers, personnel officers, housing officials or police – against the law, but always carefully disguised so as to avoid detection. Some is due to implicit racial attitudes among these 'gatekeepers' that are often so deep-rooted that they operate automatically, almost at the level of the unconscious.

Radical analysts would go further and suggest that there is also a widespread and subtle institutional racialism at work, almost invisibly built into the rules and regulations and processes that govern British society. Some say that bias is unintentional, some claim it is quite calculated and deliberate. The facts outlined above show quite clearly that our institutions *do* turn out unfavourable answers for blacks. But before attributing these outcomes to 'institutional racialism', we must acknowledge that they produce unfavourable results for disadvantaged whites, too, for semi-skilled and unskilled manual workers, for claimants, for single mothers, for the handicapped, for those with poor educational qualifications.

Take employment. The acquisition of skilled manual and better non-manual jobs in Britain depends heavily on formal educational qualifications and training. Only a small proportion of first-generation immigrants have recognized qualifications, and the children particularly of Caribbeans have fewer than average – but this is also true of less skilled white manual workers and their children.

Recession and technological change, without adequate retraining systems, have marginalized many of the less skilled and the uncertificated. Blacks, especially of West Indian origin, belong predominantly to these groups, hence they have been harder hit. Only a decade or two after importing them to do the menial jobs, the British economy proceeds to wipe out those jobs. But this same process also marginalizes unskilled and uneducated whites.

Now consider self-employment. One in four small firms owned by black people, surveyed by Hackney's Business Promotion Centre, believed that banks were operating a deliberate policy of racial discrimination over credit. Not surprisingly, the banks rejected the suggestion. They said they were simply operating hard-nosed rules of thumb to avoid losing money – insisting on fully secured loans, matching capital from borrowers, and evidence of know-how and sound ventures. Those rules happen to operate to the disadvantage of Afro-Caribbeans (though not so much of Asians). Yet they also work against undereducated, underskilled whites without business experience or capital or collateral of their own.

In housing, the level of income determines the quality of private housing that can be bought or rented. As average black incomes are lower, the quality they can afford is poorer. The mechanisms with council housing are much more complex. Immigrants are more likely to come from the worst, most insecure and over-crowded private rented accommodation, hence they are under greater pressure to accept their first offers. They are more likely to be deterred by higher rents, rates and central-heating charges for better council properties. They are more likely to be made home-less, and until recently the homeless were deliberately dumped on the hard-to-let estates. But all these factors also apply to the most disadvantaged whites. The GLC allocation survey found that the homeless, the unemployed and single parents were just as likely as black people to be found in lower-quality council housing, although, within each of these categories, blacks fared worse than whites. Two additional factors, besides overt discrimination, place blacks at a particular disadvantage here. For first-generation immigrants there is an element of cultural expectation: to someone who has come from a rural or fringe urban area in the Third World, then lived for years in rotten, overcrowded private rooms, the worst Hackney Council can offer may not at first sight seem so awful. In addition, blacks are almost certainly, on average, less aware than whites of their rights and options, and of the limited but real ways in which the system can be manipulated to their advantage.

In education, immigrants are more likely to live in poor neigh-bourhoods and hence to go to poor schools. They are less likely to be aware of their rights to keep the child at home till the school of their choice has a vacancy. Their home backgrounds are more overcrowded, more insecure. The language spoken at home may be foreign or non-standard English. Racialism among teachers seems an unlikely explanation for poor performance, since Asians often outperform whites. Children of West Indian origin suffer from additional handicaps, in particular the very high proportion of single mothers and the greater proportion of working mothers with unsocial hours of work. White children facing a similar combination of handicaps often do spectacularly badly at school, too.

In each case the institutions do operate in such a way that the outcome for the average coloured person is less favourable than the outcome for the *average* white. A part of this difference is due to widespread conscious racialism among individuals, which must be combated by stricter enforcement of the law, and unconscious racialism which can be modified by race-awareness training.

As for the rest of the difference, I believe the root of the problem is this. British society operates greatly to the disadvantage of the uncertificated, the less articulate, those who are unaware of their rights and how to assert them, those on low incomes, with low skills or outmoded skills, manual workers generally, non-property-owners, single parents, the handicapped, and the children of all these groups – whatever their colour.

Immigrants are over-represented among these groups, hence the system operates to their disadvantage too: but it is primarily because of class bias rather than racial bias. Thus institutional racialism is none other than institutional class-ism, as seen from one particular standpoint. It crushes poor working-class whites as well as blacks, and divides them against each other into the bargain.

This has important lessons for the devising of solutions to racial disadvantage. The danger in providing a privileged deal for the black marginal working class through positive discrimination is that it could well alienate the white marginal working class even further and make them more racially prejudiced than they already are. Positive discrimination in favour of the disadvantaged, regardless of their colour, would have less ambivalent results. What both groups need is roughly the same: better education, especially at the formative pre-school level; better training, pay, conditions; promotion chances less tied to formal qualifications; better information and advocacy over welfare rights; better control over the quality of services at local level; better access to housing, jobs and capital; and, in the sphere of council housing, careful and sensitive treatment by housing officials to ensure that disadvantaged groups are fully aware of their rights and options, and do not come away with a worse deal than average. Pressing for a better deal for the marginalized working class *as a whole* will automatically benefit both whites and blacks, and will help to eliminate the social and economic roots of racial prejudice and racial hatred at the same time.

The Hidden Police State

There is, however, one area in which racialism has been institutionalized and politicians of both major parties have given way to the racial prejudice of the white working class: that is, over immigration laws. No one can seriously expect a country with steadily rising unemployment, impending technological upheavals and housing shortages to keep an open door to immigration. Nor can recession itself be relied on to keep the flow to manageable proportions, for however bad things get here, they will always look rosier than the lot of the underemployed or the landless poor in many developing countries. As long as international inequalities persist, international migration will continue and is likely to be restricted in countries with a labour surplus.

But it is the manner of control in Britain that has become increasingly racialist and inhuman. As the law stood in 1982, white Common Market entrants could come and go as they pleased, while the category of 'patrial' allowed many white citizens of the dominions a similar freedom. It is on coloured people that the brunt of restrictions falls, and is intended to fall. The explicit policy of both parties has been, first, to prevent new inflows, second, to treat those already here equally and humanely. But the two objectives are hard to combine: in practice the increasingly harsh application of the first principle has interfered with the second. It has made the inner city the location of experiences unprecedented in a supposedly democratic state with a full range of human rights: of humiliations and family separations, of raids and interrogations, of detentions without trial and arbitrary expulsions.

Yasher Ishmailoglu is the Turkish community worker at the Hackney Cypriot Centre. He came to England, in 1972, because he could not get a job in Cyprus owing to the Turkish community leaders' policy of boycotting the Greek administration. His first marriage broke up because of the amount of time he was spending on community work. He met his second wife at his brother's wedding in Cyprus and sent for her in 1979. But the couple had to undergo a lengthy and unpleasant interrogation before his fiancée was admitted for residence.

Ishmailoglu remembers well: 'They took the attitude that it was not up to them to prove that my marriage was a fraud, it was up to me to prove it was genuine. They asked me all kinds of questions, where did I find her, what colour dress was she wearing when we first met. And they ask very personal questions, why was there such a big age difference between us, why my first wife left me, and stupid things, how much money I had in the bank, what TV programmes I watched. Do you watch cowboy films or the news, do you watch Dallas or Coronation Street? Are you a member of a political party? Do you belong to the Communist party, or the Labour Party? Have you committed any offences? I felt as if I was a guilty person, as if I am going through an experience where I have committed a crime and was being interrogated by the police, like in Turkey when I was interrogated by the military authorities. Then after one hour she started to ask me the same questions in a different way, to try to catch me. She said, for example, "Let me just check these points through again, now, it was at the airport you first met her wasn't it?" I said it was at my brother's wedding. She said, "Oh, sorry, I forgot."

'After that they took my wife in separately, with an interpreter. They asked her the same questions, to see if she gave the same answers as me. They asked her if she was forced by her mother or father to marry me, how much her father pay me to bring her here. Then they asked her: if we refuse and we send you home to Cyprus, what will you do? That question stayed in my wife's head for two months. She had the impression that they would refuse her, she kept this fear until the letter came saying she was free to stay. And they ask both of us, has she got a boy-friend or have I got a girl-friend? That kind of question may never occur to you, but when they ask it, afterwards it sticks in your mind. I was preparing for weeks ahead, and prepared my wife, and I know about the regulations, but still I was hurt. So what is it like for those who are not prepared?'

Relatives coming to visit, immigrants returning from extended trips back home (common for funerals and weddings), face interrogations that bring home to most of them the unambiguous message that their kind are not wanted in Britain. There is a growing incidence of passport checks at some hospitals and un-announced raids on workplaces.

One victim of such a raid was Gansuc Calane, a thirty-year-old Gujarati from the former Portuguese enclave of Daman, 150 kilometres north of Bombay, taken over by India in 1961. Calane lives with his wife Hasuben and their two sons, Arvind, eight, and Jayesh, ten months, in a single room of a typical three-storeyed rented house on Rectory Road. The ground floor is given over to a doctor's surgery. At the back is a badly constructed extension which is visibly sinking into the ground. Half the doorbells are broken. The stairs are uncarpeted and some of the floor-boards broken. Five separate households share the two upper floors: on the first floor, where washing is draped across the landing, are two East African families, each with two rooms. On the second floor, with one room each, are a Kenyan Asian (just about to be made redundant from his job at Lesney's Matchbox Toys) and his Gujarati friend, a tailor; and the Calanes. Their room measures about 3½ metres by 4 metres. A large double bed takes up half the width and breadth. Most of the remaining floor space is occupied by the baby's cot, a wardrobe, a red plastic sofa with deep holes gouged in the arms. A mauve single mattress, leaning against the wall, is put down on the floor at night for Arvind to sleep on. In winter, draughts blow along the floor through gaps in the louvred windows and holes in the floor-boards along the rear walls, and condensation – 4 or 5 litres of it every day – streams down the walls and drips from the ceiling on to the blue carpet. Not surprisingly, Arvind suffers from rheumatism. Hasuben, a pretty twenty-seven-year-old in kunta and trousers, cooks in a tiny kitchen roughly 2 metres square, with an ancient, blackened gas cooker. The toilet is one floor down, shared with the two single men, and has no seat. The bath, also on the first floor, is shared by all five households – eleven people in all.

Calane's father was a Daman smallholder. Their land, nearly a hectare in area, provided a sufficiency in rice, until Gansuc married in 1971. Then other means of survival had to be found, and local jobs were few. The Calanes decided to sell their land and go into debt to buy Gansuc a ticket out of India. As he had no relevant work experience, he could not get a British work permit. Having a Portuguese passport, he went to Lisbon. There he worked as a cook at a fried-chicken restaurant. In 1975 he got a British job through an agency, submitted references from the Lisbon restaurant to the Department of Employment, and obtained a work permit. He came over in November 1975 and started work as an assistant cook in Hammersmith. In 1976 he got a job at the Hilton Hotel and moved to Hackney, where he found his present accommodation by the simple expedient of asking Asians he met on the street if they knew of rooms to let. Every month he sent money back home to his wife and parents. His work permit was renewed from year to year until November 1979, when he was granted full resident status. In March 1980 he brought Hasuben and Arvind over from India to live with him. He was well thought of at the Hilton and got promotion.

Everything seemed to be going well, until the fateful day of Thursday, 22 May 1980. At about 3 o'clock that afternoon, an hour before Calane was due to finish work, immigration officials raided the Hilton. Upwards of a hundred immigrant workers – Poles, Chinese, Africans, Asians – were rounded up in the hotel ballroom and asked to fill in forms.

'I could not fill in form,' Calane explains. 'At that time I'm not properly reading and writing and speaking English. They say, OK fair enough, just you sitting here when it's your turn we call you. I sitting with overall, no choice to get changed, and I don't know what's going on. Then they take me and others and put us in van and take everybody to police station. They questioned me till 4 a.m., how long you lived in India, which hotel you work in India, I told them I did not work in hotel in India. They ask, how you go to Portugal, who gave you passport, who gave you permit, and this and that. That time I'm very upset, I made little mistakes, I'm not remember which year I left India. They ask which restaurant I'm working in in Lisbon, I remember the name, but not the address. I said you give me passport and I will go and look and come back in a week. They said you can't do that. Later they came in and said, we looked for this place and we didn't find it, this is wrong address, you never work in Portugal.'

Calane must have submitted a convincing reference to the Department of Employment to obtain a work permit, but the department was not in the habit at that time of keeping them for future reference. Because Calane could not prove his reference was genuine, it was assumed to be false. The onus of proof was placed on him, five years after the event, and the only evidence lay in another country which Calane was not allowed to visit to gather evidence for his case. Nor can the officials have looked very hard for the restaurant he quoted to them, for Calane was declared an illegal immigrant on the same day as the raid, and required to report weekly to the immigration office in Southwark, pending deportation. It was typical of the increasingly harsh application of the 1971 Immigration Act, directed originally at people landing in small boats in the dead of the night. After 1979, it was used with a growing lack of fairness and compassion against wider and wider categories of minor alleged irregularities.

Two years of attempts to revoke the order followed, but despite the efforts of a solicitor (which cost Calane £250), of the Joint Council for the Welfare of Immigrants and of the local MP; despite the birth, on 26 August 1981, of Calane's second son, Jayesh – proud possessor, by virtue of being born here, of a British passport – the Home Office would not shift an inch. On 26 October 1981, Timothy Raison at the Home Office wrote to Stanley Clinton Davies, MP: 'I am satisfied that Mr Calane is an illegal entrant having obtained his work permit by producing false references. Arrangements have been made for Mr Calane to be removed from the UK. His British-born child will be expected to accompany him.' At this point the Hilton Hotel, very reluctantly, gave Calane his notice, but the glowing reference they provided, typed on an impressive-looking card, showed clearly that Calane possessed the qualities which his Portuguese reference was required to prove: 'We have always found Mr Calane to be honest, extremely hard-working and courteous. He performed his duties to our entire satisfaction and we would not hesitate to recommend him highly to any future employer.'

Calane was out of work for five weeks, then found a night job at the Café Royal, working from 10 p.m. to 8 a.m., and on Fridays going straight from work to report at the immigration office. Bowing to what seemed inevitable, Calane asked to be 'removed' back to India where all his relatives lived – his wife has an Indian passport. But the immigration officials appear to have grown impatient at the interminable delays involved in getting an Indian visa, and decided to send him to Portugal. They informed him of this change of plan when he reported in on Friday, 19 March 1982 – the same day as the Holly Street stabbings.

'I say, no, I don't want to go, I no relatives there, no jobs there. If you want to send me I want to go to my own country, India. He say no. I say I don't want to go, I'm not going, that's it. So he say OK you wait, then he say, OK Mr Calane, I want to go and see your Mrs and speak with her, but when we got into car he cheat me very much, he took me to police station [it appears that the official believed Mr Calane could no longer be relied on to go on reporting to them, and used his powers under the 1971 Immigration Act to detain him without charge or other normal legal rights]. All night Mrs is not sleeping, she is thinking, where am I going? Her heart is very strong, or if another person, she would kill herself. Next day they took me to Ashford Remand Centre. People in Ashford not sleeping, worry, worry, every day. Every day they bring three, four people, every day three, four go night and day to send for their own country. My wife very worry. She went to social security, she say my husband in gaol, me and my two children got no money for food. They say no, law says we can't give you any money [illegal immigrants are not entitled to supplementary benefit but may receive a lower level of emergency payment]. JCWI gave her some money. But we didn't pay the rent for five weeks, we didn't pay the milkman, my Mrs borrow money from my friend. Just for food he loan her £127.'

At Ashford Calane was given a letter informing him, in the usual stilted officialese, that he would be sent to Lisbon on flight BA 438 on 26 March. The intention was to send the whole family to Portugal, where they knew no one, had no money, no accommodation, and little prospect of a job. Under representations from the Joint Council for the Welfare of Immigrants, the Home Office agreed to send Calane ahead, alone, so he could prepare the ground for his family. Calane was taken to a hostel at Gatwick on Wednesday, 7 April. But officials seem to have got worried that he might not send for his family, and might leave them here as a burden on the taxpayer, so he was taken back to Ashford. The JCWI persuaded officials to keep trying for a visa for India. Realizing it was pointless to keep Calane in detention indefinitely, they released him on 23 April, after thirty-seven days.

His liberty had been restored – but the loss of it for so long had cost him his job at the Café Royal. He went to the social security and was refused supplementary benefit. All he was getting when I saw him was an emergency payment of £36 a week – almost £30 a week lower than the supplementary-benefit scale. He had no success in finding another job. He was deep in debt, with little prospect of paying it off. He was no longer able to send his parents any money, though they depended entirely on his remittances: 'My father is very upset. He write that he is praying God about what happened to his son. I worry about them, how are they living. I worry, worry about my family, not just about the passport, but also about the life.' When I left him he was left hanging in suspense, threatened with eviction for rent arrears, and waiting for the visa for India to come through. Immigrants like Calane are living in what, for them at least, is a police state that denies many basic human rights. Calane was held to be guilty because he could not prove his innocence, and denied the facilities to prove his innocence. He was interrogated, confused and entrapped. He was arrested and detained without charge, and held without trial at Her Majesty's pleasure. He was deprived of a job with which he could support his dependants, and then denied the state support of even a poverty-level income.

And he still faced removal to India where there were in 1982 some 18 million unemployed, with the small consolation that one day, when he grew up, baby Jayesh would one day have the right to come and live in Britain without let or hindrance. In the year 2017, when Gansuc is an old man of sixty-five, Jayesh will have the right to apply to bring his parents over to live with him.

Prophecy is nowhere so easy as in England. The revolution must come. It is already too late to bring about a peaceful solution. I think the people will not endure more than one more crisis.

Friedrich Engels on the English working class, 1844

When people submit to force, they do not do so willingly, but because they are not strong enough.

Mencius (tr. D. C. Lau)

It was a curious feature of the second slump that, the more capitalism appeared to manifest its failure, the more proud, strident and aggressive grew the eulogies of the Western way of life, of freedom, of democracy, of human rights.

It should be clear by now that the poor of Britain, of whom the inner city contains more than its share, do not enjoy much in the way of economic and social rights. What is less widely appreciated is that they do not, in any meaningful way, enjoy the compensatory benefits of full civil rights or of freedom, democracy or equality before the law. No secret police, no written law, no overt repression, no explicit arrangements cause this state of affairs. It is simply the result of a tendency observed in almost all human societies without the strongest safeguards and common values to prevent it: political power and economic power go hand in hand. And the converse: economic weakness and political weakness are found together, clasped in a vicious circle. Economic weakness results in political weakness, which in turn prevents effective measures being taken to alleviate economic weakness.

The inner city, and the major problems of its disadvantaged residents, result from systematic defects in our society. But this is not all. It is clear, too, that even in the terms of this broad framework of legalized injustice, individual injustices arise continually:

injustices in the administration of systems that are already unfair, insults added to injuries. These are so widespread in Hackney that I have hardly met a single individual who has not been the victim of some form of maladministration, malpractice or denial of rights: pay anomalies, errors in social-security payments, non-take-up of benefit, harassment by landlords, delays in repairs, denial of effective family-planning methods, and, generally, rough and insensitive treatment.

The scale and frequency of these occurrences is such that they cannot possibly all arise by chance. Nor are they due to the fortuitous concentration in Hackney of a peculiarly nasty or in-efficient bunch of bureaucrats. I have, in fact, come across many such tales in many other poor areas. The real reason is that administrative error and inefficiency, and private torts, are far more widespread in a poor area than they would be in a wealthier place. And they add, sometimes intolerably, to the trials of already unfortunate lives.

Part of the cause lies with the sheer burden of work for agencies in poor areas: manpower is growing daily less adequate to deal with the number of cases, or with the gravity of each one. The frequency of shocking details and of emotional outbursts must, in the end, blunt the senses of officials at the receiving end, especially as many of these are themselves quite badly paid.

Yet there is a more fundamental reason. It is that the poor, who are generally also the less well-educated and less articulate, are ill informed about their rights, and are not provided with accessible channels to assert them. Faced with an official who says blandly, 'I'm afraid you are not entitled to that benefit,' or, 'Our computer records show that you owe us £50 more than you say you owe us,' there is a widespread tendency to accept what is said, partly out of deference, more commonly because the victim does not possess the back-up of education, reference books and filed records that legitimize the statements of officials even when they are mistaken.

There are, of course, many who do not accept what is said, but few of them are aware of the proper channels for asserting the rights that have been denied them. The most common approach is to protest to the person who has just denied the right, to argue, to remonstrate. This often has little effect because the official is put on the defensive, and the arguments are not presented in a form that officials consider legitimate – they may be garbled, or in poor English, emotional, founded on ideas of natural justice rather than regulations, full of irrelevancies, lacking in hard evidence. The official proceeds to deny the right again. The complainant, meeting a failure of communication, breaks down, or breaks out in abuse, occasionally in violence.

At this stage the victim of maladministration may give up and go away in disgust, unaware of alternative channels of complaint. Those channels are not usually on the same premises. They are usually at a separate address or another agency. They will involve costly journeys by public transport, lost time, nervous stress, social embarrassment, and quite possibly another failure at the end of it. Most people, even with a strong grievance, throw in the towel at this point.

Figures on official complaints tend to confirm this view. Though one might expect the number of complaints to increase at a time of shortage of resources and cuts in administrative staff, the opposite seems to be the case. Nationally, only about one in ninety claims for supplementary benefit led to an appeal in 1978, but in 1980 only one claim in 116 was appealed. Industrial tribunals heard 44,000 cases in 1978. Two years later, despite a massive increase in dismissals, only 36,100. The ombudsman structure was virtually insignificant. The central government ombudsman received only 1,031 complaints of maladministration in 1980, of which 70 per cent were rejected. The local-government ombudsman had 2,920 complaints (80 per cent were turned down). The health-service ombudsman had a mere 647 complaints, of which 87 per cent were rejected. These figures are for the whole country. Far from indicating a general level of satisfaction and good performance, they simply illustrate the very low rate at which complaints systems are used. If Hackney's residents were of the kind that registered official complaints, they could match the ombudsmen's national totals without any outside assistance.

What does make a difference, for a less-educated person dealing with the authorities, is the help of an advocate, usually an educated person, and usually middle-class, who can deal with public or private bodies on their own terms. Time and again one sees how the intercession of a social worker, a trade-union official, a councillor, MP or voluntary advice worker suddenly transforms the situation. Yet if public and private bodies were operating properly, that is, ensuring that their clients received all their rights, and policing their own activities, advocacy should make no difference whatsoever. And advocacy is not easy to come by in the inner city. All the sources of advocacy are grossly overworked, and several have been cut back because of public-spending restrictions at precisely the time when they are most needed.

Inequality before the Law

The ultimate channel of redress for the individual is the law, that august institution that allegedly balances the merits of the parties and their evidence, blind to the size of their wallets. The law in Britain is an absurdly expensive business. The legal professions enjoy a well-controlled monopoly of access to the ears of judges. Yet despite the monopoly, and despite the central importance of the matter, legal services are private. We do not have a National Legal Service.

Legal aid is meant to equalize the chances of the poor. It works well, generally, to provide them with rudimentary representation in criminal cases, and with cheap divorces. But it is of little or no assistance in a very wide range of civil-law cases of the kind that crop up frequently in a poor working-class area. Legal aid cannot be obtained for cases of unfair dismissal or disputes about redundancy money. Unions are supposed to help here, but the most vulnerable workers are usually the least unionized. Legal aid does not cover crucial types of housing cases such as those involving security of tenure or enforcement of repairs on a landlord. It cannot be obtained for complaints against the police, nor for any of the tribunals which deal with a range of matters crucial to the poor, such as supplementary benefits, national insurance, rent or industrial injuries. And it is, in practice, impossible to obtain for the vast majority of civil cases: costs cannot be recovered on claims for less than £500, and legal aid is not granted where costs cannot be recovered. Very few poor people ever spend that kind of money. In the vast majority of civil cases the poor – if they stand at all – stand alone, either as plaintiffs or as defendants, against public author- ities or private interests with greatly superior resources. It would not be an exaggeration to say that civil law is overwhelmingly used *against* the poor, and is virtually non-existent when the poor wish to use it in their favour, except for cases taken up by law centres. Hackney has an active law centre. It can take on cases that legal aid does not assist, but can cope with only a small proportion of the potential demand.

Shoreditch County Court is a good place to see the civil law in operation in Hackney. Court number two is cavernous and tall, like a church nave. Long curtains filter out the light of the morning sun. Barristers in curled wigs and gowns, ruffs and bands and stiff collars, sweep in like clergy, while at the back, on the pews, wait a large but quiet congregation, alone or in family groups, some with their babies, most in their Sunday best. Their air is of tense expectation, of faint hope, of dejection and anxiety. They stand reverently as the registrar strides in, thin-faced, aquiline and bearded.

The cases for the day are all housing cases brought by Hackney Council against tenants in rent arrears, or squatters. The vast majority of the sixty-odd defendants are unrepresented, and the cases are rattled through at the rate of one every five or ten minutes. The defendants step into the box and stand, nervous and alone, relying on memory, emotion, appeal to human fairness. They face a battalion of lawyers and housing officials armed with ribboned briefs, records and regulations. Most of the defendants are on low incomes, some are not getting rent or rate rebates. There are a number of women whose husbands have deserted them, saddling them with rent arrears. But there are also tenants who consider that they, not the council, have a grievance: people who, in total ignorance of the letter of the law, have tried to seek justice in their own manner. Most of these have withheld their rent as a protest against neglected repairs, or as a way of getting back money they claim the council owes them, for damages, or for cash out of their own pocket spent on essential repairs. There are indeed legal ways of doing this, but these people have just gone ahead and taken their own action, and it has rebounded on them. They bring in exhibits like bagfuls of defective plugs, or jam-jars full of cockroaches, to illustrate their points, but they are immaterial to the suit in hand, and the registrar does not even look at them.

Case Number 8113849, *London Borough of Hackney* v. *Bowles & Bowles*, was one such case. Joseph Bowles is a very short, soft-spoken man in his later fifties, accompanied by his sixteen-year-old daughter Andrea. Bowles had run up no less than £1,110.64 of rent arrears, more than a year's worth, in protest over the state of his council home, half of a crumbling Victorian terraced house, for which he was paying the princely sum of £19.11 a week in rent and rates. Bowles explained the problems, but they were not relevant to the council's claim. The registrar ordered Bowles to pay off the arrears at the rate of £5 a week. 'You've got to show you're willing,' says the registrar in a parental tone. 'If you show you're willing, then perhaps the council would put things right.'

Joseph Bowles is not what one would call a fortunate man. He used to work at a shoe factory, but it closed in 1972 and he was out of work for the next six years. In 1978 he got his present job as a nightwatchman at a depot for Hackney Council refuse vehicles. He works a fourteen-hour shift, five nights a week, from 5.30 p.m. to 7.30 a.m., and takes home £79 (1981) for seventy hours.

The Bowleses occupy the bottom two floors of a house in Glyn Road, Clapton, close to, and barely above the level of, Hackney Marshes, and subject to every form of damp known to man. The front gate swings on a loose post. The entrance steps down to the front door are fissured and crusted with mould. The basement bay-window frames are soft with rot, one of the front door's glass panels is smashed, the wooden doorstep is crumbling to pieces. The stench of damp hits you as the front door opens. All the basement walls have rising damp to about half a metre. In many places the plaster is broken off right through to the joists. In the lounge, the floor is bowed like a switchback and the carpet is literally as sodden as a peat bog and squelches underfoot.

'Ever since we moved in we've been getting flooded when it rains heavily,' Bowles explains. 'The drains bubble up. We have the firemen in here at least once a year. I've had to throw away several carpets and sofas.' 'I won't let my husband go into debt to get new ones now, they'll just get ruined,' says Mrs Bowles, a nervous, plump lady of forty-five.

We continue the tour. Two windows in the bathroom are smashed from break-ins the previous year, and have not been repaired. Upstairs, one of the three bedrooms is unusable. The slates fell in four years ago, and the rain has caved in about one-third of the internal ceiling and made long streaks down the walls where it courses. Because of this, the Bowleses' ten-year-old son Christopher has to share a bedroom with his older sister.

The Bowleses say they have visited the local estate office dozens of times to ask for repairs. 'Whenever I go, they tell me they can't do it, it's condemned property,' says Bowles. 'Once they did send a lad round to do the window frames, but he said they only allowed him two and a half hours to do the job and he couldn't do it in twice the time. So he didn't do it – I've still got the wood he left, it's a nice piece of mahogany, it's been here over four years [Bowles was a victim of Hackney repair-workers' bonus system, described in Chapter 5: the worker probably stood in danger of facing a bonus loss, and skipped the job, reporting it as completed]. Mrs Bowles: 'When I go over there, they keep saying they'll come, but they never do come. They make excuses, because of our dogs.'

They go on to catalogue their tribulations. The dogs, four uncouth yelping mongrels that Mrs Bowles cows with a balding broom, are kept for security. The family have suffered two break-ins in the past year. On the last occasion the electricity meter was robbed of £100, which the Bowles had to repay. Mrs Bowles has become possessed by the fear of crime. 'I went over Millfields Park with the dogs last month, and a big black boy got me on the floor and tried to have sex with me. My dogs jumped at him and scared him off. A girl got raped there, I believe she's still in a coma. I have to keep in all day, I daren't go out. My husband does all the errands. I keep the curtains closed all the time so people think there's someone in. I get nervous at night when my husband's at work. I'm terrified to go out now. I've started to smoke now, I never used to and I can't afford to, but I've got to.' She also takes a high dosage of Valium and Disipal, a drug prescribed for trembling and pre-Parkinsonism, which is associated with prolonged use of tranquillizers.

The main problem in the children's lives is that, a few metres from their bedroom window, there is a twenty-four-hour minicab base, whose drivers often play loud music in the night, and who respond to requests for quiet with counter-complaints about the Bowleses' pack of dogs. Both the children lose a lot of sleep. 'Andrea was going to stay on at school,' says her mother, 'but she said she couldn't concentrate, I wanted her to work in a bank, she would have been good enough, but she's got a job in a clothing factory. The [education] welfare officer said Christopher could do well at school, they said he might be clever enough to go to university, but he has to stay at home one or two days a fortnight because he's being kept awake all night.'

To cap it all, on the top floor of the house lives an old man, deaf, dumb, and more than a little eccentric. He gets some social work support, meals on wheels and home help, but willy-nilly the Bowleses are inevitably the first line of assistance in emergencies and bear the stigma of sharing a house with him. Bowles complains: 'He walks about with a paper bag on his head and his coat done up with a string. My kids' schoolmates say to them: "That's your dad." They have to pretend they live in another house, up the road.'

Bowles and his wife are obsessed with the injustices they have suffered, especially in connection with housing. 'We been married nineteen years. We waited twelve years before we got this place. I seen all my workmates growing up from being babies with dummies in their mouths, and now they got houses, some of them nice ones, and we got this dump. My wife gets really depressed over other people getting better accommodation. I feel choked about it. They built Clapton Park estate opposite us, and we tried to get a place in there, but we couldn't. They painted the estate two or three times since then, but they ain't done my place once. And there's people up the road have a whole house from the council and they're only paying £16 a week. It's like if you were offered rotten potatoes and you were asked to pay the same price as new. We've been in for a transfer ever since we moved in here, but they say they can't rehouse us with these arrears. I'll pay this fine money now, I don't know how, I'll scrape around and pay it somehow. Before I went to court, I said to the wife, "Well, I don't care if they send me to gaol or chuck us out. What do I want to fight to stay in this place for?" But it's the kids, I don't want them to go into care.'

Bowles had never once used the channels of complaint open to him, never once complained to the local councillor or MP or any other advice agency, never sought legal advice (though the only source, on this matter, would have been the law centre). Instead he had simply gone back again and again to the place that was the source of his problems, battering his head on a brick wall. That behaviour was entirely representative of many of those I met. But Bowles has his own theory for what has happened to him, and if it is taken metaphorically rather than literally, it comes very close to the truth: 'It's all because I'm a bit small. They always kept me down. I ain't got no push, see, that's why. If I'd been a big bloke, they'd have taken notice. If you're small, they walk all over you.'

Mass Action

So far we have looked only at individual ways of obtaining redress. The seventies saw the blossoming of new concepts of community action, of neighbourhood self-help, of the value of collective pressure, through lobbying, demonstrations, publicity, to achieve a better deal for disadvantaged groups. What chance have these methods of correcting the political imbalance? The individual story is, alas, repeated at the community level. The ability to exert pressure is inversely related to need. It depends on knowledge of ways of forming legal organizations, of drawing up well-argued, well-documented cases, of the 'right' people to contact. It demands a fairly high level of formal education among leaders (or rare talents for autodidacticism), on possession of resources such as funds to pay for stationery, access to means of printing and of transport, on a surplus of mental and physical energy over and above that needed for work and survival. All these are attributes that are very much thinner on the ground among manual workers, people on low incomes, people with poor educational backgrounds, and very much thicker among the middle classes. There is no doubt that community action and community pressure work, but middle-class areas can make them work far better for themselves than poor areas, and hence are much better able to get more resources or to divert attempts to reduce their privileges. As a general rule, the more a particular group of people need justice or reform or more resources, the less are they equipped to fight for them by conventional means. This is the principal reason why, after four decades of the welfare state, no significant inroads have been made into reducing the numbers below the official poverty line of the time, or into reducing inequality, and why the inner cities and the peripheral regions have never succeeded in securing government action on the scale needed to reverse their decline.

Hackney has an untypically active voluntary sector which does valuable work, but most of it is staffed and dominated by a highly educated minority, and funded by government Partnership grants. The most authentic and most powerful working-class community organizations in Hackney, as in most inner-city areas, are the tenants' associations on council estates. In 1981 there were fifty associations officially recognized by Hackney Council, for a total of ninety-two borough estates. Their strongest side is social: there are twenty bingo clubs, twenty pensioners' clubs, fourteen youth clubs, eleven play groups, six lunch clubs, five kung fu groups, four mother-and-toddler groups, one women's self-defence group and one Chinese boxing club. Many tenants' associations are virtually moribund, but some of them offer a stimulating programme of attractions. Fellows Court, for example, provides ladies' keep-fit classes, swimming and slimming clubs, pensioners' and youth clubs, pensioners' dancing, ballroom dancing and tap dancing. Holly Street offers netball on Mondays, bingo Tuesdays and Wednesdays, Karate Mondays, Tuesdays and Fridays, pensioners' club on Wednesdays, reading classes on Saturdays, and disco every other Friday.

But it is the political side of tenants' associations, their function as pressure groups, to demand improvements on their estates and oversee the performance of estate managers and repair departments, that is the weakest. The turn-out to general meetings is often absurdly low – even on the most active estates it rarely runs to 10 per cent; in the least active, it may be 1 per cent or less. Effectiveness therefore depends far too heavily on the quality of leadership. Often an estate may have no one willing to shoulder the burden – there have been efforts by community workers to form associations on some of the worst estates without any success. Often it is only the dedication and ability of one, two or three individuals that keeps things going, and when they move on – as the most able often do, to better housing elsewhere, or to a seat on the council – the tenants' association may collapse unless it can find a replacement.

Geffrye Court, the Hoxton block where Doris Davies* lives, did not have an association at the time of writing. But one issue galvanized the ladies into action in 1981. Tenants were paying £4 a week for hot water, but a new energy-conserving scheme, heating water by pulses rather than constantly, meant that those who got up in the early morning (as cleaners and shift-workers do) had to boil a kettle to wash or shave. Ellie Riley* complained that she could only get ankle-deep hot water for a bath and had to have a heater in her airing cupboard because her tank wasn't warm enough.

'We decided we'd have to put pressure on,' says Ellie. With great efforts, they managed to raise two petitions in June 1980 and March 1981, but although they sent these in, nothing happened – and they had not made copies. Then they contacted the Liberal councillor Jeff Roberts, who arranged for a deputation to the housing-management committee. 'We went round knocking on doors,' Ellie remembers, 'but hardly anyone would come out. They said things like "We got to cook a dinner". I said, "You'd run half-way across Hoxton to save half a penny on a pound of butter, and Hackney Council's diddling you out of £4 a week and you won't go?"' In they end they managed to find three volunteers, plus Ellie, Doris and Doris's daughter Maureen Cooper.* It speaks volumes that every one of them was female (just as it was the women – mostly the same women – who did all the work to organize an estate party for the kids on the occasion of a royal wedding the following month; the men stood around on the balconies watching).

At 7.30 p.m. on 29 June 1981 our six Hoxton ladies filed uncertainly into the wood-panelled committee room in Hackney town hall and found out that they were supposed to sit on the leather-seated chairs at one end reserved for the public. In front of them, ranged around long mahogany tables, sat the councillors

* See page 441. These are not their real names.

and higher council officials, whose pay levels and generous payments for attending evening meetings were clearly discernible in their immaculate suits, shirts and expensive ties. The standing orders put deputations firmly in their place: only six allowed (to avoid intimidation by numbers); and 'only one member thereof shall be at liberty to address the committee and for not more than ten minutes except in reply to questions from members of the committee, and the matter shall not be further considered by the committee until the deputation shall have withdrawn'. The elaborate wording, incomprehensible to our heroines, conceals the purpose: to prevent tenants and ratepayers grilling councillors and officials, to reduce their collective action to an orderly, brief oration by a single individual. Some of the most effective deputations of recent years have ignored these rules, coming in force, shouting, demanding, refusing to be shut up. But our ladies obeyed the rules.

Ellie Riley, bulky in her white raincoat, rises to address the meeting.

(*Ellie*) 'Well, we come up to find out how it is that we're paying £4 a week for hot water and we're not getting £2-worth. If I was expecting six pounds of potatoes for 30p and you only gave me three pounds, wouldn't you say you were diddling me?'

(*Councillor, putting a spoke in the wheel*) 'Could I ask how many complaints have been *officially received* on this matter? I feel sure we should have had an overwhelming supply of complaints if the allegations were true.'

(*Maureen, shouting*) 'When you lived on our estate you never did nothing for us.'

(*Chairman*) 'Only one member may address the committee.'

(*Maureen*) 'He's trying to be funny with us, that's why.'

(*Official, defensive*) 'We've not received a single complaint.'

(*Ladies*) 'You have! You have! What about our petitions?'

(*Official*) 'I don't recall any questions on this matter being put at the district liaison committee [where housing-committee members meet tenants' associations every quarter – Geffrye Court has no association and therefore does not attend]. We have looked at this estate on two occasions and not found anything that gave us cause for concern.'

The councillors then question Ellie, who explains the nature of the problem in more detail. But the delegation is not allowed to question in return. The chairman thanks Ellie paternalistically for her presentation. And the ladies leave the meeting, a good deal more angered than when they came. Maureen buttonholes Jeff Roberts outside.

(*Maureen*) 'Well, when can we come again? Because that was no use at all. They were telling lies.'

(*Ellie*) 'They've trodden Shoreditch into the ground since Hackney took it over.' .

Thus are the unlettered confused and confounded by procedures and requirements designed by the lettered. What Geffrye Court needed to match the weight of officialdom was carefully mustered evidence, copies of all correspondence, everything down in grammatical, correctly spelled writing. Instead, our ladies relied on the spoken word, dialect, anecdote, the power of truth. In a working-class area serviced by middle-class bureaucrats, it is easy for the bureaucrats to have it their own way – which is precisely why abuses do not come to light and therefore flourish more widely than in a middle-class area.

The ladies finally succeeded in having their hot-water problem sorted out, though dozens of others remained: repair delays, lack of play space or car space, poor cleaning services. The following year, Doris and Ellie leafleted the whole estate to try to form a tenants' association, but all but a handful of tenants were not interested.

The problems of organizing disadvantaged communities either to create facilities for themselves, or to exert pressure to gain a greater share of public resources, are enormous. Some of the problems stem from the structures of power: the literate, Latinate language of debate, the complexities of procedure and proper channels, the reluctance of 'representatives' to hand over any real power or concede any accountability (except to take them or leave them once every three to five years) to the people they are supposed to represent. Hackney's more radical Labour council elected in 1982 promised some interesting experiments in improving this situation.

But there are also problems stemming from within the community itself. The general level of participation in politics, unions, and social activities of most kinds decreases as you descend the social ladder. There are physical barriers to involvement, such as lack of cars and bad public transport, more people working unsocial hours, one-parent families unable to leave children, and the sheer exhaustion brought about by much manual work, all of which hold people back from evening meetings. There are psychological factors: the fear of crime, a lack of confidence in one's articulacy, a dislike of public arguments, cynicism about the responsiveness of established powers and disbelief in one's own power (both derived from long experience in every sphere of life).

There are social blocks, such the constant shifting of population, especially of those elements best suited to provide leadership. There is the mass of cleavages based on race, language, behaviour and the detailed ecological factors of the kind discussed in Chapter 12, all of which atomize communities into their constituent households. There is, as well, a deeper problem: a belief in most people, again based on experience, that it is usually more profitable to devote energies to bettering one's personal situation than to get involved in collective actions which may not move in the direction you wish, or if they do, may not succeed, or if they succeed, may produce, at best, only modest improvements. There is a widespread escapist mentality, that it is easier to try to get out of bad housing or bad employment than to fight collectively for improvements that benefit everyone, and by the same token, that it is easier to get out of the inner city than to stay and fight to change it. And if that fails, it is easier to bury your head in the sand, to slump in front of the television, to obliterate your troubles with drink or drugs, than to press on in a relentless struggle for justice.

There are a few of the tenants' associations that have had a considerable impact, usually for the good of their own estate, but not always for an increase in the general sum of happiness. The most successful of the associations over this period was at Lea View, a six-storey block built in 1939 that became a dumping-ground for homeless families and a' workshop for vandals and graffiti artists. In 1979 the moribund tenants' association was revitalized by the arrival of a housing-action project sponsored by the Mutual Aid Trust, a charity backed by the Institute of Community Studies which was working on a survey of Hackney at the time. The two paid project workers provided the energy, the expertise and the resources usually lacking in tenants' associations, and with the help of a tenant, Jack Davidson, an unemployed cabinet-maker, galvanized residents into meetings and petitions. In autumn 1980, as part of the Labour Council's programme to modernize all pre-war estates in the borough, a team of architects moved into an empty flat on Lea View and issued an invitation to tenants: 'Come and help us design the estate that you want to live in.' The plan that emerged looked leafy and utopian, having, for families, ground-floor maisonettes with their own gardens back and front. But the twilight of spending cuts began, and rumours began to spread that council officials had drawn up proposals to shelve Lea View's modernization so as to allow several hundreds of the 1,000 long-term empty council-owned houses to be rehabilitated. As a way of alleviating Hackney's housing stress, this idea made sense. But Lea View's 250 households were not going to be abandoned. On the night the issue was to be debated, the tenants' association organized a 200-strong procession to the town hall, complete with blazing torches and bawling babies, and in complete defiance of standing rules, surrounded and barracked the housing development committee. When the item was finally reached, towards midnight, the officers' report was overturned. Lea View kept its renewal programme, and the empty houses stayed empty. The campaign was a resounding success for Lea View. But as the housing budget was limited and declining, their gain could only be at the expense of others less well organized to exert pressure: estates with no tenants' associations, or weak ones, and the hundreds of scattered families without a home to call their own who would have been rehoused in the refurbished empties.

Thus the overall shortage of resources in inner-city and other poor areas, in comparison with the insatiable level of need, forces the organized poor to fight each other for priority. The winners are those who can exert the most pressure: not necessarily those in the greatest need.

Only a massive increase in the share of public funds going to deprived areas could put an end to this zero-sum game where one poor man's gain is another's loss. But so far there is only one form of collective action that has succeeded in increasing the total amount of resources available to inner cities: not peaceful demonstrations, not lobbies of Parliament, not academic reports. It is, alas, only riots and the fear of more riots that have got the inner city taken seriously. That is not a defence of rioting, but rather a condemnation of the political system that ignores and neglects urgent need until it reaches the crisis point of constituting a threat to civil order.

The Loneliness of the Long-Distance Canvasser

In the years in which it manifested its most blatant failings, the institution of representative democracy was also the focus of the most impassioned apologias. The Thatcher government under-lined that system's drawbacks more clearly than ever before: here was a government elected by only one-third of the electorate and which no less than 56 per cent of those who bothered to vote did not want. A government in which our hallowed 'representatives', supposedly voting according to their enlightened consciences, were reduced more than ever before to prime-ministerial stooges. A government which embarked on a course of wholesale economic and social destruction of which its manifesto contained not the slightest hint – for if it had, they would never have been elected.

None of these developments was unprecedented: they were simply an accentuation of what had gone before. Therefore long experience has taught the people of Hackney to harbour few illusions about the virtues of our political system. 'Politics?' said one black youth when I asked his views. 'Me no think about them thing, all them hypocrites, all them rubbish.'

Canvassing before elections, when the politically active hound the inactive into their very homes, is the time when the depth of political cynicism and apathy in a poor area become most appar-ent. Riding on his successes at Lea View, tenants' leader Jack Davidson stood as Labour candidate for Springfield ward in a borough-council by-election in 1981, and I followed him door-stepping. Eric Sheldon, a squat pensioner, opened his door in Oldhill Street on to a vista of crumbling walls and ceilings and an African doing up his trousers on the way out of the communal bathroom: 'Voting is useless, the trade unions run everything anyway. I have so many problems, my life is nothing but problems.

There is no underground here and no buses: where you have the underground, there you have also the buses.' Next to Datchler estate, a very nice one by local standards. Twenty-nine-year-old Jean Collins, standing in her postage stamp of a garden: 'It doesn't matter who gets in, it doesn't do no good. They never do what they say they will. The trouble is, I don't understand politics.' Anthony Herrick, thirtyish, peered out of his first-floor window: 'I doubt if I'll vote, I haven't voted for years. I'm not into politics. Too lazy? Yeah, that's probably it.' He is not offended by the suggestion, amused rather. 'Politics' is seen as something separate, up there, a sort of hobby, like bird-watching or classical music.

On to Fawcett estate, smeared with graffiti, courtyard walls stained with white where cisterns overflow. Here people are even more enclosed and resistant, eager to get rid of the canvassers so they can get on with surviving and fighting each other. Though they are, most of them, being minced alive by politicians, politics is not seen as something relevant to them. A man in his fifties, scabbed from shaving, in a collarless shirt, opens the door only long enough to hear who it is and slam it again as he shouts, with unaccountably bitter anger: 'I don't care who you are, I won't support any of you!' As if politicians of any shade are not only distant and alien, but bitter personal enemies, to be railed at whenever they appear.

It is one of many sad ironies in the inner city that, the poorer and more disadvantaged people are, the less likely they are to vote. The turn-out at elections in Hackney is chronically low. It is best at general elections. In 1974, for example, when the national turn-out averaged 73 per cent, only 53 per cent of voters in Hackney North and Hackney Central bothered to vote, and only 55 per cent in Hackney South. The turn-out is even lower when the voting is for the borough council, even though, among other things, it is the landlord of two out of three voters: 23 per cent in 1974 (London average, 36 per cent); 36 per cent in 1978 (London average, 43 per cent). Within Hackney, turn-out was lowest in those wards with the highest levels of council tenants, unemployed, single parents and immigrants.

Non-voting can be a healthy sign in a healthy society, arising from a general satisfaction with the way things are or a belief that the outcome will be fairly satisfactory whichever party wins. In Hackney, as in most of Britain, the opposite is the case. An immense number of people have no party preference for the very good reason that whichever party has been in power, things have gone badly for them. The attitude among many whom I asked for their views was a profound and weary cynicism and a belief that all politicians are con-men: 'A plague on both your houses.' They may be tempted into renewed hope by the Liberal–Social Democratic Alliance, but no doubt the attitude will soon revert to 'a plague on all three of your houses'. There is, as well, a low sense of efficacy, a conviction that however you vote, it will have so little effect that it is not worth going out of the relative warmth and safety of your home to do something about it. And that conviction is well founded. For the most significant power our system of democracy currently offers, the right to choose one's rulers every four or five years, is so insignificant from an individual point of view that wasting it is the act of a rational person.

The sense of powerlessness comes close to what Paulo Freire, talking of Latin America, termed the 'culture of silence' – a scepticism as to one's power to influence the course of events by any legitimate means, to make them, be it ever so little, just a little less unfavourable to one's happiness.

Inner-City MP

The linchpin of parliamentary democracy is, of course, the Member of Parliament. British MPs are generally overworked, but the burden on the inner-city member is such that even with the most heroic efforts he or she can do no more than a little to alleviate the mass of individual suffering in his or her constituency, nor can an MP influence legislation or the share-out of resources sufficiently to make much difference to the plight of his or her area.

Stanley Clinton Davis, MP for Central Hackney, does not look the inner-city type: pin-stripe suit, wavy black hair, upper-crust accent. But he has many local roots. He was born in Hackney, educated there until his school was evacuated in the war, returned there to work as a solicitor, and served on the council from 1959 until his election to Parliament in 1970. Though most of the seventies passed without much local flak, since about 1978 Davis has come under increasing fire from the expanding left wing of his constituency Labour Party. Before 1975, party membership in Hackney was overwhelmingly working class, as were the borough councillors, and the party was essentially little more than a skeletal machine that clanked into action at election time. The introduction of monetarist policies by Dennis Healey from 1976 on inevitably radicalized many party members, who saw them as a betrayal of Labour's ideals and policies, and many others who were personally affected by shrinking job opportunities and promotion blocks. It was from this feeling that the demand for MPs to be accountable to party members grew. In Hackney the radicalization process was speeded along by gentrification. The new owner-occupying intelligentsia came to dominate first the Hackney North constituency, then the centre, and in 1982 became a majority of the Labour group on the council. As happened in many parts of Britain over this period, the middle-class intelligentsia became the vanguard of the working class.

Davis became a prime target. He was no right-winger, being anti-EEC, pro unilateral disarmament, and a supporter of Labour's alternative economic programme. But as a junior minister in the 1975–9 Labour government, he had felt obliged to defend its record. He was openly opposed to the idea of accountability to his general management committee. He disregarded their recommendation to vote for Tony Benn in Labour's deputy leadership contest in 1981, and voted for Healey. And so determined efforts were made to oust Davis when he came up for reselection as parliamentary candidate on 12 November 1981, but he scraped through with twenty-nine votes to twenty-seven for his two more left-wing rivals (one of them a Militant supporter). The battle was typical of the fratricidal warfare, unleashed primarily by monetarism and recession, that split the Labour Party.*

One thing that Davis's critics cannot accuse him of is of shirking his constituency work, to which he has an unstinting commitment.

---

* The left finally ousted Davis when, in 1983, as a result of parliamentary boundary changes, his constituency was divided between North and South Hackney. Davis was not selected for either, and Hackney now had only two, instead of three, MPs.

Every Friday night he holds a surgery, either in the Labour and Trades Union Hall in Dalston Lane or, to make access easier, in a number of community halls on the larger estates.

An MP's surgery in the inner city is a distressing parade of human need in all its varieties. There is already a queue waiting when Davis's blue Ford Granada pulls up outside the Wally Foster community centre next door to Kingsmead estate at 6 p.m. on 25 June 1982. The child-health clinic serves as temporary office as the clients file in one by one. Davis hears them out, eliciting extra information, noting the salient points on a clean white sheet of paper and clipping it to any documentation they might bring, and explaining what he can, or cannot, do for them.

The first case is a lady in her sixties, who lives in a terraced council house. She has come to ask if anything can be done about her next-door neighbours, a young couple with two small children: 'They can't get a transfer because they're in rent arrears, so they're making my life hell to get themselves moved. I'm sure they're on drugs. The other night she went berserk and ran down the street screaming. She smashed our window at 4 in the morning. My husband refused to take his heart tablets. He says if it goes on like this it's not worth living anyway. I've got an ulcer, and I'm on Valium.' Davis promises to write to the council. Next are a neatly dressed, prosperous-looking couple who have four teenage children in a three-bedroomed house, and have been asking for a five-bedroomed place for six years. Some junior housing official misled them into thinking that if they spotted an empty one, they could have it. They spotted one and asked for it, only to be told that it had been allocated to another woman, with seven children. She is due to move in three days' time. Believe it or not, they have come to ask Davis if he can stop her. He tactfully points out that the woman with seven children also has problems: 'All I can do, I'm afraid, is go on nagging periodically on your behalf.'

Another man is seeking a transfer from remote Hackney Wick to 'somewhere convenient like Old Street', where he will be better placed to look for work; and a single mother is currently sharing a single bed with her three-year-old daughter in a small room in her parents' house: both of whom, like almost everyone, unaware of families living four to a room and sleeping three to a bed, believe that their own problems must be the worst in Hackney. Finally the community-centre porter nips in for a bit of free legal advice as to whether the council is liable if kids jump on his car roof while it is parked on borough property.

Davis moves on to Dalston Lane. When he arrives the small downstairs waiting-room is crowded with supplicants on steel and frayed-canvas chairs. He uses an office upstairs, so tiny that people sitting on opposite sides of it bang their knees together. Here cases concerning Hackney Council are filtered away from Davis, to borough councillors who hold surgeries in the same building. First of the MP's cases is a girl of Asian descent, in her late twenties, with two children aged ten and eleven. Her husband was sentenced to fifteen months for burglary a month ago. He's about to be transferred to the Isle of Wight. It is too far to visit; there are no educational facilities, she says, and her husband is illiterate; and, most important, her husband is said to have grassed up some people who have friends there. Davis promises to write to the Home Secretary, but holds out little hope. And so it rolls on and on: a woman who has been threatened with eviction for rent arrears – she has paid her money and had her rent book stamped, but the money never reached the town hall and the stamp turns out to be forged; a tall West Indian who wants help in a dispute over superannuation and compensation – Davis gasps as he pulls out his pay-slips for six years; another West Indian whose five teenage children are sleeping two and three to a bed, because a larger house they were allocated a year ago still has not been put in a condition where they can move in; a blonde lady in a crumpled blue mac whose landlord has had the gall to ask for *arrears* of a rent rise that is not due to *start* till ten months from now: 'I need someone of importance to write to him and tell him that I don't owe him a penny,' she says. And along with all the normal case-load an inevitable visit from one of several obsessional constituents, of whom Hackney is over-full: the wife is physically handicapped, the son is mentally handicapped, the husband, who has come tonight, has a speech defect that makes him sound like someone stammering into a microphone with intermittent current. Years of practice have enabled Davis to understand him, but the MP has still not succeeded in fathoming the full depths of the family's never-ending complex of housing and legal problems. This particular couple ring several times a week for half an hour at a time, and write long epistles running to thirty pages each. Davis simply cannot afford the time, and his secretary handles them.

Davis saw about twenty cases in all, an average night. Correspondence brings in more work. In all, Davis reckons he gets 1,500 to 2,000 new cases a year, five or six per day, equivalent to one in every ten or fifteen households in his constituency. He spends a couple of hours a day on such individual cases, plus the surgery of two to four hours a week – a rough average of twenty to thirty minutes to cover each case from start to finish. There is no time, except in the most unusual cases, for painstaking investigation of people's claims, let alone follow-up of official replies to check whether anything has been done. Special strings can be pulled occasionally, such as a personal interview with a minister, but that sort of political capital has to be carefully conserved. If Davis went demanding an interview on every case that, *per se*, merited it, he would soon lose the ability to get any interviews, where a Home Counties MP might see the minister on far less serious cases. Thus the sheer volume of desperate need in the inner city drowns out most individual cries.

What is most noticeable is the extent to which the MP is used, or abused, for cases that in a better-ordered system should never come to him, or never arise in the first place. People come, wasting their own time and the MP's, in a vain attempt to vault over impossibly long queues for housing or jobs. They come for free advice, for a sympathetic ear, for a shoulder to cry on. More frequently they come because they have been the victims of maladministration or injustice. On this type of case, Davis has most success with housing repairs, with social-security errors, and with fuel cut-offs. The degree of success he has with each agency is a direct measure of the routine inefficiency of that agency. The MP's time, thus, is diverted into providing advice and counselling services to make up for the shortage of public provision, and into correcting errors most of which should not arise if agencies were effectively managed and accountable to their users.

Sixteen hours is a massive chunk out of the precious week of an MP, but it is merely one of many calls on his time. He spends two or three hours a day at his solicitor's practice, which he has to keep going as an MP never knows, these days, when he might be unseated by electors or party members. Four or more visits are made around the constituency each week to meet organizations, businesses, or council. Then there are local Labour Party meetings – monthly reports to the general management committee, important demonstrations. And there is involvement in voluntary societies for multiple sclerosis and nuclear disarmament. Plus a role as Labour's spokesman on Latin America, the Caribbean, Canada and South Africa, involving meetings with visiting politicians and diplomats and occasional visits overseas.

The only public provision for assistance he gets is the normal MP's allowance of £8,500 a year, which leaves little after he has paid his secretary's salary. For research assistance, Britain provides nothing – Davis pays his own student children, out of his own pocket, to do odd pieces of research. He also has the help, like many other MPs, of visiting US undergraduates of mixed abilities and political leanings, assigned to British MPs for ten or twelve weeks at a time as part of their degree course at the University of Maryland, and inevitably limited as to continuity and commitment. Davis's aide in June 1982 was Dwight Sullivan, a slim, well-spoken young man. Sullivan was shocked by the relative powerlessness of British MPs compared with American legislators, who have virtually no surgery cases to deal with and publicly funded staffs of fourteen for each Congressman and thirty for each Senator.

Thus overburdened and under-resourced, our parliamentary representatives inevitably find their prime roles of legislation and invigilation severely hampered. The pace of legislation, and therefore the pace of reform, is slowed and its quality is surely reduced. Equally serious, or perhaps even more so, it is quite impossible for MPs to monitor the impact of previous legislation or to keep a watchful eye over the actions of governments and bureaucracies.

Our system of representation by single-member constituencies also militates against reforms that could help the urban or regional poor, and, indeed, against any widespread awareness of their problems. Britain's marked social segregation has created constituencies the bulk of which are either predominantly English middle class and Tory, or predominantly working class, Welsh or

Scottish, and Labour. Thus the bulk of Tory MPs, and indeed of Tory voters, have no direct experience of widespread and acute need which could awaken their compassion.

For the inner-city MP the problem of lack of widespread awareness is even more acute. Inner-city Labour MPs have trouble convincing even other Labour MPs, who do not represent inner-city areas, of the extent and gravity of problems in housing, in employment, and in law and order. Hence, despite strenuous efforts, they have been unable to secure investment incentives for inner-city areas in the South-East and Midlands to rival those available for the depressed regions.

The same problems that beset MPs also affect local councillors. The work-load is less, in terms of hours, but most councillors have full-time jobs to hold down on weekdays. Council meetings, party meetings and voluntary group meetings take up at least four nights a week for conscientious councillors. Correspondence and reading council material can take another six to eight hours a week. Agenda for committee meetings are often bulkier and more complex than full-length novels, covering everything from the minutest detail of tenders to paint a single fence, through multi-million new building or rehabilitation housing schemes, to borough-wide policy on major issues. Generally councillors do not have time to read agenda, but concentrate on those items of specific interest to them.

Most councillors now hold surgeries, and though their case-load – six or seven problems a week for the most active – is much smaller than an MP's, it takes up an equal proportion of their available time. And most of the cases should never come to them either. Anthony Kendall, Labour leader in 1982, explains: 'Mostly we are putting right what bureaucracy has done awfully: cock-ups that a bit of simple thinking could have put right, bad communications where people have not been told what's going on, often just the rude way people are treated.'

Thus councillors are hardly in a better position than MPs to check whether their decisions are having the desired effect, or whether they are being properly implemented. Peter Kahn, deputy leader in 1982, says: 'We are making policy decisions which the officers don't carry out.' In 1982, the new, more radical Labour council appointed full-time political advisers to the chairmen of committees, to get round the bureaucratic blockage and establish direct lines to local organizations and people.

But ultimately the only effective check on the day-to-day actions of central and local government is the public itself. Our present system of representative democracy provides no direct power to call officials to account for their actions. In the absence of such a power, systematic abuses generally come to light through petitions, demonstrations, press campaigns, vigilant pressure groups, all of which work less easily for the most deprived.

Press campaigns rarely focus on poverty: they are more likely to help make life harder for claimants by focusing on 'scrounging'. Pressure groups for the poor, like the Child Poverty Action Group and the Low Pay Unit, are dedicated and thorough, but they lack a vocal and active constituency among the poor, to back them up. Thus it is much easier to crush the disadvantaged without an outcry than it is to reduce the privileges of the privileged.

Conclusion:
Myths, Realities and Possibilities

I would have the reader trace the rapidly increasing disintegration, then the final collapse of the whole edifice, and the dark dawning of our modern day when we can neither endure our vices nor face the remedies needed to cure them.

Livy, History of Rome, *I, i (tr. A. de Selincourt)*

At the end of our odyssey through the inner city we can sum up some of the lessons of the experience for the wider context of British society. Seen from its lowest reaches, it diverges somewhat from the accepted myths that prevail at higher levels.

The first myth is that absolute poverty has been eradicated in Britain. In fact, it persisted quietly throughout the post-war period and became acute in recession, and under a government that seemed totally unconcerned about the fate of the unfortunate.

The International Labour Office has drawn up a list of 'basic human needs' for developing countries, to act as a target for policy. If we were to do the same for Britain, it might run roughly as follows for private requirements: enough food to maintain health and work capacity; sufficient clothing to avoid social stigma and personal shame; adequate heating and insulation to prevent excessive cold and damp; basic furnishings and floor coverings; and a tolerable home for each household. We have met in these pages many people who do not enjoy these basic needs: people who can afford only one square meal a day, who have to wear second-hand clothes, who cannot keep warm or dry in winter, who have no home. People who are spending 40 to 60 per cent of their income on housing and fuel alone, when the 'average' family spends only 21 per cent. People who have not much more than £1·00 to £1·30 per person per day to spend on food, clothing and other items, after housing and fuel costs are met. We have learned to distrust those complacent official statistics that assured us that real incomes kept rough pace with inflation, or fell by only a few per cent, for we have met people whose real incomes dropped by 20 per cent between 1979 and 1981, and others whose hourly earnings, even in money terms, dropped by a half.

The ILO adds to the private needs a list of basic social needs. Adapted to Britain, these might reasonably include: education and training, permitting full participation in society and in the economy; the right to a job; preventive and curative health care; full and equal access to the law; adequate support in disablement and old age; effective family planning; sufficient play and leisure facilities for the young within reach of the home; transport for work and leisure without excessive cost or inconvenience; freedom to walk the streets without fear; the right to participate fully, at work, in the neighbourhood and in local services, in deciding on matters that affect one's life. This list is not at all utopian. Most of its items have been recommended for poor countries, never mind rich ones, and they could be considered the minimum requirements for a civilized humane society. Yet Britain is very far from meeting these needs for the poorest 20 to 40 per cent of her population.

Those who are deprived of their basic social needs are, all too frequently, the same people who are deprived of their basic private needs. They suffer disproportionately from bad working conditions, unemployment and educational failure and, where they are concentrated geographically, from an ugly environment, crime and heavy policing, substandard health care, maladministration and injustice, and lack of access to redress. Deprivation is frequently multiple, cumulative, self-reinforcing and self-perpetuating through generations. There is indeed a cycle of deprivation, but the disadvantaged and many of their children are trapped in it less by their own personal shortcomings than by the structures of social and geographical inequality.

So much for absolute poverty. Relative poverty is felt in relation not only to the living standards of others – and hence is directly related to the level of inequality in a society – but also to the prevalent view of the minimum requirements for a socially acceptable life. Among my informants these included a three-piece suite, wall units, carpets, fridge, washing-machine and colour television; an annual holiday away from home plus several day trips a year; and at least one night out a week for teenagers. Those lacking *any* of these items felt, to that extent, deprived. Yet in this book we have met families whose homes were virtually bare of all furnishings; many who never escape the confines of Hackney; teenagers who cannot afford to go to job interviews, let alone discos. We have also seen the potent effect of the social minimum: for we have seen families willing to go without some of their basic needs in order to rent a colour television, or buy a new cooker or sofa on hire-purchase terms. We have seen teenagers ready to jeopardize their education with long hours of part-time work, to earn enough to go out. And we have met individuals willing to rob and steal, or to defraud social security, in order to come closer to the social minimum. Relative poverty also increased steeply after 1979: for real incomes fell for many – cut further by heavy taxation at lower and lower levels. Yet at the same time the pressure of advertising ensured that the social minimum continued to rise to include new and more expensive items. Inequality also worsened as the tax burden on the rich lightened and shifted on to the poor, and the costs of home ownership fell relative to the cost of renting. And tax cuts for the rich provided an incentive, not so much for hard work, as for directors to award themselves grotesque pay increases.

Most middle-class people who do not live or work in a poor area console themselves with the belief that the poor are cushioned against extreme poverty by the welfare state. This is myth number two. It is becoming increasingly clear that we no longer live in a welfare state, if indeed we ever did. For a genuine welfare state would surely make positive efforts to ensure that none of its citizens lived in want. The one we have is something different: little more than a safety net to prevent utter destitution, sometimes failing even in that, and often exacting a price in humiliation for its assistance. Little is done to ensure that the rights that exist on paper are enjoyed by all: it is left largely to the individual to assert them. A true welfare state would aim to forestall and prevent problems before they arise, but the British approach is reactive rather than active. In almost all spheres, from health to family stability, from housing to law and order, it deals in treatment of

425

acute cases rather than prevention. As most positive forms of
public spending were progressively cut, it was no longer possible
even to try to cure all those cases that presented for treatment, but
only the worst of them. Monetarism shifted the welfare state from
cure to crisis intervention. At the very same time, Conservative
governments began to undermine the foundations and question
the principles on which the welfare state had been based.

We have had more than two decades of cant about the third
myth, the idea that we live in a 'classless society'. Yet Britain is as
class-ridden as it ever was, and riven by chaotic and unspoken
class warfare. There is, first of all, the universal management/
labour cleavage, present in public enterprises just as pronouncedly
as in private, and with shifting relations of power depending on the
economic climate and the political colour of the government. The
post-war period saw a gradual advance of trade-union powers and
status, reaching a zenith in the early 1970s, when unionization
became a serious threat to company profits. This was a time of
decision. On the one hand, further advances could be made
towards industrial democracy, taking Britain down the road to a
human-faced capitalism like Sweden's. On the other hand, if
company profitability was to be restored without any worker voice
in conventional company management, the power of the trade
unions would have to be smashed. Monetarism and world recession, compounded by the anti-union legislation of the Thatcher
government, determined that the second course was followed.
Intensified global competition ensured that union power remained
weaker.

What makes the management/labour divide deeper in Britain
that in many other Western economies are the deep cultural
divisions which partly coincide with and partly cut across it –
between upper and middle classes, middle and lower classes, and
in general between manual and non-manual workers. Most factories are segregated along class lines, and neighbourhoods are
segregated by income, leading to a considerable degree of segregation in schools. This segregation has allowed the persistence of two
British cultures, as old as the Norman invasion, in an opposition
far deeper than the science/arts divide: the written semi-Latinate
culture in which the business of law, bureaucracy, academic

education and representative politics is still largely conducted, and the mainly oral Anglo-Saxon culture of the unlettered.

These central divisions are even further blurred by others that criss-cross them: landlord against tenant, home owner against council tenant, worker against claimant. This blurring confuses perceptions and allegiances, prevents the emergence of class consciousness and concerted action, and allows people to deny that class exists or, laughably, to assert that 'we're all working class now.'

Related to this is myth number four, that ours is a 'mixed economy'. In a legal sense this is, of course, true, in that some parts of industry are still publicly owned. But the requirement, progressively more stringent from the late sixties onwards, that public enterprises should make a profit, and the continued absence of meaningful industrial democracy, made most public enterprises hard to distinguish from large private concerns in terms of relations of power, status and income between workers and managers. As competition intensified and government finance dried up, nationalized industries behaved increasingly like privately owned ones. Privatization of ownership merely pursued the logic of an existing trend. Privatization of natural monopolies like telephones, electricity and water allowed private companies to extract excess profits. Privatization of public services – intended to improve 'efficiency' – merely resulted in lower standards of service and worse pay and conditions for workers.

Myth number five is that we live in a democracy. To the ancient Athenians, who invented the concept, democracy at its height meant voting in person, in an assembly of all the citizens, on all major issues. Today's equivalent – made possible in large countries for the first time by information technology – would be frequent referenda at national and local levels. But we have come to accept unthinkingly the idea that democracy can only mean representative democracy. Yet representative democracy offers people no true continuing control over the activities of their rulers. The idea that publication of a compendious and complex election manifesto – which in any case is not binding – gives any government a 'mandate' to enact everything, or anything, in it is a patent absurdity. Compounding this is the manifest distortion of our 'first

427

past the post' electoral system, which now allows governments to be 'chosen by the people' with the support of less than a third of the electorate, with the contrary votes of almost three-fifths of those who vote.

The uncomfortable reality is that we live under an oligarchy, with a periodic right to change the members of that oligarchy, but with a strong element of potential dictatorship at the heart of the prime-ministerial system. An oligarchy that, under most governments, remained to varying degrees responsive to *organized* pressure groups, but which retained the potential, that became a reality under Mrs Thatcher, of ignoring all pressure groups including even those of organized business.

Until the 1980s, our democracy functioned tolerably well for middle-class interests and middle-class areas, and for the organized labour movement. But it never served poor people and poor areas with equal effectiveness. Power is as unevenly distributed in Britain as wealth. The lower down the social scale you move, the less does Britain look like a democracy. For if there is one single experience that sums up the lives of the poor, it is powerlessness. Life becomes a succession of frustrations in which the individual seems to be subjected to unpleasant forces almost completely outside his or her effective control, and to the seemingly arbitrary (because unaccountable) power of others. There is a feeling that you are, essentially, abandoned by society, that no one gives a damn if you die like a rat in a sewer.

The powerless do not acquiesce in their predicament. They often rebel against the rules. But lacking effective class-consciousness and cohesion, their rebellion frequently takes individualist, anarchic forms which often make the situation worse for others, or indeed for themselves. There seems little prospect in the foreseeable future of mass action on a scale that would force changes to be made, or indeed on any significant scale at all.

Nor is our system well equipped to change itself effectively or rapidly, except in negative directions, for it is always easier to destroy than to create. The problems are well known and are growing more critical year by year, but it takes decades for the solutions to emerge. We still have no unified system of taxation and benefits able to adjust incomes to needs, but instead a confusing chaos of benefits and allowances and a pernicious poverty trap that was worse than supertax in its effects on 'the incentive to work'. We have an economy that adjusts to changes in world trade not positively, through the stimulation of investment and massive retraining and redeployment, but destructively, through the collapse of companies and the marginalization of communities and people. We are still nowhere near any significant progress on industrial democracy or any rational, fair and non-destructive means of determining pay increases. We have a legal system that is so expensive that most people cannot contemplate bringing a civil law case. A punitive penal system that research has shown for years to be more effective in hardening criminals than in reforming or deterring them along with the highest rate of imprisonment in Europe. A higher bureaucracy where secrecy and secretiveness take precedence over the public's right to information. An education system that bears little relation to society's needs, and that has the lowest continuation rate of any major Western economy. A health system that seems to be run more for the convenience of consultants than of consumers. A natural environment that is one of the least protected and most polluted in Western Europe.

The blockage to reform lies partly in the class-based two-party system, in which each party reverses the reforms of the other, and partly in our tradition of government by consent, which effectively gives a veto over reform to strong interest groups whose powers or privileges might be damaged by that reform. There is, too, a curious resistance to the idea of tackling problems comprehensively, root and branch, and a sad tendency to adopt piecemeal solutions without a great deal of thought or systematic feedback on their wider impact. The net result is an uncommonly rigid society, unable to alter its institutions in tune with the times, and looking every day more backward, in almost every sphere, compared with the rest of Western Europe.

What, then, is to be done?

Programmes aimed specifically at inner-city areas can, of course, help those areas. Priority must go to the massive renewal and rehabilitation of public and private housing and the improvement of amenities, transport and environment, so as to attract a more balanced mix of resident, and eliminate the localized pockets of environmental deprivation that concentrate the disadvantaged. There is no way of doing this on the cheap. The fact that public money in the past has helped to create the problems does not mean that public money in the future cannot help to solve them: architects and planners are wiser today, and humbler too, and the mistakes are far less likely to be repeated. The economic base of the inner city must also be modernized, which will mean incentives for investment comparable to those that were available in the depressed regions. Services are needed to provide small businesses with capital, credit, management consultancy, technology advice, and assistance with marketing. But efforts must be made to ensure that the new local industries and services do not simply draw in better-qualified commuters from outside the area, without benefiting the local unemployed. The renewal of the built environment will create semi- and unskilled jobs in construction. In addition, concentrated efforts must be made in training and educating the underskilled and underqualified.

Self-help has a crucial role to play in improving the environment and the morale of inner-city communities: local people must become more involved in the struggle for more resources, in planning their neighbourhoods, and in helping to improve them. But the prospects for a strategy of self-help should not be overestimated: as we have seen, the inner-city population lacks the funds and the expertise that can be found in better-off areas. Self-help in the inner city must be *assisted* self-help, with external funding and technical help. And it will, of course, get much further if it has to deal with responsive rather than insensitive local and national authorities. When government is committed to eroding welfare benefits, savaging public expenditure, and fostering real wage cuts for the less skilled, self-help can do little more than repair a small part of the damage, though it can create the structures and the practice that can be put to more productive use in better times.

But I doubt whether any policy aimed at particular deprived areas can solve the inner-city problem, because the local problem is the symptom of national diseases. Improve one particular location, and another inner-city area would burst forth elsewhere. Dress and heal Hackney's wounds, and more will appear in Tottenham or Leyton. As long as British society continues to generate an under-class on low incomes, with insecure jobs or no jobs, and without adequate education, new inner-city areas will continue to arise wherever housing is significantly worse than average. As long as the British economy adjusts to changing world-trade patterns in unplanned and destructive ways, it will continue to generate marginalized workers and marginalized areas wherever industries and plants are least competitive. As long as there are no real accountability, participation or effective legal rights, maladministration and injustice will continue to flourish.

Only a holistic approach, aimed at the whole body of the nation, can effect a cure. Many of the specific elements involved have been sketched in earlier chapters or follow logically from the analysis of the malfunctioning of institutions. What is required more than anything, for the success of specific policies, is a new consensus on values: on the importance of compassion and a far greater measure of equality and participation than we have enjoyed hitherto. Equality is now the key. The progressive reduction of gross inequalities in income and wealth, in specific, measurable steps, starting with the extremes, should become an explicit policy goal. An important aspect of equality, now and henceforth, is the fair distribution of work and its financial rewards. If advancing technology reduces the total amount of work to be done, then the work that is left should be shared around by gradual reduction in the retiring age and in hours of work, not by the division of society into workers and workless.

Britain must put an end to that other deep divide, between the classes, before it puts an end to us. This cannot be done by appealing to whatever illusory unity may be forged by any real or imagined outside threat. Nor can the class war be 'won' by crushing organized labour, for it will always persist, even if only in the form of absenteeism, low productivity, poor quality or sabotage. Class conflict will necessarily and inevitably continue until its sources are removed. First and foremost, the contradictions between management and labour, owner and employee, must be resolved. Nationalization in itself does not end those contradictions. They will only disappear when workers have a significant stake in the enterprises in which they work, sharing the profits and participating in major decisions.

Conclusion

The division of the nation into two great housing classes should be ended. It is hard to remain in favour of council housing when you have witnessed at first hand the sense of powerlessness felt by tenants unable to choose where they wish to live. The policy of selling the best council houses to the wealthiest tenants at knock-down prices could have no effect on the core of the problem; indeed, it would only make it worse. My own view is that the vast majority of council tenancies should be converted into forms of owner-occupation, with subsidies for poorer families and schemes to help those who would not qualify for normal mortgages. Local councils, housing associations or co-operatives would take a major role in providing finance, assisting in maintenance and improvement of substandard properties, and providing a much-reduced rented sector for the young or mobile.

It is quite amazing that we have passed laws against race and sex discrimination, while nothing has been done to prevent the gross discrimination that persists between manual and non-manual workers. There must be an end to discriminatory pay systems, terms of employment, holidays, hours of work, perks and pension arrangements, and to the absurd institutions of separate dining-rooms, toilets, car-parks and so on. The educational foundations of class division must be ended, with a unified, general education leading to a uniform certificate, an end to private schools, and a redrawing of school catchment areas to reach a socially balanced intake.

And it is surely time for a leap forward in the concept of democracy. We need proportional representation like the rest of Western Europe – to end the destructive polarization of British politics. Without that, we will never arrive at a new consensus. The power of representatives needs to be strengthened by the employment of full-time paid chairmen for council committees, and by the provision of staffs four or five strong to back up MPs. An elective cabinet is needed, to forestall any repeat of Thatcher's prime-ministerial dictatorship. And a Freedom of Information Act to provide the public with the ammunition to control bureaucratic abuse and laxity. But the idea of democracy must be moved forward, beyond the elitist idea of doing everything through remote representatives, towards a more meaningful involvement of people in decisions on day-to-day affairs. We need neighbour-hood, street or estate councils, with real powers and real resources; and local services of all kinds – including central-government ones such as health and social security – that are directly accountable to their immediate users, so that complaints and suggestions for improvement could be raised.

We need an extension in the concept of rights. The basic needs set out above should become universally recognized and guaran-teed rights, moving from our present system where the onus is on individuals to claim their rights, to one in which the onus is on institutions to ensure that everyone receives their rights. This would involve thorough management-control systems to eliminate error and offhand or rude service, and staff training in awareness of the dangers of class bias and in sensitivity to poor working-class needs and ways of expressing them. In the health service and in social security, there should be financial penalties for waiting times, recognizing the social and economic cost of waiting to clients. There would need to be a great expansion, especially in poor areas, in welfare-rights advice and free legal services. And much-increased public assistance to local groups in forming and running residents' and tenants' associations.

Britain must move towards a more active and preventive ap-proach to problems of all kinds. In the economy, this means planning ahead, identifying and encouraging investment in indus-tries of the future, retraining marginalized workers on a massive scale, influencing the location of new industries to compensate communities undermined by the decline of old industries. Social services and health services should set out to promote family stability and good health, and to identify problems at an earlier stage, when treatment can be less drastic and more effective. We should move to a system of clear quantitative targets for social policy: aiming at specific reductions in, for example, mortality or disease rates, or specific increases in enrolment in higher educa-tion.

During the 1980s and early 1990s, instead of moving closer towards these goals, we moved further away. Billions were poured into private pockets by selling nationalized industries on the cheap – while billions were cut from essential public services. An increasingly wealthy elite drove more and more expensive cars over deeper and deeper holes in the road. The poor were robbed to pay the rich. Statistics were doctored or suppressed to hide the realities of unemployment and poverty.

The doctrine of free markets swept all before it. As Karl Marx retreated before Adam Smith, monetarism moved from national dogma to international religion. The World Bank and the International Monetary Fund imposed privatization, public spending cuts and free trade on Third World countries. Eastern Europe leapt from Communism to Thatcherism.

Free markets do have their uses. They ensure the most efficient use of resources, and match production with consumer demand. Free trade is the best guarantor of peace as well as of efficiency. But free markets will never work in social services, health care, education, transport policy. If they are introduced, the only result will be a poorer service for those who cannot pay. They can never be made to work with monopolies like water, electricity, telephones, where the consumer has no choice of supplier: they will not bring improved services, but only higher prices.

Free markets cannot solve social or environmental problems. Indeed they create them, since free market prices do not include external costs imposed on third parties. They cannot alleviate inner-city problems. Indeed they create them, by concentrating weakest players on the labour market in the cheapest accommodation on the housing market. Extending the market to inappropriate areas merely extends the problems that markets create. When the obsession with markets has subsided, when the poor and the vulnerable pay the price of another oversimplified ideology, the need for a balance will be recognized again. It is the role of government to regulate markets in the public interest, wherever their workings produce results that are socially or environmentally undesirable.

Because the inner city derives from the combination of all of Britain's most deep-seated problems, the challenge and the opportunity it presents is this: if we can, using nation-wide measures, eliminate or greatly alleviate the inner-city problem, we shall at the same time resolve most of our other problems, with a chance of becoming not only a more humane and civilized society, but also a more stable, more efficient and more competitive economy.

But the warning that the inner city presently offers is the converse: because the weaknesses that give rise to it are so widespread in Britain, the inner-city problem could become much more widespread. An expanding proportion of manual working-class areas in Britain could come to resemble the present inner city, blighted by a decaying environment, the accelerated breakdown of families and the consequent decline in socialization of the young.

Our present situation is critical. In 1979, an extreme form of conservatism won power and proceeded to alter British society in ways that favoured its perpetuation in office. The sale of council houses and shares in privatized companies reduced the number of council tenants, and created a mass of people with a stake in voting Tory. Emasculated trade unions suffered a steep decline in membership. The poll tax led to mass self-disenfranchisement. Meanwhile, the shift from manufacturing to services swelled the ranks of those who saw themselves as middle class. And the exodus to the suburbs led, through boudnary changes, to an increase in constituencies with a Tory majority.

These factors worked heavily against the Labour Party. So, in 1992 the fourth Conservative government in a row was re-elected, with a powerful lead, in the pit of a recession, with deep public fears about health and education. When, then, would they fail to be elected? Britain seemed to have become a one-party state in which many urban areas, social groups and regions had no constitutional ways of getting their interests heard.

Only a strong electoral pact between Labour and Liberal Democrats has any good prospect of ousting the Tories. Only proportional representation can prevent them from returning again and again. Labour's concern with social justice can strengthen and be strengthened by Liberal concern with the environment and with local participation. Yet it is far from certain that such a pact could be brought about.

If these economic and political trends continue, Britain will remain the sick man of Europe, and could become a country as deeply and as destructively divided as many in Latin America.

Note on Incomes and Prices

One unfortunate side effect of inflation is the more or less rapid obsolescence of data on family incomes and expenditures. So that these may have some meaning to future or foreign readers, I quote here a small selection of mid-1981 incomes and prices.

Incomes

Social security
Supplementary benefit, national scale rates:

Single pensioner	£27·15
Pensioner couple	£43·45
Eighteen-year-old living in parents' home	£17·05
Married couple with two children, aged seven and eleven	£52·80

On top of this, rent and rates, worth an average of £18·22 per week in Hackney, are also paid. Allowing for typical deductions of 25 per cent, the married couple's rate is equivalent to a gross wage of about £95, excluding the effect of rent and rate rebates, which are often unclaimed.

Wages
Average weekly *gross* earnings of full-time workers over twenty-one, whose pay was unaffected by absence, in April 1981 (*New Earnings Survey*):

	Hackney	Greater London	Great Britain
Manual men	£119·70	£131·90	£121·90
Non-manual men	£152·30	£185·90	£163·10
All men	£133·50	£163·80	£140·50
All women	£94	£107·40	£91·40

Tax and national-insurance contributions deduct 20 to 30 per cent.

436

Expenditure

Housing etc. (weekly averages for Hackney)

Average rent, Hackney Council	£10·51
Average domestic rate bill	£7·71
Typical electricity bill, three-bed all-electric flat	£17 per week six colder months, £8 per week six warmer months
TV rental, colour	£2·20

Groceries (prices from Sainsbury's, Matthews and Ridley Road market)

White loaf (1 kg)	32p	Cheese (1 lb/454 g)	£1·14
Spaghetti (1 kg)	62p	Milk (1 pint/560 ml)	18½p
Jam (1 lb/454 g)	36p	Butter (1 lb/454 g)	93p
Sugar (2 lb/900 g)	33p	Eggs (one dozen large)	90p
Tomato soup (15 oz/420 g)	21p	Ham (1 lb/454 g tin)	£1·06
		Chicken (per lb/454 g)	55p
		Mince (per lb/454 g)	92p
Tea (125 g)	19p	Rump steak (per lb/454 g)	£1·99
Coffee (100 g)	45p		
Cola (1 litre)	29p		
Can beer (¾ pint/420 ml)	49p	Apples (per lb/454 g)	20–30p
Cheapest wine	£1·49	Carrots, onions,	
Spirits	£5–£7	spinach (per lb/454 g)	12p

Clothing (price range, market stall and chain stores)

Child's trousers	£2–£8
Child's shoes	£6–£15
Woman's skirt	£5–£18
Gent's shoes	£9–£25
Gent's shirt	£3–£8

Bibliography and Sources

The greater part of this book is based on personal observations and interviews. The major other source of information has been the reports of Hackney Borough Council, too numerous to mention, especially those of the housing, social services, planning, finance and economic development committees.

There are very few general books on Hackney's history. Besides Charles Booth, *Life and Labour of the People in London*, my main sources were *A Short History of the London Borough of Hackney*, Hackney Library Services, 1967, and Michael Hunter, *The Victorian Villas of Hackney*, The Hackney Society, 1981.

On industry and economics, the reports of the Hackney and Islington Inner City Partnership were helpful, especially the *Reports of the Employment Working Party* and the *Clothing and Footwear Industry Sector Survey*. The Low Pay Unit's 1982 report *Low Pay in Hackney* was published too late to be incorporated except in proof corrections.

On housing, see Michael Young *et al.*, *Report from Hackney*, Policy Studies Institute, 1981, and *Homeless in Hackney*, Hackney Homeless Action, 1981. The health section draws on *The State of the Health Services in City and Hackney Health District*, City and Hackney Community Health Council, 1981, and Gillian Lomas *et al.*, *Poverty and Schizophrenia*, Psychiatric Rehabilitation Association, 1973. Data given in the education chapter are from Inner London Education Authority Research and Statistics Branch, *School Exam Results in the ILEA 1978* and *Monitoring of Educational Attainment 1981*.

Other statistics were drawn from the standard sources, of which the *National Housing and Dwelling Survey* (Department of the Environment, 1978) is most useful in comparing inner-city areas. Also the early results of the 1981 Census, reported in *County Monitors: Inner London, Outer London, Hackney and Islington Special Area and Small*

Area Statistics, Office of Population Censuses and Surveys, 1982, plus *New Earnings Survey*, the *Department of Employment Gazette*, *Social Trends*, *Social Security Statistics* (various issues).

General books on the inner-city problem which I found useful were a number of reports from the excellent Community Development Projects, especially: *The Costs of Industrial Change*, CDP, 1977; *CDP Final Report*, Coventry and Hillfields CDP; *Interproject Report*, National CDP Project, 1973. Peter Hall (ed.), *The Inner City in Context*, Heinemann, 1981, provides a useful survey and analysis of the field in Britain and elsewhere.

Index

Note: Readers who might like to gather together the history of the 'Davies' family will find their stories and opinions as follows:

440